Frommer's®

Edinburgh &

ion

⊗ WILEY

A John Wiley and Sons, Ltd, Publication

Published by:

WILEY PUBLISHING, INC.

Copyright © 2011 John Wiley & Sons Ltd, The Atrium, Southern Gate, Chichester,
West Sussex PO19 8SQ, UK
Telephone (+44) 1243 779777
Email (for orders and customer service enquiries): cs-books@wiley.co.uk. Visit our Home Page on
www.wiley.com

UK Publisher: Sally Smith
Project Manager: Daniel Mersey
Commissioning Editor: Jill Emeny
Development Editor: Ismay Atkins
Content Editor: Erica Peters
Cartography: Andrew Murphy
Photo Editor: Jill Emeny

Front cover photo: © Findlay Rankin/Age footstock/Photolibrary. Description: Facades of Templetons
Carpet Factory, Glasgow
Back Cover photo: © Festivals Edinburgh. Description: © Performance on the Royal Mile during the
Edinburgh Festival

British Library Cataloguing in Publication Data
A catalogue record for this book is available from the British Library

ISBN: 978-0-470-71123-1 (pbk), ISBN 978-0-470-97808-5 (ebk)

Typeset by Wiley Indianapolis Composition Services

Printed and bound in the United States of America

5 4 3 2 1

CONTENTS

LIST OF MAPS

ABOUT THE AUTHOR

Barry Shelby was born 1960 in Berkeley, California, where he later attended the University of California. He received a master's degree in journalism in 1984 from Northwestern University in Illinois. From 1984 to June 1997, he was an editor at *World Press Review* magazine in Manhattan. He moved to Scotland in 1997, where he has worked as a food and drink writer and editor for newspapers and magazines, including the *Guardian, Glasgow Herald* and *The List.* He is married to a Scot and presently resides in Scotland's Western Isles after a decade living in Glasgow.

ACKNOWLEDGMENTS

The editor would like to thank Claudia Monteiro at Festivals Edinburgh and Alan Gordon at Festival Fringe for both images and information. Also to Naomi Kraus for her time consulting on this title, Ismay Atkins for the development work, and Erica Peters and Scott Totman for helping to bring this new edition together.

HOW TO CONTACT US

In researching this book, we discovered many wonderful places—hotels, restaurants, shops, and more. We're sure you'll find others. Please tell us about them, so we can share the information with your fellow travelers in upcoming editions. If you were disappointed with a recommendation, we'd love to know that, too. Please write to:

Frommer's Edinburgh & Glasgow, 4th Edition
Wiley Publishing, Inc. • 111 River St. • Hoboken, NJ 07030-5774

AN ADDITIONAL NOTE

Please be advised that travel information is subject to change at any time—and this is especially true of prices. We therefore suggest that you write or call ahead for confirmation when making your travel plans. The authors, editors, and publisher cannot be held responsible for the experiences of readers while traveling. Your safety is important to us, however, so we encourage you to stay alert and be aware of your surroundings. Keep a close eye on cameras, purses, and wallets, all favorite targets of thieves and pickpockets.

FROMMER'S STAR RATINGS, ICONS & ABBREVIATIONS

Every hotel, restaurant, and attraction listing in this guide has been ranked for quality, value, service, amenities, and special features using a **star-rating system.** In country, state, and regional guides, we also rate towns and regions to help you narrow down your choices and budget your time accordingly. Hotels and restaurants are rated on a scale of zero (recommended) to three stars (exceptional). Attractions, shopping, nightlife, towns, and regions are rated according to the following scale: zero stars (recommended), one star (highly recommended), two stars (very highly recommended), and three stars (must-see).

In addition to the star-rating system, we also use **seven feature icons** that point you to the great deals, in-the-know advice, and unique experiences that separate travelers from tourists. Throughout the book, look for:

 special finds—those places only insiders know about

fun facts—details that make travelers more informed and their trips more fun

kids—best bets for kids and advice for the whole family

special moments—those experiences that memories are made of

overrated—places or experiences not worth your time or money

insider tips—great ways to save time and money

great values—where to get the best deals

The following abbreviations are used for credit cards:

AE	American Express	DISC	Discover	V	Visa
DC	Diners Club	MC	MasterCard		

THE BEST OF EDINBURGH & GLASGOW

Given the contrasting reputations of Edinburgh and Glasgow, any travelers who haven't examined a map of Scotland might be forgiven for thinking that they are separated by hundreds of miles. In fact, Scotland's two primary cities are only about 74km (46 miles) apart, but almost everyone who visits them will be struck by their differences.

Both cities contribute mightily—and equally—to the cultural vibrancy of the nation. With this in mind, the country is improving the public transportation links between the two cities, first by increasing the frequency of trains and second by contemplating a high-speed rail link between them.

To the east, Edinburgh offers a famous and almost fairytale-like setting, with an imposing castle high on one of many hills. Built on ancient volcanoes and first established because of its secure and defensible position, the capital of Scotland has become a crossroads. Practically everyone who comes to Scotland today spends some time in Edinburgh—and its midsummer international arts festival is one of the biggest in the world. Edinburgh is the second most popular tourist destination in Great Britain after London, and it's not hard to see why. Compact and tidy, it is more of a big town than a small city.

In the west, Glasgow, on the other hand, is not a place that anyone might call precious. Glasgow was settled earlier than its cross-country rival because it was an ideal place to ford the mighty River Clyde, and later gained a reputation for shipbuilding and industry. For all its ancient origins, today Glasgow resembles nothing so much as a modern, cosmopolitan city, with a growing population. It has overcome its 20th-century associations with grime, grit, and gangsters—and now it is arguably more vibrant than Edinburgh, with a vigorous music and art scene. Without a picturesque castle or flamboyant palace, it exemplifies urban Scotland: Dynamic and attuned to the world. In 1990, it was named European Culture Capital; in 1999, U.K. City of Architecture and Design; and in 2014, it will host the Commonwealth Games.

Edinburgh and Glasgow have a lot to offer individually, and taken as a duo, they are more impressive still. Both cities are among Europe's most dynamic centers. Edinburgh is the seat of Scottish royalty and government, and Glasgow boasts lively urban culture mixed in with Victorian splendor.

FROMMER'S FAVORITE EDINBURGH & GLASGOW EXPERIENCES

- **Visiting a Pub:** In Edinburgh, there are a good number of traditional pubs, many of which serve hand-pulled, cask-conditioned ales. Glasgow's scene overall is more modern, with several so-called "style" bars. The preferred Scottish draught is lager, often combined with a wee dram of whisky by the traditionalists. Whether you become friendly with the locals or not, pub life is always one of the most entertaining aspects of a visit to Scotland. I list my favorite pubs in chapters 11 and 19.

- **Experiencing Edinburgh's Famous Festival:** The Edinburgh Festival is one of Europe's (if not the world's) most prestigious annual cultural events. In fact, it encompasses several "festivals" at once. The original International Festival remains primarily devoted to the high arts: Classical music and dance. Meanwhile the Fringe now dominates the month-long fest, hosting the most acts and drawing the largest audiences to hundreds of stages with comedians, music, drama, and other entertainers. Furthermore, a huge international book festival occurs virtually simultaneously, while smaller jazz and TV festivals compete at the edges. If you're planning to visit Edinburgh in August, make your hotel reservations early. See p. 103.

- **Savoring the Cuisine:** The fresh fish and seafood harvested from Scotland's icy lochs and seas is world-class. Then there is the lamb and Aberdeen Angus beef. Edinburgh has three restaurants with Michelin stars and Glasgow boasts some of the best Indian restaurants in the U.K. I review the best dining spots in chapters 7 and 15.

- **Enjoying Art Galleries & Museums:** Edinburgh is home to the National Galleries of Scotland, which contains the country's collection held in five different buildings. It ranges from Renaissance painting to pop art. Meanwhile, Glasgow has one of the best municipal holdings of art in Europe. The crowning glory for many critics is the Burrell Collection (p. 201), a host of art and artifacts bequeathed to the city by an industrialist, but the Victorian Kelvingrove Art Gallery and Museum (p. 201) has the soul of the city's collection. For the lowdown on galleries and museums in both cities, see chapters 8 and 16.

- **Playing Golf:** Sure, most people think only of St. Andrews, which frequently hosts the Open. But both Edinburgh and Glasgow (and the regions nearby) have fine courses. The birthplace of the sport's rules is Edinburgh, and its historic short course, Bruntsfield Links (p. 105), can be played during summer for free—and all you need is a ball, pitching wedge, and putter.

- **Strolling in Parks or Gardens:** In the capital, you have the option of the splendid Royal Botanic Gardens, Holyrood Park and Arthur's Seat, the Meadows, or

Calton Hill. Glasgow (which many believe means "Dear Green Place") has a host of options from Glasgow Green along the River Clyde to Kelvingrove Park in the salubrious West End. See chapters 9 and 17.

o **Shopping:** Glasgow considers itself the second biggest shopping playground in Britain after London. And, as no self-respecting city likes to be upstaged when it comes to retail therapy, so Edinburgh has given chase. There is a combination of posh department stores, such as Harvey Nichols; old favorites, such as House of Fraser or Jenners; and plenty of trendy designer shops. For more details on shopping, see chapters 10 and 18.

o **Exploring Ancient Edinburgh:** Take a wander down one of the many narrow lanes off the Royal Mile in the city's Old Town to begin to get a sense of what medieval Edinburgh was like. In addition to exploring on your own, my walking tours should help to heighten the experience. See chapter 9.

o **Admiring Victorian Glasgow:** Glasgow actually contemplated tearing down its Victorian-built heritage after World War II. It was perceived as old-fashioned. Thank goodness the city fathers were stopped and it didn't happen. For walking tours that highlight Glasgow's best architecture, see chapter 17.

THE best CASTLE & PALACE

o **Edinburgh Castle:** The Castle's earliest construction dates to around A.D. 1000, placed at the highest point of a rocky, narrow ridge—a natural fortress. The Castle has been the locus of many historic royal events and vicious battles. Extraordinarily, it remains an active military barracks, as well as a crowded tourist attraction featuring the crown jewels and the famous Stone of Scone on which ancient Scottish royalty is believed to have been coronated. See p. 87.

o **Palace of Holyroodhouse:** At the opposite end of Edinburgh's Royal Mile from the Castle, the Palace of Holyroodhouse is the historic as well as the current Royal residence (when the British monarch is occasionally in town). "Rood" means "cross," and the abbey ruins that are adjacent to the Palace date to 1128. The building's present form largely dates from the late 1600s, when it was rebuilt in a dignified neo-Palladian style. But the best bits are in the oldest wing, where Mary, Queen of Scots once stayed. See p. 94.

THE best CATHEDRALS & CHURCHES

o **Glasgow Cathedral:** In the 7th century, a Celtic religious pilgrim called St. Mungo (or St. Kentigern) is believed to have started a monastery on the site of Glasgow Cathedral, consecrated in the 1130s. This is mainland Scotland's only fully intact medieval cathedral, and while the Protestant reformation stripped it of Roman Catholic idolatry, the corpse of St. Mungo apparently lies in the crypt of this impressive cathedral. See p. 198.

o **St. Giles' Cathedral:** In Edinburgh's Old Town, the auld kirk of St. Giles was perhaps a victim of over-enthusiastic Victorian renovation, but it is still an imposing piece of ecclesiastical architecture. Here is where John Knox, Scotland's Martin Luther, preached his sermons on the Reformation. See p. 91.

- **St. Vincent Street Church:** Access is limited as the Free Church of Scotland is still using this kirk in Glasgow, but the landmark is a beautiful example of the work of Alexander "Greek" Thomson, Glasgow's largely unknown genius of the Victorian era. The clock tower is decorated in all manner of exotic yet sympathetic Egyptian, Assyrian, and even Indian-looking motifs and designs. See p. 199.

THE best GALLERIES & MUSEUMS

Edinburgh

- **Museum of Scotland:** In 1998, the collections of the Royal Museum of Scotland and the National Museum of Antiquities were united into a coherent whole. Here you'll find practically everything you ever wanted to know about Scotland from prehistory to the Industrial Age, housed in an attractive modern building. See p. 96.
- **National Galleries of Scotland:** The country's art collection is held in a set of buildings, collectively known as the National Galleries. The flagship, in Princes Street Gardens, offers paintings by artists such as Velázquez and Cézanne, plus Scottish master works. Adjacent is the Royal Academy, which has space for touring exhibits. Other branches include the National Gallery of Modern Art and the associated Dean Gallery near the Water of Leith, as well as the National Portrait Gallery on Queen Street. See p. 95 and 97.

Glasgow

- **The Burrell Collection:** The contents of this gallery were accumulated by industrialist Sir William Burrell (1861–1958), who spent much of his fortune on collecting art and artifacts—then ensuring they all went to the city of Glasgow. Now on display in a postmodern building in Glasgow's Pollok Country Park, it's one of Scotland's most admired museums, with a strong focus on medieval art, 19th-century French paintings, and Chinese ceramics. See p. 201.
- **Hunterian Art Gallery:** This museum owns much of the artistic estate of James McNeill Whistler, as well as housing a re-creation of the home of Scotland's most famous architect and designer, Charles Rennie Mackintosh. See p. 200.

Highlights of Historic Edinburgh

Gladstone's Land, owned by the National Trust for Scotland, is a 17th-century merchant's house near Edinburgh Castle. Visit it to get an impression of just how cramped living conditions were—even for the rich— some 400 years ago. On the second floor, you can also see the original exterior facade with its classical friezes of columns and arches, as well as the painted timber ceiling. Across town, the **Georgian House** is on Charlotte Square, which was designed by the great Robert Adam around the time of the American Revolution. This town house is set out and decorated in the manner of the 18th century. See p. 97.

- **Kelvingrove Art Gallery & Museum:** Reopened in 2006, this diverse collection of art and antiquaries is in the second-most visited gallery and museum in the U.K. outside of London. See p. 201.

THE best ARCHITECTURE IN GLASGOW

- **Glasgow School of Art:** Architect Charles Rennie Mackintosh's global reputation rests in large part on his magnificent Glasgow School of Art, which is still used by students and is open for guided tours. It's a highlight of a Mackintosh heritage trail, which draws legions of fans to Glasgow. Nearby is another landmark, the Willow Tea Rooms. See p. 198.
- **Holmwood House:** On the city's Southside, this villa is probably the best example of Alexander "Greek" Thomson's innovative style as applied to stately Victorian mansions. Magnificently original, its restoration (which is ongoing) has revealed that the architect was concerned with almost every element of the house's design. See p. 201.

THE best HOTELS

Edinburgh

- **Best Boutique Hotel:** In an upscale neighborhood, **The Bonham,** 35 Drumsheugh Gardens (✆ 0131/226-6050), offers some of the most alluring rooms in a city filled with fine hotels. See p. 67.
- **Best Traditional Hotel:** With a Michelin star-winning restaurant, doormen dressed in kilts, and romantic views to rival any other, **The Balmoral,** 1 Princes St. (✆ 0131/556-2414), is legendary and located in the heart of the capital. See p. 60.
- **Best Rooms near the Castle:** As its list of celebrity guests testifies, **The Witchery,** Castlehill (✆ 0131/225-5613), offers opulence and individuality in a manner not seen anywhere else in the Old Town. See p. 66.
- **Best Hotel in Leith:** About a 15-minute ride north of Edinburgh's center, **Malmaison,** 1 Tower Place (✆ 0131/468-5000), is an oasis of chic on the Leith waterfront. See p. 70.

Glasgow

- **Best Boutique Hotel:** In the city's attractive West End, **Hotel du Vin,** 1 Devonshire Gardens (✆ 0141/339-2001), stands out, boasting modern comforts. See p. 175.
- **Best Hip Hotel:** With only some 18 rooms, the **Brunswick Hotel,** 106–108 Brunswick St. (✆ 0141/552-0001), exudes cool in the city's Merchant City. The design is modern and minimalist but with character and class. See p. 169.
- **Best in the Commercial Center:** Linked to the Leith hotel with the same name, **Malmaison,** 278 W. George St. (✆ 0141/572-1000), receives and treats guests in style. See p. 173.

THE best DINING BETS

Edinburgh

- **Best Fine-Dining Restaurant:** With a precious Michelin star and the city's most talented chef/owner, **Restaurant Martin Wishart,** 54 The Shore, Leith (✆ **0131/553-3557**), is where the leading out-of-town chefs want to dine when they visit Edinburgh. See p. 83.

- **Best Cafe:** Near the heart of Old Town, **Spoon Café Bistro,** 6a Nicolson St. (✆ **0131/557-4567**), forks out some of the best soups, salads, and sandwiches in Edinburgh. See p. 82.

- **Best Vegetarian Restaurant:** Off the Royal Mile, **David Bann,** 56–58 St. Mary's St. (✆ **0131/556-5888**), continually sets the highest standards for meat-free dining. See p. 80.

- **Best Modern Scottish Restaurant:** New to the city is **21212,** 3 Royal Terrace (✆ **0845/22-21212**), an innovative fine-dining restaurant that quickly garnered a Michelin star. See p. 76.

- **Best Restaurant Views: Forth Floor,** Harvey Nichols, 30–34 St. Andrew Sq. (✆ **0131/524-8350**), offers wonderful cooking of fresh Scottish produce to go with its scenic vistas. Second best is **Oloroso,** 33 Castle St. (✆ **0131/226-7614**). See p. 76 and 77.

- **Best on a Budget:** Nothing fancy, but the **Kebab Mahal,** 7 Nicolson Sq. (✆ **0131/667-5214**), serves up good, hearty Indian food at budget prices. See p. 82.

Glasgow

- **Best Fish Restaurant:** One of the most consistently excellent restaurants in the entire city, **Gamba,** 225a W. George St. (✆ **0141/572-0899**), specializes in superb seafood, showing off some of Scotland's best natural produce. See p. 186.

- **Best Indian Restaurant:** The competition is stiff, but for this edition the nod goes to the always outstanding **Mother India,** 28 Westminster Terrace (✆ **0141/221-1663**). See p. 191.

- **Best Bistro:** More of a bistro despite its name, **Café Gandolfi,** 64 Albion St. (✆ **0141/552-6813**), offers straightforward and delicious dishes, whether a bowl of Cullen *skink* (smoked haddock chowder) or a sirloin steak sandwich. See p. 184.

- **Best Cool Cafe: Where the Monkey Sleeps,** 182 W. Regent St. (✆ **0141/226-3406**), makes sandwiches that are as delicious as their names are ridiculous.

- **Best on a Budget:** A brief stroll from the shopping precincts of Sauchiehall Street, the **Wee Curry Shop,** 7 Buccleuch St. off Cambridge St. (✆ **0141/353-0777**), is a tiny gem of a restaurant, serving freshly prepared Indian cuisine at bargain prices. See p. 188.

THE best BARS & PUBS

Edinburgh

- **Best in New Town:** In a city famous for its pubs, the **Café Royal Circle Bar,** 17 W. Register St. (© **0131/556-1884**), stands out, boasting lots of atmosphere and gas-light, frosted-glass Victorian-style design. See p. 139.
- **Best in Stockbridge:** At the heart of the village of Stockbridge, the **Bailie Bar,** 2 St. Stephen St. (© **0131/225-4673**), usually has plenty of banter between the regulars and the staff, and no music ever drowns out the conversation here. See p. 139.
- **Best in Old Town:** Just below the castle, the **Bow Bar,** 80 W. Bow (© **0131/226-7667**), pours some of the best ales in town in a traditional and comfortable pub with a good whisky selection, too. See p. 140.
- **Best in Leith: The Shore,** 3–4 The Shore (© **0131/553-5080**), fits seamlessly into the seaside port ambience, without resorting to a lot of the usual decorations of cork and netting. Excellent food, as well. See p. 141.
- **Best for Folk Music:** It is a toss-up between **Sandy Bell's,** 25 Forrest Rd. (© **0131/225-2751**), and the **Royal Oak,** 1 Infirmary St. (© **0131/557-2967**), when it comes to spontaneous Scottish folk and poetry. Try both if this is your bag. See p. 138 and 137.

Glasgow

- **Best in the Commercial Center:** With its long, horseshoe-shaped bar and central location, the **Horse Shoe,** 17 Drury St. between Renfield and W. Nile streets (© **0141/229-5711**), is a throwback to the days of so-called Palace Pubs in Scotland. See p. 243.
- **Best in the Merchant City:** Unless you are looking for a "style" bar (of which there are plenty), the **Babbity Bowster,** 16 Blackfriars St. (© **0141/552-5055**), is ideal for a drink and some conversation. See p. 243.
- **Best in the West End:** The competition is furious and the selection is vast, but I'll give the nod to **Brel,** 39–43 Ashton Lane (© **0141/342-4966**), for its combination of good ambience, excellent location, and decent Belgian-inspired grub. See p. 243.
- **Best for Whisky:** With a selection of single malts that numbers easily into the hundreds, the **Pot Still,** 154 Hope St. (© **0141/333-0980**), is the place to go for a wee dram. See p. 243.
- **Best for Rock Music:** It's between the near legendary **King Tut's Wah Wah Hut,** 272 St. Vincent St. (© **0141/221-5279**), and **Nice 'n' Sleazy,** 421 Sauchiehall St. (© **0141/333-9637**)—both draw the best in local indie band talent. See p. 242.

THE best SPA EXPERIENCES

- At the **Sheraton Grand,** 1 Festival Sq. at Lothian Rd. in Edinburgh (*©* **0131/229-9131**), the **One Spa** is located on the top floor. The highlight is undoubtedly the roof-top hydropool and glass-walled swimming pool surrounded by loungers, but the pampering is also first-rate. See p. 68.
- In Glasgow, the newest luxury hotel—**Blythswood Square,** 11 Blythswood Sq. (*©* **0141/208-2458**)—has raised the stakes when it comes to exercise, leisure, and treatments. All the guests are entitled to complimentary time slots for using the facility, although treatments are priced accordingly. See p. 173.

EDINBURGH & GLASGOW IN DEPTH

Edinburgh and Glasgow are the principal cities in Scotland: The majority of the country's five million people live in or around these two cities—each is home to a population of between 500,000 and 600,000 within city limits. The country itself occupies the northern third of Great Britain, covering about 78,725 sq. km (30,410 sq. miles)—or nearly the size of Austria. It is about 440km (275 miles) long and 248km (154 miles) wide at its widest point. As it is a modestly sized country, its two main cities are both key players in the nation's economy.

Both cities are on tidal tributaries to the sea, but across Scotland no denizen lives more than about 65km (40 miles) from salt water. Notwithstanding the size of their country, the Scots have extended their influence around the world.

Inventors Alexander Graham Bell (telephone) and John Logie Baird (television), as well as Africa explorers Mungo Park and David Livingstone, came from Scotland. Philosophers David Hume (law) and Adam Smith (economics) were key participants in the Scottish Enlightenment, which was based in Glasgow and Edinburgh. James Watt (steam engine pioneer) and John Muir (the world's first ecologist) were born near the two key cities. This country also gave the world entrepreneur Andrew Carnegie; poet Robert Burns; actors Sean Connery and Ewan McGregor; comedians Billy Connolly and Frankie Boyle; bands Belle & Sebastian and Franz Ferdinand, and singers Sheena Easton, Annie Lennox, and Shirley Manson. Edinburgh spawned novelists Sir Walter Scott and Robert Louis Stevenson, while Glasgow was home to architects Alexander "Greek" Thomson and Charles Rennie Mackintosh.

EDINBURGH & GLASGOW TODAY

The key modern event shaping Edinburgh and Glasgow—indeed all of Scotland—was the devolution settlement and the renewal in 1999 of the **Scottish Parliament,** which is based in Edinburgh near the Palace of Holyroodhouse. For the Scottish capital, it has meant a return to the forefront of governance in Scotland, rather than having things run from London, the U.K. capital. Even for Glasgow, its effects have been profound as voters in the city and its surroundings send the most Members of the Scottish Parliament—or **MSP**s—to Edinburgh. The Scottish Parliament, which is led by the party with the largest number of MSPs, can enact laws regarding health, education, transportation, and public housing, and it has limited taxing powers. But it has no authority over matters of defense, immigration, or foreign policy.

Scotland has long been the stronghold of the left-leaning **Labour Party,** but in the last Parliamentary election in May 2007, the party garnering the most votes—for the first time—was the **Scottish National Party** (SNP). Along with a few minor parties, and in contrast to the other big parties such as the Labour or **Conservative Party,** the SNP favors complete independence for Scotland.

It's important to remember that many Scots, even if they don't want independence, think of themselves as Scots first and British second. And yet, the border between England and Scotland is just a line on a map; you're hardly aware when crossing it. But while the two countries have been joined constitutionally since 1707, Scotland still has a strong cultural identity.

LOOKING BACK AT EDINBURGH & GLASGOW

The key to comprehending—and, in part, enjoying—Edinburgh and Glasgow is to know at least a bit about Scotland's long and sometimes complex history. For much of its existence, the country had full (if disputed) autonomy from England—the larger, more populous, and sometimes pushy neighbor to the south. Although the Scottish and English crowns were joined (1603) and the countries were unified into Great Britain (1707), they are distinct nations.

Although the union with England may well have saved Scotland economically in the 18th century, it also effectively relegated the country to something more akin to an administrative region within Great Britain. Even after devolution, former Prime Minister Tony Blair, while favoring devolution and even born in Edinburgh, once compared the Parliament in Scotland to a Parish Council. Although Edinburgh has long been an intellectual center and Glasgow was considered the "Second City" of the British Empire, many histories of Britain tend to ignore or anglicize developments in Scotland. If you're in any doubt about Scotland's autonomy, however, consider this: In 1320, after decades of war against English invaders and occupiers, barons loyal to Scottish King, Robert the Bruce put their names on a letter to the Pope, the **Declaration of Arbroath.** It not only clearly affirmed the country's independence but also addressed notions of freedom and liberty as Scots: Abstract ideals that most nations didn't contemplate for hundreds of years.

Independence on the Cards?

As of 2010, the SNP didn't have the votes in Parliament to make Scotland an independent country. It is trying to get support to hold a referendum, asking Scottish voters if they favor independence—as it stands, the country is divided on the matter and it is not at all clear whether they would favor it.

EARLY HISTORY Standing stones, *brochs* (circular stone towers), and burial chambers are the best remaining signs of Scotland's earliest residents, but little is known about these first tribes that were living in parts of the country hundreds, indeed thousands, of years before the Romans arrived. When the Romans invaded in about A.D. 82, much of the land was occupied by a people they called the **Picts** (the Painted Ones). Despite some spectacular bloodletting, the Romans never really conquered the indigenous people of Scotland, and the building of Hadrian's Wall (well south of the current border with England) effectively marked the northern limits of Rome's influence. Sometime before A.D. 500, however, the Irish Celtic tribes, called (confusingly) "Scots," began to successfully colonize the land, bringing Christianity and creating the kingdom **Dalriada,** west and northwest of Glasgow on the coast. Celtic Christianity, already introduced by Saints Ninian and **Mungo** to Strathclyde and Galloway, became more widespread. In Glasgow, a cathedral still stands at the spot where St. Mungo (or Kentigern) settled, established an enclave, and was later buried.

THE DARK & MIDDLE AGES The Celtic Scots and the Picts were united around 843, while pressures of invasion from the south and Scandinavia helped mold Scotland into a relatively cohesive unit. Under **Malcolm II** (1005–34), tribes who occupied the southwest and southeast parts of the Scottish mainland were merged with the Scots and the Picts. **Malcolm III** (1031–93), with his English-born wife, Margaret, drove forward church reforms that soon replaced the Gaelic form of Christianity. She led a life of great piety, founded Edinburgh on Castle Hill, and was later canonized as St. Margaret in 1251. King **David I** (1081–1153) embarked on one of the most lavish building sprees in Scottish history, erecting many abbeys, including Jedburgh, Kelso, and Melrose, while also establishing royal burghs such as Edinburgh.

Some of Scotland's most legendary heroes lived during the 13th century, particularly **William Wallace** (1270–1305), who drove the English out of Perth and Stirling. Later **Robert the Bruce** (1274–1329) beat English forces at Bannockburn in 1314. In 1320, after decades of war, barons loyal to Scottish King put their names on a letter to the Pope, the Declaration of Arbroath. In the 15th and 16th centuries, the royal **Stuart** line was established, providing a succession of kings (and one notable queen: **Mary, Queen of Scots**).

THE REFORMATION The passions of the Protestant Reformation arrived on an already turbulent Scottish scene in the 16th century. The main protagonist was undoubtedly **John Knox,** who had a peculiar mixture of piety, conservatism, strict morality, and intellectual independence that many see as a pronounced feature of the Scottish character today. From his pulpit in Edinburgh, Knox helped shape the democratic form of the Scottish Church: Primary among his tenets were provisions for a self-governing congregation, including schools. Thus, Knox effectively encouraged literacy. In Edinburgh's Old Town, visitors can see the John Knox House, where the reformer may have lived, and St. Giles Cathedral, where he most certainly preached.

Knox vehemently opposed the reign of one of Scotland's most famous (and tragic) monarchs: Mary, Queen of Scots (1542–87). When Mary eventually took up her rule, she was a Roman Catholic Scot of French upbringing trying to govern a land (about which she knew little) in the throes of the Reformation. Following some disastrous political and romantic alliances, Mary fled Scotland to be imprisoned in England—her life eventually ended by the executioner's ax on orders of her cousin, Elizabeth I. Ironically, Mary's son—**James VI of Scotland**—succeeded the childless Elizabeth and became King of England (James I) in 1603. The subsequent cult of Mary, Queen of Scots has ensured that landmarks associated with her rule and movements through Scotland, whether Stirling Castle or the Palace of Holyroodhouse, are firmly on the modern tourist trail.

UNION & THE JACOBITES   In the 17th century, Scotland's sovereignty ebbed away as the Scottish royalty spent most of their time in London instead of Edinburgh. In 1689, the final Stuart monarch, the staunchly Catholic James VII (and II of England) fled to France, ending the rule of Scottish kings. In 1707, Scotland had little choice but to merge with England in a constitutionally united Great Britain. This union abolished the Scottish Parliament in Edinburgh, and those loyal to the Stuarts (known as the "Jacobites" from the Latin for James) could only vainly attempt to restore the Stuart line of royalty. Charles Edward Stuart (the Young Pretender), better known as **Bonnie Prince Charlie,** picked up the gauntlet in 1745. He was the central figure in a revolt that nearly worked. Initially successful, starting from the Highlands, Stuart and his supporters easily reached Derby, only 201km (125 miles) from London. The British capital was reportedly in a panic. But Charlie

---

A Few Famous Scots

- Robert Burns (1759–96): Scotland's ploughman poet, known in many languages and countries
- Sir Alexander Fleming (1881–1955): Nobel Prize winner who discovered penicillin
- David Hume (1711–76): Laid the foundation for intellectual and philosophical pursuits using the concept of secular morality
- David Livingstone (1813–73): Medical missionary and African explorer who named Victoria Falls on the Zambezi River
- Flora Macdonald (1725–90): Key person in rescuing Bonnie Prince Charlie from British troops after his defeat at Culloden
- John Muir (1834–1914): Pioneering conservationist who discovered California's Yosemite Valley and founded the Sierra Club
- Sir Walter Scott (1771–1832): Romantic novelist and poet who occupies a position of preeminence in English literature
- Adam Smith (1723–90): Author of the book *The Wealth of Nations,* which underpins the modern science of economics
- Muriel Spark (1910–2006): Author whose classic tale, *The Prime of Miss Jean Brodie,* puts her among the elite of 20th-century novelists

and the Jacobites made an ill-conceived tactical retreat to Scotland, where they were eventually crushed at the **Battle of Culloden,** near Inverness, in 1746.

THE SCOTTISH ENLIGHTENMENT & ECONOMIC GROWTH   During the 18th century, the union began to reap dividends, and the Scottish economy underwent a radical transformation. As trade with British colonies increased, the port of Glasgow flourished. Its merchants grew rich on the tobacco trade with Virginia and the Carolinas. Ships from Glasgow (where they were often constructed, too) were making the trip back and forth to the New World much faster than competitors elsewhere in Great Britain. The **Merchant City** district of the city center is named after the tobacco and cotton barons. The River Clyde became world-famous for shipbuilding. Of course, many industrial inventions that altered the history of the developing world—such as the steam engine—were either invented or perfected by Scottish genius and industry. The ground-breaking movement in philosophy now known as the Scottish Enlightenment, which was established at Glasgow University and based largely in Edinburgh, brought forward important thinkers, such as David Hume and Adam Smith. Edinburgh's **New Town** was begun in the mid-1700s and today is a World Heritage Site recognized by the United Nations. Later, Victorian builders turned Glasgow into a showcase of 19th-century architecture.

RECENT HISTORY   By the 1960s and 1970s, Scotland found that its industrial plants couldn't compete with the emerging industrial powerhouses of Asia and elsewhere. A glimmer of light appeared on the Scottish economic horizon in the 1970s: The discovery of **North Sea oil** lifted the British economy considerably. Edinburgh also became a center for global banking (though more recently, this has proved to be a mixed blessing). In 1997, under a newly elected Labour government in London, the Scottish electorate voted on **devolution**—a fancy word for limited sovereignty. The referendum passed, allowing Scotland to have its own legislature for the first time since the 1707 union with England. The Scottish Parliament has since passed laws that differ from practice in England and Wales, such as ensuring free higher education for Scots or offering home care for the elderly. Whether the country can afford these benefits is hotly debated.

SCOTTISH MUSIC

Scottish music is considerably more than "Scotland the Brave" played on bagpipes, although you may well hear the song during your stay. The Gaelic-influenced songs and sounds of the Hebridean Islands and the Highlands have been around for centuries—and today many Scottish folk musicians live and play most often in Edinburgh or Glasgow. The fiddle, accordion, guitar, flute, and Celtic drum are all part of the musical tradition. The best chance to hear the real deal is at a jam session in a pub or at a more formal (but still fun) *ceilidh* (pronounced *kay*-lee). Traditionally, *ceilidhs* were community gatherings, with music, dance, singing, and story-telling. More often today, they are reduced to Scottish country dances, such as the Gay Gordon or Stripping the Willow. Bagpipes and the rousing, indeed ear-shattering, sounds they can create are entrenched in the national identity. Every summer, Glasgow hosts an international piping competition that draws thousands of pipers (many of whom also perform as part of Edinburgh's Military Tattoo, a show featuring music, marching, and military exercises). But a lone piper may pop up anytime, anywhere.

EATING & DRINKING

In the past 20 years, Scottish restaurants, especially in Edinburgh and Glasgow, have garnered significant attention for their culinary excellence, using the best ingredients—whether West Coast langoustines (aka Dublin Bay Prawns) or Perthshire raspberries—that the country produces in a variety of styles.

Let's begin with traditional Scottish cooking, which is hearty. Staples include **fish** (such as salmon, oysters, or haddock, often smoked), **potatoes** (*tatties*), **turnips or swedes** (*neeps*), **oatcakes, porridge oats,** and local game such as **grouse** or **venison.** And, of course, **haggis,** which remains Scotland's national dish—though it's perhaps more symbolic than gustatory. **Fish and chips** is also common, though up north it is called a fish supper if you're taking it away and a fish tea if you're eating in.

But modern Scottish cuisine is more diverse and innovative, borrowing from French and even Far Eastern techniques, using local produce such as scallops or lamb. One of Scotland's best-known food exports is **Aberdeen Angus** beef, but equally fine is free-range Scottish **lamb,** known for its tender, tasty meat. Fish, in this land of seas, rivers, and lochs, is a mainstay, from wild halibut to the herring that's transformed in the smokehouse into the elegant **kipper.** Scottish **smoked salmon** is, of course, a delicacy known around the globe. Scottish shellfish is world-class, whether oysters, mussels, clams, and crabs, or lobsters and their smaller or delicate relative, **langoustines,** which have become a hit in upmarket restaurants. Ranging from pheasant and grouse to rabbit and venison, game is also a key feature of the Scottish natural larder.

Scottish **raspberries** are among the finest in the world. You should definitely try some of Scotland's excellent **cheeses** as well. One of the best is *Criffel,* from the south of the country: A creamy and rich semi-soft cheese made from the milk of shorthorn cows that graze only in organic pastures. Delicious.

At your hotel or B&B, the morning meal is almost insured to include the Scottish breakfast (which is essentially the same as the English breakfast) or the **full fry-up,** as the locals may call it. Expect most or all of the following: Eggs, bacon, and sausage; black pudding; very occasionally haggis; grilled tomatoes; mushrooms; sometimes fried bread; toast with marmalade or jam; juice; and coffee or tea.

These days, "eclectic" best describes Scotland's metropolitan **restaurant scene**. While perhaps not as varied as England's biggest cities, Indian restaurants abound, as do French, Italian, and Thai options. But Edinburgh currently has more Michelin-starred restaurants than any other U.K. city, excluding London. In rural areas, the selection can be more hit or miss, while the English gastro-pub phenomenon has not really spread north of the border. But stick to my recommendations and you should do just fine.

PUB LIFE IN SCOTLAND Much socializing in Scotland centers on the local pub. It can be the gathering place for an entire community, the place where locals go to share news and exchange gossip. At certain pubs, pickup sessions of traditional and folk music are common. Even if you're not a big drinker, going out for a pint of lager, a dram of whisky, or a bite to eat at a Scottish *howff* can be a memorable part of your trip.

The most widely available, mass-produced Scottish beers are Tennent's lager and McEwan's ale, but from region to region, you may find a number of local breweries, making anything from light-colored lagers to dark ales. Among them, Deuchars IPA (Edinburgh), Black Isle Organic, and Orkney's Dark Island are standouts. The most

> ## Whisky Galore
>
> While blends such as Famous Grouse or Johnny Walker are best known, most connoisseurs prefer varieties of single malt whisky, the taste of which depends largely on where it's distilled: Sweet Lowland, peaty Island, or smooth and balanced Highland. Single malts are seen as sipping whiskies and can be diluted with a few drops of tap water. If you want a cocktail made with whisky, expect it to be a blend, such as Whyte & MacKay or Bell's, and not single malt like Glenmorangie or Laphroaig. If you want a North American bourbon, rye, or sour-mash whisky, you need to name the brand: For example, Jack Daniel's or Maker's Mark.

popular stout remains Ireland's Guinness, while the potent Stella Artois, from the Continent, is the best-selling premium lager.

SCOTLAND IN POPULAR CULTURE

MOVIES The movies listed below are among the best and most popular made about Scotland and its people.

Braveheart (1995): This movie—hardly historically accurate but moving nonetheless—probably did more to stir overseas interest in Scotland than any promotional campaign ever cooked up by the tourist board. Mel Gibson stars as the 13th-century patriot William Wallace in this sweeping Academy Award-winning epic.

Gregory's Girl (1981): A simple comedy about an awkward high school student (played by gawky John Gordon-Sinclair) in a modern (and mostly hideous) 20th-century New Town near Glasgow.

I Know Where I'm Going! (1945): This is a charming, funny, World War II-era black-and-white movie from the great British team Powell and Pressburger. It takes a young English fiancée on a suspenseful, romantic adventure to the Hebridean isles.

Local Hero (1983): In this sweetly eclectic comedy—possibly the best Scottish movie ever made—villagers on a gorgeous stretch of coastline (filmed near Mallaig) expect to cash in big time because of Texan oil-industry interest, but events conspire against them.

Morvern Callar (2002): An excellent adaptation directed by Lynne Ramsay of Alan Warner's affecting contemporary story of an unusual turn of events in the life of a young woman from a Scottish town.

My Name is Joe (1998): Although not entirely lacking humor and romance, this movie paints a rather grim, if accurate, picture of Glaswegians struggling with their addictions and inner demons.

Orphans (1997): Actor Peter Mullan (star of *My Name is Joe*) wrote and directed this outlandish and very, very dark comedy about the day the Flynn family in Glasgow tried to bury their recently deceased mother.

The 39 Steps (1935): Director Alfred Hitchcock and scriptwriter Charles Bennett almost completely reset John Buchan's tale of spies and intrigue. Instead of sticking to the borders, the film transports the hero to the Highlands.

Trainspotting (1996): Based on one of the most popular contemporary books by Scottish author Irvine Welsh, *Trainspotting* is a gritty and often hilarious account of a group of unrepentant drug-addled characters in Edinburgh in the late 1980s.

Whisky Galore! (1949): Retitled *Tight Little Island* in the U.S., this classic movie is based on a true story. The residents of a small Scottish isle get an intoxicating windfall when a ship carrying 50,000 cases of whisky crashes off their coast during World War II.

The Wicker Man (1973): A cult classic of cinema about a strange New Age community on a picturesque Scottish island—and the secrets they keep from a mainland constable.

BOOKS   There are too many books about Scotland to mention, so this is a concise list to get interested visitors going.

Black & Blue—An Inspector Rebus Novel (Orion, 1997) by Ian Rankin is one of many in the best-selling modern crime mystery series by this prolific author. Lots of fans visit sites in Edinburgh, such as the Oxford Bar, frequented by the fictitious Rebus and the real Rankin.

The Heart of Midlothian by Sir Walter Scott (Penguin Classics) was declared a masterpiece in 1818 and remains Scott's seminal piece of fiction, influencing the later works of authors such as Balzac, Hawthorne, and Dickens.

Kidnapped by Robert Louis Stevenson (Penguin Classics) follows the adventures of young David Balfour after he's spirited out of Edinburgh and ends up on the wrong side of the law in the Western Highlands. The story is as entertaining today as it was upon publication in 1886.

Lanark: A Life in Four Books by Alasdair Gray (Pub Group West, 2003) is perhaps the most important contemporary novel to be published in Scotland in the last 100 years. Gray is an eccentric of the first order, but this work of fiction (first published in 1981 and illustrated by the author), despite some fantastical detours, gets to the core of urban Scotland.

The Prime of Miss Jean Brodie by Muriel Spark (Perennial Classics, 1999) and *Trainspotting* by Irvine Welsh (W. W. Norton & Company, 1996) are both better known for their cinematic adaptations, but in their own very different ways, both novels manage to capture elements of Edinburgh life.

HISTORY   *Scotland: A New History* by Michael Lynch (Pimlico, 1992) is a good take on Scottish history from ancient times up to the 1990s.

The Scottish Enlightenment: The Scot's Invention of the Modern World by American historian Arthur Herman (Crown, 2001) offers a clear and extremely readable explanation of the impact that Scottish thinkers had on the world.

The Scottish Nation: 1700–2000 by academic Tom Devine (Penguin, 2001) is a good, fairly recently published historical overview of Scotland. Devine is one of the few historians to examine how people were driven from the Scottish Lowlands, as well as more famous and lamentable clearances from the Highlands.

Stone Voices: The Search for Scotland by Neal Ascherson (Hill & Wang, 2003) is a quest for the national character of Scotland. In a series of anecdotes and reflections, journalist Ascherson helps readers understand the worthy sentiments behind Scottish independence and begins to redress the imbalance of Scottish histories so often written by the English.

PLANNING YOUR TRIP TO EDINBURGH & GLASGOW

Edinburgh and Glasgow, separated by less than 74km (46 miles), are, of course, the primary cities of Scotland, as well as significant metropolises in the United Kingdom. Each has an increasingly busy international airport and a city center railway terminal that regularly receives trains from London and other cities in England, and from elsewhere in Scotland.

Although Scotland likes to think of itself as a separate country, the central United Kingdom government in London regulates all issues regarding international visitors and immigrants, and the same rules apply to travel to Scotland as to traveling in any part of England, Wales, and Northern Ireland.

This chapter is devoted to the when, where, and how of your trip—as well as the advanced planning required to get your traveling act together and take it, literally, on the road.

For additional help in planning your trip and for more on-the-ground resources in Edinburgh and Glasgow, please turn to the "Fast Facts" on p. 263.

WHEN TO GO
Weather

The Lowlands of Scotland usually have a moderate year-round temperature. In spring, the average is around 53°F (12°C), rising to about 65°F (18°C) in summer. By the time the crisp fall has arrived, the temperatures have dropped to spring levels. In winter, the average temperature is 43°F (6°C), but can be colder and sub-freezing days are not unheard of, but not the norm, either. Temperatures of northern Scotland and the Highlands are generally lower, especially in winter, and you should dress

Scotland

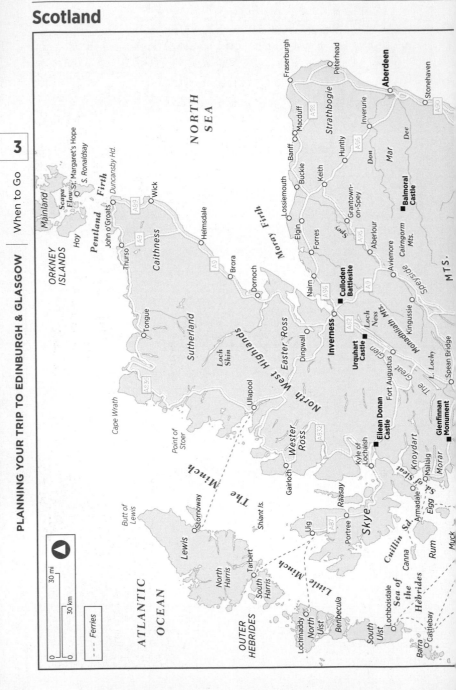

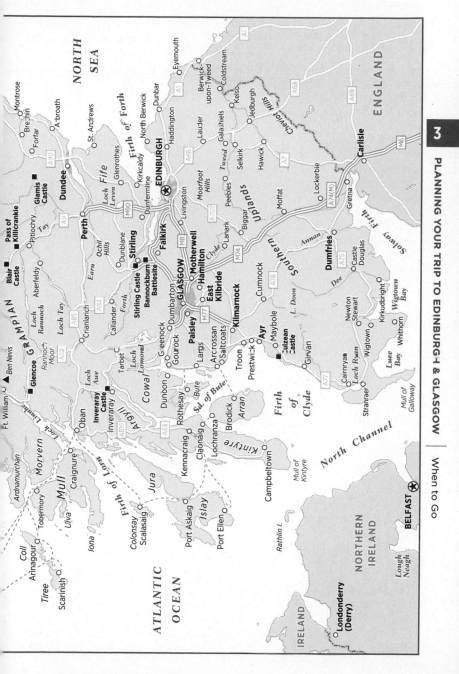

3

ATLANTIC
OCEAN

NORTH
SEA

NORTH
CHANNEL

ENGLAND

NORTHERN
IRELAND

IRELAND

accordingly. On the islands, the weather is just a bit more temperate, but can be typically windy. In the cities, daytime temperatures are higher.

It rains a fair amount in Scotland, but perhaps not as much as age-old myths would have it: The average annual rainfall in Edinburgh is about the same as that in London. September can be the sunniest month.

Average Temperature & Rainfall in Edinburgh and Glasgow

	JAN	FEB	MAR	APR	MAY	JUNE	JULY	AUG	SEPT	OCT	NOV	DEC
Temp. (°F)	38	38	42	44	50	55	59	58	54	48	43	40
Temp. (°C)	3	3	6	7	10	13	15	14	12	9	6	4
Rainfall (in.)	2.2	1.6	1.9	1.5	2.0	2.0	2.5	2.7	2.5	2.4	2.5	2.4

When You Find Bargains

The cheapest time to travel is off-season: Late **October** up to **Easter** (excluding Christmas and New Year). Rates for hotels hit their peak in the high season from **June** through **September,** and particularly in Edinburgh during the Festival in **August** rates at some hotels rise noticeably. Mid-July and August are when many locals take their holidays, which are increasingly spent inside the U.K., so besides the higher prices, you'll have to deal with bigger crowds and greater demand for hotel rooms.

Those coming from abroad should note that airlines are known to offer cut-rate fares during off-periods. Weekday flights are generally cheaper than weekend fares, often by at least 10%. The best news for bargain hunters is that many tourist attractions in Edinburgh and Glasgow are free. Most remain open year-round, which is not always the case outside these cities.

Spring offers the countryside at its greenest, fall brings on steely skies, and summer's warmth gives rise to the music and theater festivals. But winter offers savings across the board and a chance to see Scots going about their everyday lives largely unhindered by tourist invasions.

Holidays

The following holidays are celebrated in Scotland, although individual cities and regions will have their public holidays, too: New Year's Day (Jan 1–2), Good Friday and Easter Monday, May Day (first Mon in May), spring bank holiday (last Mon in May), summer bank holiday (last Mon in Aug), Christmas Day (Dec 25), and Boxing Day (Dec 26).

Edinburgh & Glasgow Calendar of Events

For an exhaustive list of events beyond those listed here, check http://events.frommers. com, where you'll find a searchable, up-to-the-minute guide to what's happening in cities all over the world.

JANUARY

Celtic Connections, Glasgow. This celebration of folk and traditional music is becoming one of the largest of its kind in the world, drawing musicians from throughout Scotland, Wales, and Ireland, as well as further afield—such as the Basque country and North America. Call ✆ **0141/353-8000.** Two weeks toward the end of January.

Burns Night. Naturally, during the celebrations to honor Robert Burns, there's much toasting with whisky and eating of haggis, the arrival of which is announced by a bagpipe. January 25.

FEBRUARY

New Territories, Glasgow. An international festival of performance arts, especially contemporary dance and theater. Early February to mid-March.

MARCH

Glasgow Comedy Festival. Inaugurated in 2003, this festival brings a diverse range of funny men and women to stages around the city. Call ☎ **0141/552-2070.** Mid-March.

APRIL

Glasgow Art Fair. Galleries from across the U.K. set up stalls in big tents on George Square. First weekend in April.

Glasgow International. A fortnight-long celebration of contemporary visual art at a host of local galleries. Last 2 weeks of April.

Triptych. As the name implies, this is a contemporary and avant-garde music festival that takes place in three cities: Edinburgh, Glasgow, and Aberdeen. Last weekend in April.

Beltane Fire Festival, Edinburgh. This one celebrates paganism and the alleged arrival of summer on Calton Hill with primal drums and dancing. A bit of nudity is almost guaranteed. April 30.

MAY

Burns an' A' That, Ayr, south of Glasgow. A celebration of the life of Robert Burns with contemporary artists and performers—mainly musicians. For details, call ☎ **0129/229-0300.** Late May.

JUNE

Edinburgh International Film Festival. Moved to June from its traditional dates in August, this is the oldest continually running film festival in Europe. ☎ **0131/623-8030.** Mid-late June.

Royal Highland Show, at the Ingliston Showground, outskirts of Edinburgh. This show is devoted to agriculture and commerce. For details, call ☎ **0131/335-6200.** Mid- late June.

Pride. Scotland's annual gay celebration alternates between Edinburgh and Glasgow. You'll see a quirky, boisterous parade through the heart of Glasgow or along Princes Street in Edinburgh. Some time in June.

West End Festival, Glasgow. The city's most vibrant neighborhoods throw a party that includes live music, a street parade, and other events. Throughout most of June.

Glasgow International Jazz Festival. Jazz musicians from all over the world come together to perform at various venues around the city. End of June.

JULY

Glasgow River Festival. A 2-day event with exhibitions, sailings, and other festivities on the River Clyde. Mid-July.

Edinburgh International Jazz & Blues Festival. Of the various events that dominate the Edinburgh social calendar in summer, this one is the first to kick off. End of July into August.

AUGUST

Edinburgh Festival. Scotland's best-known event is actually a number of festivals in one—Jazz, Book, International, and Fringe—taking place concurrently in the Scottish capital. The Fringe alone encompasses some 1,800 performances. An arts bonanza, it draws major talent from around the world. For more information, visit www.edinburgh festivals.co.uk. Throughout August.

Edinburgh Military Tattoo. A spectacular every evening at Edinburgh Castle Esplanade, featuring precision marching and army bands from across the globe. Call ☎ **0870/755-5118.** Throughout August.

Piping Live! Glasgow. Bagpipe players and bagpipe bands from around the world gather in the city for a week-long festival that culminates with the **World Pipe Band Championships**—an orgy of bagpiping, as up to 1,000 kilted participants strut their stuff. Call ✆ **0141/241-4400.** Mid-August.

SEPTEMBER

Doors Open Day, Edinburgh and Glasgow. One weekend in the month, the public is given unique access to landmark buildings that are normally off limits.

OCTOBER

Glasgay! Glasgow. One of the U.K.'s largest festivals of gay, lesbian, and transgender culture, with club nights, music, and performance art. Mid-October–mid-November.

International Story Telling Festival, Edinburgh. Events at various venues in the capital help to celebrate the oral tradition of Scotland and other nations. Call ✆ **0131/556-9579.** Last 2 weeks in October.

NOVEMBER

Edinburgh Christmas. The capital gets an early start on the holiday season with outdoor markets and fairground rides. Late November–Christmas.

Glasgow on Ice. An outdoor ice-skating rink is set up in George Square, along with carnival rides and gift booths. Late November to Christmas Eve.

DECEMBER

Hogmanay, Edinburgh and Glasgow. New Year's Eve—Hogmanay—is traditionally bigger for the Scots than Christmas. Events in the capital include a torchlight procession, a fire festival along Princes Street, a carnival, and a street theater spectacular. Both cities stage outdoor concerts on Hogmanay. The celebration in Edinburgh begins in the last week of December and continues past New Year's Day.

Visitor Information

Before you travel from abroad, you can get information from **VisitBritain** (www.visitbritain.com or **VisitScotland** (www.visitscotland.com).

In the **United States:** 551 Fifth Ave., Suite 701, New York, NY 10176-0799 (✆ **800/462-2748,** or 212/986-2200 in New York; fax 212/986-1188); 625 N. Michigan Ave., Suite 1001, Chicago, IL, 60611-1977 (✆ **800/462-2748**); 10880 Wilshire Blvd., Suite 570, Los Angeles, CA, 90024 (✆ **310/470-2782**). In **Canada:** 5915 Airport Rd., Suite 120, Mississauga, ON L4V 1T1 (✆ **888/VISIT-UK** in Canada; fax 905/405-1835 in Toronto). In **Australia:** Level 2, 15 Blue St., North Sydney NSW 2060 (✆ **02/9021-4400;** fax 02/9377-4499). In **New Zealand:** c/o British Consulate General Office, Level 17, IAG House, 151 Queen St., Auckland 1 (✆ **09/303-1446;** fax 09/309-1899).

If you're in London, you can visit **VisitScotland,** 19 Cockspur St., London SW1Y 5BL (✆ **020/7930-8661**); it's near Trafalgar Square, open May to September Monday through Friday from 9:30am to 6:30pm and Saturday from 10am to 5pm. October to April the hours are Monday through Friday 10am to 6pm and Saturday noon to 4pm.

Once in Edinburgh or Glasgow, you will find the Tourist Information Centres more useful. In the capital, the main office is the **Edinburgh Information Centre,** atop the Princes Mall near Waverley Station (✆ **0131/473-3800** or 0845/225-5121; fax 0131/473-3881; www.edinburgh.org). It can give you sightseeing information and also arrange lodgings. The center sells bus tours, theater tickets, and souvenirs of Edinburgh. It also has racks and racks of free brochures. It's open year-round, though hours vary from month to month. The summer hours are slightly longer and winter times shorter, but typically you'll find the office open Monday through Saturday from 9am to 7pm and Sunday from 10am to 7pm. There is an information desk at Edinburgh International Airport, open typically Monday through Sunday 7am to 6:30pm.

In Glasgow, the **Greater Glasgow and Clyde Valley Tourist Board,** 11 George Sq. (**© 0141/204-4480;** www.seeglasgow.com), is in the heart of the city. In addition to piles of brochures, there is a small bookstore, *bureau de change,* and hotel reservation service. During peak season, it's open Monday to Saturday from 9am to 7pm and Sunday from 10am to 6pm. Hours are more limited during winter months.

WHAT'S ON THE WEB? There is naturally a host of websites that vary in usefulness. The British tourist board's **www.visitbritain.org** has the overall U.K. picture. But for information on Scotland, it's probably better to go directly to **www. visitscotland.com** or **www.toscotland.com,** both of which have detailed information, offer brochures online, provide trip-planning hints, and answer e-mail queries. A slightly more corporate view is at **www.scotexchange.net.** The other useful and official tourism websites for Edinburgh and Glasgow are **www.edinburgh.org** and **www.seeglasgow.com.**

For the most up-to-date events listings, go to **www.list.co.uk,** which also publishes a fortnightly cultural magazine. The two organizations that operate most of Scotland's historical sites have websites as well: **www.historic-scotland.gov.uk** for Historic Scotland and **www.nts.org.uk** for the National Trust for Scotland.

For an independent and eccentric view, search blogs in Edinburgh and Glasgow. Finally, though it is not clear how often they are updated, you might also have a look at **www.scotland-info.co.uk, www.undiscoveredscotland.co.uk,** or **www.ram pantscotland.com.**

Entry Requirements
PASSPORTS

All visitors entering from abroad must have a valid passport with at least 2 months' validity remaining. No visa is required. An immigration officer may also want proof of your intention to return to your point of origin (usually a round-trip ticket). If you're planning to fly from the United States or Canada to the United Kingdom and then on to a country that requires a visa (India, for example), you should secure that visa before you arrive in Britain.

OBTAINING A PASSPORT

For Residents of the United States: Whether you're applying in person or by mail, you can download passport applications from the U.S. State Department website at **http://travel.state.gov.** For general information, call the **National Passport Agency** (**© 202/647-0518**). To find your regional passport office, either check the U.S. State Department website or call the **National Passport Information Center** (**© 900/225-5674**); the fee is 55¢ per minute for automated information and $1.50 per minute for operator-assisted calls.

For Residents of Canada: Passport applications are available at travel agencies throughout Canada or from the central **Passport Office,** Department of Foreign

Affairs and International Trade, Ottawa, ON K1A 0G3 (© **800/567-6868;** www. dfait-maeci.gc.ca).

For Residents of Ireland: You can apply for a 10-year passport at the **Passport Office,** Setanta Centre, Molesworth Street, Dublin 2 (© **01/671-1633;** www.irlgov.ie/ iveagh). Those under age 18 and over 65 must apply for a €12 3-year passport. You can also apply at 1A South Mall, Cork (© **021/272-525**) or at most main post offices.

For an up-to-date country-by-country listing of passport requirements around the world, go the "Foreign Entry Requirement" web page of the U.S. State Department at http://travel.state.gov.

CUSTOMS

WHAT YOU CAN BRING INTO SCOTLAND   The same rules for travel to any part of the U.K. apply to travel to Scotland. From outside the European Union, you can bring in the following for your own use without paying tax or duty: 200 cigarettes, 100 cigarillos, 50 cigars, or 250 grams (9 oz.) of smoking tobacco; 60cc of perfume; 2 liters of still table wine; 250cc eau de toilette; 1 liter of spirits or strong liqueurs or 2 liters of fortified wine; £145 worth of all other goods, including gifts and souvenirs. Any amounts over these limits should be declared.

If you bring in goods from a European Union member country on which tax has been paid in that country, no tax or duty is due (as long as they are for your own personal use). Some special rules may apply, however, for tobacco from some E.U. countries.

For up-to-date information on customs, go to www.hmrc.gov.uk and search for "information for travelers."

WHAT YOU CAN TAKE HOME FROM SCOTLAND   **Canadian Citizens:** For a clear summary of Canadian rules, write for the booklet *I Declare,* issued by the Canada Border Services Agency (© **800/461-9999** in Canada, or 204/983-3500; www.cbsa-asfc.gc.ca).

U.K. Citizens: For information, contact **HM Customs & Excise** at © **0845/ 010-9000** (from outside the U.K., 020/8929-0152), or consult their website at www.hmce.gov.uk.

Australian Citizens: A helpful brochure available from Australian consulates or Customs offices is *Know Before You Go.* For more information, call the **Australian Customs Service** at © **1300/363-263,** or log on to www.customs.gov.au.

New Zealand Citizens: Most questions are answered in a free pamphlet available at New Zealand consulates and Customs offices: *New Zealand Customs Guide for Travellers, Notice no. 4.* For more information, contact **New Zealand Customs,** The Customhouse, 17–21 Whitmore St., Box 2218, Wellington (© **04/473-6099** or 0800/428-786; www.customs.govt.nz).

Calling Scotland from Abroad

To call Scotland from outside the U.K., dial the **international prefix,** for example **011** in the U.S.; then U.K.'s **country code, 44;** then the **city code,** for example, **131** for Edinburgh and **141** for Glasgow; and then the local **phone number.** Inside the U.K. you add a zero before the local or city code, so **0131** for Edinburgh and **0141** for Glasgow.

Getting to Edinburgh & Glasgow

BY PLANE   British Airways (✆ **800/247-9297,** or 0870/850-9850 in the U.K.; www.ba.com) offers frequent nonstop flights daily from London's Heathrow Airport to both Edinburgh and Glasgow. **BMI** (formerly British Midland; ✆ **0870/607-0555;** www.flybmi.com) also flies from Heathrow to both Edinburgh and Glasgow. It is a member of the international "Star Alliance," which includes carriers such as Air Canada, Air New Zealand, United, and US Airways. From overseas, carriers that fly directly to Edinburgh and Glasgow from the U.S. have changed over the past few years. What long-haul flights there are tend to arrive and depart from Glasgow's airport.

London, of course, has flights from all corners of the globe. Internally, it is worth remembering **Ryanair** (✆ **0871/246-0000;** www.ryanair.com), which is a budget airline that flies from Stansted outside London to Prestwick south of Glasgow. Also **Flybe,** another discount carrier, with flights into Edinburgh and Glasgow from other U.K. airports.

BY CAR   If you're driving north to Scotland from England, it's fastest to take the **M1 Motorway** (freeway or expressway) north from London. You can reach the M1 by driving to the ring road from any point in the British capital. Southeast of Leeds, you'll need to connect with the **A1** (not a motorway), which you take north to Scotch Corner. Here the **M1** resumes, ending south of Newcastle-upon-Tyne. Then you can take the **A696,** which becomes the **A68,** for its final run north into Edinburgh.

If you're in the west of England, go north along the **M5,** which begins at Exeter (Devon). Eventually this will merge with the **M6.** Continue north on the M6 until you reach a point north of Carlisle. From Carlisle, cross into Scotland near Gretna Green. Continue north along the **A74** via Moffat. The A74 soon becomes the **M74** heading toward Glasgow. If your goal is Edinburgh, not Glasgow, various roads will take you east to the Scottish capital, including the **M8,** which goes part of the way, as do the **A702, A70,** and **A71** (all these routes are well signposted).

BY TRAIN OR BUS   From England, two main rail lines link London to Scotland. The most popular and fastest route is the one departing **King's Cross Station** in London to Edinburgh's **Waverley Station,** going by way of Newcastle. This is the so-called **East Coast Mainline.** Trains cross from England into Scotland at Berwick-upon-Tweed. But future attention is on the **West Coast Mainline,** where trains leave **Euston Station** in London for Glasgow's **Central Station,** by way of Carlisle. The line has been upgraded once for faster trains and there has been some talk (but no money) of building a high-speed line like the ones you see in France or Japan, cutting the travel time from London to Glasgow to about 2 hours. Most of the current trains still take at least 4 hours to reach the heart of Scotland's main city centers. Fares vary quite widely but advance reservations for non-flexible tickets are the cheapest and as low as about £10 each way. Bought on the day or for a ticket offering travel any time with no restrictions, the price will be considerably more expensive.

The journey from London to Glasgow and Edinburgh by bus or coach can take up to 12 long hours, although express buses can make the trip in fewer than 10 hours. **National Express** (✆ **0870/580-8080;** www.nationalexpress.com) runs buses daily (typically 9:30am, noon, and 11pm for direct services) from London's Victoria

Coach Station to Edinburgh's Bus Station near St. Andrew Square; while direct buses for Glasgow's **Buchanan Street Bus Station,** north of the Queen Street Station on North Hanover Street (© 0870-608-2608), leave London's Victoria Coach Station at 9am and 11:30pm. The standard fare is around £35, though Internet and advance purchase discounts are available. Scottish **CityLink** (© **0870/550-5050;** www.citylink.co.uk) also has a frequent bus service between Edinburgh and Glasgow, with a standard one-way ticket costing £6.

Getting Around

See p. 57 and 165 in chapters 5 and 13.

FLYING FOR LESS: TIPS FOR GETTING THE BEST AIRFARE

- Passengers who can book their ticket either **long in advance or at the last minute,** or who **fly midweek** or **at less-trafficked hours** may pay a fraction of the full fare. If your schedule is flexible, say so, and ask if you can secure a cheaper fare by changing your flight plans.

- Search **the Internet** for cheap fares (see "What's on the Web," earlier in this chapter).

- Keep an eye on local newspapers for **promotional specials** or **fare wars,** when airlines lower prices on their most popular routes. You rarely see fare wars offered for peak travel times, but if you can travel off-season, you may snag a bargain.

- Try to book a ticket **in its country of origin.** If you're planning a one-way flight from Johannesburg to Bombay, a South Africa-based travel agent will probably have the lowest fares. For multi-leg trips, book in the country of the first leg; for example, book New York–London–Amsterdam–Rome–New York in the U.S.

- **Consolidators,** also known as bucket shops, are great sources for international tickets, although they usually can't beat Internet fares within North America. Start by looking in Sunday newspaper travel sections; U.S. travelers should focus on the *New York Times, Los Angeles Times,* and *Miami Herald.* U.K. travelers should search in *The Independent, The Guardian,* or *The Observer.* For less-developed destinations, small travel agents who cater to immigrant communities in large cities often have the best deals. *Beware:* Bucket shop tickets are usually nonrefundable or rigged with stiff cancelation penalties, often as high as 50% to 75% of the ticket price, and some put you on charter airlines, which may leave at inconvenient times and experience delays. Several reliable consolidators are worldwide and available online. **STA Travel** has been the world's leading consolidator for students since purchasing Council Travel, but their fares are competitive for travelers of all ages. **ELTExpress** (**Flights.com;** © 800/8782-800) has excellent fares worldwide, particularly to Europe. They also have "local" websites in 12 countries. **FlyCheap** (© 800/359-24327; www.1800flycheap.com), owned by package-holiday megalith MyTravel, has especially good fares to sunny destinations. **Air Tickets Direct** (© 800/778-3447; www.airticketsdirect.com), based in Montreal, offers low international fares; they also book trips to places that U.S. travel agents won't touch, such as Cuba.

- Join **frequent-flier clubs.** Frequent-flier membership doesn't cost a cent, but it does entitle you to better seats, faster response to phone inquiries, and prompter service if your luggage is stolen or your flight is canceled or delayed, or if you want to change your seat. And you don't have to fly to earn points; **frequent-flier credit cards** can earn you thousands of miles for doing your everyday shopping. With more than 70 mileage awards programs on the market, consumers have never had more options. Investigate the program details of your favorite airlines before you sink points into any one. Consider which airlines have hubs in the airport nearest you, and, of those carriers, which have the most advantageous alliances, given your most common routes. To play the frequent-flier game to your best advantage, consult Randy Petersen's **Inside Flyer** (www.insideflyer.com). Petersen and friends review all the programs in detail and post regular updates on changes in policies and trends.

LONG-HAUL FLIGHTS: HOW TO STAY COMFORTABLE

- Your choice of airline and airplane will definitely affect your leg room. Find more details about U.S. airlines at **www.seatguru.com.** For international airlines, the research firm Skytrax has posted a list of average seat pitches at **www.airline quality.com.**

- Emergency exit seats and bulkhead seats typically have the most legroom. Emergency exit seats are usually left unassigned until the day of a flight (to ensure that someone able-bodied fills the seats); it's worth getting to the ticket counter early to snag one of these spots for a long flight. Many passengers find that bulkhead seating (the row facing the wall at the front of the cabin) offers more legroom, but keep in mind that bulkheads are where airlines often put baby bassinets, so you may be sitting next to an infant.

- To have two seats for yourself in a three-seat row, try for an aisle seat in a center section toward the back of coach. If you're traveling with a companion, book an aisle and a window seat. Middle seats are usually booked last, so chances are good you'll end up with three seats to yourselves.

- Ask about entertainment options. Many airlines offer seatback video systems where you get to choose your movies or play video games—but only on some of their planes. (Boeing 777s are your best bet.)

- To sleep, avoid the last row of any section or the row in front of an emergency exit, as these seats are the least likely to recline. Avoid seats near highly trafficked lavatory areas. Avoid seats in the back of many jets—these can be narrower than those in the rest of coach. You also may want to reserve a window seat so you can rest your head and avoid being bumped in the aisle.

- Get up, walk around, and stretch every 60 to 90 minutes to keep your blood flowing. This helps avoid **deep vein thrombosis,** or "economy-class syndrome." See the box "Avoiding 'Economy Class Syndrome,'" p. 31.

- Drink water before, during, and after your flight to combat the lack of humidity in airplane cabins. Avoid alcohol, which will further dehydrate you.

- If you're flying with kids, don't forget to carry on toys, books, pacifiers, and chewing gum to help them relieve ear pressure buildup during ascent and descent.

MONEY & COSTS

Pounds & Pence

Britain's decimal monetary system is based on the pound sterling (£), which is made up of 100 pence (written as "p"). Scotland issues its own currency, but English and

Coping with Jet Lag

Jetlag is a pitfall of traveling across time zones. If you're flying north–south and you feel sluggish when you touch down, your symptoms will be the result of dehydration and the general stress of air travel. When you travel east–west or vice versa, your body becomes confused about what time it is, and everything from your digestive system to your brain is knocked for a loop. Traveling east is more difficult on your internal clock than traveling west because most people's bodies are more inclined to stay up late than to fall asleep early.

Here are some tips for combating jet lag:

o **Reset your watch** to your destination time before you board the plane.
o **Drink lots of water** before, during, and after your flight. Avoid alcohol.
o **Exercise and sleep well** for a few days before your trip.
o If you have trouble sleeping on planes, **fly eastward on morning flights.**
o Daylight is the key to resetting your body clock. At the website for **Outside In** (www.bodyclock.com), you can get a customized plan of when to seek and avoid light.

Scottish money are interchangeable (although using Scottish notes in England can be problematic). There are £1 and £2 coins, as well as coins of 50p, 20p, 10p, 5p, 2p, and 1p. Banknotes come in denominations of £5, £10, £20, and £50. Unlike in England, Scots still use £1 notes, as well.

THE VALUE OF THE POUND VS. OTHER POPULAR CURRENCIES

UK£	US$	Can$	Euro (€)	Aus$	NZ$
1	$1.55	C$1.60	€1.15	A$1.60	NZ$2.10

Frommer's lists prices in the local currency. The currency conversions quoted above were correct at press time. But after the financial turmoil of 2008–09, Britain's bailout of the country's largest banks has meant the currency is under threat (as is the euro), while the U.S. dollar has been more stable. As rates fluctuate, consult a currency exchange website such as www.oanda.com/convert/classic to check up-to-the-minute rates.

For visitors from North America, prices in Scotland will make it seem like an expensive destination, on par with visiting major U.S. cities, for example, rather than Central European countries. That is particularly true with hotels, dining out, and drinking in pubs. In general, goods and services are priced in the same amount as they would be in U.S. dollars, but because of the exchange rate this means they really cost nearly one-third to one-half more. Exceptions to this general rule are theater and cinema tickets, which are about the same and sometimes cheaper given the exchange rate.

In Edinburgh and Glasgow, as well as in most towns around these cities, there are as many ATMs (or cash points) as you would find in any major city.

ATMs

The easiest and best way to get cash away from home is from a cash machine or cash point. The **Cirrus** (℃ **800/424-7787;** www.mastercard.com) and **PLUS**

(© 800/843-7587; www.visa.com) networks span the globe; look at the back of your bank card to see which network you're on, then call or check online for ATM locations at your destination. Be sure you know your personal identification number (PIN) and daily withdrawal limit before you depart. **Note:** Remember that many banks impose a fee every time you use a card at another bank's ATM, and that fee can be higher for international transactions than for domestic ones. In addition, the bank from which you withdraw cash may charge its own fee. For international withdrawal fees, ask your bank.

Credit Cards

Credit cards are another safe way to carry money. They also provide a convenient record of all your expenses, and they generally offer relatively good exchange rates. You can withdraw cash advances from your credit cards at banks or ATMs, provided you know your PIN. Keep in mind that you'll pay interest from the moment of your withdrawal, even if you pay your monthly bills on time. Also, note that many banks now add a 1% to 3% "transaction fee" on **all** charges you incur abroad (whether you're using the local currency or your native currency).

Credit cards universally accepted are MasterCard and Visa, with American Express allowed less frequently. In the past few years, Scotland has imposed a "Chip and Pin" system, which means that all credit cards issued in Scotland have a computer chip embedded in them and users must know their PIN. In effect, the PIN has replaced the signature on credit card purchases. Many businesses can override the "Chip and Pin" requirement and revert to the once common "swipe" of credit cards—although it often depends on staff's knowledge of the equipment that the business uses.

Traveler's Checks

Traveler's checks are becoming something of an anachronism. These days, traveler's checks are less necessary because 24-hour ATMs allow you to withdraw small amounts of cash as needed. You can buy traveler's checks at most banks. They are most commonly offered in denominations of £50, £100, and £200. Generally, you'll pay a service charge ranging from 1% to 4%.

The most popular traveler's checks are offered by **American Express** (© 800/807-6233 or 800/221-7282 for cardholders—this number accepts collect calls, offers service in several foreign languages, and exempts Amex gold and platinum cardholders from the 1% fee); **Visa** (© 800/732-1322)—AAA members can obtain Visa checks at most AAA offices or by calling © 866/339-3378; and **Mas-terCard** (© 800/223-9920).

American Express (see chapter 21 for addresses), **Thomas Cook, Visa,** and **MasterCard** offer **foreign currency traveler's checks,** which are useful if you're

WHAT THINGS COST IN EDINBURGH & GLASGOW	UK£ POUNDS STERLING
Taxi from the airport	15–20
Double room, moderate	120
Double room, inexpensive	60
Three-course dinner for one, without wine, moderate	20–30
Bottle of Imperial beer (in a bar)	3
Bottle of Coca-Cola (in a bar)	2
Cup of coffee	1.50
1 liter of unleaded gas (petrol)	1.25
Admission to most museums	free

traveling to one country, or to the euro zone; they're accepted at locations where dollar checks may not be.

If you carry traveler's checks, keep a record of their serial numbers separate from your checks in the event that they are stolen or lost. You'll get a refund faster if you know the numbers.

HEALTH
Staying Healthy

Scotland poses no particular health risks. The crisis over so-called mad-cow disease has passed and in fact it apparently never affected cattle in Scotland. Restrictions have been lifted, but it has been suggested that it's safer to eat beef cut from the bone instead of served on the bone. Avian flu remains a concern here as almost everywhere, but the country is not particularly vulnerable.

In general, contact the **International Association for Medical Assistance to Travelers** (**IAMAT**; ℰ **716/754-4883,** or 416/652-0137 in Canada; www.iamat. org) for tips on travel and health concerns in the countries you're visiting, and for lists of local, English-speaking doctors. The U.S. **Centers for Disease Control and Prevention** (ℰ **800/311-3435**; www.cdc.gov) provides up-to-date information on health hazards by region or country and offers tips on food safety. The website www. tripprep.com, sponsored by a consortium of travel medicine practitioners, may also offer helpful advice on traveling abroad. You can find listings of reliable clinics overseas at the **International Society of Travel Medicine** (www.istm.org).

WHAT TO DO IF YOU GET SICK AWAY FROM HOME

If you need a doctor, your hotel can recommend one, or you can contact your embassy or consulate. If you need an ambulance, dial **999**. *Remember:* U.S. visitors are eligible for free emergency care. For follow-up care, you should expect to be asked to pay. I list **hospitals** and **emergency numbers** under "Fast Facts," p. 261 and 21.

If you suffer from a chronic illness, consult your doctor before your departure. Pack **prescription medications** in your carry-on luggage, and carry them in their

Avoiding "Economy Class Syndrome"

Deep vein thrombosis, or as it's known in the world of flying, "economy-class syndrome," is a blood clot that develops in a deep vein. It's a potentially deadly condition that can be caused by sitting in cramped conditions—such as an airplane cabin—for too long. During a flight (especially a long-haul flight), get up, walk around, and stretch your legs every 60 to 90 minutes to keep your blood flowing. Other preventative measures include frequent flexing of the legs while sitting, drinking lots of water, and avoiding alcohol and sleeping pills. If you have a history of deep vein thrombosis, heart disease, or another condition that puts you at high risk, some experts recommend wearing compression stockings or taking anticoagulants when you fly; always ask your physician about the best course for you. Symptoms of deep vein thrombosis include leg pain or swelling, or even shortness of breath.

original containers, with pharmacy labels—otherwise they might not make it through airport security. Carry the generic name of prescription medicines, in case a local pharmacist is unfamiliar with the brand name.

I list **additional emergency numbers** in the "Fast Facts" appendix, p. 264.

SAFETY

STAYING SAFE   Like most big cities, Edinburgh and Glasgow have their share of crime. Handguns are banned by law, however, and shootings are exceedingly rare. Knives present a problem but one largely confined to youth gangs. Fights can flare up unexpectedly in either city, but in Glasgow, particularly, during heated soccer matches; exercise caution if any are being played during your stay. Marches of the Orange Order in June and July can also be scenes of random aggression.

In general, however, compared to most large cities of Europe, Edinburgh and Glasgow are equally safe, and violent crime against visitors is extremely rare. The same precautions prevail in these larger cities as they do elsewhere in the world. Tourists are typically prey to incidents of pickpocketing; mugging; "snatch and grab" theft of cell phones, watches, and jewelry; and theft of unattended bags, especially late at night, in poorly lit areas of the city. Also avoid visiting ATMs if it is late and there aren't many people around.

Visitors should take steps to ensure the safety of their passports. In Scotland, you are not expected to produce photo identity to police authorities, and passports may be more secure in locked hotel rooms or safes.

Dealing with Discrimination

Both Edinburgh and Glasgow are progressive cities and, in Scotland, discrimination is punishable by law. Racial flare-ups have occurred in housing projects on the cities' outskirts where asylum seekers have been sent. Travelers are unlikely to experience any discrimination, although gay and lesbian tourists do occasionally report cool receptions at smaller hotels and B&Bs.

SPECIALIZED TRAVEL RESOURCES

Travelers with Disabilities

Most disabilities shouldn't stop anyone from traveling. There are more options and resources out there than ever before.

Many Scottish hotels, museums, restaurants, and sightseeing attractions have wheelchair ramps and toilets for people with disabilities. Recent changes in Scottish law have also put the onus on all new premises to have wheelchair accessibility. At historical sites, however, and in older buildings, access can be limited. Not all public transport is accessible for travelers with disabilities.

Many travel agencies offer customized tours and itineraries for travelers with disabilities. Among them are **Flying Wheels Travel** (✆ 507/451-5005; www.flying wheelstravel.com), **Access-Able Travel Source** (✆ 303/232-2979; www.access-able.com), and **Accessible Journeys** (✆ 800/846-4537 or 610/521-0339; www.disabilitytravel.com). **Avis Rent a Car** has an "Avis Access" program that offers such services as a dedicated 24-hour toll-free number (✆ 888/879-4273) for customers with special travel needs; special car features such as swivel seats, spinner knobs, and hand controls; and accessible bus service.

Organizations that offer assistance to travelers with disabilities include **Moss-Rehab** (www.mossresourcenet.org), the **American Foundation for the Blind** (**AFB;** ✆ 800/232-5463; www.afb.org), and **SATH** (**Society for Accessible Travel & Hospitality;** ✆ 212/447-7284; www.sath.org). **AirAmbulanceCard. com** is now partnered with SATH and allows you to preselect top-notch hospitals in case of an emergency.

The community website **iCan** (www.icanonline.net/channels/travel) has destination guides and several regular columns on accessible travel. Also check out the quarterly magazine *Emerging Horizons* (www.emerginghorizons.com), and *Open World* magazine, published by SATH.

Gay & Lesbian Travelers

Bars, clubs, and hotels catering exclusively to gay and lesbian travelers do exist in Edinburgh and Glasgow. For advice and information on local events, call the **Lothian Gay and Lesbian Switchboard** (✆ 0131/556-4049) or the **Strath-clyde Gay and Lesbian Switchboard** (✆ 0141/847-0447). Scotland allows civil partnerships, but gay discrimination does occasionally occur.

The International Gay and Lesbian Travel Association (**IGLTA;** ✆ 800/448-8550 or 954/776-2626; www.iglta.org) is the trade association for the gay and lesbian travel industry, and offers an online directory of gay- and lesbian-friendly travel businesses; go to their website and click on "Members."

Many agencies offer tours and travel itineraries specifically for gay and lesbian travelers. Among them are **Above and Beyond Tours** (✆ 800/397-2681; www.abovebeyondtours.com), **Now, Voyager** (✆ 800/255-6951; www.nowvoyager.com), and **Olivia Cruises & Resorts** (✆ 800/631-6277; www.olivia.com).

Gay.com Travel (✆ 800/929-2268 or 415/644-8044; www.gay.com/travel or www.outandabout.com) is an excellent online successor to the popular *Out &*

About print magazine. It provides regularly updated information about gay-owned, gay-oriented, and gay-friendly lodging, dining, sightseeing, nightlife, and shopping establishments in every important destination worldwide.

The following travel guides are available at many bookstores, or you can order them from any online bookseller: *Frommer's Gay & Lesbian Europe* (www. frommers.com), an excellent travel resource to the top European cities and resorts; *Spartacus International Gay Guide* (Bruno Gmünder Verlag; www.spartacus world.com/gayguide), and *Odysseus: The International Gay Travel Planner* (Odysseus Enterprises Ltd.); and the *Damron* guides (www.damron.com), with separate, annual books for gay men and lesbians.

Senior Travelers

Many discounts are available to seniors. Even if discounts aren't posted, ask if they're available. Seniors should always exercise caution in historic sites, where the ground can be uneven, and on cobbled streets in Edinburgh.

Members of **AARP** (formerly known as the American Association of Retired Persons), 601 E St. NW, Washington, DC 20049 (✆ **888/687-2277**; www.aarp.org), get discounts on hotels, airfares, and car rentals. AARP offers members a wide range of benefits, including *AARP The Magazine* and a monthly newsletter. Anyone over 50 can join.

Many reliable agencies and organizations target the 50-plus market. **Elderhostel** (✆ **877/426-8056;** www.elderhostel.org) arranges study programs for adults 55 and up. **ElderTreks** (✆ **800/741-7956;** www.eldertreks.com) offers small-group tours to off-the-beaten-path or adventure-travel locations, restricted to travelers aged 50 and older. **INTRAV** (✆ **800/456-8100;** www.intrav.com) is a high-end tour operator that caters to the mature, discerning traveler (not specifically seniors), with trips around the world that include guided safaris, polar expeditions, private-jet adventures, and small-boat cruises down jungle rivers.

Recommended publications offering travel resources and discounts for seniors include: The quarterly magazine *Travel 50 & Beyond* (www.travel50andbeyond. com); *Travel Unlimited: Uncommon Adventures for the Mature Traveler* (Avalon); *101 Tips for Mature Travelers,* available from Grand Circle Travel (✆ **800/221-2610** or 617/350-7500; www.gct.com); and *Unbelievably Good Deals and Great Adventures That You Absolutely Can't Get Unless You're Over 50* (McGraw-Hill), by Joan Rattner Heilman.

Family Travelers

When booking overnight rooms, ask whether family suites are available. Historical attractions in Edinburgh and Glasgow often offer family tickets. Finally, look for the "Kids" icon, indicating attractions, restaurants, and hotels that are especially family-friendly.

Familyhostel (✆ **800/733-9753;** www.learn.unh.edu) takes the whole family, including kids 8 to 15, on moderately priced U.S. and international learning vacations. Lectures, field trips, and sightseeing are guided by a team of academics.

Recommended family travel websites include **Family Travel Forum** (www. familytravelforum.com), **Family Travel Network** (www.familytravelnetwork.com),

Traveling Internationally with Your Kids (www.travelwithyourkids.com), and **Family Travel Files** (www.thefamilytravelfiles.com).

Student Travelers

If you're traveling internationally, you'd be wise to arm yourself with an **International Student Identity Card (ISIC),** which offers substantial savings on rail passes, plane tickets, and entrance fees. It also provides you with basic health and life insurance and a 24-hour helpline. The card is available from **STA Travel** (**© 800/781-4040** in North America; www.sta.com or www.statravel.com; or www.statravel.co.uk in the U.K.), the biggest student travel agency in the world. If you're no longer a student but are still under 26, you can get an **International Youth Travel Card (IYTC)** from the same people; this entitles you to some discounts (but not on museum admissions). **Travel CUTS** (**© 800/667-2887** or 416/614-2887; www.travelcuts.com) offers similar services for both Canadians and U.S. residents. Irish students may prefer to turn to **USIT** (**© 01/602-1600;** www.usitnow.ie), an Ireland-based specialist in student, youth, and independent travel.

SUSTAINABLE TOURISM

Sustainable tourism is conscientious travel. It means being careful with the environments you explore, and respecting the communities you visit. Two overlapping components of sustainable travel are **ecotourism** and **ethical tourism. The International Ecotourism Society** (TIES) defines ecotourism as responsible travel to natural areas that conserves the environment and improves the well-being of local people. TIES suggests that eco-tourists follow these principles:

- Minimize environmental impact.
- Build environmental and cultural awareness and respect.
- Provide positive experiences for both visitors and hosts.
- Provide direct financial benefits for conservation and for local people.
- Raise sensitivity to host countries' political, environmental, and social climates.
- Support international human rights and labor agreements.

Should They Stay or Should They Go?

Psychologically speaking, Scotland is a politically conflicted place. In 1999, its Parliament was restored after being dissolved for nearly 300 years following the union between England and Scotland in 1707. Most Scots have a fierce pride in their country, which is every bit as old as its larger and more dominant neighbor to the south. But whether that self-belief will ever translate into complete self-government is open to debate.

The traditional political parties—Labour, Conservative, and Liberal Democrat—remain staunchly in favor of the current union, while the leading independence group, the Scottish National Party, has seen its percentage of the vote drop in 21st-century elections. But SNP members are not the only ones who advocate Scottish independence: New parties with growing electoral success, such as the Greens and Scottish Socialists, also back full autonomy from rule in London.

IT'S EASY BEING green

Here are a few simple ways you can help conserve fuel and energy when you travel:

- Each time you take a flight or drive a car, greenhouse gases release into the atmosphere. You can help neutralize this danger to the planet through "carbon offsetting"—paying someone to invest your money in programs that reduce your greenhouse gas emissions by the same amount you've added. Before buying carbon offset credits, just make sure that you're using a reputable company, one with a proven program that invests in renewable energy. Reliable carbon offset companies include **Carbonfund** (www.carbonfund.org), **TerraPass** (www.terrapass.org), and **Carbon Neutral** (www.carbonneutral.org).

- Whenever possible, choose non-stop flights; they generally require less fuel than indirect flights that stop and take off again. Try to fly during the day—some scientists estimate that nighttime flights are twice as harmful to the environment. And pack light—each 7kg (5 pounds) of luggage on a 5,000-mile flight adds up to 22kg (50 pounds) of carbon dioxide emitted.

- Where you stay during your travels can have a major environmental impact. To determine the green credentials of a property, ask about trash disposal and recycling, water conservation, and energy use; also question if sustainable materials were used in the construction of the property. The website **www.greenhotels.com** recommends green-rated member hotels around the world that fulfill the company's stringent environmental requirements. Also consult **www.environmentallyfriendly hotels.com** for more green accommodation ratings.

- At hotels, request that your sheets and towels not be changed daily. (Many hotels already have programs like this in place.) Turn off the lights and air-conditioner (or heater) when you leave your room.

- Use public transport where possible—trains, buses, and even taxis are more energy-efficient forms of transport than driving. Even better is to walk or cycle; you'll produce zero emissions and stay fit and healthy on your travels.

- If renting a car is necessary, ask the rental agent for a hybrid, or rent the most fuel-efficient car available. You'll use less gas and save money at the tank.

- Eat at locally owned and operated restaurants that use produce grown in the area. This contributes to the local economy and cuts down on greenhouse gas emissions by supporting restaurants where the food is not flown or trucked in across long distances.

You can find some eco-friendly travel tips and statistics, as well as touring companies and associations—listed by destination under "Travel Choice"—at the **TIES** website, www.ecotourism.org. Also check out **Ecotravel.com,** which lets you search for sustainable touring companies in several categories (water-based, land-based, spiritually oriented, and so on).

FROMMERS.COM: THE COMPLETE
travel resource

Planning a trip or just returned? Head to **Frommers.com,** voted Best Travel Site by *PC Magazine*. We think you'll find our site indispensable before, during, and after your travels—with expert advice and tips; independent reviews of hotels, restaurants, attractions, and preferred shopping and nightlife venues; vacation giveaways; and an online booking tool. We publish the complete contents of over 135 travel guides in our **Destinations** section, covering over 4,000 places worldwide. Each weekday, we publish original articles that report on **Deals and News** via our free **Frommers. com Newsletters.** What's more, **Arthur**

Frommer himself blogs 5 days a week, with cutting opinions about the state of travel in the modern world. We're betting you'll find our **Events** listings an invaluable resource; it's an up-to-the-minute roster of what's happening in cities everywhere—including concerts, festivals, lectures, and more. We've also added weekly **podcasts, interactive maps,** and hundreds of new images across the site. Finally, don't forget to visit our **Message Boards,** where you can join in conversations with thousands of fellow Frommer's travelers and post your trip report once you return.

While much of the focus of eco-tourism is about reducing impacts on the natural environment, ethical tourism concentrates on ways to preserve and enhance local economies and communities, regardless of location. You can embrace ethical tourism by staying at a locally owned hotel or shopping at a store that employs local workers and sells locally produced goods.

Responsible Travel (www.responsibletravel.com) is a great source of sustainable travel ideas; the site is run by a spokesperson for ethical tourism in the travel industry. **Sustainable Travel International** (www.sustainabletravelinternational.org) promotes ethical tourism practices, and manages an extensive directory of sustainable properties and tour operators around the world.

In the U.K., **Tourism Concern** (www.tourismconcern.org.uk) works to reduce social and environmental problems connected to tourism. The **Association of Independent Tour Operators** (**AITO;** www.aito.co.uk) is a group of specialist operators leading the field in making holidays sustainable.

PACKAGES FOR THE INDEPENDENT TRAVELER

Package tours are simply a way to buy the airfare, accommodations, and other elements of your trip (such as car rentals, airport transfers, and sometimes even activities) at the same time and often at discounted prices.

One good source of package deals is the airlines themselves. Most major airlines offer air/land packages, including **American Airlines Vacations** (© 800/321-2121; www.aavacations.com), **Delta Vacations** (© 800/221-6666; www.deltavacations.com), **Continental Airlines Vacations** (© 800/301-3800; www.covacations.com), and **United Vacations** (© 888/854-3899; www.unitedvacations.com). Several big

online travel agencies—Expedia, Travelocity, Orbitz, Site59, and Lastminute.com—also do a brisk business in packages.

Travel packages are also listed in the travel section of your local Sunday newspaper. Or check ads in travel magazines such as *Arthur Frommer's Budget Travel Magazine, Travel + Leisure, National Geographic Traveler,* and *Condé Nast Traveler.*

ESCORTED GENERAL-INTEREST TOURS

Escorted tours are structured group tours, with a group leader. The price usually includes everything from airfare to hotels, meals, tours, admission costs, and local transportation. While you are not likely to need such services in either Edinburgh or Glasgow, for information on tours to regions of Scotland, please see p. 149 in chapter 12.

Despite the fact that escorted tours require big deposits and predetermine hotels, restaurants, and itineraries, many people derive security and peace of mind from the structure they offer. Escorted tours—whether they're navigated by bus, motor coach, train, or boat—let travelers sit back and enjoy the trip without having to drive or worry about details. They take you to the maximum number of sights in the minimum amount of time with the least amount of hassle. They're particularly convenient for people with limited mobility and they can be a great way to make new friends.

On the downside, you'll have little opportunity for serendipitous interactions with locals. The tours can be jam-packed with activities, leaving little room for individual sightseeing, whim, or adventure—plus they often focus on the heavily touristed sites, so you miss out on many a lesser known gem. For more information on escorted general-interest tours, including questions to ask before booking your trip, see frommers.com.

STAYING CONNECTED

Telephones

Telephones in Scotland operate pretty much like telephones in the U.S. or anywhere in the Western world. Pay phones are less common, given that the telephone companies say they're expensive to maintain and an estimated 90% of the population now have mobile (cell) phones. For calls within Scotland, England, Wales, and Northern Ireland, you need to know the local or city codes, such as 0141 for Glasgow. They always start with zero but sometimes they are five digits long. For international calls, you need to know the country code of the place you are calling. For assistance in making calls outside the U.K., dial 155 for an international operator.

Cellphones

First, cellphones are called mobiles in Scotland. The three letters that define much of the world's wireless capabilities are GSM (Global System for Mobiles), a big, seamless network that makes for easy cross-border cellphone use throughout Europe and dozens of other countries worldwide. In the U.S., T-Mobile and AT&T Wireless/

Cingular use this quasi-universal system; in Canada, Microcell and some Rogers customers are GSM, and all Europeans and most Australians use GSM. If your cellphone is on a GSM system, and you have a world-capable multiband phone, such as many Sony Ericsson, Motorola, or Samsung models, you can make and receive calls across civilized areas around much of the globe. Just call your wireless operator and ask for "international roaming" to be activated on your account. Unfortunately, per-minute charges can be high—usually $1 to $1.50 in Western Europe.

For many, **renting** a phone is a good idea. (Even world phone owners will have to rent new phones if they're traveling to non-GSM regions, such as Japan or Korea.) While you can rent a phone from any number of overseas sites, including kiosks at airports and at car-rental agencies, I suggest renting the phone before you leave home. North Americans can rent one before leaving home from **InTouch USA** (𝄐 **800/872-7626;** www.intouchglobal.com) or **RoadPost** (𝄐 **888/290-1606** or 905/272-5665; www.roadpost.com). InTouch will also, for free, advise you on whether your existing phone will work overseas; simply call 𝄐 **703/222-7161** between 9am and 4pm EST, or go to www.intouchglobal.com/travel.htm.

Buying a phone can be economically attractive, as many nations have cheap prepaid phone systems. Once you arrive at your destination, stop by a local cellphone shop and get the cheapest package; you'll probably pay less than $100 for a phone and a starter calling card. Local calls may be as low as 10¢ per minute, and in many countries incoming calls are free.

Voice-Over Internet Protocol (VOIP)

If you have web access while traveling, consider a broadband-based telephone service (in technical terms, **Voice-over Internet Protocol,** or **VoIP**) such as Skype (www.skype.com) or Vonage (www.vonage.com), which allow you to make free international calls from your laptop or in a cybercafe. Neither service requires the people you're calling to also have that service (though there are fees if they do not). Check the websites for details.

Internet & E-mail

WITH YOUR OWN COMPUTER   More and more hotels, cafes, and retailers are signing on as Wi-Fi (wireless fidelity) "hotspots." Mac owners have their own networking technology: Apple AirPort. **Boingo** (www.boingo.com) and **Wayport** (www.wayport.com) have set up networks in airports and high-class hotel lobbies. iPass providers (see below) also give you access to a few hundred wireless hotel lobby setups. To locate other hotspots that provide **free wireless networks** in cities around the world, go to www.personaltelco.net/index.cgi/WirelessCommunities.

For dial-up access, most business-class hotels throughout the world offer dataports for laptop modems, and a few thousand hotels in the U.S. and Europe now offer free high-speed Internet access. In addition, major Internet Service Providers (ISPs) have **local access numbers** around the world, allowing you to go online by placing a local call. The **iPass** network also has dial-up numbers around the world. You'll have to sign up with an iPass provider, who will then tell you how to set up your computer for your destination(s). For a list of iPass providers, go to www.ipass.com and click on "Individuals Buy Now." One solid provider is **i2roam** (𝄐 **866/811-6209** or 920/235-0475; www.i2roam.com).

ONLINE traveler's TOOLBOX

- **Airplane Food** (www.airlinemeals.net)
- **Airplane Seating** (www.seatguru.com; and www.airlinequality.com)
- **Foreign Languages for Travelers** (www.travlang.com)
- **Maps** (www.mapquest.com)
- **Subway Navigator** (www.subwaynavigator.com)
- **Time and Date** (www.timeanddate.com)
- **Travel Warnings** (http://travel.state.gov, www.fco.gov.uk/travel, www.voyage.gc.ca, www.smartraveller.gov.au)
- **Universal Currency Converter** (www.oanda.com)
- **Weather** (www.intellicast.com; and www.weather.com)

Wherever you go, bring a **connection kit** of the right power and phone adapters, a spare phone cord, and a spare Ethernet network cable—or find out whether your hotel supplies them to guests.

TIPS ON ACCOMMODATIONS

Edinburgh

Edinburgh offers a huge choice of places to stay, from the super posh and ridiculously pricey five-star hotels to rock-bottom bunkhouses and youth hostels. It is a city that anticipates bundles of tourists and travelers, whether backpackers, families, or business types in the Scottish capital on commercial or governmental matters. But be warned, however: During the 3- to 4-week period of the Edinburgh Festival every summer, the hotels fill up. If you're planning a visit at that time, be sure to reserve your room as far in advance as possible. Otherwise you'll end up in a town or village as much as 40km (55 miles) from the city center. And don't be surprised if the rates in Edinburgh are higher during August, particularly at guesthouses and smaller hotels.

The **Edinburgh Information Centre,** near Waverley Station, atop the Princes Mall shopping center, 3 Princes St. (© **0131/473-3800** or 0845/225-5121; fax 0131/473-3881; www.edinburgh.org; Bus: 3, 8, 22, 25, or 31), compiles a lengthy list of small hotels, guesthouses, and private homes providing bed and breakfast for as little as £20 per person. A £4 booking fee is charged, and a 10% deposit is expected. Allow about 4 weeks' notice, especially during summer. It's open year-round; typically the hours are Monday through Saturday from 9am to 7pm and Sunday from 10am to 7pm, though it is open later during the Festival and closes earlier in the winter months.

Glasgow

The tourist trade in Glasgow is less seasonal than in Edinburgh, with fewer visitors in general coming to Scotland's largest city. However, it has become a popular spot for business conferences while the increase in budget-airline flights from the European continent seems to have increased the overall number of visitors. So if, for example, an international association of dentists is in town, finding a room can be difficult.

Until recently, many tourism industry observers said Glasgow suffered from a shortage of hotel rooms, but new places such as the Radisson SAS have changed the equation. Whenever you're coming, it's recommended that you reserve a room in advance. Some rates are predictably high, but many business-oriented hotels offer bargains on weekends, and the number of budget options is increasing.

The Glasgow and Clyde Valley tourism office (www.visitscotland.com) offers an **Information & Booking Hot Line** (© **0845/225-5121** from within the U.K., or 01506/832-121 from outside the U.K.). Lines are open (local time) Monday to Friday from 8am to 8pm, Saturday from 9am to 5:50pm, and Sunday from 10am to 4pm. The fax number is 01506/832-222. The fee for this booking service is £4.

Tourist Board Rankings

VisitScotland ranks the lodgings at hundreds of hotels, guesthouses, B&Bs, and self-catering apartments. While helpful, these stars are largely based upon available amenities, such as 24-hour room service, ironing boards, or spas, which may not be relevant for each and every traveler. Also, not all hotels and guesthouses are part of the scheme, which costs them money to join, although they may be no less attractive.

Saving on Your Hotel Room

The **rack rate** is the maximum rate that a hotel charges for a room. Hardly anybody pays this price, however, except in high season or on holidays. To lower the cost of your room:

- **Ask about special rates or other discounts.** You may qualify for corporate, student, military, senior, frequent flyer, trade union, or other discounts.
- **Dial direct.** When booking a room in a chain hotel, you'll often get a better deal by calling the individual hotel's reservation desk rather than the chain's main number.
- **Book online.** Many hotels offer Internet-only discounts, or supply rooms to Priceline, Hotwire, or Expedia at rates much lower than the ones you can get through the hotel itself.
- **Remember the law of supply and demand.** Resort hotels are most crowded and therefore most expensive at weekends, so discounts are usually available for midweek stays. Business hotels in downtown locations are busiest during the week, so you can expect big discounts over the weekend. Many hotels have high-season and low-season prices, and booking even 1 day after high season ends can mean big discounts.
- **Look into group or long-stay discounts.** If you come as part of a large group, you should be able to negotiate a bargain rate. Likewise, if you're planning a long stay (at least 5 days), you might qualify for a discount. As a general rule, expect 1 night free after a 7-night stay.
- **Avoid excess charges and hidden costs.** When you book a room, ask whether the hotel charges for parking. Use your own cellphone, pay phones, or prepaid phone cards instead of dialing direct from hotel phones, which usually have exorbitant rates. Finally, ask about local taxes and service charges, which can increase the cost of a room by 15% or more.

House-Swapping

House-swapping is becoming a more popular and viable means of travel; you stay in their place, they stay in yours, and you both get an authentic and personal view of the area, the opposite of the escapist retreat that many hotels offer. Try **HomeLink International** (www.homelink.org), the largest and oldest home-swapping organization, founded in 1952, with over 11,000 listings worldwide ($75 for an annual membership). **HomeExchange.org** (6,000 listings) and **InterVac.com** (over 10,000 listings) are also reliable. Many travelers find great housing swaps on Craigslist (www.craigslist.org), too, though the offerings cannot be vetted or vouched for. Swap at your own risk.

○ **Book an efficiency apartment.** A room with a kitchenette allows you to shop for groceries and cook your own meals. This is a big money saver, especially for families on long stays.

○ **Consider enrolling in hotel "frequent-stay" programs,** which are upping the ante lately to win the loyalty of repeat customers. Frequent guests can now accumulate points or credits to earn free hotel nights, airline miles, in-room amenities, merchandise, tickets to concerts and events, discounts on sporting facilities—and even credit toward stock in the participating hotel, in the case of the Jameson Inn hotel group.

Landing the Best Room

Somebody has to get the best room in the house. It might as well be you. You can start by joining the hotel's frequent-guest program, which may make you eligible for upgrades. A hotel-branded credit card usually gives its owner "silver" or "gold" status in frequent-guest programs for free. Always ask about a corner room. They're often larger and quieter, with more windows and light, and they often cost the same as standard rooms.

When you make your reservation, ask if the hotel is renovating; if it is, request a room away from the construction. Ask about rooms for non-smokers, ones with views, or with twin, queen- or king-size beds. If you're a light sleeper, request to be a distance from vending machines, elevators, restaurants, bars, and discos. Ask for a room that has been most recently renovated or redecorated.

If you aren't happy with your room when you arrive, ask for another one. Most lodgings will be willing to accommodate you. For tips on surfing for hotel deals online, visit frommers.com.

3

PLANNING YOUR TRIP TO EDINBURGH & GLASGOW

Tips on Accommodations

SUGGESTED EDINBURGH & GLASGOW ITINERARIES

Few travelers have unlimited time, and so some suggested itineraries for 3-day and weeklong visits to Edinburgh and Glasgow may be helpful. This chapter will also help you to plan your time if you want to venture further afield to see the outstanding sights in the areas around Edinburgh and Glasgow. These itineraries incorporate information found in chapters 8 and 16, and also include ideas from chapters 12 and 20. Most of the attractions below have cross-references to the pages with listing information and more details.

These itineraries highlight major sights, such as Edinburgh's Royal Mile, but also direct you to less celebrated spots, such as Alexander "Greek" Thomson's Holmwood House on Glasgow's Southside. The pace may look a bit breathless for some visitors. If you prefer a more relaxed pace, then skip an attraction or two: These plans are suggestions, not requirements. You may also mix bits of one itinerary with highlights of another.

By combining the first and second itineraries, you'll have an instant plan for visiting both Glasgow and Edinburgh in 1 week (with a day to spare). **Note:** Visiting most attractions in Edinburgh and Glasgow can be done on foot and by using public transportation; excursions outside the cities may well require a car. For car hire advice, see p. 58.

EDINBURGH IN 3 DAYS

Although it's impossible to see all of Edinburgh in 3 days, you can still get a good feel for the city. The city center is compact, with Old and New

Edinburgh in 3 Days

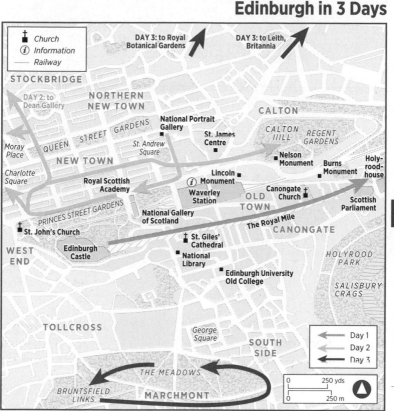

Legend:
- ✝ Church
- ⓘ Information
- — Railway

DAY 3: to Royal Botanical Gardens

DAY 3: to Leith, Britannia

STOCKBRIDGE

DAY 2: to Dean Gallery

NORTHERN NEW TOWN

CALTON

QUEEN STREET GARDENS

National Portrait Gallery

St. James Centre

CALTON HILL

REGENT GARDENS

Moray Place

St. Andrew Square

NEW TOWN

Nelson Monument

Burns Monument

Holyroodhouse

Charlotte Square

Royal Scottish Academy

Lincoln Monument

ⓘ

Waverley Station

Canongate Church ✝

OLD TOWN

Scottish Parliament

PRINCES STREET GARDENS

National Gallery of Scotland

The Royal Mile

CANONGATE

✝ St. John's Church

St. Giles' Cathedral

WEST END

Edinburgh Castle

National Library

HOLYROOD PARK

Edinburgh University Old College

SALISBURY CRAGS

TOLLCROSS

George Square

SOUTH SIDE

BRUNTSFIELD LINKS

THE MEADOWS

MARCHMONT

Day 1
Day 2
Day 3

0 — 250 yds
0 — 250 m

4

SUGGESTED ITINERARIES | Edinburgh in 3 Days

Towns only separated by a quarter of a mile or so. The historic Port of Leith is a bit further afield, but still only a couple of miles, and 10–15 minutes by bus.

Day 1: The Royal Mile & Old Town ★★★

On your first day, head straight to the **Royal Mile** (p. 106) in Edinburgh's Old Town. It stretches from **Edinburgh Castle** (p. 87) to the **Palace of Holyroodhouse** (p. 94). Along the way you can stop at the historic **Gladstone's Land** (p. 91) or **St. Giles' Cathedral** (p. 91), as well as the modern **Scottish Parliament** (p. 93) building. Be sure to wander down at least one of the narrow alleys and passageways that extend down the hill on either side of the Royal Mile, like ribs from a spine. Also, if you have time left over, check out the **Grassmarket** and take a detour to the **Museum of Scotland** (p. 96).

Day 2: New Town & Scotland's National Galleries ★★

Having a grip on Edinburgh's Old Town, it's time to move to the city's **New Town,** which dates to the late 1700s. Begin with the **Princes Street Gardens** (p. 101) and then move on to **George Street,** with its panoply of shops and stylish bars. Climb up to **Calton Hill** (p. 100) at the eastern end of New Town for the views, and from the western side of the district, take in **Charlotte Square** (p. 118) or wander down to **Stockbridge** on the Water of Leith. If you're still going strong, you can follow a path along the Water of Leith to the **Dean Gallery** (p. 95), part of the capital **National Galleries of Scotland** (p. 95). Catch the shuttle bus to any of the others, including the **National Portrait Gallery** (p. 96) or the main **National Gallery of Scotland** (p. 95), back on Princes Street Gardens.

Day 3: To Leith & the Southside ★

It's your last day, so let's move out of the city center and head to the sea. First stop, however, is the marvelous **Royal Botanic Garden** (p. 101), where you might well spend a few hours wandering about the verdant paths. In **Leith** (p. 121) you'll find the original port of Edinburgh, once an independent town in its own right. Two big attractions of Leith are its pubs and restaurants—several of which are considered to be among the city's finest. Come back toward central Edinburgh, but detour south to the **Meadows** and see some of the fine residential neighborhoods of Marchmont or Bruntsfield and get an idea of how Edinburghers live.

GLASGOW IN 3 DAYS

Even with only 3 days, you can still see a good portion of Scotland's largest city. While Glasgow is much larger than Edinburgh, most of the important attractions are in the city center, and those that aren't are easily accessible. A quick trip on the underground takes you to the West End, the most desirable district of the city, while a bus ride across the river brings you to the Southside, with its key destination, the Burrell Collection.

Day 1: Central Glasgow ★★

Start off in the heart of Glasgow. The bustling **city center** offers a host of monumental Victorian buildings and a couple of landmarks designed by the great **Charles Rennie Mackintosh,** such as his **Glasgow School of Art** (p. 198). The city also boasts another great 19th-century design genius, **Alexander "Greek" Thomson.** Have a gander at his **St. Vincent Street Church** (p. 199) with its exotic mix of Central Asian, Middle Eastern, and Mediterranean influences. Just east of the city's commercial center is **Merchant City,** with its trendy bars, good restaurants, art galleries—such as the **Glasgow Print Studio** (p. 231)—and performance spaces such as the **City Halls** (p. 238). This is the historic core of the city, but alas most of its historic buildings are long gone. The strongest-surviving remnant of Glasgow's rich medieval history is **Glasgow Cathedral** (p. 198).

Glasgow in 3 Days

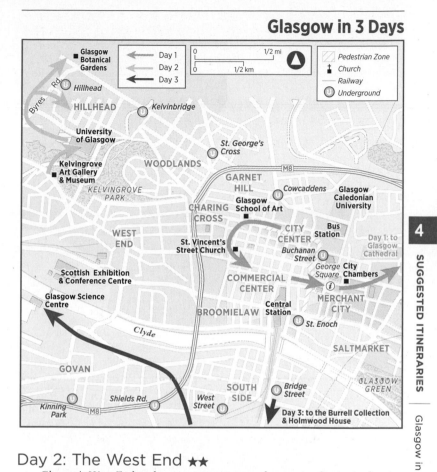

Day 2: The West End ★★

Glasgow's West End is the most prosperous and attractive district in the city. Not only is the **Kelvingrove Art Gallery & Museum** (p. 201) a fine piece of Victorian architecture, it also has an expansive collection of paintings and artifacts—one of the best held by any city in Europe. Take a stroll through adjacent **Kelvingrove Park** and then stop at the **University of Glasgow,** where you can see the complete interiors of the home where Mackintosh lived at the **Hunterian Art Gallery** (p. 200). The West End's "Main Street" is **Byres Road,** with bars, restaurants, shops, and more. Detour onto cobbled **Ashton Lane,** or, on fine days, take in the city's **Botanic Gardens** (p. 205) at the top of Byres Road.

Day 3: The Southside ★

Glasgow is bisected by the River Clyde, and the city's Southside is considered, by some, to be the real Glasgow. A highlight of the area is the **Burrell Collection** (p. 201), a custom-made museum holding the vast collection of art and artifacts amassed by an industrialist who bequeathed the entire wonderful lot to the city. If you find that "Greek" Thomson intrigues you, then definitely go to **Holmwood House** (p. 201); it's the best example of his sumptuous and timeless villas. Families will enjoy the **Science Centre** (p. 204) on the southern banks of the Clyde.

EDINBURGH & SIDE TRIPS IN 1 WEEK

With more time, you can see some of the picturesque countryside that surrounds the capital of Scotland. I have devised these trips for travel by car. See chapter 5 on p. 58 for information on renting cars.

Days 1 to 3

Follow "Edinburgh in 3 Days" itinerary, above.

Day 4: Kingdom of Fife & Linlithgow ★

If you're up very early and it's a dry day, you might scale **Arthur's Seat,** the ancient volcano that rises up above Edinburgh. From there you can see across the Firth of Clyde and the so-called **Kingdom of Fife** (p. 152)—your next destination. First head north to the seaside town of **St. Andrews** (p. 153), about a 1-hour drive once you're out of Edinburgh. World famous for its golf, this seaside town is also an important historic site of Christian pilgrimage and home of the first university in Scotland. You might wish to come back south along the coast, stopping briefly, if you're interested in Scottish art, to see the excellent **Kirkcaldy Museum** (p. 155), with its priceless collection of the Colourists, Joan Eardley, and even a Vettriano. After this, you should have enough time to head back across the Forth (20 minutes) and get to **Linlithgow** (p. 143) and its ancient palace, the birthplace of one of Scotland's most iconic figures: Mary, Queen of Scots.

Day 5: East Lothian Coast ★

In the morning, head east out of the city for the town of North Berwick and its popular **Scottish Seabird Centre** (p. 147), where, thanks to a host of video cameras dotting the nearby islands and coastal cliffs, you can see a range of avian and sea-life colonies. Other highlights of the region include two castle ruins, the romantic **Dirleton** (p. 147), in the cute village of the same name, as well as the magnificent **Tantallon** (p. 148) on bluffs above the sea. Golf buffs may want to see **Muirfield,** although others will settle happily for a stroll around nearby **Gullane** village and its sandy beaches (p. 148).

Day 6: South into the Borders ★★

Make another early start and head south toward Melrose, which takes about 1 hour by car. This village has **Melrose Abbey** (p. 151), which has inspired many—including writer Sir Walter Scott. His home, **Abbotsford** (p. 139), is next on the agenda. This mansion has a host of historical artifacts collected by Scott, and it is where he wrote many of his most enduring tales. Next up is the

Edinburgh & Side Trips in 1 Week

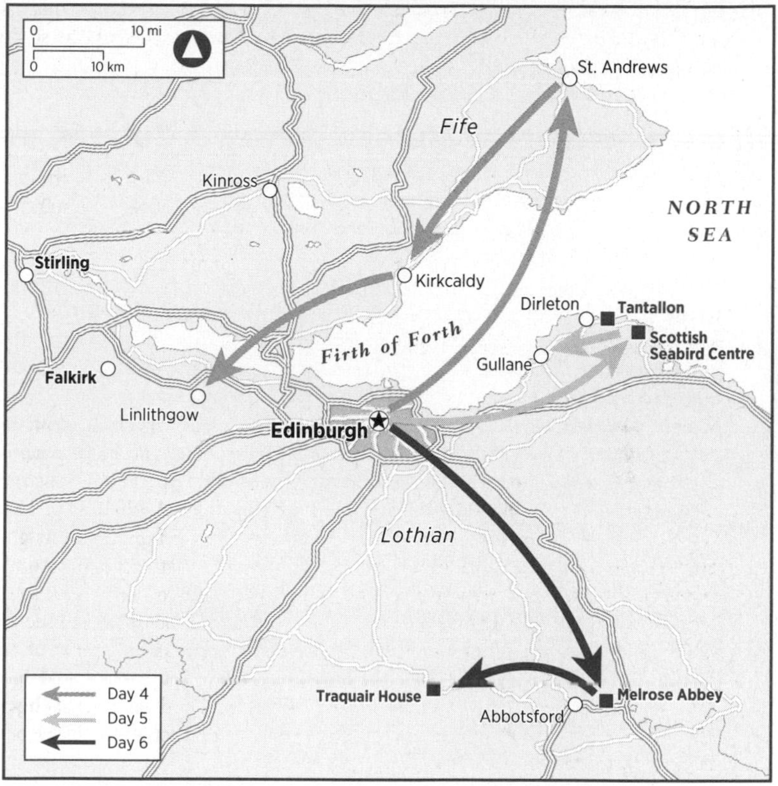
0
10 mi
0
10 km
St. Andrews
Fife
Kinross
NORTH
SEA
Stirling
Kirkcaldy
Dirleton
Tantallon
Scottish
Seabird Centre
Firth of Forth
Gullane
Falkirk
Linlithgow
Edinburgh
Lothian
Day 4
Day 5
Day 6
Traquair House
Melrose Abbey
Abbotsford

oldest continuously inhabited home in Scotland, the alluring **Traquair House** (p. 152).

Day 7: Edinburgh's Other Attractions

Take it easy—you've had a busy week. It's time to see some of the other attractions that Edinburgh has to offer. Take in any museums or galleries not yet hit, such as the **Writer's Museum** (p. 91). How about the **Edinburgh Zoo** (p. 97)? Or if you really enjoyed *The Da Vinci Code,* then you had better make the pilgrimage to **Rosslyn Chapel** (p. 144) on the southern fringes of the city. Otherwise, just hang out in Old Town or New Town.

GLASGOW & SIDE TRIPS IN 1 WEEK

Glasgow is a fairly big city with lots to offer, but one of its additional attractions is the ease with which you can escape the metropolis, finding fresh air and memorable scenery. Each day of the side trips involves driving, but for no more than an hour or so out of the city. For information on car rental firms, see chapter 21, p. 267.

Days 1 to 3

Follow the "Glasgow in 3 Days" itinerary, above.

Day 4: Clyde Coast, Burns Country & Culzean ★★

Set out for the Clyde coast, which opens up rather spectacularly into the Irish Sea. Ayrshire is the principal county and so start with the town of **Ayr,** on the coast southwest of Glasgow. This is the beginning of your tour of **Burns Country**—the historic stomping ground of Scotland's most famous "ploughman poet." In nearby Alloway, you'll find the bard's birthplace, the **Burns Cottage** (p. 257), which has been recently restored, and the **Burns Museum,** which was undergoing major improvements in 2010. Depending on your time and interest, you can also visit other landmarks, such as **Souter Johnnie's Cottage** in Kirkoswald (p. 259). But leave time for **Culzean Castle** and its magnificent **Country Park** (p. 260), with acres and acres to explore from sandy beachhead to a walled garden with exotic plants. If you fancy golf, however, you might prefer seeing world-famous **Troon** and **Turnberry** (p. 260).

Day 5: Stirling, the Trossachs & Loch Lomond ★

About a 35–45-minute drive northwest of Glasgow, **Stirling** has played a key part in Scottish history and was the one-time home to royalty. The Old Town has the impressive **Stirling Castle** (p. 253), where the buildings are currently being restored in keeping with their historic appearance. Children will enjoy nearby **Stirling Jail** (p. 253), but history buffs should try to visit **Bannockburn** (p. 253) on the southern outskirts of Stirling, where the Scots defeated English invaders in the 14th century. Stirling also has the towering monument to **William Wallace** (p. 253). Head west and see the well-preserved ruins of **Doune Castle** (p. 253) before hitting the rolling hills and small mountains of the Trossachs and then lovely **Loch Lomond** (p. 252) in the shadows of the southern Highlands.

Day 6: The West Coast ★★

This tour may take 2 days, depending on your ambitions, and whether you're knocked sideways by the scenery of the Clyde coast. Here are just some of the highlights. Head-clearing ferry rides take passengers to the isles of either **Arran** (p. 248) or **Bute** (p. 249). You can visit the stately mansions of **Brodick Castle** (p. 248) or **Mount Stuart** (p. 249), or walk on quiet beaches. From either island, you can head farther west to the Argyll peninsulas of **Cowal** and **Kintyre** (p. 250), both remote and sparsely settled. **Tighnabruaich** and **Tarbert** are two picturesque harbor villages worth stopping in. Finally, you might wish to really leave it all behind and go to the small island of **Gigha** (p. 251). Owned by a community trust, it is the southern-most of Scotland's Inner Hebrides. Closer to Glasgow, on the north shores of the Clyde as it widens to the sea, is Helensburgh and the superlative **Hill House** (p. 248), designed by Charles Rennie Mackintosh.

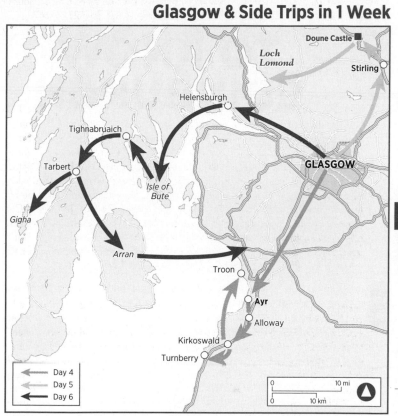

Glasgow & Side Trips in 1 Week

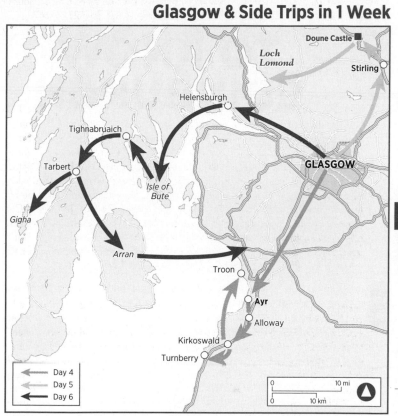

Doune Castle
Loch Lomond
Stirling
Helensburgh
Tighnabruaich
Tarbert
GLASGOW
Isle of Bute
Gigha
Arran
Troon
Ayr
Alloway
Kirkoswald
Turnberry

Day 4
Day 5
Day 6

0   10 mi
0   10 km

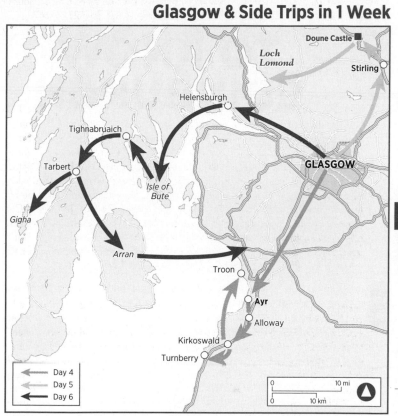

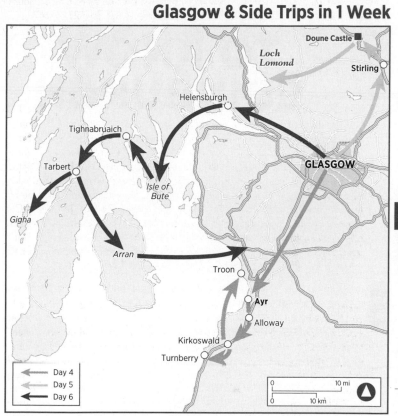

Day 7: Glasgow's Other Attractions

Unless you're still absorbing the refreshing air of the west coast and haven't made it back to Glasgow, pick up where you left off in the city. Revisit the **West End** for lunch and a bit of shopping, or stay in the city center and see any museums missed earlier, such as the **Gallery of Modern Art** (p. 198) or the more contemporary offerings at the **CCA** (p. 202). If the weather's fine and dry, hike up to the **Central Necropolis,** (p. 198) near Glasgow Cathedral, or stroll through **Glasgow Green** (p. 205), along the River Clyde.

GETTING TO KNOW EDINBURGH

E dinburgh is one of Europe's fairest cities and has even been called the Athens of the North. And what most experienced travelers to the U.K. say is true: If you can visit only two cities in all Great Britain, it's London first and Edinburgh second.

5

Built on extinct volcanoes atop an inlet from the North Sea (the Firth of Forth), the Scottish capital began as a small and fortified settlement on a craggy hill. Indeed, because of its defensive attributes, Edinburgh became an important, protected place for the country's often besieged rulers. Somewhat ironically, the city today represents the crossroads of Scotland for visitors: The spot that they are likely to pass through while in Scotland.

Edinburgh (remember "burgh" is always pronounced more like "*burr*-a" with the "a" at the end quite clipped and softly guttural) abounds with historic, intellectual, and literary associations. Names such as Mary, Queen of Scots and her nemesis, Protestant reformer John Knox; pioneering economist Adam Smith and philosopher David Hume; authors Sir Walter Scott, Robert Louis Stevenson, Muriel Spark, and Sir Arthur Conan Doyle; as well as inventor Alexander Graham Bell are all part of Edinburgh's past.

Today the city is famous for its world-class cultural festival. The **Edinburgh Festival** is actually several festivals at once: Books, comedy, drama, classical music, dance, and more. But this ancient seat of Scottish royalty has a year-round interest. When the festival-goers aren't swarming the city center, Edinburgh's pace is more relaxed, its prices are lower, and the inhabitants are under less pressure and offer a more relaxed welcome.

Edinburgh is a city that lends itself to walking. The **Old Town** and **New Town** offer moody cobbled alleys, elegant streetscapes, handsome squares, and placid parks. From several hilltops, panoramic views can be enjoyed—and the city at sunset can be a romantic sight.

Even though Glasgow might trump it when it comes to the contemporary arts, Edinburgh has traditionally been considered the cultural capital of the north. It will always be home to the **National Galleries of**

Greater Edinburgh

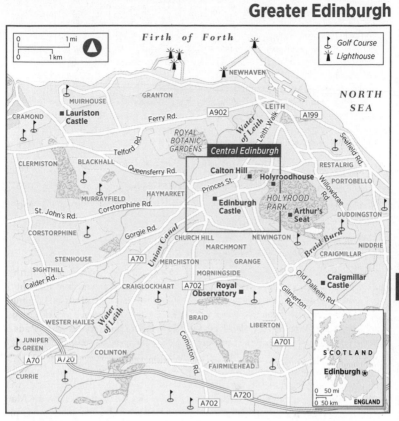

Scotland. And as a point for excursions, it's well placed. Notable nearby attractions include Linlithgow, the Borders to the south; the Kingdom of Fife on the opposite shore of the Firth of Forth; and even St. Andrews is not far.

ORIENTATION

Arriving

For information on arriving by plane, train, car and more, see "Getting to Edinburgh & Glasgow," p. 25 in chapter 3.

Visitor Information

Edinburgh Information Centre, atop the Princes Mall near Waverley Station (VisitScotland; ✆ **0131/473-3800** or 0845/225-5121; fax 0131/473-3881; www. edinburgh.org; Bus: 3, 8, 22, 25, or 31), can give you sightseeing information and also arrange lodgings. The center sells bus tours, theater tickets, and souvenirs of Edinburgh. It also has racks and racks of free brochures. It's open year-round;

5

GETTING TO KNOW EDINBURGH | Orientation

Edinburgh Festival ★

The world-famous Edinburgh Festival draws in visitors and performers from all over the globe in August. Their presence alone transforms this small city, making it feel like one of the most cosmopolitan-feeling communities on the planet. The city center buzzes with people, although you may find that places like Leith remain relatively calm.

In addition to the principal International Festival, there is the more popular Fringe. Also coinciding with them is the Book Festival and a Jazz Festival. The city's International Film Festival used to take place then too, but it has been moved to earlier in the summer. For more details see p. 103.

typically the hours are Monday through Saturday from 9am to 7pm and Sunday from 10am to 7pm, though it is open later during the Festival and closes earlier in the winter months.

City Layout
MAIN DISTRICTS & ARTERIES

Central Edinburgh is divided into the **Old Town,** where the city began, and the larger **New Town,** where it expanded in the 1700s. Many visitors find lodgings in New Town and tend to visit Old Town for sightseeing, dining, and drinking (note that the local parlance generally drops the definite article "the" when referring to the Old Town or the New Town; henceforth so shall I). There are hotels, however, in the historic core of the city on **High Street** and in the **Grassmarket.**

Almost everyone planning to travel to Edinburgh has heard of the **Royal Mile,** the main thoroughfare of Old Town, running from Edinburgh Castle in the west to the Palace of Holyroodhouse in the east. Because of its once smoky skies, Old Town earned the city the nickname "Auld Reekie." Today, the air is fine and the district is chock-a-block with tourist attractions, shops, and sidewalks full of out-of-town visitors for most months of the year. Both British royalty and Scotland's **Parliament** (revived in 1999) are based in Old Town, as are city government offices and the country's legal elite. An altogether more infamous street at the southern base of the castle is the Grassmarket, where convicted criminals were once hanged on the gallows—now it's home to restaurants, pubs, and hotels.

New Town is actually fairly old. North of Old Town, on the other side of the **Princes Street Gardens,** New Town was first settled in the 18th century—about one decade before the American Declaration of Independence was signed. By the end of the 1700s, classic squares, streets, and town houses had been completed, and the first New Town was soon expanded with more Georgian designs. New Town's development was part of a "Golden Age of Edinburgh."

New Town is the city's main shopping precinct today, with broad sidewalks and smart shops, bars, and restaurants. Its busiest boulevard, **Princes Street,** offers panoramic views of Old Town and Edinburgh Castle. Parallel to Princes Street is New Town's second great boulevard, **George Street,** which begins at St. Andrew Square and runs west to Charlotte Square. You may also hear a lot about **Rose**

Street, a narrow car-free lane between Princes and George streets—with many more pubs, shops, and restaurants.

Edinburgh's **Southside** and **West End** are primarily residential. The former is home to the well-regarded **University of Edinburgh** (founded in the 16th century) and the sprawling park known as the **Meadows.** The West End includes the last of New Town developments started at the beginning of the 19th century. It has theaters, several small B&Bs, and swank boutique hotels, as well as the city's most exclusive central neighborhoods.

North of the central city is **Leith,** Edinburgh's historic port where the Water of Leith (a small river that meanders through the city) meets the Firth of Forth. Leith briefly served as the Scottish capital, and its strategic location attracted Oliver Cromwell's invading forces to build a citadel here. It remained an independent burgh until the 20th century. Fans of Irvine Welsh (the author of *Trainspotting*) will know that it has a rough and tumble reputation. But today most of its shipping and the sailors have gone, and lots of luxury apartments are being built. But it hasn't lost all of its atmosphere, and it offers a good selection of restaurants and pubs. Leith is also the home of the Royal Yacht *Britannia*.

Neighborhoods In Brief

Edinburgh has a host of districts—some of which appear to be only a few streets, and many that can be folded into the broader areas of Old and New Towns.

Old Town This is where Edinburgh began. Its spine is the **Royal Mile,** a medieval thoroughfare stretching for about a few kilometers from Edinburgh Castle downhill to the Palace of Holyroodhouse. The Royal Mile is one boulevard with four segments bearing different names: Castlehill, Lawnmarket, High Street, and Canongate. "This is perhaps the largest, longest, and finest street for buildings and number of inhabitants in the world," wrote English author Daniel Defoe. Old Town also includes the Grassmarket and Cowgate.

New Town Situated north of Old Town, the first New Town bloomed between 1766 and 1840, and is one of the largest Georgian developments in the world. It grew to encompass the northern half of the heart of the city. Home to at least 25,000 residents, it's also the largest historic conservation area in Britain. New Town is made up of a network of squares, streets, terraces, and circuses (circular open spaces where several streets meet), reaching from Haymarket in the west almost to Leith Walk in the east. New Town also extends from Canonmills in the north to Princes Street, its most famous artery, on the south.

Stockbridge Part of New Town today, northwest of the castle, Stockbridge was once a village, and it still rather feels like a small town near the heart of the city, with its own tight-knit community. Straddling the Water of Leith, it is a good place for visitors to the city to relax, with some friendly cafes, pubs, restaurants, and shops.

Haymarket & Dalry West of the city center by about a few kilometers, these two districts may be off the beaten path for most visitors. Haymarket centers on the railway station (an alternative to Waverley for travelers to and from Glasgow or places

Edinburgh Neighborhoods

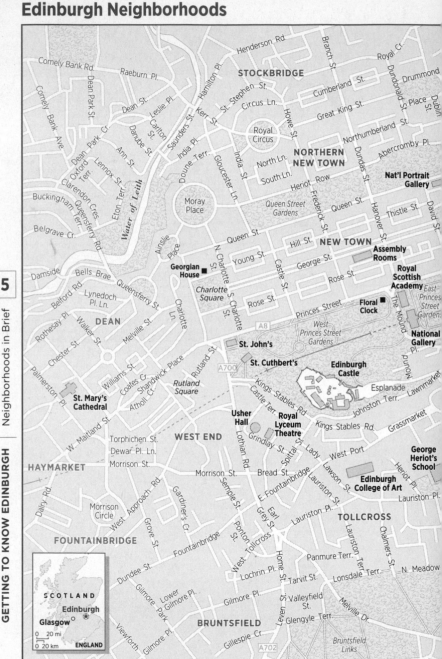

Comely Bank Rd.
Raeburn Pl.
Comely Bank Ave.
Comely Bank St.
Dean Park St.
Dean St.
Leslie Pl.
Carlton St.
Danube St.
Dean Park Cr.
Oxford Terr.
Lennox St.
Ann St.
Clarendon Cres.
Buckingham Terr.
Queensferry Terr.
Queensferry Rd.
Belgrave Cr.
Eton Terr.
Water of Leith
Damside
Bells Brae
Belford Rd.
Lynedoch Pl. Ln.
Rothesay Pl.
Walker St.
Chester St.
Palmerston Pl.
DEAN
Melville St.
Williams St.
Coates Cr.
Shandwick Place
Atholl Cr.
St. Mary's Cathedral
W. Maitland St.
Torphichen St.
Dewar Pl. Ln.
Morrison St.
HAYMARKET
Dalry Rd.
Morrison Circle
West Approach Rd.
FOUNTAINBRIDGE
Dundee St.
Gilmore Park
Lower Gilmore Pl.
Viewforth
Gilmore Pl.
Gillespie Cr.

Henderson Rd.
Branch St.
Royal Cr.
Dundonald St.
Dublin
Drummond
STOCKBRIDGE
Hamilton Pl.
St. Stephen St.
Cumberland St.
Great King St.
Kerr St.
Circus Ln.
Howe St.
Northumberland St.
Abercromby Pl.
Dundas St.
Saunders St.
India Pl.
Royal Circus
North La.
South Ln.
Heriot Row
Frederick St.
Queen St.
Hanover St.
Nat'l Portrait Gallery
Thistle St.
David St.
NORTHERN NEW TOWN
Moray Place
Doune Terr.
Gloucester Ln.
India St.
Queen Street Gardens
Ainslie Place
Queen St.
Hill St.
NEW TOWN
Assembly Rooms
Georgian House
N. Charlotte St.
Young St.
George St.
Rose St.
Royal Scottish Academy
East Princes Street Garden
Charlotte Square
S. Charlotte St.
Rose St.
Castle St.
The Mound
Charlotte Ln.
Princes Street
Floral Clock
National Gallery
A8
West Princes Street Gardens
The Mound
Melville St.
St. John's
A700
St. Cuthbert's
Edinburgh Castle
Esplanade
Lawnmarket
Rutland Place
Kings Stables Rd.
Castle Terr.
Johnston Terr.
Grassmarket
Rutland Square
Usher Hall
Royal Lyceum Theatre
Kings Stables Rd.
WEST END
Lothian Rd.
Grindlay St.
Spittal St.
Lady Lawson St.
West Port
George Heriot's School
Heriot Pl.
Morrison St.
Bread St.
E. Fountainbridge
Lauriston St.
Edinburgh College of Art
Lauriston Pl.
Dewar Pl.
Semple St.
Earl Grey St.
Lauriston Pl.
TOLLCROSS
Lauriston Terr.
Chalmers St.
Gardiner's Cr.
Grove St.
Fountainbridge
Ponton St.
Home St.
Panmure Terr.
Lonsdale Terr.
N. Meadow
Gilmore Pl.
West Tollcross
Lochrin Pl.
Tarvit St.
Leven St.
Valleyfield St.
Melville Dr.
BRUNTSFIELD
Glengyle Terr.
Bruntsfield Links
A702

SCOTLAND
Edinburgh
Glasgow
0   20 mi
0   20 km
ENGLAND

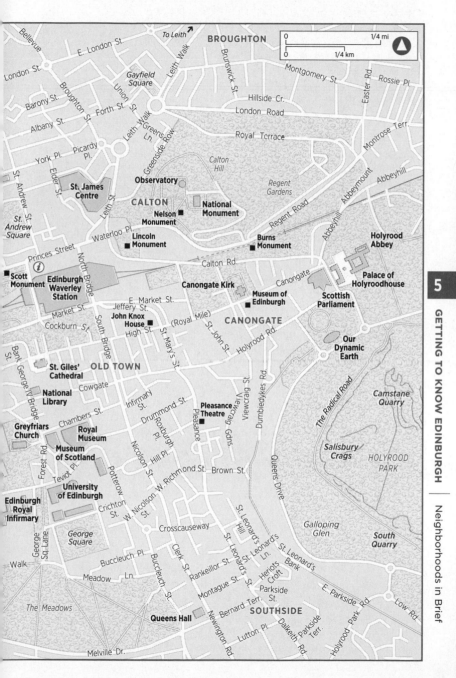

much further north). Near the station is the Scottish national rugby stadium: Murrayfield. Dalry is slowly being gentrified.

Tollcross & West End   Edinburgh's theater district and conference center are located in the area west of the castle. While the West End neighborhoods near Shandwick Place are rather exclusive, the district of Tollcross might appear a bit rough by contrast. However, it is rapidly changing, with redevelopment moving it upmarket.

Marchmont   A kilometer or two south of High Street, this suburb was constructed between 1869 and 1914, offering new housing for people who could no longer afford to live in New Town. Its northern border is the Meadows. Sometimes visitors go south to this neighborhood for affordable B&Bs and guesthouses.

Bruntsfield   This suburb to the west of the Meadows is named after Bruntsfield Links. Now a residential district, it is where James IV gathered the Scottish army he marched to its defeat at Flodden in 1513.

Church Hill & Morningside   South of Bruntsfield, Church Hill has the area nicknamed "holy corner" because of the concentration of churches at the junction of Bruntsfield, Colinton, and Chamberlain roads. Morningside is probably the poshest old suburb in the city, with leafy streets. If you venture this far, be sure and visit the historic pub Canny Man.

Calton   Encompassing Calton Hill, with its Regent and Royal terraces, Calton skirts the so-called Pink Triangle. Edinburgh has a lively and engaged gay population, which focuses socially on an area from the top of Leith Walk to Broughton Street. It is not, however, a dedicated gay district such as San Francisco's Castro or Christopher Street in Manhattan's Greenwich Village. It is just part and parcel of this lively area with its bars, nightclubs, and restaurants.

Leith Walk   Not precisely a neighborhood, but the main artery that connects Edinburgh's city center to Leith. Off it are Easter Road (home of Hibernian Football Club) and the districts of Pilrig and South Leith. An honest cross-section of Edinburgh can be seen during a walk down Leith Walk.

Leith   The Port of Leith lies only a couple of kilometers north of Princes Street and is the city's major harbor, opening onto the Firth of Forth. The area is currently being gentrified, and many visitors come here for the restaurants and pubs, many of which specialize in seafood. The port isn't what it used to be in terms of maritime might; its glory days were back when stevedores unloaded cargoes by hand.

Newhaven   Newhaven is a fishing village west of Leith. Founded in the 1400s, this former little harbor with a bustling fish market was greatly altered in the 1960s. Many of its "bow-tows" (a nickname for closely knit, clannish residents) were uprooted, like the Leithers, in a major gentrification program.

📎 **All-Day Tickets & Edinburgh Pass Cards**

Lothian buses in Edinburgh offer all-day tickets, which are handy if you plan several rides across town. For unlimited travel, the price is £3 for adults, £2.40 for children. Another way to both get around and get into some 30 attractions that charge admission (although many attractions are free) is the Edinburgh Pass. It is priced on a sliding scale depending on the number of days you wish to use it. For example, a 3-day adult pass is £51.50 and a 3-day child pass is £33. The pass gets you onto tour buses and boat rides. For more information call ✆ **0845/225-5121.**

GETTING AROUND

Because of its narrow lanes, known as "wynds" and closes, you can only explore Old Town in any depth on foot. Edinburgh is fairly convenient for the visitor who likes to walk (see chapter 9 for some suggested strolls), as many of the attractions are on or near the Royal Mile and close to one of the major streets of New Town. Remember, if you're here from overseas, the cars drive on the left. If you're crossing, traffic closest to you approaches from the right.

BY BUS   Until the new trams are completed (see below), the city's numerous buses will continue to provide the chief method of public transportation in Edinburgh. Fares depend on the distance traveled, with the adult one-way (single) **minimum fare** of £1.20 covering the principal Edinburgh districts. If you plan multiple trips in 1 day, purchase a **Day Ticket** (see above) that allows unlimited travel. Be advised that bus drivers will not give change, so carry the correct amount in coins or purchase a pack of 20 tear-off tickets (called "City Singles") for £24. At Travelshops, 1-week **Ridacard** passes, which allow unlimited travel on buses, can be purchased for £13 adults, £11 students, and £9 juniors.

In addition, the tourist buses that terminate at Waverley Bridge offer hop-on, hop-off at any of their stops on the set circuit of primarily Old and New Towns. See p. 101 in chapter 8 for details.

Visitors can find advance tickets and further information in the city center at the **Waverley Bridge Travelshop,** Waverley Bridge, open Monday to Saturday 8:15am to 6pm and Sunday 9:30am to 5:15pm, or at **27 Hanover Street Travelshop,** open Monday to Saturday 8:15am to 6pm. For details on fares and timetables, call ✆ **0131/555-6363,** or visit **www.lothianbuses.co.uk.**

BY TAXI   You can hail a "black" taxi similar to those in London, or pick one up at a taxi stand. Fares start at around £1.50 in the day, and a typical trek across town might cost about £7. Taxi ranks are at High Street near North Bridge, Waverley and Haymarket stations, Hanover Street, North Street, Andrew Street, and Lauriston Place. Fares are displayed in the front of the taxi and charges are posted, including extra fees for night drivers or destinations outside the city limits. You can also call a taxi. Try **City Cabs** at ✆ **0131/228-1211** or **Central Taxis** at ✆ **0131/229-2468.**

Edinburgh's Controversial Trams

As I write, Edinburgh is constructing a new **tram** system. Since mid-2009, Edinburgh has suffered the same torn-up streets as other cities while they wait for tram systems, whether Manchester or Bordeaux. Eventually, the Edinburgh tram will take passengers up or down Princes Street and Leith Walk. It will cross Leith into Newhaven and Granton, and may circle back to Haymarket—if there is enough money. No trams are expected to be operational until 2011, and until then bus routes along the streets where track is being laid will be disrupted.

BY CAR Unless absolutely necessary, I suggest that you simply don't drive in Edinburgh—it can prove to be a tricky business. Traffic-calming systems, round-abouts, one-way streets, narrow and cobbled roads, dedicated bus lanes, and construction works for the new tramways—as well as driving on the left for visitors not used to it—are all good reasons to forego the automobile. Parking is expensive and can also be difficult to find. Some zones are marked PERMIT HOLDERS ONLY, meaning your vehicle will be towed if you have no permit. A double yellow line along the curb indicates no parking at any time. A single yellow line along the curb indicates restrictions, too, so be sure to read the signs for details of limitations. Major car parks (parking lots) are at Castle Terrace (near Edinburgh Castle), Waverley Station, and St. James Centre (close to the east end of Princes St.).

You may want a rental car for touring the countryside or for heading onward. Many agencies grant discounts to those who reserve in advance. Most will accept your foreign driver's license, provided you've held it for more than a year and are over 21. Major car-rental companies have offices at the Edinburgh airport should you want to rent a car on the spot. In the city, try **Avis** on West Park Place near Haymarket Station (© **0870/153-9103**), **Hertz** on Picardy Place (© **0870/864-0013**), or **Thrifty** at 42 Haymarket Terrace (© **0131/337-1319**). For more agencies, see p. 265.

BY BICYCLE Bicycles are more common in Edinburgh than in Glasgow. Do bear in mind that the city has several steep hills and the streets are often cobbled. For information on bike rental see p. 105 in chapter 8.

WHERE TO STAY IN EDINBURGH

Edinburgh offers all kinds of accommodation, from the super posh and fabulously pricey five-star hotels to youth hostels. It's a city that anticipates bundles of tourists and travelers, whether seasonal backpackers, school groups, and families—or professional types in the Scottish capital on commercial and governmental matters.

During the Edinburgh Festival (p. 103)—from late July to early September—the hotels, guesthouses, hostels, and B&Bs fill up. If you're planning a visit at that time, be sure to reserve your room as far in advance as possible. Otherwise you may end up in a town or village as many as 40km (55 miles) from the city center. And don't be surprised if the standard room rates in Edinburgh are higher—in isolated cases twice as high—during August, particularly at smaller hotels.

The tourist board's **Edinburgh Information Centre** is near Waverley Station, atop the Princes Mall shopping center, 3 Princes St. (© **0845/ 225-5121** or 0131/473-3800, or 44-150/683-2121 from overseas; www. edinburgh.org or www.visitscotland.com; Bus: 3, 8, 22, 25, or 31). The local information center, in conjunction with the Scottish tourist board, compiles a lengthy list of small hotels, guesthouses, and private homes providing a bed and breakfast for as little as £30 per person. A booking fee is charged for reservations made using the Booking Hotline, and a 10% deposit is expected. It's open year-round; typically the hours are Monday to Saturday from 9am to 7pm and Sunday from 10am to 7pm, though it's open later during the Festival and closes earlier in the winter months.

The Scottish Tourist Board is also a source of star ratings, which traditionally have been based largely on a tick-list of amenities, such as TVs, telephones, kettles, ironing boards, and so forth. Thus, the stars can be limited for smaller operations that may not offer all the modern conveniences but are still perfectly good places to stay.

The Internet can be a trove of discounted rates if you have the time and inclination to surf the net. In some cases, the bargains are only available through web-based booking services. Some of these special prices and promotions are noted below. Often, there are onerous cancelation terms. Also check the Edinburgh Principal Hotel Association website, www.stayin edinburgh.net. Finally, booking for multiple nights in one hotel is another way to reduce your bill.

If you have an early flight out and need a hotel convenient to the airport, consider the 244-unit **Edinburgh Marriott,** 111 Glasgow Rd. (✆ **0131/334-9191**), off the A8 on Edinburgh's western outskirts. It offers doubles from about £85 to £150, including breakfast. Facilities include an indoor pool, gym, sauna, and restaurant.

The overnight room prices quoted below are standard rates and carry no special cancelation fees. Last-minute and Internet bookings may get you cheaper tariffs (but may also carry penalties for cancelation). Also, note that in compliance with Scottish law, all premises are nonsmoking (though some will have designated outdoor smoking areas).

BEST HOTEL BETS

- **Best Boutique Hotel: The Bonham,** 35 Drumsheugh Gardens, Edinburgh EH3 7RN (✆ **0131/226-6050**), is first class in all areas, from the ground-floor lounges and restaurant to stylish rooms. See p. 67.
- **Best Traditional Hotel: The Balmoral,** 1 Princes St., Edinburgh EH2 2EQ (✆ **800/223-6800** in the U.S., or **0131/556-2414**), sets the standard for big, classic hotels in Edinburgh. See p. 60.
- **Best Hotel for Business Travelers:** For convenience, try the **Radisson Blu Hotel,** 80 High St., Edinburgh EH1 1TH (✆ **0131/557-9797**), which offers a business center, conference rooms, and has a decent gym and pool, too. See p. 66.
- **Best Hotel for Romance: The Witchery by the Castle,** Castlehill, The Royal Mile, Edinburgh EH1 2NF (✆ **0131/225-5613**), by **Edinburgh Castle,** practically specializes in creating a romantic retreat with sumptuous rooms. See p. 66.
- **Best Hotel Spa Facilities: Sheraton Grand Hotel,** 1 Festival Sq., Edinburgh EH3 9SR (✆ **800/325-3535** in the U.S. and Canada, or **0131/229-9131**), edges out the competition with its indoor/outdoor rooftop pool. See p. 68.
- **Best B&B/Guesthouse: 23 Mayfield,** 23 Mayfield Gardens, Edinburgh EH9 2BX (✆ **0131/667-5806**), remains a Frommer's favorite. See p. 69.
- **Best Discreet Luxury Hotel: The Howard,** 34 Great King St., Edinburgh EH3 6QH (✆ **0131/557-3500**), can even offer you your own butler. See p. 61.
- **Best Hotel in Historic Building: Prestonfield,** Priestfield Rd., Edinburgh EH16 5UT (✆ **0131/225-7800**), is housed in a mansion that dates to the 17th century, amid lovely country parkland. See p. 68.
- **Best Hotel in Leith: Malmaison,** 1 Tower Place, Leith, Edinburgh EH6 7DB (✆ **0131/468-5000**), is walking distance to three Michelin-starred restaurants. See p. 70.

NEW TOWN
Very Expensive

The Balmoral ★★★ Almost directly above Waverley railway station, The Balmoral's soaring clock tower is a city landmark, famously set a few minutes fast for the benefit of those on the way to the train. The plushest accommodation—such as room 520, aka the Dee Suite—are sumptuously furnished, with an ample sitting room and a huge, well-appointed bathroom; not to mention fabulous views toward the castle. Dining options at The Balmoral include the elegant and Michelin-star-earning **Number One** (p. 73). Kilted doormen supply the Scottish atmosphere from the start, and afternoon tea is served in the high-ceilinged Palm Court.

1 Princes St., Edinburgh EH2 2EQ. ⓒ **800/223-6800** in the U.S., or 0131/556-2414. Fax 0131/557-3747. www.thebalmoralhotel.com. 188 units. £220–£290 double with breakfast. AE, DC, MC, V. Valet parking £15. Bus: 3, 8, 22, 25, or 30. **Amenities:** 2 restaurants; 2 bars; concierge; health club; indoor pool; room service; sauna; spa. *In room:* A/C, TV/DVD, fax, hair dryer, Internet, minibar.

Caledonian Hilton Edinburgh ★   This hotel is another of the city's landmarks with commanding views toward the nearby Edinburgh Castle and over the western fringe of Princes Street Gardens. The public rooms are reminiscent of Edwardian splendor, and the guest rooms (many of which are exceptionally spacious) are traditionally styled with reproduction furniture. Fine-dining meals are served in the Pompadour Restaurant. A traditional tea is served in the high-ceilinged lounge.

Princes St., Edinburgh EH1 2AB. ⓒ **0131/222-8888.** Fax 0131/222-8889. www.caledonian.hilton.com. 251 units. £175–£250 double with breakfast. Children 15 and under stay free in parent's room. AE, DC, MC, V. Parking £10 per day. Bus: 12, 25, or 33. **Amenities:** 2 restaurants; 3 bars; indoor pool; exercise room; room service. *In room:* TV/DVD, hair dryer, Internet, minibar.

The Howard ★★   One of the most discreet luxury hotels in the city, The Howard links a set of Georgian terraced houses in northern New Town, and is sister hotel to the highly desirable The Bonham (p. 67) and Channings (see below). Rooms here are individually and elegantly decorated, and some feature a Jacuzzi. Excellent service is a hallmark of The Howard—a group of butlers tend to your individual needs, from parking your car to unpacking your luggage, should you so desire.

34 Great King St., Edinburgh EH3 6QH. ⓒ **0131/557-3500.** Fax 0131/557-6515. www.thehoward.com. 18 units. £190–£275 double with breakfast. AE, DC, MC, V. Free parking. Bus: 23 or 27. **Amenities:** Restaurant; room service. *In room:* TV/DVD, hair dryer, Internet.

Expensive

Channings ★   Five Edwardian town houses were knocked together in this tranquil residential area on the edge of the city center to create this hotel, which maintains the atmosphere of a Scottish country house. Most of the furniture has been personally collected by the company's owner over the years. Guest rooms are modern in style; the front units get the views of the neighboring Georgian architecture, while the rear ones offer vistas toward the Firth of Forth and have a more secluded feel.

12–16 S. Learmonth Gardens, Edinburgh EH4 1EZ. ⓒ **0131/623-9302.** Fax 0131/332-9631. www. channings.co.uk. 46 units. £99–£139 double with breakfast. AE, DC, MC, V. Parking on street. Bus: 37. **Amenities:** Restaurant; bar; room service. *In room:* TV/DVD, hair dryer, Internet.

The George Hotel   A traditional yet modern hotel in the heart of New Town. The buildings that house this hotel on posh George Street were first erected in the 1780s, transformed with alterations of Corinthian and neo-Renaissance style during the next 150 years or so before becoming the exclusive George Hotel in 1950. In 2006–07, another major renovation took place, bringing with it the stylish new restaurant and bar, Tempus.

Where to Stay in Edinburgh

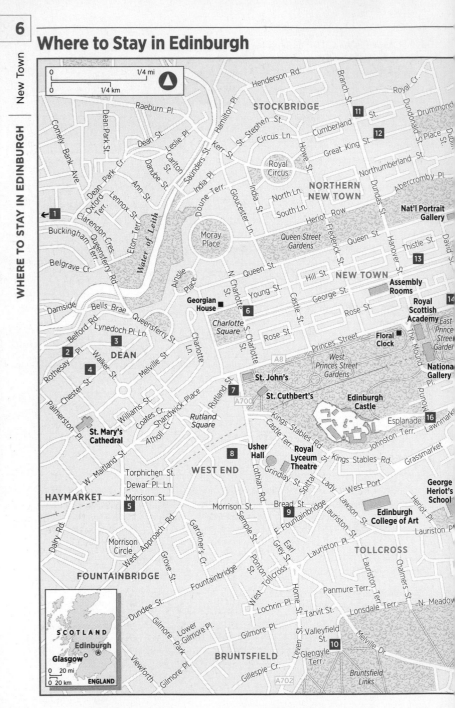

0 .... 1/4 mi
0 .... 1/4 km

Henderson Rd.

STOCKBRIDGE

Raeburn Pl.

Comely Bank Ave.

Dean Park St.

Dean St.

Leslie Pl.

Carlton

Danube St.

Ann St.

Dean Park Cr.

Oxford Terr.

Lennox St.

Eton Terr.

Clarendon Cres.

Queensferry Rd.

Buckingham Terr.

Belgrave Cr.

1

Hamilton Pl.

Saunders St.

Kerr St.

St. Stephen St.

India Pl.

Doune Terr.

Gloucester Ln.

India St.

Water of Leith

Moray Place

Ainslie Place

Circus Ln.

Royal Circus

Cumberland St.

Great King St.

Howe St.

North Ln.

South Ln.

Heriot Row

Queen Street Gardens

North Charlotte St.

Young St.

Queen St.

Hill St.

George St.

Rose St.

NORTHERN NEW TOWN

Dundas St.

Frederick St.

Hanover St.

Northumberland St.

Abercromby Pl.

Thistle St.

NEW TOWN

11

12

Dundonald St.

Drummond

Royal Cr.

St.

Place

David St.

Nat'l Portrait Gallery

13

Assembly Rooms

Royal Scottish Academy

14

Damside

Bells Brae

Belford Rd.

Lynedoch Pl. Ln.

Rothesay Pl.

Walker St.

Chester St.

Palmerston Pl.

DEAN

2

3

4

Queensferry St.

Melville St.

Williams St.

Coates Cr.

Shandwick Place

Atholl

Charlotte Ln.

Charlotte St.

Georgian House

Charlotte Square

S. Charlotte St.

Rose St.

Rutland St.

Princes Street

A8

West Princes Street Gardens

St. John's

St. Cuthbert's

Floral Clock

East Prince Street Garden

National Gallery

The Mound

6

7

A700

Rutland Square

Rutland St.

Kings Stables Rd.

Castle Terr.

Usher Hall

Royal Lyceum Theatre

Edinburgh Castle

Esplanade

Johnston Terr.

Lawnmarket

16

St. Mary's Cathedral

W. Maitland St.

Torphichen St.

Dewar Pl. Ln.

Morrison St.

HAYMARKET

WEST END

5

8

Grindlay St.

Spittal

Lothian Rd.

Lady Lawson

St. Kings Stables Rd.

West Port

Bread St.

E. Fountainbridge

Lauriston St.

9

Grassmarket

George Heriot's School

Edinburgh College of Art

Lauriston Pl.

TOLLCROSS

Dalry Rd.

Morrison Circle

West Approach Rd.

Gardiner's Cr.

Fountainbridge

Grove St.

Semple St.

Ponton St.

Morrison St.

FOUNTAINBRIDGE

Dundee St.

Gilmore Park

Lower Gilmore Pl.

Viewforth

Gilmore Pl.

West Tollcross

Lochrin Pl.

Earl Grey St.

Home St.

Tarvit St.

Valleyfield St.

Glengyle Terr.

Leven St.

Panmure Terr.

Lauriston Terr.

Lonsdale Terr.

Chalmers St.

N. Meadow

Lauriston Pl.

Heriot Pl.

Lauriston Pl.

Melville Dr.

10

BRUNTSFIELD

Gillespie Cr.

A702

Bruntsfield Links

SCOTLAND

Edinburgh

Glasgow

0 .... 20 mi
0 .... 20 km

ENGLAND

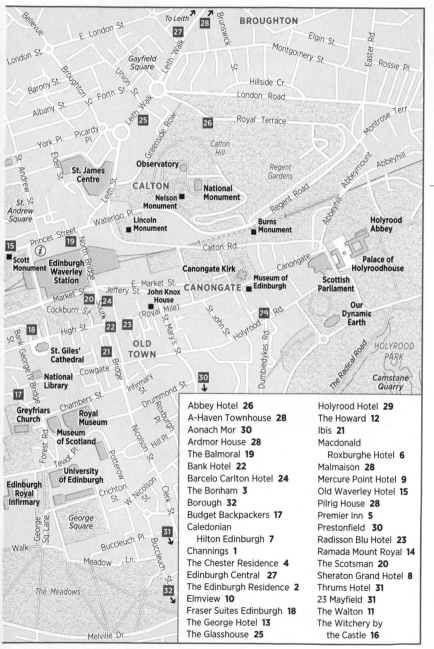

Abbey Hotel **26**	Holyrood Hotel **29**
A-Haven Townhouse **28**	The Howard **12**
Aonach Mor **30**	Ibis **21**
Ardmor House **28**	Macdonald
The Balmoral **19**	Roxburghe Hotel **6**
Bank Hotel **22**	Malmaison **28**
Barcelo Carlton Hotel **24**	Mercure Point Hotel **9**
The Bonham **3**	Old Waverley Hotel **15**
Borough **32**	Pilrig House **28**
Budget Backpackers **17**	Premier Inn **5**
Caledonian	Prestonfield **30**
Hilton Edinburgh **7**	Radisson Blu Hotel **23**
Channings **1**	Ramada Mount Royal **14**
The Chester Residence **4**	The Scotsman **20**
Edinburgh Central **27**	Sheraton Grand Hotel **8**
The Edinburgh Residence **2**	Thrums Hotel **31**
Elmview **10**	23 Mayfield **31**
Fraser Suites Edinburgh **18**	The Walton **11**
The George Hotel **13**	The Witchery by
The Glasshouse **25**	the Castle **16**

19–21 George St., Edinburgh EH2 2PB. ✆ **0131/225-1251.** Fax 0131/226-5644. www.principal-hayley. com. 195 units. £149–£210 double with breakfast. AE, DC, MC, V. Limited free parking. Bus: 24, 28, or 45. **Amenities:** Restaurant; bar; concierge. *In room:* TV/DVD, hair dryer, Internet.

The Glasshouse ★   Among the top "boutique" hotels of Edinburgh, the Glass-house combines old and new, with an impressive stone church facade harmonizing surprisingly seamlessly with a modern glass structure. Many of the sleek bedrooms offer panoramic views of the city and a special feature of the Glasshouse is the rooftop bar and garden for hotel guests. Advance Internet bookings can get you sav-ings of 50% on published rates.

2 Greenside Place, Edinburgh EH1 3AA. ✆ **0131/525-8200.** Fax 0131/525-8205. www.theetoncollection. com/hotels/glasshouse. 65 units. £295 deluxe double with continental breakfast. AE, DC, MC, V. Parking available nearby. Bus: 5, 14, or 22. **Amenities:** Bar; babysitting; concierge; health club; room service; laundry service. *In room:* A/C, TV/DVD, hair dryer, Internet, minibar.

Macdonald Roxburghe Hotel ★   Housed in Georgian buildings designed by the great 18th-century architect Robert Adam just adjacent to Charlotte Square, the Roxburghe creates a classy atmosphere—reflected in the elegant drawing room with its ornate ceiling and woodwork, antique furnishings, and tall arched windows. The largest guest rooms have traditional features such as imposing fireplaces.

38 Charlotte St. (at George St.), Edinburgh EH2 4HG. ✆ **0870/194-2108** or 888/892-0038 (U.S. only). Fax 0131/240-5555. www.macdonaldhotels.co.uk/roxburghe. 198 units. From £115 double with break-fast. AE, DC, MC, V. Parking £12. Bus: 13, 19, or 41. **Amenities:** Restaurant; bar; concierge; health club; indoor pool; spa, sauna. *In room:* TV/DVD, hair dryer.

Old Waverley Hotel   Some corner guest rooms at this popular hotel on busy Princes Street look directly onto Princes Street Gardens and the castle beyond. Located opposite the Scott Monument, the Old Waverley Hotel actually isn't very elderly by Edinburgh standards—it only dates to 1848. The guest rooms are well maintained and comfortable, but you're mainly paying for a location in the heart of the action. Advance Internet booking can mean savings of 70% on the published tariff as listed below.

43 Princes St., Edinburgh EH2 2BY. ✆ **0131/556-4648.** Fax 0131/557-6316. www.oldwaverley.co.uk. 66 units. £229 double with breakfast. AE, DC, MC, V. Parking £10. Bus: 4, 12, 31, or 44. **Amenities:** Restau-rant; bar; room service. *In room:* TV, hair dryer, Internet.

Ramada Mount Royal   There aren't necessarily a lot of frills with the Ramada, but the comfort is genuine in the streamlined guest rooms. The reception area, up one flight of stairs from the street entrance, offers floor-to-ceiling windows that frame classic views of Old Town and Edinburgh Castle. Be aware that this hotel is traditionally a favorite of large bus-tour groups.

53 Princes St., Edinburgh EH2 2DG. ✆ **0131/225-7161.** Fax 0131/220-4671. www.ramadajarvis.co.uk. 158 units. £125–£180 double with breakfast. AE, DC, MC, V. Parking available nearby. Bus: 4, 12, 31, or 44. **Amenities:** Restaurant; bar; room service. *In room:* TV, hair dryer.

Moderate

The Walton   This guesthouse with Georgian character and elegant features sits at the heart of Edinburgh's less frenetic northern New Town—a short walk up the hill to the busy streets of New Town proper. There are limited hotel amenities, so if you require an in-house restaurant or a full-service desk 24/7, look elsewhere. A sister

FAMILY-FRIENDLY hotels

A-Haven Townhouse With some guest rooms large enough to accommodate families, this small hotel in Leith should make any brood feel right at home. See p. 70.

Barcelo Carlton Hotel Kids will love the indoor pool. Parents will love the availability of extra-large units and the fact that cots are readily provided. It's right in the heart of town to boot. See p. 65.

Thrums Hotel This Southside hotel takes its moniker from *Peter Pan* author J. M. Barrie's nickname for his hometown of Kirriemuir. No sign of Tinker Bell, but kids are made especially welcome here, and there is room for them to play outside. See p. 69.

hotel, The Glenora, offers alternative rooms on Rosebery Crescent, near the Haymarket railway station.

79 Dundas St., Edinburgh EH3 6SD. ☎ **0131/556-1137.** Fax 0131/557-8367. www.waltonhotel.com. 10 units. £85–£140 double with breakfast. MC, V. Limited free parking. Bus: 23 or 27. *In room:* TV, hair dryer, Wi-Fi.

Inexpensive

Abbey Hotel On the slopes of Calton Hill, this small four-story hotel, once called the Greenside, gets mixed reviews. On the plus side, it is well located and the building retains traditional features such as high ceilings, cove moldings, and elaborate trim. The Firth of Forth and the dramatic Forth bridges are just about seen from the uppermost front rooms; a sloping tiered garden, with a patio at the bottom, is the view from the rear units.

9 Royal Terrace, Edinburgh EH7 5AB. ☎/fax **0131/557-0022.** 15 units. £45–£130 double with breakfast. AE, MC, V. Parking on street. Bus: 1, 4, 5, or 15. **Amenities:** Bar. *In room:* TV, hair dryer.

OLD TOWN

Very Expensive

Barcelo Carlton Hotel ☺ This baronial Victorian pile (once an exclusive department store) rises from the east side of North Bridge, between the Royal Mile and the cavernous gap that separates Old Town from New Town. Some recent investment in the Carlton removed bedrooms to create more space in the remaining units, and bathrooms that have both a tub and shower. Among the leisure facilities is an indoor pool. Some complain of the noise from the busy street in front of the hotel: Light sleepers should request rooms at the rear.

19 North Bridge, Edinburgh EH1 1SD. ☎ **0131/472-3000.** Fax 0131/556-2691. www.barcelo-hotels.co.uk. 189 units. £120–£180 double with breakfast. Children 15 and under stay free in parent's room. AE, DC, MC, V. Parking free for Premium room guests. Bus: 3, 8, 14, or 29. **Amenities:** Restaurant; bar; babysitting; health club; indoor pool; Jacuzzi; sauna; limited room service; squash courts. *In room:* TV/DVD, hair dryer, Wi-Fi.

The Scotsman ★ Located almost directly across the street from the Carlton (above), this stylish hotel honors the newspaper that was published in this building for nearly a century. Guest rooms include state-of-the-art bathrooms and some offer such extras as two-way service closets, meaning any laundry can be picked up and delivered virtually unnoticed. The Scotsman's two-floor penthouse suite is in a category of its own, with a private elevator and balcony with barbecue. The spa occupies a vast space, with a 60-station gym and stainless steel swimming pool, while the hotel's Northbridge restaurant serves modern Scottish cuisine. Similar to its sister hotel The Glasshouse, advance Internet bookings can save you more than 50% on published rates.

20 North Bridge, Edinburgh EH1 1DF. ✆ **0131/556-5565.** Fax 0131/652-3652. www.theetoncollection. com. 68 units. £150–£300, including breakfast. AE, DC, MC, V. Valet parking. Bus: 3, 8, 14, or 29. **Amenities:** Restaurant; bar; babysitting; health club; indoor pool; room service; sauna; spa; salon. *In room:* TV/DVD, hair dryer, minibar, Wi-Fi.

The Witchery by the Castle ★★   Part of the famous Edinburgh restaurant of the same name (p. 80), the overnight accommodation at the Witchery is romantic and sumptuous—the rooms decorated with Gothic antiques and elaborate tapestries. Each lavishly decorated suite (named the Library, Vestry, Armoury, and the like) has its own character, for example an oak four-poster bed in a red-velvet-lined bedroom.

Castlehill, The Royal Mile, Edinburgh, EH1 2NF. ✆ **0131/225-5613.** Fax 0131/220-4392. www.the witchery.com. 7 suites. From £300, including continental breakfast and champagne. AE, DC, MC, V. Parking nearby. Bus: 28. **Amenities:** Restaurant. *In room:* A/C, TV/DVD, fridge, hair dryer.

Expensive

Fraser Suites Edinburgh   Opened in February 2010, this boutique hotel is located just off the Royal Mile near St. Giles' Cathedral. All rooms have designer furniture, plush carpeting, and the latest in bathroom features (including a "rainfall shower"). There are also suites with full kitchens and dining space. The worst it seems one can say is that some of the rooms have quite restricted views (which means they are the least expensive). Its restaurant—Glasshouse Off the Mile—offers contemporary Scottish cuisine, such as rump of Perthshire lamb rubbed in cumin rock salt.

12–26 St. Giles St., Edinburgh EH1 PT. ✆ **0131/221-7200.** http://edinburgh.frasershospitality.com. 75 units. From £250, including breakfast. AE, MC, V. Parking nearby. Bus: 28. **Amenities:** Restaurant; gym. *In room:* TV/DVD, Internet, MP3 dock.

Holyrood Hotel ★   This impressive and stylish hotel in the Macdonald chain is near the Scottish Parliament and the Palace of Holyroodhouse, as well as being only a few minutes' walk from the heart of Old Town. Bedrooms have deluxe furnishings and elegant toiletries. The Club Floor is geared toward luxury-minded guests: It has a dedicated elevator, butler service, lounge, and library, along with a champagne and canapé reception every night.

81 Holyrood Rd., Edinburgh EH8 8AU. ✆ **0844/879-9028.** Fax 0131/550-4545. www.macdonaldhotels. co.uk. 156 units. From £110–£250 double with breakfast. AE, DC, MC, V. Limited parking £15. Bus: 35. **Amenities:** Restaurant; bar; indoor pool; health club; sauna; room service; laundry service; dry cleaning; club-level rooms. *In room:* A/C, TV/DVD, fax, hair dryer, Internet, minibar.

Radisson Blu Hotel ★   Formerly the Crowne Plaza, this is the preferred big hotel in Old Town for many, as it is halfway between Edinburgh Castle and Holyroodhouse on the Royal Mile. It offers first-class facilities, including a jet-stream pool, a

Basic Chain Hotels & Hostels

If you're the type of traveler who thinks of hotels as just places to lay your head at night, it's worth checking out the deals available with some of the town's no-frills chains. In the heart of Old Town, try the **Ibis**, 6 Hunter Sq., Edinburgh EH1 1QW (© **0131/240-7000**; www.ibishotel.com), where rooms generally are below £100. In the West End, the **Premier Inn**, 1 Morrison Link, Edinburgh EH3 8DN (© **0870/238-3319**; www.premiertravelinn.co.uk), is modern and functional with rooms at around £85, although its Leith branch is cheaper still at £65.

A few hostels have private rooms, too. Your best bets include the **Edinburgh Central**, a five-star hostel, which is part of the Scottish Youth Hostel Association. Single rooms with en-suite facilities start at £34 and twins are £51 and upwards, depending on the season. It is located at 9 Haddington Place, Edinburgh EH7 4AL (© **0845/293-7373**; www.edinburgh central.org). Another option is **Budget Backpackers** at 37–39 Cowgate, Edinburgh EH1 1JR (©**0131/226-6351**; www.budgetbackpackers.com). Twin rooms are around £25 per person but don't leave your booking until the last minute.

restaurant (called the Restaurant), and the less formal Itchycoo Bar and Kitchen, which offers tapas-style sharing platters and drinks.

80 High St., Edinburgh EH1 1TH. © **0131/557-9797.** Fax 0131/557-9789. www.radissonblu.co.uk/hotel-edinburgh. 238 units. From £120 double with breakfast. AE, DC, MC, V. Parking £8.50. Bus: 35. **Amenities:** 2 restaurants; bar; concierge; health club; indoor pool; room service; sauna. *In room:* TV/DVD, hair dryer, minibar, Wi-Fi.

Moderate

Bank Hotel 🥄   This hotel on the Royal Mile offers good value. You enter the hotel via the informal Bank Bar and once inside you'll discover high ceilings, well-chosen furnishings, and king-size beds; all but one of the guest rooms have both a shower and a bath tub.

1 South Bridge St., Edinburgh EH1 1LL. © **0131/556-9940.** Fax 0131/558-1362. www.festival-inns.co.uk. 9 units. £100–£150 double with breakfast. AE, MC, V. Bus: 35. **Amenities:** Bar; Wi-Fi. *In room:* TV, hair dryer.

WEST END

Very Expensive

The Bonham ★★★   One of Edinburgh's most stylish hotels, The Bonham is arguably the jewel in the shimmering crown of the Townhouse Group of hotels in Edinburgh (which also includes The Edinburgh Residence, The Howard, and Channings). Its rooms have individual themes with plush contemporary furniture and upholsteries. Bathrooms are state of the art, with expensive toiletries. The Restaurant at The Bonham is elegant, yet modern.

35 Drumsheugh Gardens, Edinburgh EH3 7RN. © **0131/226-6050.** Fax 0131/226-6080. www.thebonham.com. 48 units. £100–£250 small double with breakfast. AE, DC, MC, V. Free parking. Bus: 19 or 37. **Amenities:** Restaurant; room service. *In room:* TV, hair dryer, Internet, minibar.

The Chester Residence One option between a fully self-catered rental home and a hotel room is to rent one of the city's "serviced apartments"; those at the Chester Residence rate five stars according to the tourist board. Each luxury flat (save the studio-size "patio apartment") has a kitchen, separate sitting room, and full bathroom. The "garden apartment" includes a private walled garden. You can cook for yourself but the suites are serviced daily.

9 Rothesay Place, Edinburgh EH3 7SL. ✆ **0131/226-2075.** Fax 0131/226-2191. www.chester-residence. com. 19 units. £165–£499 per apartment, including continental breakfast. MC, V. Parking on street. Bus: 13. *In apartment:* TV/DVD, Internet, CD, MP3 dock, Wi-Fi.

The Edinburgh Residence ★ Part of the Townhouse Group, this is a fine luxury hotel, and sibling to The Bonham, The Howard, and Channings. Grand staircases and classic wood paneling greet guests and the suites are traditional but with all modern conveniences. All units are spacious: The smallest suite is 40 sq. m (430 sq. ft.).

7 Rothesay Terrace, Edinburgh EH3 7RY. ✆ **0131/226-3380.** Fax 0131/226-3381. www.theedinburgh residence.com. 29 units. £125–£400 suite, including breakfast. AE, MC, V. Free parking. Bus: 13. **Amenities:** Bar; Internet; room service. *In room:* TV/DVD, hair dryer, minibar.

Sheraton Grand Hotel ★ The modern exterior of the Sheraton Grand belies the elegant, even a bit old-fashioned, interior—think soaring public rooms and rich carpeting. With a good location and state-of-the-art spa and leisure facilities (including a rooftop indoor/outdoor pool), this hotel pretty much has it all. The castle-view rooms on the top floors are the best (and most expensive). The main restaurant, with views of Festival Square, presents well-prepared meals and a lavish Sunday buffet, while an annex houses the fine-dining Italian **Santini** restaurant (p. 77) below the spa.

1 Festival Sq., Edinburgh EH3 9SR. ✆ **800/325-3535** in the U.S. and Canada, or 0131/229-9131. Fax 0131/228-4510. www.sheratonedinburgh.co.uk. 260 units. £180–£360 double with breakfast. AE, DC, MC, V. Parking nearby. Bus: 10, 22, or 30. **Amenities:** 3 restaurants; 2 bars; babysitting; concierge; exercise room; indoor and outdoor pools; massage; spa; sauna; room service. *In room:* A/C, TV/DVD, hair dryer, Internet, minibar.

Expensive

Mercure Point Hotel The Point has been listed among the 50 premier hotel designs in the world. The guestrooms are equally attractive. Standard ones may feel a bit small, but the premium units are spacious. Many units have views of the castle, but those at the rear do not. If you like stainless steel and brushed chrome instead of Scottish tartan and antiques, this might be the place for you.

34 Bread St., Edinburgh EH3 9AF. ✆ **0131/221-5555.** Fax 0131/221-9929. www.accorhotels.com. 139 units. From £105 double with breakfast. AE, DC, MC, V. Parking on street. Bus: 2 or 28. **Amenities:** Restaurant; bar; limited room service. *In room:* TV, hair dryer, Wi-Fi.

SOUTHSIDE

Expensive

Prestonfield ★★ Prestonfield, rising in baroque Jacobean splendor amid 5.3 hectares (13 acres) of gardens, pastures, and woodlands below Arthur's Seat, has entertained such luminaries as Sean Connery and Minnie Driver. All guests should appreciate the traditional atmosphere and 1680s' architecture, as well as the peacocks and Highland cattle that strut and stroll across the grounds. In the spacious bedrooms, modern media conveniences such as DVD players and flat-screen plasma TVs are hidden in bespoke cabinets. The hotel's Rhubarb restaurant is among the city's most theatrical looking and serves high-class food.

Priestfield Rd., Edinburgh EH16 5UT. *℃* **0131/225-7800.** Fax 0131/668-3976. www.prestonfield.com. 18 units. £285 double with breakfast. AE, MC, V. Free parking. Bus: 2, 14, or 30. **Amenities:** Restaurant; bar; babysitting; concierge; room service. *In room:* TV/DVD, minibar, Wi-Fi.

Moderate

Aonach Mor   Named after a West Highland mountain, this basic but comfortable guesthouse is located in a proud, if short, row of three-story Victorian terraced houses. Away from the hustle and bustle of the city center, some of the rooms offer views toward the impressive escarpment of Arthur's Seat.

14 Kilmaurs Terrace, Newington, Edinburgh EH16 5DR. *℃* **0131/667-8694.** www.aonachmor.com. 7 units. £60–£140 double with breakfast (depending on season). MC, V. Parking on street. Bus: 30 or 33. *In room:* TV, hair dryer.

Borough   This boutique hotel southeast of the Meadows was designed by Britain's Ben Kelly, who was best known in the 1980s and 90s for designing the famous Hacienda nightclub in Manchester. The rooms are admittedly on the small side, but they are individually designed and at least have high ceilings and casement windows as well as stylish looks. The bar and restaurant on the ground floor are equally fashionable.

72 Causewayside, Edinburgh EH9 1PY. *℃* **0131/668-2255.** www.theboroughhotel.com. 11 units. £50–£150 double with breakfast. Limited parking. Bus: 42. **Amenities:** Restaurant; bar. *In room:* TV/DVD/CD, WI-Fi.

Elmview   This luxurious bed-and-breakfast in a row of Victorian town houses is on the edge of Bruntsfield Links, at the northwest corner of the Meadows. Each of the rooms is well furnished with en suite bathrooms. The only possible hang-up is that immediate street parking is reserved for permanent residents.

15 Glengyle Terrace, Edinburgh EH3 9LN. *℃* **0131/228-1973.** www.elmview.co.uk. 3 units. £90–£120 double with breakfast. MC, V. Bus: 11, 15, or 17. *In room:* TV, hair dryer.

23 Mayfield ★ 🍴   Run since June 2008 by the former owners of Aonach Mor, this handsome three-story sandstone guesthouse is about a mile from the city center. Not all of the units are large, but they tend toward the plush side—and are affordable. Family rooms have one double and two single beds; the deluxe four-poster rooms have mahogany furniture.

23 Mayfield Gardens, Edinburgh EH9 2BX. *℃* **0131/667-5806.** Fax 0131/667-6833. www.23mayfield. co.uk. 9 units. £80–£130 double with breakfast. MC, V. Free parking. Bus: 5, 7, 8, or 29. **Amenities:** Lounge. *In room:* TV, hair dryer, Wi-Fi.

Inexpensive

Thrums Hotel ☺   Thrums Hotel has high-ceilinged guest rooms with some antique furnishings. Children are particularly welcomed here: Some rooms are set aside for families, while the garden has an outdoor play area. Six units come with a shower-only bathroom; the rest are equipped with combination tub and shower.

14–15 Minto St., Edinburgh EH9 1RQ. *℃* **0131/667-5545.** Fax 0131/667-8707. www.thrumshotel.com. 15 units. £55–£110 double with breakfast. MC, V. Free parking. Bus: 5, 7, 8, or 29. *In room:* TV, hair dryer.

LEITH & NORTH OF NEW TOWN

Expensive

Malmaison ★★   Leith's stylish branch of this well-known U.K. boutique hotel brand was once a seamen's mission, capped by a stately, stone clock tower. This hip, yet unpretentious inn has made good use of the 19th-century baronial dormitory for salty dogs. Many rooms are average in size but individually designed and well equipped. For extra space, reserve a suite.

1 Tower Place, Leith, Edinburgh EH6 7DB. ℂ **0131/468-5000.** Fax 0131/468-5002. www.malmaison-edinburgh.com. 100 units. From £125 double with breakfast. AE, DC, MC, V. Free parking. Bus: 16 or 35. **Amenities:** Restaurant; bar; exercise room; room service. *In room:* TV, hair dryer, Internet, minibar.

Moderate

A-Haven Townhouse ☺   The A-Haven is a classy ivy-covered Victorian with rooms outfitted in mostly traditional furnishings. Some units overlook the Firth of Forth; others offer views of Arthur's Seat. There are also rooms large enough to accommodate families.

180 Ferry Rd., Edinburgh EH6 4NS. ℂ **0131/554-6559.** Fax 0131/554-5252. www.a-haven.co.uk. 14 units. £70–£130 double with breakfast. AE, MC, V. Free parking. Bus: 7, 11, or 14. **Amenities:** Bar. *In room:* TV, hair dryer, Internet.

Ardmor House   This gay-owned, straight-friendly guesthouse with nice gardens is a stylish boutique B&B. It has five guest rooms, all with modern bathrooms. Bay windows and period settees befit this restored Victorian house, just about halfway between the city center and Leith. There is a very pleasant garden reserved for guests.

74 Pilrig St. (near Leith Walk), Edinburgh EH6 5AS. ℂ **0131/554-4944.** www.ardmorhouse.com. 5 units. £75–£145 double with breakfast. MC, V. Free parking. Bus: 11. *In room:* TV, hair dryer, Wi-Fi.

Pilrig House   The self-catering apartments in this historic home just south of Leith will suit those travelers who want a bit of independence as well as comfort, and peace and quiet. Its literary heritage is an added bonus: Robert Louis Stevenson often played in this house and its grounds as a child.

Pilrig House Close, Bonnington Rd. (north side of Pilrig Park), Edinburgh EH6 5RF. ℂ **0131/554-4794.** www.pilrighouse.com. 3 units. £80–£250. MC, V. Free parking. Bus: 11 or 36. **Amenities:** TV/DVD/CD player, kitchenette, hair dryer.

WHERE TO DINE IN EDINBURGH

Edinburgh boasts some of the best restaurants in the country—five restaurants have a Michelin star and the selection is more diverse than ever. You'll find an array of contemporary Scottish restaurants; French, fish, and brasserie-style eateries; along with cuisine from around the world, particularly Indian and Thai food; and increasing vegetarian options.

Scotland's reputation for excellent fresh produce is growing. So look out for the following in season: shellfish such as langoustines (aka Dublin Bay Prawns), oysters, mussels, or exquisite hand-dived scallops; locally landed finned fish (such as halibut, bream, and sea bass); as well as heather-fed lamb and Aberdeen Angus beef. Fresh vegetables include asparagus, peas, and, of course, potatoes—some claim that the spuds grown in Ayrshire's sandy soils are unparalleled for their fluffy texture and rich taste.

A lot of restaurants still close for a few hours every afternoon but bistro-style operations and pubs often serve food right through the day. The hours given in the information below reflect when food may be ordered; bars on the premises may keep longer hours. During the annual Edinburgh Festival from late July to the end of August, many dining options offer extended hours. Given the crowds, always reserve a table in advance.

For ideas on dining options, take a look at **The List** magazine's comprehensive **Eating & Drinking Guide,** an annually updated publication that lists and reviews hundreds of restaurants, bars, and cafes in Edinburgh (and Glasgow). It is available to buy or online.

PRICES In Edinburgh, prices don't quite rival London, but are not far off—especially at the top end. If you're looking for bargains, set-price lunches and pre-theater menus always offer discounts, sometimes almost half the price of the regular a la carte dinner menu. For more special offers, log onto **www.5pm.co.uk** for a selection of restaurants offering deals.

SMOKING All restaurants and bars are nonsmoking by law. Some have outdoor dining areas, however, where smoking is allowed.

TIPPING   As is the rule across most of Britain, a gratuity of 10% is the average for service, although you can leave nothing if you feel service was poor. On the other hand, if you were truly impressed, leaving up to 20% can be considered. At a few restaurants, service is included in the check automatically, so there's no need to add a gratuity on top of that.

BEST DINING BETS

o **Best Dining Experience: Restaurant Martin Wishart,** 54 The Shore (C 0131/553-3557), is one of the best restaurants in the U.K., let alone Edinburgh and Scotland. See p. 83.

o **Best Hotel Restaurant: Number One,** The Balmoral, 1 Princes St. (C 0131/557-6727), is another Michelin star holder, with memorable cuisine. See p. 73.

o **Best Innovative Cooking: 21212,** 3 Royal Terrace, Calton Hill (C 0845/22-21212), has been turning heads since opening in 2009. See p. 76.

o **Best Restaurant with Great Views Too: Forth Floor Restaurant & Brasserie,** Harvey Nichols, 30–34 St. Andrew Sq. (C 0131/524-8350), is a marvelous place for a meal with views over the city. See p. 76.

o **Best Thai Food: Dusit,** 49a Thistle St. (C 0131/220-6846), manages to maintain authenticity while using great local produce. See p. 78.

o **Best Vegetarian Restaurant: David Bann,** 56–58 St. Mary's St. (C 0131/556-5888), proves that meat-free meals are not only good for you but can taste fantastic, too. See p. 80.

o **Best for Late-Night Supper: The Witchery by the Castle,** Boswell Court, Castlehill, Royal Mile (C 0131/225-5613), is unparalleled for a meal in the run-up to midnight. See p. 80.

o **Best for a Casual Meal: Spoon Café Bistro,** 6a Nicolson St. (C 0131/557-4567), is owned by a classically trained chef who knows just which ingredients work brilliantly together. See p. 82.

o **Best Modern Scottish Restaurant: The Kitchin,** 78 Commercial Quay (C 0131/555-1755), has in chef/owner Tom Kitchin one of the most talented young cooks in the country. See p. 83.

o **Best Indian Restaurant: Khushi's Diner,** 32b West Nicolson St. (C 0131/667-4871), is one of the longest continually operating Indian restaurants in the U.K. See p. 83.

RESTAURANTS BY CUISINE

AMERICAN
Bell's Diner ★ (New Town, $, p. 79)

CAFES
Spoon Café Bistro ★★ (Old Town, $, p. 82)

FISH/SEAFOOD
Café Royal Oyster Bar ★ (New Town, $$, p. 78)

Fishers Bistro (Leith and New Town, $$, p. 84)

KEY TO ABBREVIATIONS:
$$$$** = Very Expensive   **$$$** = Expensive   **$$** = Moderate   **$ = Inexpensive

Ondine ★ (Old Town, $$$, p. 80)
Seadogs (New Town, $-$$, p. 78)
The Shore Bar & Restaurant (Leith, $$, p. 84)
Sweet Melindas ★ (Southside, $$, p. 82)

FRENCH
Café St. Honoré (New Town, $-$$, p. 78)
La Garrigue ★ (Old Town, $$, p. 81)
The Kitchin ★★ (Leith, $$$, p. 83)
Plumed Horse ★ (Leith, $$$, p. 84)
Restaurant Martin Wishart ★★★ (Leith, $$$$, p. 83)
The Vintners Rooms ★ (Leith, $$$, p. 84)

INDIAN
Kebab Mahal ★ (Old Town, $, p. 82)
Khushi's Diner (Southside, $, p. 83)

INTERNATIONAL
Atrium ★ (West End, $$$, p. 76)
blue (New Town, $$, p. 77)
Dome Grill Room & Bar (New Town, $$, p. 76)
Oloroso ★ (New Town, $$$, p. 77)

ITALIAN
Santini (West End, $$, p. 77)

SCOTTISH/MODERN BRITISH
Atrium ★ (West End, $$$, p. 76)
blue (New Town, $$, p. 77)

Forth Floor Restaurant & Brasserie ★★ (New Town, $$$, p. 76)
The Grain Store ★ (Old Town, $$$, p. 79)
Haldanes Restaurant (New Town, $$$, p. 77)
Howies (Old Town, $$, p. 81)
The Kitchin ★★ (Leith, $$$, p. 83)
Number One ★ (New Town, $$$$, p. 73)
Oloroso ★ (New Town, $$$, p. 77)
Rhubarb (Southside, $$$, p. 82)
The Shore Bar & Restaurant (Leith, $$, p. 84)
Sweet Melindas ★ (Southside, $$, p. 82)
Tower Restaurant (Old Town, $$, p. 81)
21212 ★★ (New Town, $$$$, p. 76)
Wedgwood the Restaurant ★ (Old Town, $$$, p. 81)
The Witchery by the Castle (Old Town, $$$, p. 80)

SPANISH
Barioja (Old Town, $$, p. 80)

THAI
Dusit ★ (New Town, $$, p. 78)
Time 4 Thai (New Town, $$, p. 78)

VEGETARIAN
David Bann ★★ (Old Town, $$, p. 80)
Henderson's Vegetarian Restaurant (New Town, $, p. 79)

NEW TOWN & WEST END

Very Expensive

Number One ★ SCOTTISH/MODERN BRITISH   One of the plushest dining spaces in the city center, the premier restaurant in the city's best hotel also has a Michelin star to its name. You can sample the likes of scallop and cauliflower risotto, or perhaps venison loin with juniper jus. Dessert brings some exotic choices, such as mulled wine parfait with a cinnamon sauce. A special treat while you're in Edinburgh.

The Balmoral, 1 Princes St. © **0131/557-6727.** www.restaurantnumberone.com. Reservations required. Fixed-price dinner £58. AE, DC, MC, V. Daily 6:30–10pm. Bus: 3, 8, 19, or 30.

Edinburgh Dining

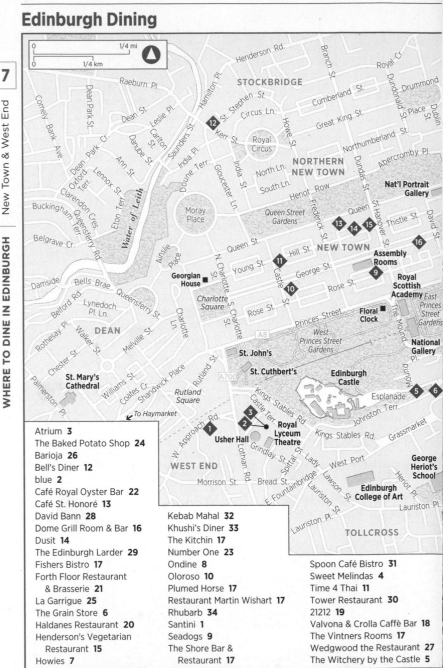

Atrium **3**
The Baked Potato Shop **24**
Barioja **26**
Bell's Diner **12**
blue **2**
Café Royal Oyster Bar **22**
Café St. Honoré **13**
David Bann **28**
Dome Grill Room & Bar **16**
Dusit **14**
The Edinburgh Larder **29**
Fishers Bistro **17**
Forth Floor Restaurant
  & Brasserie **21**
La Garrigue **25**
The Grain Store **6**
Haldanes Restaurant **20**
Henderson's Vegetarian
  Restaurant **15**
Howies **7**

Kebab Mahal **32**
Khushi's Diner **33**
The Kitchin **17**
Number One **23**
Ondine **8**
Oloroso **10**
Plumed Horse **17**
Restaurant Martin Wishart **17**
Rhubarb **34**
Santini **1**
Seadogs **9**
The Shore Bar &
  Restaurant **17**

Spoon Café Bistro **31**
Sweet Melindas **4**
Time 4 Thai **11**
Tower Restaurant **30**
21212 **19**
Valvona & Crolla Caffè Bar **18**
The Vintners Rooms **17**
Wedgwood the Restaurant **27**
The Witchery by the Castle **5**

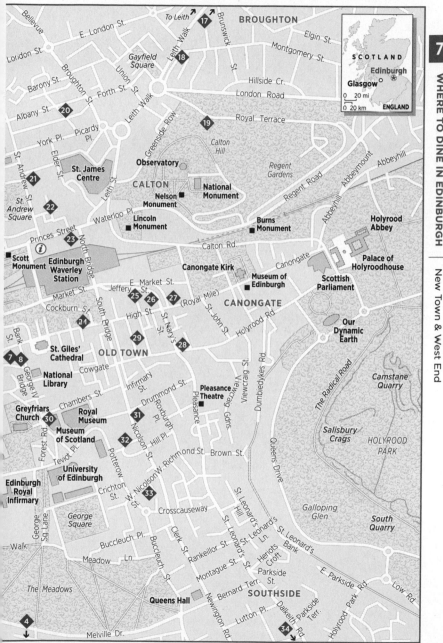

21212 ★★ FRENCH   Chef Paul Kitching left a top restaurant in Manchester to set up this Michelin star operation with partner Katie O'Brien in the Scottish capital. Although Kitching has dispensed with some of his more extravagant ideas, such as a 45-course meal, he is still astounding food critics. The choices here are five: Two options for the opener, one for the first intermediate, two choices for a middle course. And if you see a pattern emerging, check the name of the restaurant. Gentle, slow cooking is a signature, as are seemingly odd but successful combinations of ingredients, such as beef with tart lemon curd or a bread and butter pudding with cucumber, dried cherries, and sunflower seeds.

3 Royal Terrace, Calton Hill ℂ **0845/22-21212.** www.21212restaurant.co.uk. Reservations required. Fixed-price lunch £25; fixed-price dinner £65. MC, V. Tues–Sat noon–1:45pm, 6:45–9:30pm.

Expensive

Atrium ★ SCOTTISH/INTERNATIONAL   Since 1993, this has been one of the most acclaimed and stylish restaurants in Edinburgh. Dishes often feature local and organic ingredients, displaying flair but not excessive amounts of fuss or fancy presentation. Main courses might include Perthshire lamb cooked pink with an accompanying mini shepherd's pie, or Gressingham duck with roast squash. Or how about seared scallops served with chilies and garlic on lemon linguini? Desserts are equally superb.

10 Cambridge St. (adjacent to the Traverse Theatre). ℂ **0131/228-8882.** www.atriumrestaurant.co.uk. Reservations recommended. Fixed-price lunch £15; main courses £18–£22. AE, MC, V. Mon–Fri noon–2pm and 5:30–10pm; Sat 5:30–10pm. Bus: 1, 10, 15, or 24.

Dome Grill Room & Bar INTERNATIONAL   Many people come here to soak in the Dome's style: Relaxed elegance on a Victorian-era bank with Corinthian columns, intricate mosaic-tile flooring, marble-topped bar, potted palms, and towering flower arrangements—all under an elaborate domed ceiling. It oozes class. The selection of food includes smoked salmon starters, bowls of mussels, or breast of duck. At the rear of the building is a garden cafe, which backs onto Rose Street.

14 George St. ℂ **0131/624-8624.** www.thedomeedinburgh.com. Reservations recommended. Main courses £9–£20. AE, DC, MC, V. Daily noon–10pm; bar Fri–Sat until 1am. Bus: 45.

Forth Floor Restaurant & Brasserie ★★ SCOTTISH/MODERN BRITISH At the top of the Harvey Nichols boutique department store, this restaurant has excellent views of the Firth of Forth. It matches the commanding vistas with excellent contemporary Scottish cooking. While you do feel a little like you're dining in a department store annex (despite the slick, minimalist decor), the food can be phenomenal, whether it's roast monkfish with chorizo and red-wine butter or a light salad with endive and seasonal truffles. The produce used by the kitchen is notably well-sourced and fresh, such as West Coast langoustines as an *amuse-bouche* to start your meal or beef certified by the Scottish Beef Club. The brasserie menu, while less extensive than the restaurant's selections, offers good value, especially on the fixed-price lunch.

Harvey Nichols, 30–34 St. Andrew Sq. ℂ **0131/524-8350.** www.harveynichols.com. Reservations recommended for restaurant. Fixed-price lunch £15; main courses £16–£22. AE, DC, MC, V. Tues–Sat noon–10pm; Sun and Mon lunches only. Bus: 8, 10, 12, or 45.

Haldanes Restaurant 🍴 SCOTTISH Haldanes serves dinners conducted like meals in a private country house, with polite and deferential service. Run by chef George Kelso and wife Michelle, the restaurant offers cooking with a light touch despite using robust and mostly traditional ingredients, whether venison, wood pigeon, or salmon. The dining room's layout and candlelit decor with deep carpets and wood paneling is excellent for a romantic meal, even if the location underneath the Albany Hotel is a little unprepossessing.

39a Albany St. ✆ **0131/556-8407.** www.haldanesrestaurant.com. Reservations recommended. Main courses £16–£20. MC, V. Daily 5:30–9pm (9:30pm Fri and Sat). Bus: 23 or 27.

Oloroso ★ SCOTTISH/INTERNATIONAL Though they're fantastic, it's not all about the vistas from this restaurant in the heart of Old Town. Oloroso's chef and owner, Tony Singh, is a Scottish-born Sikh with an imaginative approach to cooking Scottish produce. Here, in his rooftop restaurant with an ample veranda and excellent panoramic views, the feeling is contemporary and swanky. Frequently changing menus include dishes such as veal T-bones or fresh fish from the grill menu, or pan-fried breast of duck with puy lentils and black pudding. The bar, which mixes some mean cocktails, is usually open until 1am.

33 Castle St. ✆ **0131/226-7614.** www.oloroso.co.uk. Reservations recommended. Fixed-price lunch £18.50; main courses £15–£25. MC, V. Daily noon–2:30pm and 7–10pm. Bus: 24, 29, or 42.

Santini ITALIAN This modern West End restaurant in the Sheraton Grand (on the ground floor under the hotel's One Spa) offers some of the capital's classiest, most authentic Italian cooking. Part of a small international chain, with branches in Milan and London, Santini serves dishes such as fish antipasti with seared whitefish and chargrilled shrimps or venison and pork belly. For lunch, in addition to a well-priced two-course meal, it has introduced an Italian version of the Japanese bento box.

8 Conference St. ✆ **0131/221-7788.** Fixed-price lunch £9.50; main courses £15–£22. AE, MC, V. Mon–Fri noon–2:30pm and 6:30–9:30pm; Sat 6:30–10pm. Bus: 1, 2, 10, 24, or 34.

Moderate

blue INTERNATIONAL/MODERN BRITISH This attractive bistro above the Traverse Theatre is the less expensive sibling of Atrium (p. 76). You'll find a minimalist look with touches of azure hues and a cheerful staff. The menu has dishes that tend to always highlight local and seasonal produce. Solid options include organic

---

Haggis: The King o' the Puddin' Race

The much-misunderstood traditional dish of Scotland, haggis may be an acquired taste, but a well-made one is delicious with mashed potatoes and swede. Macsween of Edinburgh (www.macsween.co.uk) is a long-established family business specializing in Robert Burn's "King o' the Puddin' Race." Macsween haggis includes lamb, beef, oatmeal, onions, and a special blend of seasonings and spices cooked together and stuffed into a natural casing. They also make a popular vegetarian version. Both are sold in vacuum-packed plastic bags and require only reheating in a microwave or simmering pot of water. You can find this company's product at a range of food stores and supermarkets throughout Edinburgh.

chicken stew with herb gnocchi or pan-fried mackerel with lentil broth. There are good pre-theater options if you're heading out for a show.

10 Cambridge St. ✆ **0131/221-1222.** www.bluescotland.co.uk. Reservations recommended. Main courses £10–£15. AE, MC, V. Mon–Sat noon–2:30pm and 6–10:30pm. Bus: 1, 10, 15, or 24.

Café Royal Oyster Bar ★ SEAFOOD/FISH   The Café Royal first opened in 1862, and after some 140 years its splendorous Victorian touches remain intact. The main menu offers more than just oysters: Salmon, langoustines, and lobsters—as well as beef and rabbit—might feature. If the restaurant's dining room is closed (between lunch and dinner), head for the neighboring Circle Bar, which serves food and beverages throughout the day. Its menu is more limited but also less pricey. A highlight of the bar is the collection of tile pictures of notable inventors.

17a W. Register St. ✆ **0131/556-1884.** Reservations recommended. Main courses £14–£22. AE, MC, V. Daily noon–2pm and 6–10pm (bar open daily 11am–11pm). Bus: 8 or 29.

Café St. Honoré FRENCH   A New Town favorite, this Parisian-style brasserie with a classic black-and-white-checkered floor is deliberately rapidly paced at lunch and more sedate in the evening. An upbeat and usually enthusiastic staff serves French cuisine with Scottish influences, such as Borders beef with Dauphinoise potatoes and bon bons made of Stornoway black pudding from the Outer Hebrides.

34 N.W. Thistle St. ✆ **0131/226-2211.** www.cafesthonore.com. Reservations recommended. Fixed-price lunch £16.50; main courses £8–£20. AE, MC, V. Daily noon–2pm and 6–10pm. Bus: 24, 29, or 42.

Dusit ★ 🍴 THAI   Thistle Street, although little more than a slender lane with narrow sidewalks, has become something of a hot bed for restaurants. This rather unassuming restaurant has a reputation for being one of the best in the city for Thai cuisine—some say the best in Scotland for any style of cuisine. The menu is not typical and has a tendency toward modern dishes—many of which incorporate Scottish produce, such as venison and Jerusalem artichokes. Recommended are hoi yang scallops or stir-fried guinea fowl. The wines are plentiful and matched to the cuisine.

49a Thistle St. ✆ **0131/220-6846.** www.dusit.co.uk. Reservations recommended. Fixed-price lunch £11; main courses £12–£18. AE, MC, V. Mon–Sat noon–3pm and 6–11pm; Sun noon–11pm. Bus: 24, 29, or 42.

Seadogs FISH   Owner David Ramsden historically has worked so hard to keep his restaurants affordable that they have sometimes not been able to survive. Fingers crossed for this new place. There's a coziness to the mismatched furniture and cutlery, while decoration is pretty much limited to doggy motifs and images. Fish 'n' chips here offers a variety of fish, while sharing platters might offer paella or fish pie. More innovative recipes include smoked mackerel on toast with rhubarb jam.

43 Rose St. ✆ **0131/225-8028.** www.seadogsonline.co.uk. Main courses £10. MC, V. Daily noon–4pm and 5–10pm. Bus: 22 (alight at Princes Street).

Time 4 Thai THAI   There was an extraordinary boom in Edinburgh's Thai restaurant scene before the recession of 2008/2009. This stylish New Town restaurant was one of them, featuring well-made and attractively presented curries and other Thai specialties. Everything is served with extra doses of grace and courtesy.

45 N. Castle St. ✆ **0131/225-8822.** Reservations recommended. Fixed-price lunch £9.50; main courses £8–£16. AE, MC, V. Mon–Thurs noon–2:30pm and 5–11pm; Fri–Sun 1–11pm. Bus: 24, 29, or 42.

FAMILY-FRIENDLY fare

The Baked Potato Shop This is a favorite lunch spot located at 56 Cockburn St., just off High St. in Old Town (ⓒ **0131/225-7572**). Here kids can order fluffy potatoes with a choice of hot fillings along with other dishes, including chili and salads. It's inexpensive, too. Open daily 9am to 9pm.

Valvona & Crolla Caffè Bar ★ Located at 19 Elm Row, at the top of Leith Walk (ⓒ **0131/556-6066**), this place is best known as one of the U.K.'s finest Italian delis. But if you can get past the tempting salamis, cheeses, and other delicacies, V&C also has a welcoming cafe that handles children in that way that Italians seem to do best.

Inexpensive

Bell's Diner ★ 👜 AMERICAN   If you're a connoisseur of the burger, consider a visit to Bell's Diner in Stockbridge. Open for some 30-odd years, it is an institution in Edinburgh. The diner's chargrilled patties of real ground beef (available in three different weights) are hand-made and cooked to order, and served with a variety of toppings (cheese to garlic butter). They come with fries, salad, and a full array of condiments. The operation's only drawback, aside from its rather compact space, is the limited hours of operation. On a Saturday it only opens for lunch, which seems a shame.

17 St. Stephen St. ⓒ **0131/225-8116.** Reservations recommended. Main courses £6.50–£9. Sun–Fri 6–10pm; Sat noon–10pm. Bus: 24, 29, or 42.

Henderson's Vegetarian Restaurant 🍴 VEGETARIAN   Right in the heart of New Town, Henderson's is another bona fide institution in the Scottish capital. Once called the "Salad Table," the business (which includes Henderson's Bistro around the corner and another outlet on Lothian Road) recently went for a more formal title, and added an art gallery, too. Regardless, Henderson's is a long-standing purveyor of healthy, relatively inexpensive meat-free food. Dishes, such as vegetable stroganoff or mushroom and spinach crepe, complement a choice of a dozen different salads, from Greek to spicy bean. Wines include organic options.

94 Hanover St. ⓒ **0131/225-2131.** www.hendersonsofedinburgh.co.uk. Fixed-price lunch £9.50; main courses £6–£8. MC, V. Mon–Sat 8am–10:30pm. Bus: 13, 23, or 27.

OLD TOWN

Expensive

The Grain Store ★ SCOTTISH/MODERN BRITISH   With its dining room up some stairs, and wooden tables set amid raw stone walls, the Grain Store capably captures some Old Town essence and atmosphere. The cooking of owner Carlo Coxon is often ambitious and innovative, using Scottish produce whenever possible. For example, the menu might include dishes such as a saddle of Highland venison with a beetroot fondant, or Pithivier (a French tart) of brown hare with a puff pastry shell.

📷 **Tea for Two?**

New in town is **The Edinburgh Larder,** 15 Blackfriars St. (📞 **0131/556-6922**), for specially sourced teas (and coffees), as well as rich cakes such as dark chocolate and beetroot. For a formal venue, try the Palm Court at the **The Balmoral,** 1 Princes St. (📞 **0131/556-2414**).

30 Victoria St. 📞 **0131/225-7635.** www.grain store-restaurant.co.uk. Reservations recommended. Fixed-price lunch £12.50; main courses £17–£25. AE, MC, V. Daily noon–2pm and 6–10pm (till 11pm Fri and Sat). Bus: 2, 41, or 42.

Ondine ★ SEAFOOD/FISH   This newcomer to the Edinburgh dining scene has perhaps made the biggest splash with its fresh seafood and fish dishes, using sustainably caught produce. Chef Roy Brett moves comfortably from fish soup to clam linguini with garlic and red chilies to lemon sole (fillet or whole), served with shrimp and capers. Diners can enjoy a nicely informal atmosphere that seafood restaurants should have but with plenty of class, too.

2 George IV Bridge. 📞 **0131/226-1888.** www.ondinerestaurant.co.uk. Reservations recommended. Fixed-price lunch £15; main courses £15–£22. MC, V. Daily noon–10pm (till 4pm on Sun). Bus: 2, 41, or 42.

The Witchery by the Castle ★ MODERN SCOTTISH/ BRITISH   The restaurant, so named because of historical connections to medieval executions nearby and rumors of lingering ghosts, serves classy Scottish food in classier still surroundings, with dishes that feature ingredients such as Angus beef, Scottish lobster, and Loch Fyne oysters. Well-prepared old-time British favorites, such as an omelet Arnold Bennett (made with cream and smoked fish) or beef Wellington for two (with accompanying jug of red wine *jus*), mashed potatoes, and green beans, contrast with a list of more contemporary specials—a starter of hot-smoked salmon with beetroot puree, for example. Atmospheric and good for special occasions, the Witchery is also ideal for a sumptuous late meal and then lingering over a postprandial drink until midnight or so. In addition to the dark and lavish dining room near the street, there is also the "Secret Garden" further down the narrow close. The premises also house a boutique hotel (see chapter 6).

Boswell Court, Castlehill, Royal Mile. 📞 **0131/225-5613.** www.thewitchery.com. Reservations required. Fixed-price 2-course lunch, pre- and post-theater dinner £13; main courses £18–£25. AE, DC, MC, V. Daily noon–4pm and 5:30–11:30pm. Bus: 23, 27, 41, or 45.

Moderate

Barioja 👬 SPANISH   Just off the Royal Mile with views north towards Calton Hill and the Royal High School, this tapas bar is the partner to the fine-food Spanish restaurant IGGS next door. Casual and staffed by natives of Spanish-speaking nations, Barioja is fun, friendly, and often lively. The kitchen's tapas come in reasonably substantial portions, whether tender fried squid, garlicky king shrimps, or spicy chorizo sausages. Wine prices are somewhat more pricey than the food options.

19 Jeffrey St. 📞 **0131/557-3622.** www.barioja.co.uk. Tapas £4–£10. AE, MC, V. Daily noon–11pm (10pm on Sun). Bus: 36.

David Bann ★★ VEGETARIAN   Chef David Bann has been at the forefront of meat-free cooking in Edinburgh for more than a decade. He comes from the school of thought that insists (and proves) vegetarian meals can be *both* tasty and healthy: No need to sacrifice the former for the latter. The menu at his eponymous restaurant (located just a short stroll south of Royal Mile) is internationally eclectic: From Mexico to Thailand, India to the Med. The dining room is as stylish as the cooking, and to top it off, the prices are very reasonable.

56–58 St. Mary's St. ✆ **0131/556-5888.** www.davidbann.com. Reservations recommended. Main courses £7.50–£12. AE, MC, V. Daily noon–10pm. Bus: 36.

Howies SCOTTISH/MODERN BRITISH   David Howie Scott started his eponymous restaurant with modest ambitions (for example, guests brought their own wine). He went on to create a minor empire in Edinburgh, where there are now four branches, some 20 years after the business was founded. The one on Victoria Street, in Old Town, is probably the most convenient for tourists. The company's motto is "fine food without the faff"—and I might add "sold at reasonable prices," as well. Typical dishes include pan-seared supreme of chicken, honey-cured Scottish salmon, or gnocchi with fresh basil pesto.

10–14 Victoria St. ✆ **0131/225-1721.** www.howies.uk.com. Reservations recommended. Fixed-price lunch £10; main courses £10–£15. AE, MC, V. Daily noon–2:30pm and 6–10pm. Bus: 2, 41, or 42.

La Garrigue ★ 🛉 FRENCH   The chef and proprietor of La Garrigue, Jean Michel Gauffre, hails from the southern French region of Languedoc and he effectively re-creates the fresh and rustic cooking of his birthplace. The feeling of the dining room is informal but still smart, with some stylish hand-crafted timber furniture. The menu can feature a hearty roast or cassoulet (stew) with beans, confit duck, Toulouse sausage, pork, or lamb. In addition to such hearty dishes, expect something more delicate, such as pan-fried filet of bream. The wines are from southern France, too. Often, chef Gauffre will come in the dining room to see how it is going and have a friendly chat—he knows that small touches go a long way. La Garrigue is well worth a detour off the Royal Mile.

31 Jeffrey St. ✆ **0131/557-3032.** www.lagarrigue.co.uk. Reservations recommended. Fixed-price lunch £14; fixed-price dinner £25.50. AE, MC, V. Mon–Sat noon–2:30pm and 6:30–10:30pm. Bus: 36.

Tower Restaurant SCOTTISH/MODERN BRITISH   Because the Tower is set at the top of the Museum of Scotland, it's worth requesting a window seat when making a reservation here. A sister operation to The Witchery by the Castle (p. 80) and Rhubarb (see below), the kitchen here employs local ingredients to create some tasty fare: Hearty portions of steak, roast venison, and excellent seafood are typically featured on the menu. In addition to a daytime tea menu and evening a la carte, there is the proprietor's fixed-price (£30) three-course James Thomson Celebration menu.

In the Museum of Scotland, Chambers St. ✆ **0131/225-3003.** www.tower-restaurant.com. Reservations required. Fixed-price lunch £13; main courses £14–£22. AE, DC, MC, V. Daily noon–11pm. Bus: 2, 41, or 42.

Wedgwood the Restaurant ★ SCOTTISH/MODERN BRITISH   Perhaps the next place to earn an internationally recognized accolade will be this small restaurant run by chef Paul Wedgwood (no connections with the famous bone china producers). The menus change with the seasons, and recipes combine Scottish ingredients with some Asian influences here and there. A popular signature dish has been salmon done three ways: poached, smoked, and cured, each with different accompaniments. Expect a glass of sparkling wine and an appetizing *amuse-bouche* to start the evening, with intermediate palate cleansers such as a bubbly raspberry and ginger beer concoction. Given the restaurant's cozy confines, booking is effectively mandatory.

267 Canongate. © **0131/558-8737.** Reservations required. Fixed-price lunch £10; main courses £15–£20. MC, V. Daily noon–3pm and 6–10pm. Bus: 35 or 36.

Inexpensive

Kebab Mahal ★ 🍴 INDIAN   The kebab, of course, is the late-night staple for many a university student. While the late weekend hours of this simple diner means it attracts that clientele, Kebab Mahal is much more. The counter is full of hot food, but most of the main courses are prepared separately in a kitchen to the rear. True to its Islamic owner's faith, Kebab Mahal doesn't have a license to serve alcohol, doesn't allow diners to bring their own, and closes every Friday from 1 to 2pm for prayers.

7 Nicolson Sq. © **0131/667-5214.** Main courses £4–£6. No credit cards. Sun–Thurs noon–midnight; Fri–Sat noon–2am (except for Fri prayers). Bus: 3, 5, 29, 31, or 35.

Spoon Café Bistro ★★ CAFE   This particular "spoon" is far from greasy. The contemporary cafe moved into new premises in 2009, thus fulfilling the long-standing ambitions of a bistro that originally lacked the facilities in its first location on Blackfriars Street. Owner Richard Alexander could cook at the best restaurants in town—instead, he has opted for his own operation that combines a relaxed ambience, first-rate espresso-based coffees, and the sure hand of a classically trained chef. The soups are always superb, whether meat-free options—such as lentil and red onion or a roast pepper and eggplant—or Italian ham and pea soup. Sandwiches are prepared freshly, and now you can get more elaborate dishes like crispy pan-seared trout fillet with a cider vinegar dressing or braised beef with baby potatoes. Alternatively, you can still simply drop in for a piece of homemade cake: Moist carrot or rich chocolate.

6a Nicolson St. © **0131/557-4567.** www.spooncafe.co.uk. Soups from £3; sandwiches and salads from £4.50; main courses £10. MC, V. Mon–Sat 10am–10pm; Sun noon–6pm. Bus: 3, 5, 29, 31, or 35.

SOUTHSIDE

Expensive

Rhubarb SCOTTISH/MODERN BRITISH   Standing proud amid 5.3 hectares (13 acres) of private parkland and gardens, 17th-century Prestonfield House is the elegant home of a five-star hotel (p. 68) that boasts this posh, almost theatrical, restaurant. Another venture from the owner of The Witchery by the Castle (p. 80), Rhubarb shares its sense of drama and flair. One signature dish is the chef's rhubarb dessert with jelly, custard, and tiny baked Alaska.

Priestfield Rd., about 5km (3 miles) south of Edinburgh city center. © **0131/225-1333.** www.prestonfield.com. Reservations recommended. Fixed-price lunch £17; main courses £18–£25. AE, DC, MC, V. Daily noon–2pm and 6–10pm. Bus: 2, 14, or 30.

Moderate

Sweet Melindas ★ 🍴 SCOTTISH/FISH   The capital's Marchmont neighborhood, although just south of the Meadows, is far enough from the well-trod traveler's trail to feel like miles away from touristy Edinburgh. This locally owned and operated restaurant is a neighborhood favorite but merits a trip across town. The cooking tends to emphasize fish—which the chefs purchase from the shop next door—in dishes such as Thai fish cakes or roast cod with crab linguini. Often there is seasonal game, whether wood pigeon or venison, and a reasonable selection of vegetarian options, as well.

11 Roseneath St. © **0131/229-7953.** www.sweetmelindas.co.uk. Reservations recommended. Fixed-price lunch £12.50; fixed-price dinner £22.50. AE, MC, V. Mon 6–10pm; Tues–Sat noon–2pm and 6–10pm. Bus: 24 or 41.

Inexpensive

Khushi's Diner INDIAN   Khushi is said to be the longest continually run Indian restaurant in Edinburgh. But over the past half decade, due to aspiration and then a fire, the operation has been moving around a bit. Now, back where Old Town becomes the Southside near the University of Edinburgh, it continues to offer home-style curries and South Asian cuisine at very reasonable prices. No alcohol is sold, but you can bring your own and no corkage is charged.

32b West Nicolson St. © **0131/667-4871.** www.kushisdiner.com. Main courses £8–£11. No credit cards. Mon–Sat noon–11pm; Sun 5–10pm. Bus: 3, 5, 29, 31, or 35.

LEITH

Very Expensive

The Kitchin ★★ MODERN SCOTTISH/FRENCH   After opening this contemporary restaurant in 2006, the appropriately named chef/owner Tom Kitchin quickly garnered a Michelin star, among other awards. Now he is among the catering business's professional elite, appearing on national TV and in the broadsheets. The chef's motto is "from nature to plate" and his French-inspired recipes capture the attention. He likes to use top seasonal Scottish ingredients—sometimes daring ones—whether fricasseed lamb's sweetbreads or wild halibut carpaccio. Terrine of pig's head meat might be served with a mustard dressing and root vegetable remoulade. Less challenging but no less appealing is hake fillet atop pasta with braised fennel. Kitchin combines youth, talent, and ambition—one to watch. Note that The Kitchin is closed Sunday and Monday.

78 Commercial Quay. © **0131/555-1755.** Reservations required. Fixed-price lunch £25, main courses £30. MC, V. Tues–Sat 12:30–2pm and 6:30–10pm. Bus: 16, 22, 35, or 36.

Restaurant Martin Wishart ★★★ MODERN FRENCH   Despite a Michelin star and a host of local awards, chef/owner Martin Wishart is the antithesis of the high-profile prima donna or loud-mouthed TV chef. His menu, which changes frequently, is kept short and sweet, taking advantage of the best of the season; think John Dory with leeks, salsify, and mussel and almond gratin. Flavors are notoriously intense—sometimes almost unfathomable—but always imaginative and completely memorable. Celeriac puree and pumpkinseed crisps might accompany braised ox cheek or a seared scallop might arrive with Bellota ham and Parmesan velouté. Staff are everywhere and totally understand both the food and wine they serve. If you're not on a budget, push the boat out and go for the tasting menu. If money is tight, try the set lunches. Alas, it's closed Sunday and Monday, which means getting a table is always difficult.

54 The Shore. © **0131/553-3557.** www.martin-wishart.co.uk. Reservations required. Fixed-price lunch £24.50; main courses £40. AE, MC, V. Tues–Fri noon–2pm and 6:45–9:30pm; Sat noon–1:30pm and 6:45–9:30pm. Bus: 22 or 36.

Expensive

Plumed Horse ★ MODERN SCOTTISH/FRENCH   This restaurant arrived in Edinburgh in 2006 with chef/owner Tony Borthwick at the helm. The dining space feels quite compact and despite a traditional ambiance Borthwick's cooking is as contemporary as his rivals (and just a little bit less expensive, too). Dishes such as rose veal with mushrooms and Madeira cream sauce are elegantly and attractively plated up. It too is closed both Sunday and Monday.

50–54 Henderson St. © **0131/554-5556.** www.plumedhorse.co.uk. Reservations required. Fixed-price lunch £24.50; fixed-price dinner £45. MC, V. Tues–Sat noon–1:30pm and 7–9pm. Bus: 22 or 36.

The Vintners Rooms ★ FRENCH   Housed in an impressive 17th-century stone building, this restaurant is one of the most romantic in Edinburgh. The kitchen uses Scottish produce in a host of confidently modern Gallic dishes. The menu might feature carpaccio of octopus with lobster, chili-caramelized belly of pork, or rack of lamb with cabbage and polenta parcel.

The Vaults, 87 Giles St. © **0131/554-6767.** www.thevintnersrooms.com. Reservations recommended. Main courses £18–£23. AE, MC, V. Tues–Sat noon–2pm and 7–10pm. Bus: 22 or 36.

Moderate

Fishers Bistro FISH   This place is a favorite for its seafood and view of the harbor at Leith. The Miller family founded the restaurant in the early 1990s, and their chefs offer such enticing dishes as fresh Loch Fyne oysters and mussels in a white-wine sauce, or breaded and crispy fish cakes. Of course, the fresh fish depends on what's been landed: It might be trout or turbot. There is also a branch, **Fishers in the City,** in New Town on Thistle Street (© **0131/225-5109**).

1 The Shore. © **0131/554-5666.** www.fishersbistros.co.uk. Reservations suggested. Main courses £12–£16. AE, MC, V. Daily noon–10:30pm. Bus: 16, 22, 35, or 36.

The Shore Bar & Restaurant SCOTTISH/FISH   Whether diners eat in the pub or in the only slightly more formal dining room to one side, they should appreciate the simplicity and ease of this operation. The menu moved away from its dedication to fish in 2008, and now also includes steaks, lamb shanks, and roast duck. The bar is still one of the best in Leith. It often has live music in the evenings, good ale on tap, and a sincere seaport ambience all the time.

3/4 The Shore. © **0131/553-5080.** Reservations recommended. Main courses £10–£15. AE, MC, V. Daily noon–10pm. Bus: 16, 22, 35, or 36.

PICNIC FARE

The Edinburgh weather doesn't always lend itself to outdoor dining on an expanse of lawn, but there are certainly days when the sun shines warmly enough to enjoy a picnic at Princes Street Gardens, the Meadows, and Holyrood Park—or along the Water of Leith and in the Botanic Garden.

If you're in the central area of town, the best place for deli goods is undoubtedly **Valvona & Crolla Caffè Bar** ★★ 19 Elm Row (at the top of Leith Walk; ✆ 0131/556-6066). This Italian shop has an excellent reputation across the U.K., with a wonderful range of cheeses and cured meats, fresh fruit and vegetables, plus baked goods from rolls to sourdough loaves, all the condiments you might need, and wine as well. Another option in New Town is the food hall at the top of **Harvey Nichols** department store, 30–34 St. Andrews Square (✆ 0131/524-8388). Freshly prepared salads, lots of dried goods, plus fresh fruit and vegetables are stocked here.

In Stockbridge, **I.J. Mellis Cheesemongers** ★★ on Bakers Place (✆ 0131/225-6566) sells award-winning British and Irish cheeses. The Mellis staff members really know their stuff, and there are other shops in Old Town on Victoria Street and south of the city center on Morningside Road.

If you're on the south side of the city near the Meadows, **Peckham's** on Bruntsfield Place (✆ 0131/229-7054) is a solid choice for filling a picnic basket. But if you like Mexican food—Monterey Jack cheese, real tortillas, and the like—find **Lupe Pintos** ★ in Tollcross at 24 Leven St. (near the King's Theatre; ✆ 0131/228-6241). The shop also stocks American goods, such as beef jerky, dill pickles, and peanut butter.

Heading toward the Botanic Garden on the other side of town in Canonmills, at the roundabout, there is a Spanish deli called **Dionika** (✆ 0131/652-3993).

EXPLORING EDINBURGH

Edinburgh's reputation is enormous, and the city essentially lives up to it. The second-most popular destination after London for visitors to Great Britain, the Scottish capital is one of the most picturesque cities in Europe. Built on a set of steep hills, Edinburgh is unarguably dramatic.

Old Town lies at the heart, with Edinburgh Castle at one end of the **Royal Mile,** which follows the spine of a hill down to the Palace of Holyroodhouse. For many visitors, this *is* Edinburgh, with its mews, closes, and alleyways. But across the valley to the north, now filled by the verdant Princes Street Gardens, is the city's **New Town,** which dates to the 1770s. Here are tidy streets and broad avenues, another popular focal point in Edinburgh, with restaurants, bars, shops, squares, and attractions, such as the **National Portrait Gallery.** New Town reaches out to the village-like setting of **Stockbridge**—from which one can walk along the city's narrow meandering river, the Water of Leith—to **Dean Village** (another district that feels almost rural in nature) and the **National Gallery of Modern Art** and its sister arts venue, the Dean Gallery.

Between the city center and Haymarket is the **West End.** It has more outstanding examples of New Town–styled buildings, as well as a cluster of performance spaces such as **Usher Hall** and the **Traverse Theatre.**

Edinburgh's **Southside** is mostly residential, but offers the sprawling park known as the **Meadows,** the precincts of Edinburgh University, as well as suburbs such as Marchmont. North of the city center is the now vibrant district around the port of **Leith** on the Firth of Forth, which empties into the North Sea.

Edinburgh's world-famous annual cultural celebration—the **Edinburgh Festival**—brings in tourists and lovers of art of all forms from around the world. But if you prefer a bit more space and smaller crowds, avoid the month of August in Edinburgh.

Suggested Itineraries

IF YOU HAVE 1 DAY

Stick to the city's famous Royal Mile and Edinburgh's Old Town. It is every bit a day's worth of activity, with plenty of history and attractions from **Edinburgh Castle** to the **Palace of Holyroodhouse,** shops, restaurants, and pubs. Wander down some of the alleys off the Royal Mile, too.

IF YOU HAVE 2 DAYS

Take the hop-on, hop-off bus tour that emphasizes New Town (see p. 101). Your ticket is good for 24 hours (although the buses stop running in the late afternoon or early evening). Get off at **Calton Hill** for the views, which Robert Louis Stevenson said were the best in the city. Amble down Princes Street for a bit of shopping, and afterwards, rest in **Princes Street Gardens.** Admire some art at one of the branches of the National Gallery.

IF YOU HAVE 3 DAYS

Take in **Leith,** Edinburgh's once rough-and-tumble port. Now increasingly gentrified, it is still evocative of a historic seaside village. The **Royal Botanic Garden** on your way back into the city center is worth a visit. It is one of the best in Britain—and that's saying something. If you have any time to spare, take one of the strolls outlined in chapter 9, and visit Stockbridge or the Meadows, which feel off the main tourist tracks.

IF YOU HAVE 4 DAYS OR MORE

Climb **Arthur's Seat** for views of the city and the sea, or if you have children, take the family to the **Edinburgh Zoo.** Explore the regions around the city, with excursions up to St. Andrews, to the coast and North Berwick, or west to nearby, historic Linlithgow.

TOP ATTRACTIONS
Along the Royal Mile

Old Town's **Royal Mile ★★★** is an attraction in itself, stretching down the spine of a ridge from Edinburgh Castle to the Palace of Holyroodhouse. The street bears four names along its length: Castlehill, Lawnmarket, High Street, and Canongate. Walking along, you'll see some of the most interesting old structures in the city, with turrets, gables, and towering chimneys. Some of the highlights are listed here, in order from west to east.

Edinburgh Castle ★   Few locations in Scotland have lore equal to that of Edinburgh Castle. The very early history is somewhat vague, but in the 11th century, Malcolm III and his Saxon queen, later venerated as St. Margaret, founded a building on this spot. There's only a fragment of their original pile in St. Margaret's Chapel, which dates principally to the 1100s. After centuries of destruction, demolitions, and upheavals, the buildings that stand today are basically those that resulted from the castle's role as a military garrison over the past 300-odd years. It still barracks soldiers. And many of the displays are devoted to military history, which might limit the place's appeal for some. The castle vaults served as prisons for foreign soldiers in the 18th century, and these great storerooms held hundreds of Napoleonic soldiers in the early 19th century. Some prisoners made wall carvings still seen today.

However, it is not all about war. Visitors can see where Mary, Queen of Scots gave birth to James VI of Scotland (later James I of England) in 1566. Scottish Parliaments used to convene in the Great Hall of the castle. Another highlight for visitors is the Scottish Crown Jewels, used at the coronations, along with the scepter and

Edinburgh Attractions

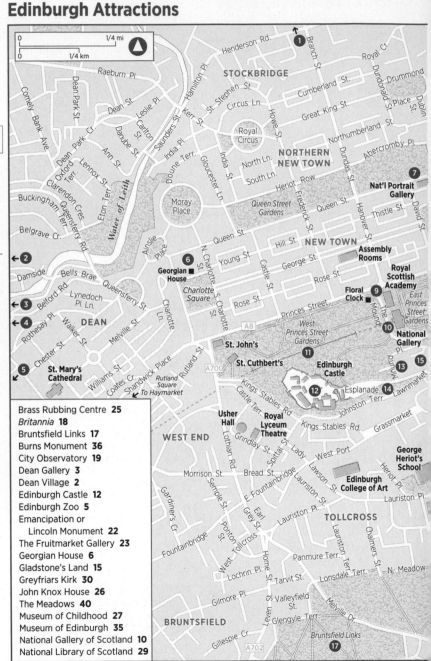

Brass Rubbing Centre **25**
Britannia **18**
Bruntsfield Links **17**
Burns Monument **36**
City Observatory **19**
Dean Gallery **3**
Dean Village **2**
Edinburgh Castle **12**
Edinburgh Zoo **5**
Emancipation or
 Lincoln Monument **22**
The Fruitmarket Gallery **23**
Georgian House **6**
Gladstone's Land **15**
Greyfriars Kirk **30**
John Knox House **26**
The Meadows **40**
Museum of Childhood **27**
Museum of Edinburgh **35**
National Gallery of Scotland **10**
National Library of Scotland **29**

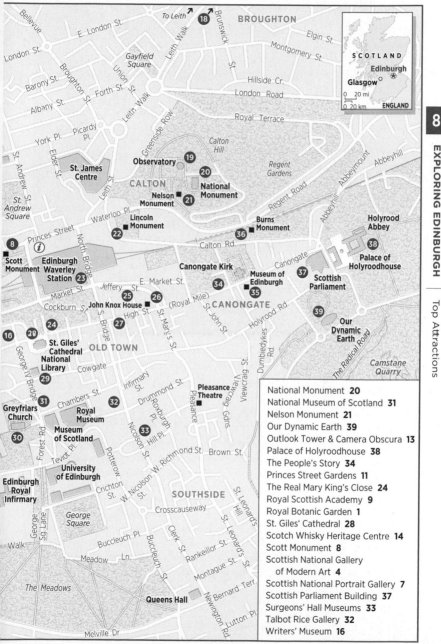

To Leith ↗ 18 ↗

BROUGHTON

Elgin St.

E. London St.

Bellevue

London St.

Montgomery St.

Hillside Cr.

London Road

Gayfield Square

Barony St.

Broughton St.

Forth St.

Union St.

Leith Walk

Royal Terrace

Albany St.

York Pl.

Picardy Pl.

Greenside Row

Calton Hill

Regent Gardens

St. Andrew St.

Elder St.

Leith St.

Observatory 19

20

St. James Centre

St. Andrew Square

CALTON

Nelson Monument 21

National Monument

Regent Road

Abbeyhill

Abbeyhill

Waterloo Pl.

Lincoln Monument

Burns Monument

Holyrood Abbey

Princes Street

22

36

38

8 ℹ

Scott Monument

Edinburgh Waverley Station 23

North Bridge

Calton Rd.

Canongate

Canongate Kirk

37

Scottish Parliament

Palace of Holyroodhouse

Market St.

Jeffery St.

E. Market St.

34

Museum of Edinburgh

Cockburn St.

25

26

John Knox House

35

Holyrood Rd.

39

Our Dynamic Earth

24

27

High St.

(Royal Mile)

CANONGATE

St. Mary's St.

St. John St.

Dumbiedykes Rd.

The Radical Road

Camstane Quarry

10

29

St. Giles' Cathedral

National Library

OLD TOWN

Cowgate

Infirmary St.

Pleasance Theatre

Pleasance

Viewcraig St.

St. Leonard's St.

31

Greyfriars Church

Chambers St.

32

Royal Museum

Drummond St.

Roxburgh Pl.

Brown St.

30

Museum of Scotland

Nicolson St.

33

Hill Pl.

W. Richmond St.

Teviot Pl.

University of Edinburgh

Potterow

Crichton St.

W. Nicolson St.

SOUTHSIDE

St. Leonard's Hill

Edinburgh Royal Infirmary

Crosscauseway

George Sq. Lane

George Square

Clerk St.

St. Leonard's St.

Walk

Buccleuch Pl.

Buccleuch St.

Meadow Ln.

Montague St.

Newington Rd.

Lutton Rd.

The Meadows

Queens Hall

Bernard Terr.

Melville Dr.

Newington Rd.

SCOTLAND

Edinburgh

Glasgow ○

ENGLAND

0   20 mi
0   20 km

FROMMER'S FAVORITE EDINBURGH
experiences

Contemplating the City and Environs from up High. At 250m (823 ft.), Arthur's Seat is presumably the best—unless you want your panorama to include Arthur's Seat, in which case you might prefer Castle Hill. But then you will miss the castle. Calton Hill affords views of all. And if you are not up for climbing, take the elevator in the Museum of Scotland, which has an observation deck atop its magnificent modern building.

Downing a Pint in an Edinburgh Pub. Whether sampling a pint—look out for stout-like Dark Island from Orkney, organic pale ale from Black Isle brewery, and Edinburgh's own Deuchars IPA—or a dram of whisky (peaty island Laphroaig or smooth Highland Dalwhinnie), Edinburgh has numerous traditional pubs. My favorites include the Bow Bar, Café Royal Circle Bar,

and, for something a bit more hip, Black Bo's.

Strolling in Old Town or New Town. Take your pick of these two central and historically preserved districts, and don't be afraid to get off the beaten track of their main roads and boulevards. Explore a few of the many cobbled side streets and alleyways for a feel of the real Edinburgh. Get a little lost.

Visiting the Royal Botanic Garden & National Galleries. This botanic garden is not just for plant lovers. There are paths and paths to stroll amid a variety of foliage and settings: From redwoods in a miniforest to rock gardens with a waterfall. The art collections of the National Gallery are split between different museums, and while the size of them is not exceptional, some of the works hanging in them are.

sword of state of Scotland and the infamous Stone of Scone. Note that last entry is 45 minutes before closing and buying tickets online in advance will save time during busy periods.

Castlehill. ☏ **0131/225-9846.** www.edinburghcastle.gov.uk. Admission £13 adults, £10.40 seniors, £7 children 5–15. MC, V. Apr–Sept daily 9:30am–6pm; Oct–Mar daily 9:30am–5pm. Bus: 23, 27, 41, or 45.

Outlook Tower & Camera Obscura ☺   The 150-year-old periscope-like lens at the top of the Outlook Tower throws an image of nearby streets and buildings onto a circular table, and the moving "picture" can be magically magnified with just a bit of cardboard. Guides reveal this trick, help to identify landmarks, and discuss highlights of Edinburgh's history. In addition, the observation deck offers free telescopes, and there are several exhibits in the "World of Illusions" with an optical theme that will keep some children occupied. What is disappointing, however, is the dearth of information on the man responsible for the Camera Obscura, Sir Patrick Geddes, a polymath who worked tirelessly to improve the fortunes of Old Town in the 19th and 20th centuries and kept it from being torn down. The last camera presentation begins 1 hour before closing.

Castlehill. ☏ **0131/226-3709.** www.camera-obscura.co.uk. Admission £9 adults, £7.25 seniors and students, £6.50 children 5–15. MC, V. Apr–June and Sept–Oct daily 9:30am–6pm; July–Aug daily 9:30am–7:30pm; Nov–Mar daily 10am–5pm. Bus: 23, 27, 41, or 45.

Gladstone's Land ★ Run by the National Trust for Scotland, which rescued the property from demolition in the 1930s, this 17th-century merchant's house is decorated in period-style furnishings. It's not big and is worth a visit if only to get a feeling of the confined living conditions 400 years ago—even for the reasonably well off. Gladstone (then spelled Gledstane) expanded the original 16th-century structure he purchased in 1617 both upwards and toward the street. Above the ground floor, in the front room that he added, you can see the original exterior with its classical friezes of columns and arches. Here, as well, is the sensitively restored timber ceiling, looking suitably weathered and aged, with colorful paintings of flowers and fruit. Last admission is 30 minutes prior to closing.

477B Lawnmarket. ✆ **0131/226-5856.** www.nts.org.uk/visits. Admission £5.50 adults, £4.50 seniors, students, and children, £15 families. MC, V. Apr–June and Sept–Oct daily 10am–5pm; July–Aug daily 10am–6:30pm. Bus: 23, 27, 41, or 45.

Writers' Museum 🗡 This remnant of a 17th-century house contains a trove of portraits, relics, and manuscripts relating to Scotland's greatest men of letters: Robert Burns (1759–96), Sir Walter Scott (1771–1832), and Robert Louis Stevenson (1850–94). The Writers' Museum is often a surprisingly uncrowded space. The basement is perhaps best, with a good deal of items from the life of Stevenson (including his fishing rod and riding boots), as well as a gallery of black-and-white photographs taken when he lived in the South Pacific. The main floor is devoted to Scott with his dining room table from 39 Castle St., his pipe, chess set, and original manuscripts. Another set of rooms gives details of Burns's life (note his page-one death notice in a copy of London's *Herald* on July 27, 1796), along with his writing desk, rare manuscripts, portraits, and other items. The premises, Lady Stair's House, with its narrow passages and low clearances, was originally built in 1622 for Edinburgh merchant Sir William Gray. Outside in the Makars Close, flagstones have been engraved with the words of Scotland's best writers.

Lady Stair's Close, off Lawnmarket. ✆ **0131/529-4901.** www.cac.org.uk. Free admission. Mon–Sat 10am–5pm (also Sun noon–5pm in Aug). Bus: 23, 27, 41, or 45.

St. Giles' Cathedral ★ A brief walk downhill from Edinburgh Castle, this church—and its steeple in particular—is one of the most important architectural landmarks along the Royal Mile. Here is where Scotland's equal to Martin Luther, John Knox, preached his sermons on the Reformation. Also known as the High Kirk of St. Giles, the building combines a dark and brooding stone exterior (the result of a Victorian-era restoration) with surprisingly graceful buttresses. Only the tower represents the medieval era of the church. One of its outstanding features is the Thistle Chapel, housing beautiful stalls and notable heraldic stained-glass windows.

High St. ✆ **0131/225-9442.** www.stgilescathedral.org.uk. Free admission, but £3 donation suggested. May–Sept Mon–Fri 9am–7pm, Sat 9am–5pm, Sun 1–5pm (and for services); Oct–Apr Mon–Sat 9am–5pm, Sun 1–5pm (and for services). Bus: 23, 27, 28, 35, 41, or 42.

The Real Mary King's Close Beneath Edinburgh's City Chambers lies a warren of now hidden alleys where once people lived and worked. When the Royal Exchange (now the City Chambers) was constructed in 1753, the top floors of the existing buildings were torn down and the lower sections were left standing to be used as the foundations. This left a number of dark, mysterious passages largely intact. These underground "closes," originally very narrow walkways with houses on

For Fans of Mr. Hyde

Not far from Gladstone's Land is **Brodie's Close,** a stone-floored alley off the Lawnmarket. It was named after the well-respected cabinet-making father of the notorious William Brodie, who was a respectable councilor and deacon of trades by day—but a notorious thief and ne'er-do-well by night. Brodie's apparent split personality (actually he was simply calculating and devious) was possibly part of the inspiration for Robert Louis Stevenson's *The*

Strange Case of Dr. Jekyll and Mr. Hyde. Brodie was finally caught and hanged in 1788. In a final irony, the mechanism used in the hangman's scaffold was perfected by none other than Brodie himself—and he tried to defy its action by secretly wearing a steel collar under his shirt. It didn't work. Across the street from Brodie's Close is one of the more famous pubs along the Royal Mile: **Deacon Brodie's Tavern,** 435 Lawnmarket (✆ **0131/225-6531**).

either side, date back centuries. Led by guides dressed up as characters from the past, you can revisit the turbulent and plague-ridden days of the 17th century. Dim lighting and an audio track are intended to add to the experience. But of course in their day, these lanes weren't covered by a massive building. Still, this is a popular attraction so booking in advance is recommended.

2 Warriston's Close, High St. ✆ **0870/243-0160.** www.realmarykingsclose.com. Admission £11 adults, £10 seniors, £6 children 5–15. Advance reservations requested. Apr–July and Sept–Oct daily 10am–9pm; Aug 9am–9pm; Nov–Mar Sun–Thur 10am–5pm and Fri–Sat 10am–9pm. Closed Christmas Day. Bus: 23, 27, 28, 35, 41, or 42.

Brass Rubbing Centre 🎁   Down Chalmers Close from the High Street (or pass through the breezeway of the Jury's Hotel from Jeffrey St.) is the Brass Rubbing Centre, located in the remnants of the Holy Trinity church, founded in the 1460s. At this lesser-known and calm attraction, visitors make a wax rubbing (impression) from all sorts of designs, whether prehistoric Pictish motifs or Celtic crosses. Costs start from about £2 for simple rubbings that might take an hour or less to execute, though the cost is much more for elaborate brass plates that may occupy an entire day.

Chalmers Close. ✆ **0131/556-4364.** www.cac.org.uk. Free admission. Apr–Sept Mon–Sat 10am–5pm (also Sun noon–5pm in Aug); closed Oct–Mar. Bus: 36.

Museum of Childhood ☺   Allegedly the world's first museum devoted solely to the history of childhood, this popular and free museum is just past the intersection of High and Blackfriars streets. The contents of its four floors range from antique toys to games to exhibits on health, education, and costumes, plus video presentations and an activity area. Not surprisingly, this is often the noisiest museum in town. There is a good shop for toys and games.

42 High St. ✆ **0131/529-4142.** www.cac.org.uk. Free admission. Mon–Sat 10am–5pm; Sun noon–5pm. Bus: 35.

John Knox House ★   This is arguably the most picturesque dwelling house in Edinburgh's Old Town. It's characteristic of the "lands" that used to flank the Royal Mile, and the interior is noteworthy for the painted ceiling. John Knox is acknowledged as the father of the Presbyterian Church of Scotland, the Protestant tenets of which he established in 1560. While some regard him as a prototypical Puritan, he actually proposed progressive changes in the ruling of the church and in education. But Knox lived at a time of great religious and political upheaval; he spent 2 years as a galley slave and later lived in exile in Geneva. Upon his return, he became minister of St. Giles and worked to ensure the Reformation's success in Scotland.

Even if you're not overly interested in the firebrand reformer (who may have never lived here anyway), this late-15th-century house still merits a visit. Before Knox allegedly moved in, it was the home of James Mosman, goldsmith to the Catholic Mary, Queen of Scots (no friend of Knox). The house is now integrated into the completely modernized **Scottish Storytelling Centre.**

43–45 High St. ✆ **0131/556-9579.** www.scottishstorytellingcentre.co.uk. Admission £4 adults, £3.50 seniors, £1 children 7–15. MC, V. Mon–Sat 10am–6pm (also Sun noon–6pm July–Aug). Bus: 35 or 36.

The People's Story ✋ One of the most handsome buildings along the Royal Mile is the Canongate Tolbooth. Built in 1591, it was once the courthouse, prison, and center of municipal affairs for the burgh of Canongate. It now contains this rather pedestrian museum, which celebrates the social history of the inhabitants of Edinburgh from the late 18th century to the present, with lots of display cases and dressed-up mannequins. Still, it offers a chance to get inside the old tolbooth.

163 Canongate. ✆ **0131/529-4057.** www.cac.org.uk. Free admission. Mon–Sat 10am–5pm (also Sun noon–5pm in Aug). Bus: 35 or 36.

Museum of Edinburgh Across from the Canongate Kirk and housed in part of historic Huntly House is the Museum of Edinburgh, another free museum run by the city. It, too, concentrates on the capital's history with a set of rooms on different levels featuring reproductions and original items to represent the city and its traditional industries, whether glassmaking or cabinetry. It even has Greyfriars Bobby's collar and feeding bowl.

142 Canongate. ✆ **0131/529-4143.** www.cac.org.uk. Free admission. Mon–Sat 10am–5pm (also Sun noon–5pm in Aug). Bus: 35 or 36.

Scottish Parliament Building ★ After much controversy over its cost—the better part of £500 million and delays in its construction, the new Scottish Parliament opened in the fall of 2004. Designed by the late Barcelona-based architect Enric Miralles, it is a remarkable piece of modern design—to many worth the

---

📷 Canongate Kirkyard & Dunbar's Close

Take a few minutes to get off the well-trodden Royal Mile. Wander about the peaceful graveyard that surrounds the Canongate Church and go into the neighboring walled garden of Dunbar's Close. The kirkyard has views back toward Calton Hill as well as the graves of some notable people, such as David Rizzio confidant to Mary, Queen of Scots (p. 12), ground-breaking economic philosopher Adam Smith, and 18th-century poet Robert Fergusson, whose headstone was paid for by his more famous admirer, Robert Burns. If you use your imagination, a stop here might evoke the past in a way that museums, audio loops, videos, and tour guides can't do half as well.

expense and overruns. The abstract motif repeated on the facade facing the Canongate was apparently inspired by Raeburn's painting *Rev. Walker Skating on a Duddingston Loch,* which hangs in the National Gallery of Art. The public can visit for free and get tickets to seats in the main debating chamber or take a guided tour, which ventures into the bowels of Scottish political life. Guided tours are free, but reserve in advance.

Holyrood Rd. ✆ **0131/348-5000.** www.scottish.parliament.uk. Tues–Thurs 9am–7pm (all year when parliament is in session); Mon and Fri (and weekdays when Parliament not in session) 10am–6pm (Nov–Mar 10am–4pm); 10am–4pm weekends and public holidays. Last admission 45 min. before closing. Closed on Dec 25–26 and Jan 1–2. Bus: 35 or 36.

Palace of Holyroodhouse ★★ King James IV established this palace at the beginning of the 16th century adjacent to an abbey that a distant predecessor, King David I, had founded in 1128. What you see today was mostly built for Charles II in the 1670s. The northwest tower is the oldest part of the palace still intact and this wing provides the most interesting part of the tour inside. Here was the scene of Holyroodhouse's most dramatic incident. Mary Stuart's closest courtier, David Rizzio, was stabbed repeatedly (allegedly in front of the pregnant queen) on March 9, 1566 by accomplices of her jealous husband, Lord Darnley. There are several diverting Stuart relics, curios, and bits of history in Mary's Outer Chamber. One of the more curious exhibits is a piece of needlework done by Mary depicting a cat-and-mouse scene. (Her cousin, Elizabeth I, is the cat.)

The palace suffered long periods of neglect, but it basked in brief glory during a ball thrown by Bonnie Prince Charlie in the mid-18th century, during the peak of his feverish (and doomed) rebellion to restore the Stuart line to monarchy. Today the royal family stays here whenever they visit Edinburgh. When they're not in residence, the palace is open to visitors, and you see the various reception rooms where the queen dines, entertains, and meets Scottish government leaders. Some of the rich tapestries, paneling, massive fireplaces, and antiques from the 1700s are still in place. In addition to daytime hours, visitors can book exclusive evening tours at £30 per person, where you get your own expert guide.

More recently, the modern **Queen's Gallery** (additional admission) opened to display works from the royal collection, whether Mughal art or Dutch paintings. All that remains of the original **Abbey** is the ruined nave: still, you can imagine its grandeur and see a few tombstones, as well as the vault where the remains of King James V were once kept. On the path behind the nave, remnants of the foundations of other ecclesiastical buildings are apparent.

Behind Holyroodhouse is **Holyrood Park,** Edinburgh's largest. With rocky crags, a loch, sweeping meadows, and the ruins of a chapel, it's a wee bit of the Scottish countryside in the city, and a great place for a picnic. If you're fit and ambitious, climb up to the summit of 250-m (823-ft) high **Arthur's Seat,** from which the panorama is breathtaking. The name doesn't refer to King Arthur, as many people assume, but perhaps is a reference to Prince Arthur of Strathclyde or a corruption of *Ard Thor,* Gaelic for "height of Thor."

Canongate, at the eastern end of the Royal Mile. ✆ **0131/556-5100.** www.royalcollection.org.uk. Admission (includes audio tour) £10.25 adults, £9.30 seniors and students, £6.20 children 5–17, £27 families. MC, V. Apr–Oct daily 9:30am–6pm; Nov–Mar 9:30am–4:30pm. Closed when Royal Family in residence, typically a few weeks from mid-May to late June, mid-July, and Christmas. Bus: 35, 36, or open-top tours.

Top Museums & Monuments

Dean Gallery ★ Opened in 1999 across the road from the Scottish National Gallery of Modern Art, the Dean provides a home for surrealist art and includes an exact replica of the studio of Leith-born pop art pioneer Eduardo Paolozzi. He gave an extensive body of his private collection to the National Galleries of Scotland, including prints, drawings, plaster maquettes, and molds. The artist's mammoth composition of the robotic Vulcan dominates the entrance hall. Elsewhere works by Salvador Dalí, Max Ernst, and Joan Miróare are displayed, while the Dean also hosts traveling and special exhibitions of modern art.

73 Belford Rd. ℂ **0131/624-6200.** www.nationalgalleries.org. Free admission, except for some temporary exhibits. Daily 10am–5pm. Closed Dec 25-26. Bus: 13 or National Galleries shuttle.

The Fruitmarket Gallery Near Waverley railway station, this is the city's leading independent, contemporary art gallery housed in a cavernous old market dramatically updated and modernized by architect Richard Murphy in the early 1990s. It hosts exhibits from both local and internationally renowned modern and conceptual artists, whether Louise Bourgeois, Cindy Sherman, and Yoko Ono—or Chad McCail and Nathan Coley. The Fruitmarket's bookshop and cafe are equally appealing. Across the street is the less innovative but still worthy city-run **City Art Centre** (2 Market St.; ℂ **0131/529-3993**).

45 Market St. ℂ **0131/225-2383.** www.fruitmarket.co.uk. Free admission. Mon–Sat 11am–6pm; Sun noon–5pm. Closed Dec 25-27. Bus: 36.

National Gallery of Scotland ★★ Although the fine-art collection held by Scotland is small by the standards of larger countries, it has been chosen with great care and expanded by bequests, gifts, loans, and purchases. There's only enough space to display part of the entire collected works. One recent major acquisition was Botticelli's *The Virgin Adoring the Sleeping Christ Child.* The Duke of Sutherland has lent the museum two Raphaels, two of Titian's *Diana* canvases, and *Venus Rising from the Sea.* The gallery also has works by El Greco and Velázquez, and Dutch art by Rembrandt and van Dyck.

Impressionism and post-Impressionism are represented by Cézanne, Degas, van Gogh, Monet, Renoir, Gauguin, and Seurat. In a basement wing (opened in 1978), Scottish art is highlighted. Henry Raeburn is at his best in the whimsical *Rev. Robert Walker Skating on Duddingston Loch,* while the late-19th-century Glasgow School is represented by artists such as Sir James Guthrie.

Next door on the Mound is the **Royal Scottish Academy** (ℂ **0131/624-6200**), now connected by the Weston Link, which opened in summer 2004. The RSA was renovated and now hosts blockbuster exhibitions, such as works by Monet, Titian, or the 20th-century virtuoso, Joan Eardley.

2 The Mound. ℂ **0131/624-6200.** www.nationalgalleries.org. Free admission, except for some temporary exhibits. Fri–Wed 10am–5pm (till 6pm Aug); Thurs 10am–7pm. Closed Dec 25-26. Bus: 23, 27, 41, 42, 45, or National Galleries shuttle.

National Museum of Scotland ★★   Opened in 1998, this impressive museum housed in an effective, modern, sandstone building not far from the Royal Mile follows the story of Scotland with exhibits on archaeology, technology, science, the decorative arts, royalty, and geology. Hundreds of millions of years of Scottish history are distilled in this collection of some 12,000 items, which range from 2.9-billion-year-old rocks found on the island of South Uist to a cute Hillman Imp, one of the last 500 automobiles manufactured in Scotland. One gallery is devoted to Scotland's centuries as an independent nation. Another gallery, devoted to industry and empire from 1707 to 1914, includes exhibits on shipbuilding, whisky distilling, and the railways. The roof garden has excellent views, the **Tower Restaurant** (📞 **0131/225-3003**) offers superb lunches and fine dinners, and the adjacent **Royal Museum** (whose 3-year upgrade ends sometime in 2011) includes a well-preserved and airy Victorian-era Main Hall and some 36 more galleries.

Chambers St. 📞 **0131/247-4422.** www.nms.ac.uk. Free admission. Daily 10am–5pm. Bus: 2, 7, 23, 31, 35, 41, or 42.

Scott Monument   Resembling a church spire taken from a Continental European cathedral, the Gothic-inspired Scott Monument is one of Edinburgh's most recognizable landmarks. Not everyone appreciated the monument when first erected a few years after Scott's death in 1832, but it is now difficult to imagine the city's Princes Street Gardens without it. In the center of the 60m-tall (200-ft.) spire is a large seated statue of Sir Walter Scott and his dog, Maida. You can climb 287 steps to the top for a worthwhile view: Look east and you can clearly see the **Burns Monument,** dedicated to Robert Burns and designed by Thomas Hamilton in 1830, along Regent Road.

East Princes St. Gardens, near Waverley Station. 📞 **0131/529-4068.** Admission £3. Apr–Sept Mon–Sun 10am–7pm; Oct–Mar Mon–Sat 9am–4pm, Sun 10am–4pm. Bus: 3, 10, 12, 17, 25, 29, 33, 41, or 45.

Scottish National Gallery of Modern Art ★   Scotland's national collection of 20th-century art occupies a gallery converted from an 1828 school set on 4.8 hectares (12 acres) of grounds, about a 20-minute walk from the Haymarket train station. The collection is international in scope and quality, despite its modest size, with works ranging from Matisse, Braque, Miró, and Picasso to Balthus, Lichtenstein, and Hockney. The grounds in front of the museum have been dramatically landscaped with a swirl of grassy terraces and a pond: a piece of art itself called "Landform" by Baltimore-born Charles Jencks.

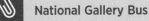
National Gallery Bus

If you plan to visit the various branches of the Scottish National Gallery, from the Dean to the Portrait, a good way to get around is by using the free shuttle bus service that stops at them all.

75 Belford Rd. 📞 **0131/624-6200.** www.nationalgalleries.org. Free admission, except for some temporary exhibits. Daily 10am–5pm. Closed Dec 25–26. Bus: 13 or National Galleries shuttle.

Scottish National Portrait Gallery ★   Housed in a red-stone, Victorian, neo-Gothic pile designed by Robert Rowand Anderson at the east end of Queen Street, this is the first purpose-built portrait gallery in the world. Until late 2011, it is closed for its first major refurbishment. Meanwhile, you can follow its progress on the museum's blog.

1 Queen St. ✆ **0131/624-6200.** www.nationalgalleries.org. Free admission, except for some temporary exhibits. From late 2011: Fri–Wed 10am–5pm; Thurs 10am–7pm. Closed Dec 25–26. Bus: 4, 10, 12, 16, 26, or National Galleries shuttle.

MORE ATTRACTIONS

Edinburgh Zoo ☺ Scotland's largest animal collection is 4½ km (3 miles) west of Edinburgh's city center on 32 hectares (80 acres) of hillside parkland. The zoo contains more than 1,500 animals, including white rhinos, pygmy hippos, and chimps. It also boasts the largest penguin colony in Europe housed in the world's biggest penguin enclosure. From April to September, a penguin parade is held daily at 2:15pm. Run by the Royal Zoological Society of Scotland, it highlights its role in wildlife conservation.

134 Corstorphine Rd. ✆ **0131/334-9171.** www.edinburghzoo.org.uk. Admission £15.50 adults, £13 seniors, £11 children, £47.50 families (2 adults and 2 children). MC, V. Apr–Sept daily 9am–6pm; Oct and Mar daily 9am–5pm; Nov–Feb daily 9am–4:30pm. Bus: 12, 26, 31, or 100 (Airlink).

Georgian House Charlotte Square, designed by the great Georgian architect Robert Adam, was the final piece of the city's first New Town development. The National Trust for Scotland runs this restored town house as an example of how people lived in that prosperous era of the city. The furniture is mainly Hepplewhite, Chippendale, and Sheraton, mostly from the 1700s. A sturdy old four-poster bed with an original 18th-century canopy occupies a ground-floor bedroom. The nearby dining room has a table set with fine Wedgwood china and also contains a chamber pot that was passed around by the gents after the women folk had retired. Last admission 30 minutes before closing.

7 Charlotte Sq. ✆ **0131/226-3318.** www.nts.org.uk/visits. Admission £5.50 adults; £4.50 seniors, students, and children, £15 families. MC, V. July and Aug 10am–7pm; Apr–Jun and Sept–Oct daily 10am–5pm; Mar 11am–4pm; and Nov daily 11am–3pm; closed Dec–Feb. Bus: 10, 19, or 41.

Greyfriars Kirk Although the churches of Scotland are not generally on the same scale as the cathedrals of the Continent, they do have their own slightly austere allure. Dedicated in 1620, this kirk was the first "reformed" church in Edinburgh and became the center of a good bit of history. It was built amid a cemetery that Queen Mary proposed in 1562 because there was no more burial space at St. Giles' Cathedral on the Royal Mile. In 1638, the National Covenant, favoring Scottish Presbyterianism to the English Episcopacy, was signed here, and an original copy is displayed. In the 18th century, the original tower exploded when gunpowder stored there caught fire. Among the many restorations, one in the 1930s brought in California redwood to create the current ceiling. The kirkyard has a bit of the Flodden Wall and it was the site of a prison for Covenanters. The most celebrated grave contains a 19th-century policeman whose faithful dog, Bobby, reputedly stood watch for years. The tenacious terrier's first portrait (painted in 1867) hangs in the church while a statue of the wee dog—made famous by Hollywood—is nearby at the top of Candlemaker Row, just outside a pub named in his honor.

Greyfriars Place. ✆ **0131/225-5429.** www.greyfriarskirk.com. Free admission. Apr–Oct Mon–Fri 10:30am–4:30pm, Sat 10:30am–2:30pm; Nov–Mar Thurs 1:30–3:30pm. Bus: 2, 23, 27, 41, 42, or 45.

THE father OF DR. JEKYLL & MR. HYDE

Robert Louis Stevenson (1850–94) was a restless character. Born in Edinburgh, he found the place unsuitable for his frail constitution. This, combined with his wanderlust, meant that he spent much of his life traveling and living outside his native Scotland. The author has been alternately hailed as Scotland's greatest writer and dismissed as nothing more than the creator of tall tales for children, though surely the former is more accurate.

He was the son of Margaret and Thomas Stevenson, born into a family famed for its civil engineering projects, especially lighthouses. R.L.S. was a sickly toddler and something of a disappointment to his father as a youth. After he was allowed to bow out of engineering and the lucrative family business, Robert attended law school. Thomas vowed that "the devious and barren paths of literature" were not suitable for his heir. R.L.S., undaunted, became a writer and a bit of a rogue. One of his favorite bars still stands today: Rutherford's on Drummond Street near South Bridge.

Determined to roam ("I shall be a nomad") and write, he went to France where he met and later married an American, Fanny Osborne, with whom he traveled to California. Following the success of *The Sea-Cook* (1881), which became the ever-popular *Treasure Island,* Stevenson produced *The Strange Case of Dr. Jekyll and Mr. Hyde,* an instant best-seller. That was quickly followed by the classic *Kidnapped* (1886), recounting the troubled political times in Scotland after the failed 1745 rebellion of Bonnie Prince Charlie. The book's 16-year-old hero is snatched and finds himself on an adventure across the Western Highlands and Islands.

Eventually R.L.S. and Fanny settled in Samoa, hoping to find a climate that would suit his scarred lungs. While here, Stevenson worked on the unfinished classic, *Weir of Hermiston* (published posthumously in 1896). On December 3, 1894, at only 43 years old, he collapsed and died.

National Library of Scotland   The country's central library hosts a year full of readings, activities, and exhibitions, such as one on the story of news, retracing its history from hand-printed single sheet circulars to the advent of the Internet. Each and every book published in the U.K. and Ireland is on the shelves here. Just don't expect to be able to check one out.

George IV Bridge. ℂ **0131/623-3700.** www.nls.uk. Exhibitions Mon–Fri 10am–8pm; Sat 10am–5pm; Sun 2–5pm. Bus: 2, 23, 27, 41, 42, or 45.

Our Dynamic Earth ☺   Under a futuristic tent-like canopy near the new Scottish Parliament, Our Dynamic Earth celebrates the evolution and diversity of the planet, with emphasis on the seismological and biological processes that led from the Big Bang to the world we know today. There is the slimy green primordial soup where life began and a series of specialized aquariums, some with replicas of early life forms, and a simulated tropical rainforest where skies darken at 15-minute intervals, there are torrents of rainfall, and creepy-crawlies underfoot. On the premises, there is a restaurant, cafe, children's play area, and gift shop. Last entry is 1 hour and 10 minutes before closing.

Holyrood Rd. ☏ **0131/550-7800.** www.dynamicearth.co.uk. Admission £10.50 adults; £9 seniors and students; £7 children 3-15. July and Aug daily 10am-6pm; Sept-Jun daily 10am-5pm. Bus: 35 or 36.

Scotch Whisky Heritage Centre   This center makes the case for the Scottish national drink by illuminating the traditions associated with its making. A holographic master blender's ghost and a whisky barrel ride showing historic moments in the whisky industry are included in the admission. Last tours are 1 hour prior to closing.

354 Castlehill, near Edinburgh Castle. ☏ **0131/220-0441.** www.whisky-heritage.co.uk. Admission £11.50 adults, £9 seniors, £6 children 6-17. AC, MC, V. Sept-May daily 10am-6pm, Jun-Aug 9:30am-6:30pm. Closed Dec 25. Bus: 23, 27, 41, or 45.

Surgeons' Hall Museums   Scotland's largest medical museum includes 18th-century anatomical specimens (which some might find distressing) as well as a section devoted to "Sport, Surgery, and the Well Being" that gives visitors a chance to use a keyhole surgery-training unit. There are also visiting exhibitions, such as a recent one on the history of cosmetic surgery. It's housed in a great Greek revival building by William Henry Playfair that was opened in 1832.

9 Hill Sq. ☏ **0131/527-1649.** www.museum.rcsed.ac.uk. Tickets £5 adults, £3 children. MV, V. Mon-Fri noon-4pm. Bus: 3, 8, 14, 31, or 33.

Talbot Rice Gallery   Part of the University of Edinburgh, housed in a wing of the Old College, the Talbot Rice contains the university's art collection with works by modern Scottish artists such as Joan Eardley and earlier pieces by the Scottish Colourists. Old Master paintings hang in the Georgian Gallery. The gallery's boxy, modern exhibition space—the White Gallery—is reserved for temporary shows by significant contemporary artists, such as Jenny Holzer.

Old College, South Bridge. ☏ **0131/650-2211.** www.trg.ed.ac.uk. Free admission. Tues-Sat 10am-5pm. Bus: 3, 8, 14, 31, or 33.

BRITANNIA: THE royal YACHT

The royal yacht *Britannia* was launched on April 16, 1953, and traveled more than a million miles before it was decommissioned in December 1997. Several cities then competed to permanently harbor the ship as a tourist attraction. The port of Leith won, and today the ship is moored next to the Ocean Terminal shopping mall about 3km (2 miles) from Edinburgh's center. Once on board, you'll see where Prince Charles and Princess Diana strolled the deck on their honeymoon, visit the drawing room and the Royal apartments, as well as explore the engine room, galleys, and captain's cabin.

The yacht is open daily except Christmas and New Year's Day, with the first tour from April to May and June to October beginning at 10am, the last tour at 4pm. In summer, July to September, the yacht is open from 9:30am to 4:30pm. From November to March, the hours are 10am to 3:30pm. Lasting at least 90 minutes, the tour is self-guided with the use of an audio headset. Adults pay £10.50, seniors £9, and children ages 5 to 17 £6.75. A family pass is £31. Advanced tickets are recommended in August (☏ **0131/555-5566;** www.royalyachtbritannia.co.uk). From Waverley Bridge, take either Lothian buses 1, 11, 22, 34, or 35, or the Majestic City Tour Bus.

The Monuments on Calton Hill ★★

Calton Hill ★ is partially responsible for Edinburgh's nickname—the "Athens of the North." Rising 106m (350 ft.), it's a bluff of rock and grass that's home to a host of monuments. The unfinished colonnade at the summit is the so-called **National Monument,** meant to honor the Scottish soldiers killed during the Napoleonic wars. The money ran out in 1829, and the William H. Playfair-designed structure (sometimes then referred to as "Edinburgh Disgrace") was never finished.

The **Nelson Monument,** containing relics of the hero of Trafalgar, dates from 1815 and rises more than 30m (100 ft.) above the hill. At the top, a large white ball drops a few yards every day at 1pm (noon GMT) Monday through Saturday; historically it helped sailors in Leith set their timepieces. The monument is open April to September, Monday from 1 to 6pm and Tuesday through Saturday from 10am to 6pm; and October to March, Monday through Saturday from 10am to 3pm. Admission is £3.

The old **City Observatory** along the western summit of Calton Hill was designed in 1818 by Playfair, whose uncle happened to be the president of the Astronomical Institute. Nearby, the circular **Dougal Stewart's Monument** of 1831 (by Playfair, as well) is not dissimilar to the 1830 **Burns Monument** designed by Thomas Hamilton on the southern slopes of Calton Hill. It replicates the Choragic Monument of Lysicrates in Athens, which was also the inspiration for his earlier attempt to honor the poet in Alloway (p. 257). But visit Calton Hill not only to see these monuments up close but also to enjoy the panoramic views of the Firth of Forth and the city spread beneath it.

Down the hill toward Princes Street, in the Old Calton Burial Grounds, is a curiosity of special note to those with an interest in North American history. The **Emancipation** or **Lincoln Monument,** erected in 1893, is dedicated to soldiers of Scottish descent who lost their lives in the U.S. Civil War. It has a statue of President Abraham Lincoln with a freed slave at his feet. Some famous Scots are buried in this cemetery, too, with elaborate tombs honoring their memory (notably the Robert Adam-designed tomb for philosopher David Hume).

Dean Village ★★

Dean Village is a former grain-milling settlement that goes back to the 12th century. Its picturesque buildings nestle in a valley about 30m (100 ft.) deep along the Water of Leith. Originally called the Water of Leith Village, its principal landmark is nearby: The soaring arches of Dean Bridge ★★ (1833), designed by the incredibly talented engineer Thomas Telford.

The village has been restored, the historic buildings (dating mainly from the 17th to 19th century) converted into private residences. Look particularly at the stonework on the yellow-washed facade of the building at the foot of Bell's Brae, with its 17th-century panel of cherubs and milling imagery, as well as the well-worn inscription blessing the "Baxters" (bakers) of Edinburgh. But don't come here for any one particular site. Stroll around and enjoy the ambience, which feels a hundred miles away from bustling Princes Street or the Royal Mile. From Dean Village you can also walk for kilometers along the Water of Leith, one of the most tranquil strolls in the greater Edinburgh area.

GARDENS & PARKS

The Meadows ★ This expansive public park south of Old Town separates the city center from the leafy neighborhoods that popped up in the 18th and 19th centuries. Tree-lined paths crisscross playing fields, whether soccer, rugby, or cricket, with plenty of additional space for having a picnic or flying a kite. The park dates to the 1700s, when a loch here was drained. At the far western end of the Meadows is Bruntsfield Links, a short-hole golf course which has a hallowed place in the history of the sport and can still be played today during the summer.

Melville Dr. Free admission. Daily dawn–dusk. Bus: 24 or 41.

Hume in Nor' Loch

When Princes Street Gardens were still a stinking bog, the great secular thinker David Hume accidently slipped into the banks of the mire. He couldn't get out and called for help from a passing woman. Recognizing the philosopher, she instead denounced Hume as an atheist and offered assistance only if he recited the Lord's Prayer. He presumably did so.

Princes Street Gardens ★★ By draining the then-fetid Nor' Loch below the Royal Mile, between Old and New Towns, the city created its most magnificent outdoor public space: The Princes Street Gardens. The banks are steep but grassy and great for a quick bit of sun, should it shine. In wintertime, there is usually an ice rink set up and often part of the park is used for various food and gift markets. With Edinburgh Castle above, this has to be one of the most photographed parks in Europe.

Princes St. Bus: 3, 10, 12, 17, 25, or 44. Free admission. Daily dawn–dusk.

Royal Botanic Garden ★★★ This is one of the grandest botanic gardens in all of Great Britain, rivaling the better known Kew Gardens near London. Sprawling across 28 hectares (70 acres), it dates from the late 17th century, when it was originally used for medical studies of useful herbs. Even today, when it comes to plant research in the U.K., only Kew does more. In spring, the various rhododendrons, from low ground cover to towering shrubs, are reason alone to visit the Royal Botanic Garden in Edinburgh. But the planting in various areas assures year-round interest, whether in the rock garden or the wide and long "herbaceous" borders elsewhere. The grounds include numerous glass houses: The Palm House (Britain's tallest) being foremost among them. Inverleith House is a venue for art exhibitions and has the Terrace Cafe, too.

20A Inverleith Row. ✆ **0131/552-7171.** www.rbge.org.uk. Free admission to garden; glasshouses £3.50 adults, £3 children. Daily Apr–Sept 10am–7pm; Oct 10am–6pm; Nov–Feb 10am–4pm; Mar 10am–6pm (glasshouses close 30 min. earlier). Bus: 8, 17, 23, or 27.

ORGANIZED TOURS

Edinburgh Bus Tours For an entertaining and informative overview of and introduction to the principal attractions of Edinburgh, consider the tour buses that leave every 20 minutes or so from Waverley Bridge (near Waverley railway station). The double-decker open-top motor coaches pass many of the major sights along the Royal Mile, the Grassmarket, Princes Street, and George Street. Three tours—Edinburgh Tour (green buses), City Sightseeing (red buses), and Mac Tours (vintage buses)—all cover roughly the same ground in Old Town and New Town. The Majestic Tour makes shorter work of the city center but includes Leith. Tickets can be used for 24 hours, and you can hop on and hop off the bus at designated stops.

Waverley Bridge. ✆ **0131/220-0770.** www.edinburghtour.com. Daily 9:30am–5:30pm (later in summer) mid-Mar–Oct £12 adults; £11 seniors and students; £5 children 5–15; £28 families.

Edinburgh Literary Pub Tour ★ Trace the footsteps of such literary greats as Robert Burns and Robert Louis Stevenson on this tour, which goes into the city's taverns, highlighting the tales of Dr. Jekyll and Mr. Hyde and the erotic love poetry of Burns. They leave nightly at 7:30pm from the Beehive Inn on the Grassmarket from May to September (7:45pm in August only); Thursday to Sunday in March, April, and October; and just on Friday from November to February. Tickets can be purchased at the Beehive on the evening or in advance on the website, which has information on Literary Bus Tours and Makars' Court literary performances outside the Writers Museum.

97b West Bow. ✆ **0131/226-6665.** www.edinburghliterarypubtour.co.uk. Reservations recommended in high season. Tickets £8.50.

Mercat Tours This well-established company conducts six different walking tours of the city, covering a range of interests from "Secrets of the Royal Mile" to "Ghosts & Ghouls," which takes place only in the evenings. The tours leave from the Mercat Cross, outside of St. Giles' Cathedral on the Royal Mile.

Mercat House, 28 Blair St. ✆ **0131/255-5443.** www.mercattours.com. Reservations recommended. Tickets from £8.50 adults, £5 children.

The Witchery Tours Edinburgh's history is filled with tales of ghosts, gore, and witchcraft, and this tour is enlivened by characters who leap out of seemingly nowhere when you least expect it. Two tours—the 90-minute "Ghost & Gore" and the 75-minute "Murder & Mystery"—overlap in parts. Scenes of horrific torture, murder, and supernatural occurrence in Old Town are visited, under the cloak of darkness. The ghost tour (May–Sept) departs nightly at 7 and 7:30pm, with the murder tour (year-round) leaving at 8:30, 9, and 9:30pm, all from the outside of the Witchery restaurant on Castlehill.

84 West Bow. ✆ **0131/225-6745.** www.witcherytours.com. Reservations required. Tickets £7.50 adults, £5 children.

SPECIAL EVENTS & FESTIVALS

Burns Night Not an occasion limited to Edinburgh, on January 25, Scots the world over gather to consume the traditional supper of haggis, *neeps* (swede or turnips), and tatties (potatoes), accompanied by a dram of whisky, while listening to recitals of the works of Scotland's Bard, Robert "Rabbie" Burns, whose birthday is being celebrated. Burns suppers are held all over town.

The Edinburgh Festival ★★★

WHEN THE WORLD COMES TO SCOTLAND

The cultural highlight of any year in Edinburgh arrives every summer with the famous Edinburgh Festival. The center of the Scottish capital, which is already busy with tourists, becomes chock-a-block with gawking visitors and savvy residents, maneuvering amid all sorts of street performers, who try to cajole and lure people to come to the stages where they are performing properly.

The Festival (as everyone simply calls it) centers today on the **Festival Fringe ★★★**. As the name implies, this was not originally the focus of the event. Indeed the Festival began with the **Edinburgh International Festival ★★**, which was inaugurated in 1947. It continues to attract internationally accomplished performers in classical music, opera, ballet, and drama.

But the Fringe has eclipsed it in popularity and scope. Initially it was avant-garde theater and topical drama. The notoriety—indeed fame—of the Fringe was cemented by the now legendary revue act called Beyond the Fringe, which featured the talents of Peter Cook, Dudley Moore, Alan Bennett, and Jonathan Miller. Additionally, other early stars at the Fringe became members of comedy group Monty Python.

Today, the Fringe presents some 2,000 shows at nearly 250 venues. It provides an opportunity for almost anybody—professional or nonprofessional, an individual, a group of friends, or a whole company—to put on a show wherever they can find an empty stage or street corner. The range is mind-boggling: A gospel choir from Soweto, penis puppetry, or avant-garde theater.

Comedy still dominates the Fringe, which always draws some of the top English-speaking funny men and women, whether Americans Rich Hall and Janeane Garofalo or Britain's Stephen K. Amos and Bill Bailey. For up-and-coming jokesters and comedic actors, a breakthrough and critically acclaimed run at the Fringe can help establish a successful international career. Such was the case for Demetri Martin recently and Lee Evans, Emma Thompson, Stephen Fry, Robbie Coltrane, Frank Skinner, Billy Connolly, Rowan Atkinson, Jo Brand, Lily Savage (Paul O'Grady), Steve Coogan, and Paul Merton over the years. The Fringe has become increasingly established and corporate-sponsored, but it retains its aura of the experimental and unexpected.

My advice when faced with a mind-boggling array of performances all at one time is to 1] take recommendations from the *List* magazine, *The Guardian*, and other media coverage; 2] combine some very cheap shows with some top-name acts, 3] keep going until you cannot go any further, and 4] go a bit further and hit a pub in the small hours to share your experiences with others.

The International Festival generally highlights classical music, performed by orchestras and chamber groups. Queen's Hall on the city's Southside usually has day-long schedules of concerts. As if all this wasn't enough, Edinburgh also hosts other festivals in the period between late July and early September. In Charlotte Square, the international **Book Festival ★★** has become a large annual event, drawing authors such as J. K. Rowling and Toni Morrison. Big top tents are thrown up to house hundreds that come for readings and lectures. The venue also includes an excellent temporary bookshop, good for finding gems too often not available in the big corporate bookshops. Finally, the Festival also incorporates an international **Jazz & Blues Festival ★**, a visual **Art Festival,** and a more industry-oriented **Television Festival.** Until a few years ago, an international Film Festival was held concurrently, but it is now held in June.

There's more. One of the hardest tickets to get is the annual military Tattoo on the Castle esplanade for impressive precision marching and pipe playing (see below).

And the Festival always ends with some awe-inspiring fireworks and a concert in Princes Street Gardens. Do make any hotel or overnight reservations as far as possible in advance if you plan to be in Edinburgh anytime between the end of July and the first week of September.

The International Festival box office is at the Hub, Castle Hill ((📞 0131/473-2000; www.eif.co.uk). The Fringe is based in 180 High St. ((📞 0131/226-0000; www.edfringe.com).

Information on all the festivals is found at **www.edinburghfestivals.co.uk.** Ticket prices vary for Festival, Fringe, and other shows or events. Some Fringe performances are free, but expect to pay £5 to £15 for most of them. The International Festival is pricier: £10–£50. The Book Festival admission is about £5–£10. For Jazz & Blues shows, tickets are around £10–£15. The Tattoo is more expensive: £15–£50—and again shows sell out in advance.

Hogmanay   New Year's Day in Scotland is historically a bigger deal than Christmas, and Edinburgh now hosts one of the largest New Year's Eve parties on the planet. In Scotland, the festivities traditionally don't really even begin until the clock strikes midnight (the "bells"), and then the celebration can continue until daybreak. In 1993, the Edinburgh City Council began a 3-day festival that features rock and pop bands, street theater, a lively parade, and, of course, spectacular fireworks over the castle. By 1997, the event had become so big that participation is reserved for ticket holders. Storms, however, have been known to lead to cancelations as all of it is held outdoors. For information, visit **www.edinburghshogmanay.com.**

Military Tattoo   Occurring at approximately the same time as the Festival, this is one of the more popular traditional spectacles. It features precision marching of not only Scottish regiments but also soldiers and performers (including bands, drill teams, and gymnasts) from dozens of countries on the floodlit esplanade of Edinburgh Castle. The Tattoo Office, 32 Market St. 📞 **0131/225-1188.** www.edinburgh-tattoo.co.uk. Ticket prices vary (£13–£44); advance reservations essential.

SPORTS & OUTDOOR ACTIVITIES

Spectator Sports

FOOTBALL (SOCCER)

You might get swept up by the zeal that some residents have for their local football clubs: **Hearts** and **Hibs.** Heart of Midlothian Football Club (just Hearts or occasionally the Jambos) home field is Tynecastle stadium on Gorgie Road (📞 **0131/200-7201;** www.heartsfc.co.uk), near Haymarket railway station. Hibernian FC (simply Hibs or sometimes Hibbies) play at Easter Road stadium, toward Leith (📞 **0131/661-2159;** www.hibs.co.uk). These cross-town rivals, when not battling each other in the Edinburgh Derby, take on other teams in the top-flight Scottish soccer league. The season usually runs from August through May, and traditional playing time is Saturday afternoon at 3pm, although mid-week evenings and Sunday matches (which begin a bit after noon) are now common. Tickets range from £10 to £50.

HORSE RACING

Place your bets at the **Musselburgh Racecourse,** Musselburgh Park (📞 **0131/665-2083;** www.musselburgh-racecourse.co.uk), about 6.5km (4 miles) east of Edinburgh. Admission is £15 to £20.

CITY STROLLS IN EDINBURGH

Because central Edinburgh is compact, walking is one of the best ways to see it. This is especially true in the city's Old Town, where narrow passages and alleys—or in the local vernacular *closes* (pronounced "clozes") and *vennels*—run off both sides of the main street. Wander down a few of them to appreciate the medieval feel of the Scottish capital.

9

Beyond Old Town to the north is the classic Georgian-era New Town—another part of the city that has UNESCO World Heritage Site status. Edinburgh's tourist attractions are also quite close together and the strolls are intended to offer a good sample of the city's key districts. Aside from Walk 1, they are virtually circular, so that you end up near to where you began your walk. Walk 3 is the longest, includes a few hills, and should be done in segments if too strenuous.

WALKING TOUR 1: THE ROYAL MILE

START:	**Edinburgh Castle Esplanade.**
FINISH:	**Holyrood Park.**
TIME:	**About 1½ to 2 hours.**
BEST TIME:	**Daytime.**
WORST TIME:	**Late at night.**

This walk crosses the historic heart of Edinburgh Old Town, the medieval town elevated to royal burgh by King David I in the 12th century. Situated on a mile-long ridge, Old Town (whose protective walls were knocked down and refortified throughout history) is, for many visitors, the most evocative district in Edinburgh. In large part, the city's current reputation for beauty and romance rests upon the appearance of the Royal Mile, which runs along the spine, and its surrounding streets, which come off it like ribs.

RUGBY

The home field of Scotland's national rugby team is **Murrayfield Stadium** (© 0131/346-5000; www.scottishrugby.org), about 3km (2 miles) west of Edinburgh's city center (walking distance from Haymarket station). The sport is usually played from fall to spring, generally on Saturdays. Some of the most passionate matches are those among teams in the annual Six Nations competition comprising Scotland, Wales, England, Ireland, Italy, and France. Ticket prices range from around £25 to £40.

Other Activities

BICYCLING

Bicycles are used by a surprising number of people in Edinburgh, despite the many hills and cobbled streets. The city is linked to the national cycle path system, and you can use it to get to many places on off-road and on-road lanes. Rent bikes from **Rent-a-Bike Edinburgh,** 29 Blackfriars St., near High Street (© 0131/556-5560; www.cyclescotland.co.uk; bus: 35). Depending on the type of bike, charges range between £10 to £15 per day or up to £70 for the week. Part-day rentals are possible. A credit card imprint will be taken as security. The same company runs **Scottish Cycle Safaris,** which organizes tours in the city and across Scotland.

GOLF

Aside from the **Bruntsfield Links,** where all you need is a ball, one lofted club, and a putter, Edinburgh's environs offer a host of attractive golf clubs and courses. It always pays to call a day or two, preferably, in advance to reserve a tee time and confirm greens fees. Among those run by the city are **Silverknowes Golf Course,** Silverknowes Parkway (© 0131/336-3843), a 6,202-yard course above the Firth of Forth; **Braid Hills** (© 0131/447-6666), about 5km (3 miles) south of Edinburgh's city center, just beyond Morningside; and **Carrick Knowe,** Glen Devon Park (© 0131/337-1096), just west of Murrayfield Stadium. Weekday rates for 18 holes are typically about £15, with rental clubs for about £16.

SAILING

Not far from Edinburgh is the **Port Edgar Sailing Centre** in South Queensferry (© 0131/331-3330; www.portedgar.co.uk). From spring to fall, it offers sailing instruction and boat rental to qualified sailors.

SPORTS COMPLEXES, GYMS & POOLS

The **Meadowbank Sports Centre,** London Road (© 0131/661-5351; www.edinburghleisure.co.uk), was built when the city hosted the Commonwealth Games in 1970. Then state-of-the-art, it still offers a good gym, track, and soccer fields. It costs about £5 to use the weight room. For swimming, the Olympic-size indoor pool at the **Royal Commonwealth Pool,** 21 Dalkeith Rd. (© 0131/667-7211), is the best in the city.

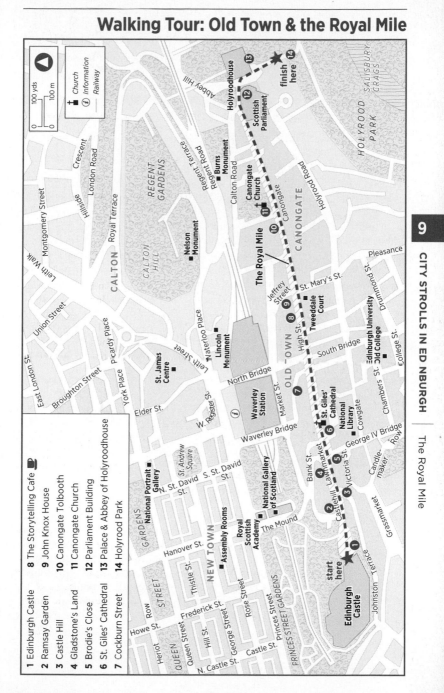

Walking Tour: Old Town & the Royal Mile

Legend
- Church
- Information
- Railway

0   100 yds
0   100 m

Map labels (numbered):
1 Edinburgh Castle
2 Ramsay Garden
3 Castle Hill
4 Gladstone's Land
5 Brodie's Close
6 St. Giles' Cathedral
7 Cockburn Street
8 The Storytelling Cafe
9 John Knox House
10 Canongate Tolbooth
11 Canongate Church
12 Parliament Building
13 Palace & Abbey of Holyroodhouse
14 Holyrood Park

start here
Edinburgh Castle

finish here

The Royal Mile

OLD TOWN
NEW TOWN
CANONGATE
CALTON
CALTON HILL
REGENT GARDENS
HOLYROOD PARK
SALISBURY CRAGS
PRINCES STREET GARDENS

Holyroodhouse
Scottish Parliament
Canongate Church
Burns Monument
Nelson Monument
Lincoln Monument
Waverley Station
National Gallery of Scotland
National Portrait Gallery
Royal Scottish Academy
Assembly Rooms
St. James Centre
National Library
Edinburgh University Old College
St. Giles' Cathedral
Tweedale Court

Street names:
Abbey Hill, Royal Terrace, London Road, Montgomery Street, Hillside Crescent, Leith Walk, Union Street, East London St., Broughton Street, Picardy Place, York Place, Elder St., Waterloo Place, Regent Terrace, Regent Road, Calton Road, Canongate, Holyrood Road, Pleasance, Jeffrey Street, St. Mary's St., High St., South Bridge, Cowgate, Drummond St., Chambers St., College St., George IV Bridge, Row, Candlemaker Row, Grassmarket, Johnston Terrace, Castle St., Castlehill, Lawnmarket, Victoria St., Bank St., The Mound, Market St., North Bridge, Waverley Bridge, W. Register St., Leith Street, N. St. David St., S. St. David St., St. Andrew Square, Hanover St., Thistle St., Frederick St., Rose Street, Castle St., George Street, Queen Street, Hill St., Howe St., Heriot Row, N. Castle St., Princes Street

9

CITY STROLLS IN EDINBURGH

The Royal Mile

1 Edinburgh Castle

The esplanade of Edinburgh Castle (p. 87) has the most accessible views of the city in practically all directions. Evidence of buildings elsewhere on the castle site dates to the 11th century, although fortifications of some kind on this mount, known as Castle Rock, may go back as far as the 6th century. In 1542, the castle ceased being a royal residence, becoming an ordinance factory. Today, military barracks are still on the grounds, although it is mainly a tourist attraction.

At the northeast corner of the esplanade is:

2 Ramsay Garden

Not a garden but an innovative and charming set of buildings that date to the end of the 19th century, this bright place was the brainchild of Sir Patrick Geddes. A polymath and city planner, Geddes almost single-handedly revived the fortunes of Old Town, working to rid it of squalid living conditions while saving it from total destruction and redevelopment. Ramsay Garden's architecture is a beautiful mix of Scottish baronial and English cottage, combining corbels (the cantilevered round extensions), conical roofs, crow steps, and half-timber gable construction.

Move from the esplanade to:

3 Castle Hill

Although the road that runs from the castle to the palace is called the Royal Mile, it has various names along the way. The first short section is Castle Hill, followed by the Lawnmarket, High Street, and Canongate. On the right as you move away from the castle grounds are Cannonball House and Castlehill School, the Scotch Whisky Heritage Centre, and then Boswell's Court, which was originally built around 1600 and now is the site of a sumptuous restaurant called the Witchery (p. 80). Across the street is Geddes's observatory, which has his camera obscura, for unique views of the city.

At the next roundabout, which marks the end of Castlehill, is the Tolbooth Church (now called the Hub). Completed in 1844, it doubled as a meeting hall for the General Assembly of the Church of Scotland.

Continue down the Royal Mile to the Lawnmarket and:

4 Gladstone's Land

Lands are buildings, and between the 14th and 15th centuries, the plots (or *tofts*) on the Royal Mile were subdivided into forelands and backlands. Just past the entrances to James Court, Gladstone's Land (p. 91) dates to at least the 16th century and was purchased by Thomas Gladstone (then spelled Gledstane) in 1617. He expanded the building upward and forward toward the street. Inside, you can see both the original frontage as well as a painted ceiling of the once "new" addition in the second-floor front room. Nearby, Lady Stair's Close has the early-17th-century Lady Stair's House, the remnants of which now contain the Writer's Museum with exhibits dedicated to Burns, Scott, and Stevenson (p. 98).

Across from Gladstone's Land is:

5 Brodie's Close

Edinburgh's history has its fair share of infamous characters. None more so than craftsman William Brodie: upstanding gentleman and deacon of trades by day but thief and ne'er-do-well by night. Once captured, Deacon Brodie escaped arrest and fled to Holland, where he betrayed himself by his letter writing. Brought back to Edinburgh, in 1788 he was hung, ironically, on gallows of his own design. Robert Louis Stevenson is said to have had a childhood nightmare about the two-faced Brodie, which later became inspiration for Dr. Jekyll and Mr. Hyde. Lest you worry about the morality of Edinburgh, the close is actually named after Brodie's father, Francis, a gifted cabinetmaker who obeyed the law.

Continue down the Royal Mile, crossing Bank Street on the left and George IV Bridge on the right, to:

6 St. Giles' Cathedral

You're now on High Street. There is nearly as much history around St. Giles, or the High Church, as the city itself (p. 91). It has its origins in the 12th century. It was burned by the English when they overran the city in 1385. Here, in the 1500s, John Knox laid down his uncompromising Protestant reforms, and, later, zealous followers destroyed Catholic alters and revered relics. It's been rebuilt and renovated repeatedly. All that really remains of the 15th-century church is the spire, a familiar landmark of the city. Around St. Giles are the Law Courts of Parliament Square, featuring (since 1838) the designs of Robert Reid, though they were inspired by drawings by the great architect Robert Adam. In the sidewalk near the Royal Mile, note the heart-shaped arrangement of cobbles. This is meant to mark the site of the old tolbooth (where taxes were collected) and a city prison, the latter of which was made famous by Sir Walter Scott's *The Heart of Midlothian*. Spitting in the heart is said to bring good luck. Nearby in the Anchor Close, the first edition of the *Encyclopaedia Britannica* was printed.

Continue down the Royal Mile to:

7 Cockburn Street

Curving down the hill to the left, Cockburn Street is a relatively recent addition to the neighborhood, built in 1856 to improve access to Waverley railway station. The road interrupts the old closes and steps (such as those in the macabre-sounding **Fleshmarket Close**) that descend straight and precipitously down the hill from the Royal Mile. Cockburn Street has a bohemian feel with a variety of bars and restaurants, CD shops, tattoo parlors, bookshops, and art galleries. Across High Street is the Tron Kirk, a center for Old Town information. A tron was the beam used to weigh goods. The church was built atop a very old lane that today has been excavated.

Continue down the Royal Mile, crossing North Bridge on the left and South Bridge on the right to Blackfriars Street and:

This cafe at the Scottish Storytelling Centre (43 High St.; ℂ 0131/556-1229) was established by the same folk behind Spoon Café Bistro (p. 82). It's a modern and casual cafe with a talented chef in charge of the small, open kitchen. Food is all freshly prepared using some excellent ingredients.

Return to High Street, turning right to:

9 John Knox House

Jutting out into the wide sidewalk on the left side of High Street is this photogenic and apparently genuine 16th-century house. Although any real link to Knox the firebrand Protestant reformer has been debated over the years, that perceived connection did ensure that this attractive building was preserved (p. 92). Next door (to the left) is Moubray House, which has some of the same late medieval details of Gladstone's Land. The rear portion (not open to the public) might actually date to 1530, making it perhaps the oldest-surviving dwelling in the city. Across the street, Tweeddale Court leads to Tweeddale House, a 16th-century survivor with the Doric porch added in the 18th century just before the printers Oliver & Boyd (whose name remains on the facade) occupied the building.

The patio here is the site of the infamous robbery and murder of one William Begbie in 1806. Apparently most of the stolen money was quickly recovered— but the assassin escaped justice. Next door is the World's End Close, the final alley on this stretch of the Royal Mile, and indeed the last one before the city's old protective wall, which safeguarded "the world" within it.

Continue down the Royal Mile to:

10 Canongate Tolbooth

Now, having crossed an intersection with Jeffrey Street on the left and St. Mary's Street to the right, you are on the portion of the Royal Mile known as the Canongate. Here, outside the town's old protective walls, the original settlement of Canongate was only formally incorporated into the city of Edinburgh in 1856. Most of the buildings along the Canongate have been rebuilt over the years. The tower of the Tolbooth (built circa 1590) remains, however. The attractive clock that extends out over the street was added to the building in the 1880s, now housing a not-terribly-impressive museum called the People's Story (p. 93).

Next door is:

11 Canongate Church

The original parish church for the Canongate burgh was Holyrood Abbey (see below), but eventually a new kirk became necessary, and this one, with its bell-shaped roofline, was christened in 1691. The churchyard, with good views of the Royal High School on Calton Hill, has numerous monuments. Pioneering economic philosopher Adam Smith is buried here and possibly the murdered confidant to Mary, Queen of Scots, David Rizzio. Aficionados of the poet Robert Burns will know that he wrote the tribute on the headstone of fellow poet Robert Fergusson and that Mrs. Agnes McLehose (to whom Burns addressed umpteen letters as "Clarinda") was laid to rest in this cemetery, as well.

Continue on down the Royal Mile to the:

12 Parliament Building

The new Parliament Building for Scotland, (designed by Spanish Catalan architect Enric Miralles), was initially intended to open in 2001, but didn't host its first session until autumn 2004. In 2006, the building suffered another setback when a beam in the main debating chamber came loose. The abstract motif, repeated on the facade along the Canongate, was apparently inspired by Raeburn's painting of *Reverend Walker skating on Duddingston Loch*, which hangs in the National Gallery of Art. Whatever critics have said about it, it is undoubtedly one of the most impressive modern public buildings to have been built in the U.K. since the turn of the century.

Continue to the foot of the Canongate and the:

13 Palace & Abbey of Holyroodhouse

Rood means cross, and the ruined abbey on the grounds of Holyroodhouse dates to King David I and 1128. Between 1426 and 1460, James II was born, crowned, married, and buried at the Palace (p. 94). Later, James IV expanded the buildings, as did his heir—all to be redone again in the 17th century by King Charles II, who never apparently visited. A critical episode in the fraught reign of Mary, Queen of Scots was played out here: The assassination of her loyal assistant David Rizzio. Young Pretender Bonnie Prince Charlie stayed at the Palace briefly in 1745 during his nearly successful, but ultimately disastrous, rebellion. For many years, the Palace remained empty most of the time. Only since the first visit by Queen Victoria in 1842 have its lodgings been regularly used by members of the royal family. The Queen's Gallery opened in 2002 for exhibitions, featuring works from the vast royal collection of art.

Adjacent is:

14 Holyrood Park

If you have any energy left, these 160 plus hectares (400 acres) of open space allow plenty of ground to roam. From here you can scale Salisbury Crags and mount the high hill known as Arthur's Seat, which rises some 251m (825 ft.) above Edinburgh. Nearby is the science- and family-oriented tourist attraction, Our Dynamic Earth (p. 94).

WALKING TOUR 2: **SOUTH OF THE ROYAL MILE**

START:	**West Bow.**
FINISH:	**Grassmarket.**
TIME:	**About 1½ hours.**
BEST TIME:	**Daytime.**
WORST TIME:	**Late at night.**

The walls surrounding medieval Edinburgh (first erected as much to deter smuggling as to protect inhabitants from enemy armies) were generally expanded to include more ground each time the fortifications needed improving. So, eventually they extended past the original Old Town boundaries to include surrounding districts such as the Grassmarket and ancient routes such as the Cowgate. This walk combines parts of Old Town with the historic settlements south of the original burgh, an area now dominated by the University of Edinburgh.

Start the walk at:

1 West Bow

Initially this street zigzagged right up the steep slope from the Grassmarket to Castlehill. With the 19th-century addition of Victoria Street, however, it is linked curvaceously and more gently to the Royal Mile via George IV Bridge. The combination of Victoria Street and West Bow creates a charming and winding road with unpretentious shops, bars, and restaurants. At the base of the street is the West Bow well, which was built in 1674. To the west is the Grassmarket.

But our walk goes southeast from Cowgate. Head up Candlemaker Row to:

2 Greyfriars Church

Not the church you see when ascending Candlemaker Row, but to the right at the top, Greyfriars Kirk (p. 97) was completed in 1620. Although Greyfriars was the first post-Reformation church constructed in Edinburgh, by the middle of the 17th century, it was being used as barracks. In 1718, the original tower exploded when gunpowder stored in it (a remnant of the 1715 rebellion) was ignited. The kirkyard has a bit of the infamous Flodden Wall, built after the Scots' disastrous defeat by England in 1513, and is full of 17th-century monuments and gravestones. Its most celebrated plot, however, contains a 19th-century policeman whose faithful dog, Bobby, reputedly stood watch for 14 years. Bobby's statue is at the top of Candlemaker Row, just outside the pub named in his honor.

Cross George IV Bridge to Chambers Street and the:

3 Museum of Scotland

Directly in front of you as you leave Greyfriars is the impressive and modern Museum of Scotland (p. 96). Entered off Chambers Street, it was designed by architects Benson and Forsyth and constructed mostly with sandstone from the northeast of Scotland. Opened in 1998, it was purpose-built for permanent exhibitions that chart the history of Scotland: The land, wildlife, and its people. Next door is the Royal Museum. Chambers Street is named after a 19th-century lord provost (the rough equivalent of ceremonial mayor), whose statue stands in front of the museum's Victorian Great Hall. Further down off Chambers Street, on what is today Guthrie Street, is where Sir Walter Scott was born.

Continue east on Chambers Street to South Bridge, turn right (south), and at this corner is the:

4 Old College

The 1781 exteriors of the University of Edinburgh Old College have been called the best public work by leading Georgian architect Robert Adam. The university was first established in 1583 by James VI (James I of England), and this "Old College" actually replaced an earlier one. Today modern buildings

Walking Tour: South of the Royal Mile

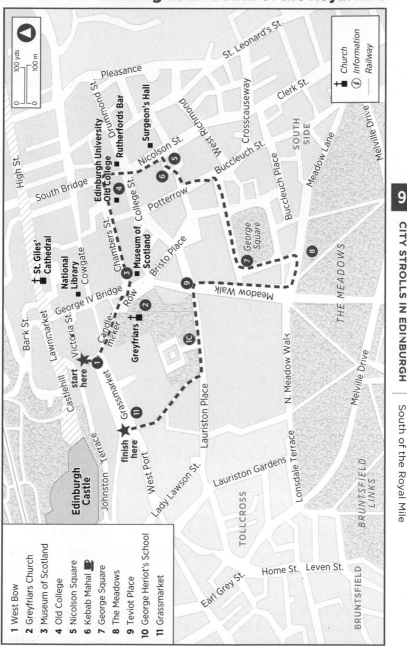

Church
(i) Information
—— Railway

100 yds
100 m

St. Leonard's St.

Pleasance

St. Richmond

Drummond St.

Surgeon's Hall

Rutherfords Bar

Edinburgh University Old College

Nicolson St.

Crosscauseway

Buccleuch St.

Clerk St.

SOUTH SIDE

Melville Drive

Meadow Lane

High St.

South Bridge

St. Giles' Cathedral

National Library

Cowgate

Chambers St.

College St.

Potterrow

Buccleuch Place

Bark St.

Lawnmarket

George IV Bridge

Victoria St.

Candlemaker Row

Greyfriars

Bristo Place

George Square

THE MEADOWS

Castlehill

start here

Grassmarket

Meadow Walk

N. Meadow Walk

Melville Drive

Johnston Terrace

finish here

West Port

Lauriston Place

Lauriston Place

Edinburgh Castle

Lady Lawson St.

Lauriston Gardens

Lonsdale Terrace

BRUNTSFIELD LINKS

TOLLCROSS

Home St.   Leven St.

Earl Grey St.

BRUNTSFIELD

Museum of Scotland

1 West Bow
2 Greyfriars Church
3 Museum of Scotland
4 Old College
5 Nicolson Square
6 Kebab Mahal 📖
7 George Square
8 The Meadows
9 Teviot Place
10 George Heriot's School
11 Grassmarket

dotted over the area with university classrooms have overtaken these premises. On nearby Drummond Street is one of Robert Louis Stevenson's favorite drinking spots—the Rutherford Bar—and a plaque commemorating his admiration for it is at the corner. Across Drummond Street there is more literary history— but of more recent vintage. A cafe once here, one flight up, is reputedly where J. K. Rowling began writing the *Harry Potter* series. No plaque, yet.

At Drummond Street, South Bridge becomes Nicolson Street. Continue south on it to:

5 Nicolson Square

The impressive neoclassical building you pass on the left (across from the modern Festival Theatre) before arriving at Nicolson Square is the Surgeons' Hall, designed by William H. Playfair in the 1830s. Nicolson Square is older, dating to 1756, and the buildings along its north fringe apparently were the first to be built. The monument in the square is called the Brassfounders' Column, designed by James Gowans in 1886.

6 Kebab Mahal 🍴

Along the north side of the square, Kebab Mahal (7 Nicolson Sq.; ✆ 0131/622-5214) serves up inexpensive but tasty and generous portions of Indian food. Its simple and unpretentious surroundings draw a real cross-section of Edinburgh: Professors, students, construction workers, and visitors to the nearby central mosque. See p. 82 for a full review. Alternatively, you might try the cafe called Elephants & Bagels at the west side of the square.

Leave the square at the west on Marshall Street, turn left (south) onto Potterrow, turning right (west) at the parking lot entrance and Crichton Street to:

7 George Square

Almost entirely redeveloped (and arguably ruined) by Edinburgh University in the 20th century, George Square originally had uniform, if less than startling, mid-18th-century town houses. It predates the city's New Town developments north of Old Town, and some of the early buildings are still standing on the western side of the square. The park provides a quiet daytime retreat. The square was named after the brother of its designer, James Brown, and not a king. The writer Walter Scott played in the park as a child.

Exit the square at the southwest corner, turning right (west) into:

8 The Meadows

This sweeping park separates the southern suburbs such as Marchmont, which were largely developed in the 19th century, from central Edinburgh. The area once had a loch, but today it is a green expanse criss-crossed by tree-lined paths (p. 101). At the western end is Bruntsfield Links, which some speculate entertained golfers as far back as the 17th century and still has a short course with many holes today.

Turn right after a short distance (at the black cycle network marker) onto a wide path for pedestrians and bicyclists—Meadow Walk—and follow it north to:

9 Teviot Place

The triangle of land formed by Teviot Place, Forrest Road, and Bristo Place is a hotbed of university life today, with its cafes and bars. To the right (east) is the Medical School. To the left (west) on Lauriston Place is the Royal Infirmary of Edinburgh. George Watson's Hospital on the grounds dates to the 1740s, but Scots baronial buildings superseded it in the 19th century, adopting the open-plan dictates of Florence Nightingale.

Walk west on Lauriston Place to:

10 George Heriot's School

Heriot was nicknamed the Jinglin' Geordie, and as jeweler to James VI, he exemplified the courtiers and royal hangers-on who left Scotland and made their fortunes in London after the unification of the crowns. Heriot, at least, decided to pay something back by bequeathing several thousand pounds to build this facility for disadvantaged boys. Of the 200-odd windows in the Neo-Renaissance pile, only two are exactly alike. Today, it is a private school for young men and women.

Continue on Lauriston Place to the edge of the campus, turn right on Heriot Place, and continue down the steps and path called the Vennel to the:

11 Grassmarket

On your way to the Grassmarket just at the top of the steep steps of the footpath called the Vennel, is another identified piece of the Flodden Wall. It was part of the southwest bastion, indicating how the Grassmarket, a small district and short street with a tree-lined median strip, was enclosed within the fortified city by the 16th century. Now home to loads of bars and restaurants in the shadow of the castle, the Grassmarket held a weekly market for more than 400 years. It also was the site of public gallows until the 1780s, where zealous Protestants—known as the Covenanters—were hanged. So was Maggie Dickson, who according to legend, came back to life. There is a pub named after her today in the Grassmarket. At the nearby White Hart Inn, both Burns and William Wordsworth are said to have lodged.

WALKING TOUR 3: NEW TOWN

START:	**Royal Scottish Academy.**
FINISH:	**East Princes Street Gardens.**
TIME:	**About 2 to 3 hours.**
BEST TIME:	**Daytime.**
WORST TIME:	**Late at night.**

In 1767, the city fathers realized that the best way to relieve the increasingly cramped and unhygienic Old Town was to create a New Town. It is a definitive example of rational Georgian town planning. Major expansion well outside the walls of the fortified city became possible as hostilities with England (or between rebellious groups within Scotland) had ended. The loch north of Old Town was drained (becoming Princes Street Gardens), and the new roads on the other side were laid out in a strict grid. Subsequent additions to the original New Town created a new city center with fine housing, offices, and commercial space. Along with Edinburgh's Old Town, today it is a U.N. World Heritage site.

Begin the walk opposite the corner of Princes Street and Hanover Street at the:

1 Royal Scottish Academy

Bisecting Princes Street Gardens, a hill called the Mound was created by earth moved during the development of Edinburgh's New Town, and it effectively forms a ridge linking New and Old towns. At the lower end of this hump are two galleries: The Royal Scottish Academy and, to the south, the National Gallery of Art. Both buildings were designed with strong Greek Doric and Ionic styling by William H. Playfair around 1825 and 1850, respectively.

Cross Princes Street north to Hanover Street, walking up Hanover Street, and turning left (west) onto:

2 Rose Street

Not particularly significant historically, this lane was simply intended for a better class of artisans and at one point in the 1780s, a two-story height limit was placed upon its buildings. The conversion of the street into an open-air pedestrian mall began in the late 1960s. Today Rose Street is best known for many popular pubs, such as the Abbotsford, Milne's, and the Kenilworth. The area has retail shops and restaurants, too.

Continue east on Rose Street to Frederick Street, turning right (north) to:

3 George Street

All the street names in the first New Town were intended to celebrate the Hanoverian reign of George III (he who lost America). George Street is the central of three principal avenues that run parallel through New Town, and it runs along the wide ridge of the hill. Looking down it to the west you can see the dome of West Register House in the distance, and to the east is the column with Melville in St. Andrew Square at the other end of George Street. To the north are views of the Forth River. Today the wide boulevard (with parking down the center) is where most of the city's expensive clothing shops are located. At the intersection with Frederick Street is the statue of Prime Minister William Pitt (1759–1806).

From the corner of Frederick Street, turn left and go west on George Street, turning left (south) on Castle Street, and proceeding back to:

4 Princes Street

Like Queen Street on the northern boundary of the first New Town, buildings on Princes Street were constructed intentionally only on one side of the boulevard. That has insured practically uninterrupted views of Old Town rising up to the Castle: One of the most iconic panoramas in all of Europe. Despite the views, the original three-story homes on Princes Street were apparently not as nice or as desirable as the ones on George and Queen streets. Today, a lot of Princes Street, a key shopping street, is dominated by unattractive modern storefronts and some ghastly 20th-century monstrosities. But at the western corner of Princes and Castle streets are three original buildings buried behind the much more recent facades.

Walking Tour: New Town

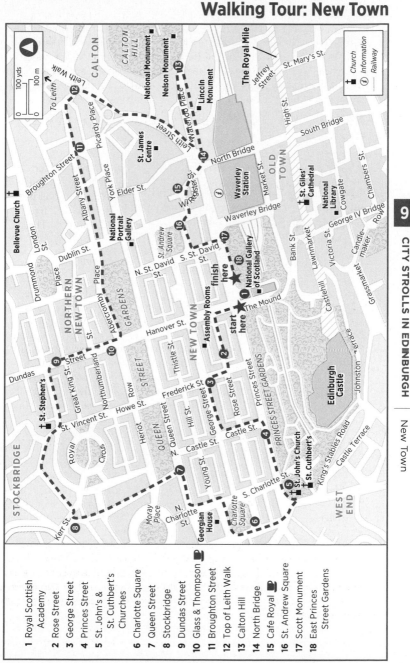

1 Royal Scottish
   Academy
2 Rose Street
3 George Street
4 Princes Street
5 St. John's &
   St. Cuthbert's
   Churches
6 Charlotte Square
7 Queen Street
8 Stockbridge
9 Dundas Street
10 Glass & Thompson
11 Broughton Street
12 Top of Leith Walk
13 Calton Hill
14 North Bridge
15 St. Andrew Square
16 Scott Monument
17 East Princes
   Street Gardens
18

Cross Princes Street to the statue of Guthrie and turn right (west), continuing to:

5 St. John's & St. Cuthbert's Churches

Episcopalians are Scottish (and American) Anglicans, and at the end of West Princes Street Gardens is St. John's Church, a Gothic house of Episcopal worship completed in 1818. Behind it is St. Cuthbert's Parish Church, which you enter from Lothian Road. Here, at the base of Castle Rock, a medieval church was apparently established in the 12th century. This one, dating to the 1890s, was at least the third to be constructed on the site. The churchyard offers plenty of handsome monuments and has the graves of painter Alexander Nasmyth and writer (as well as noted opium eater) Thomas De Quincey. In St. Cuthbert's vestibule is a memorial to John Napier of Merchiston, who invented logarithms. During the day, you can walk via a rear gate into West Princes Street Gardens.

But our stroll returns to Princes Street, crossing it, turning left (west), going a short distance, and then turning right (north) on Hope Street to:

6 Charlotte Square

This was the final piece of the original New Town development designed by the preeminent Georgian-era architect Robert Adam in 1791 just before his death. A circular park was expanded into an octagon in 1873, with a statue of Prince Albert added. On the west side, with the aforementioned green copper dome, is West Register House, which was originally built as St. George's Church in 1814. It is worth detouring behind the building to see the charming and unlikely half-timber, red-roofed house on Randolph Place by architect T. Duncan Rhind. On the north side of Charlotte Square is Bute House, the official residence of the Scottish First Minister, and the National Trust tourist attraction, Georgian House (p. 97).

From the northeast corner of the square, go north one short block to North Charlotte Street, turning right at Albyn Place, which then quickly becomes:

7 Queen Street

This northernmost street of the original New Town has the greatest amount of original buildings. Like Princes Street, town houses were built on only one side of what is today a very busy boulevard, with the private Queen Street Gardens running the length of the opposite side. At the eastern end is the Scottish National Portrait Gallery, in a smart red sandstone palace designed by R. Rowand Anderson in the 1880s. Nearby, north of the park on Heriot Row, Robert Louis Stevenson lived as a young man.

Turn left (north) on Wemyss Place, and continue on down the hill using Gloucester Lane and Gloucester Street to Bakers Place and:

8 Stockbridge

Stockbridge, a charming village within the city along a bend in the Water of Leith, was something of a hippie enclave in the 1960s and 1970s. But today's property prices ensure that it is primarily home to the well-heeled. Its name comes from the Stock Bridge, which crosses the Water of Leith. Across it, Deanhaugh Street serves as the local main street. St. Stephen Street has a variety of places to shop and eat.

Leave Stockbridge via St. Stephen Street to St. Vincent Street, turning left (east) on Cumberland Street, and proceeding to:

9 Dundas Street

Having passed Playfair's St. Stephen's church, you are now in the heart of the Northern New Town. Separated from the capital's first New Town by Queen Street Gardens, it was planned in the first years of the 19th century by Robert Reid and William Sibbald. The architecture remains uniform. At the bottom of Dundas Street, which has several art and antique shops, is Canonmills—originally the site of a milling settlement for the Abbey of Holyroodhouse.

Go up the hill of Dundas Street and stop by at:

10 Glass & Thompson ☕

This is a classic, upmarket cafe that feels part and parcel of Edinburgh's rather posh New Town. Local ingredients and Continental goods are combined on platters of cheese, seafood, cold meats, and salad. The cake selection is renowned. Open from 8am to late afternoon (2 Dundas St.; ✆ 0131/557-0909).

You can call it a day if you're tired and return to Princes Street by following Dundas Street through Queen Street Gardens (after which the road becomes Hanover St.).

Or, if you're still willing, carry on by turning left (east) on Abercromby Place, which (after crossing Dublin St.) becomes Albany Street, continuing to:

11 Broughton Street

This is one of the key places for nightlife in Edinburgh today, with traditional pubs, stylish bars, and some restaurants. At the bottom of the street at the roundabout is the former Bellevue Reformed Baptist Church (and before that, Catholic Apostolic), which the local community has actively tried to preserve, mainly for the sake of some colorful neo-Florentine interior murals by artist Phoebe Traquair (1852–1936). At the top of the street is Picardy Place, named after a small village that was established here in 1730 for immigrant silk weavers from France.

Cross Broughton Street to Forth Street, turning right on Union Street to Baxter's Place and the:

12 Top of Leith Walk

If you were to continue north on Leith Walk you would end up fairly soon at the port of Leith (See "Walking Tour 4: Leith," p. 121). At the top of Leith Walk is the Playhouse theater, designed by a Glaswegian architect for films and dramatic productions in the late 1920s (p. 136). They no longer screen films at the Playhouse, but the glass Omni Centre just up the road has a multiplex cinema.

Having crossed Leith Walk, continue up the hill past the Omni Centre and further to Waterloo Place, turning left to reach:

13 Calton Hill

The first comparison of Edinburgh to Athens apparently was made in the mid-1700s, and given the city's key role in the Scottish Enlightenment, the nickname "Athens of the North" stuck. But the city only made vain attempts to match the splendor of the Greek Acropolis, ending up with the National Monument, a never finished facsimile of the Parthenon on Calton Hill (p. 100). Nearby is the towering Nelson Monument, resembling an inverted telescope, whose ball drops every afternoon. Robert Louis Stevenson reckoned the views from Calton Hill were the best as you can see both the castle and Arthur's Seat. On its southern flank, facing Old Town, is the monumental Royal High School, a key Greek Revival building by Thomas Hamilton completed in 1829. Back along Waterloo Place is the Old Calton Burying Ground and its Emancipation Monument and statue of Abe Lincoln to honor Scottish-American Civil War soldiers. The cemetery also features Robert Adam's 1777 David Hume Monument.

Follow Waterloo Place west toward Princes Street and:

14 North Bridge

North Bridge offers another superb vantage point for looking toward the castle. Curiously, this span, like most of Edinburgh's many bridges, doesn't cross water. Instead they link hills. The first North Bridge took some 9 years to complete in the 1760s, a first step toward creating New Town. This broad span was designed in 1894.

Cross Princes Street, taking West Register Street (to the left of Wellington's statue), following the lane and stop by the:

15 Cafe Royal ☕

An oyster bar and restaurant at the Cafe Royal (17 West Register St.; ✆ 0131/556-4124) has traded continuously since 1863. It retains a good deal of Victorian splendor. The restaurant closes after lunch and reopens for dinner, but the Circle Bar is open throughout the day. Some highlights of the room are the tile pictures of notable inventors. See p. 78 for a full review.

Continue west on West Register Street to:

16 St. Andrew Square

Named for the patron saint of Scotland, this square is the eastern bookend to George Street. Compared to Charlotte Square at the avenue's other terminus, the surrounding architecture doesn't offer as much Georgian character. Up the column in the middle of the gated garden, some 38m (125 ft.) or more above, is Lord Melville, aka Henry Dundas, who was a leading politician in the late 18th and early 19th centuries.

From the southwest corner of the square, walk south on St. David Street, crossing Princes Street to the:

17 Scott Monument

Eminent Victorian art and architecture critic John Ruskin hated this monument to Scotland's greatest novelist, describing it as a church spire plunked on the ground. Never mind, the neo-Gothic structure (p. 96) remains one of the city's most notable landmarks. The design was by George Meikle Kemp, who, apparently, was third in the 1836 competition but somehow got the commission after the committee requested more drawings. It was meant to stand in Charlotte Square. The statue of Scott (with his trusty deerhound Maida) was hewn from a 30-ton block of marble by John Steell. From here you have good views up to Calton Hill's monuments.

Adjacent is:

18 East Princes Street Gardens

It took many years to completely drain the old Nor' Loch, and the park that now fills the valley was begun in 1830. The designs had to be altered in the wake of the construction of the railway lines into Waverley Station. The panoramic view of Old Town rising to Ramsay Garden and the Castle are memorable. West on the other side of the Mound, where this stroll began, is West Princes Street Gardens, with a band shell, fountain, carousel ride, and paths that scale Castle Rock.

WALKING TOUR 4: LEITH

START:	**Foot of Leith Walk.**
FINISH:	**Newkirk Shopping Mall.**
TIME:	**About 1 hour.**
BEST TIME:	**Daytime.**
WORST TIME:	**Late at night.**

Edinburgh's port was established at a natural harbor, formed where the Water of Leith feeds into the sea at the broad Firth of Forth. Briefly, Leith was Scotland's de facto capital during the interim rule of Mary of Guise. Her daughter, Mary, Queen of Scots landed famously at the town in 1561. Almost a century later, Oliver Cromwell built a fort at the port, later used by Highlanders trying in vain to reinstate the Stuart line of kings. Leith was long an independent burgh, only incorporated into Edinburgh in the 20th century. Today it is a diverse area and something of a foodie paradise, with three restaurants considered among the best in Britain.

From the statue of Queen Victoria, walk north on Constitution Street, turning right (east) at Links Lane, which leads to:

1 Leith Links

Older than Bruntsfield Links in Edinburgh's Southside, Leith Links is, by some accounts, the birthplace of golf. A version of the sport was possibly first played here in the 1400s. King Charles I apparently got in a round or two in the early 1640s. In 1744, the first rules of the game were laid down at Leith Links by the Honourable Company of Edinburgh Golfers. It was then a 5-hole course. Today it's just a public park, but running adjacent to John's Place you might just make out the first hole's fairway.

Go north down the west side of the park, turning left (west) on Queen Charlotte Street, and return to:

2 Constitution Street

At the intersection of Queen Charlotte and Constitution streets is Leith Town Hall. Originally constructed as the Leith Sheriff Court in 1828, adjoining property was incorporated later when the town became a parliamentary burgh. To the left, looking south down the street, is the fittingly named St. Mary Star of the Sea Catholic church as well as the modern Port of Leith Housing Association building.

Go right (north) on Constitution Street and continue to:

3 Bernard Street

Bernard Street has been termed, architecturally speaking, Leith's "most formal space." At the east end is a statue of Robert Burns and the Leith Assembly Rooms, which include the original merchant's meeting place built in the 1780s. The Burns Monument was erected in 1898, and the buildings from here west to the Water of Leith are Georgian and 19th-century commercial buildings, such as the former Leith Bank.

Go left from Constitution Street and walk west on Bernard Street, turning left on Carpet Lane (marked by tiles in the pavement) to:

4 Lamb's House

Carpet Lane soon becomes Water Street, facing a handsome, harled (lime, and gravel or sand wall covering), red-roofed building with an odd window built into the corner of the facade. This is Lamb's House: A 17th-century merchant's home and a masterpiece of its type, with crow-stepped gables and corbels. It has been restored repeatedly and new private owners promise more maintenance work.

At Burgess Street, turn right to:

5 The Shore

Leith's first main street, running along the river to the Firth of Forth, the road known as The Shore is now home to Michelin-star-winning Restaurant Martin Wishart (p. 83) and a clutch of bars with outdoor seating. At Bernard Street, the King's Wark is a pub within a restored 18th-century building. The original King's Wark was believed to be a palace and arsenal that James VI had rebuilt and given over to tavern-keeper Bernard Lindsay.

Cross Bernard Street and follow the Shore north and drop by:

6 The Shore Bar & Restaurant 🍵

(3/4 The Shore; ✆ 0131/553-5080) feels as if it has been sitting here and receiving seafarers for years. In fact, it opened in the 1980s, but it remains the best unpretentious pub in Leith. Food—primarily fi—is served at the bar or in the adjoining dining room. See p. 84 for a full review.

Return to the bridge, turn right crossing it to Commercial Street and the:

7 Customs House & Dock Place

Designed by Robert Reid in 1810, the Customs House has strong fluted columns. Nearby is the original entrance to the Old East Dock established by John Rennie at the start of the 19th century and the modern Commercial Quay development, which features another Michelin-star-holding restaurant, The Kitchin (p. 83). This area also skirts the walls of the citadel built for Cromwell, with fragments apparently still part of Dock Street.

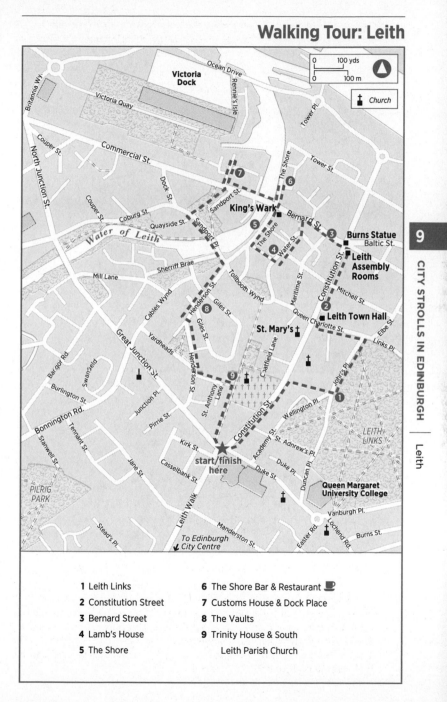

1 Leith Links
2 Constitution Street
3 Bernard Street
4 Lamb's House
5 The Shore
6 The Shore Bar & Restaurant ☕
7 Customs House & Dock Place
8 The Vaults
9 Trinity House & South Leith Parish Church

Cross Commercial Street to Sandport Street, going left on Sandport Place crossing the Water of Leith to the top of the Shore, turning right on Henderson Street to:

8 The Vaults

Having passed the modern new apartments that are changing Leith's character, this handsome and broad stone warehouse dates to 1682. The vaulted passage and cellar underneath may be 100 years older. Leith is where bottles and bottles of French wine were shipped. A link to that history is maintained by the Vintners Rooms restaurant and wine tastings that are held there. The Scotch Malt Whisky Society is located on the second floor. Just up the street on this tour is yet another Michelin-star restaurant, the Plumed Horse (p. 84).

Continue up Henderson Street, turning left at St. Anthony Place, passing the back of the Lidl supermarket to the Kirkgate and:

9 Trinity House & South Leith Parish Church

Trinity House is an early-19th-century survivor amid the urban renewal and tall apartment buildings of the 20th century. Owned by Historic Scotland, it is open to group tours by reservation. Across from it, a church has been standing since about 1480, the one now standing here was built in 1848. A plaque in the kirkyard details the intervening history. Almost back to the foot of Leith Walk (and the beginning of this perambulation), go through the Newkirkgate Shopping Mall, a mid-1960s' development that now feels quite outdated.

Continue north through the mall and you're back where you started at the intersection of streets and the statue of Queen Victoria.

Several buses go up Leith Walk to the city center.

EDINBURGH SHOPPING

Edinburgh may not have the shopping status of Glasgow, a city with a large appetite for the latest styles, but the Scottish capital does have a well-rounded selection of newfangled boutiques, souvenir shops, and traditional department stores, such as the classic Jenners. With the addition a few years ago of the fashionista's favorite, Harvey Nichols, Edinburgh is certainly starting to challenge its more trend-conscious counterpart to the west.

New Town's **Princes Street** is a primary shopping artery, with leading department stores, such as Marks & Spencer, major bookshops, and plenty of tourist tat. For the posher shops, such as Cruise or Laura Ashley, **George Street** tops the lot. For tourists, Old Town's **Royal Mile** is the place to find Scottish souvenirs, whether you're looking for tartan or whisky. If you're from a country outside the EU, take along your passport when you go shopping in case you make a purchase that entitles you to a **VAT (value-added tax)** refund.

THE SHOPPING SCENE

Edinburgh used to be the poorer relation to Glasgow when it came to shopping, particularly in the realm of fashion and boutique clothing. Less distance separates them now, though, as Edinburgh's style credentials are on the up. For visitors from abroad, prices in the U.K. may seem high. But after a few years when the pound was strong relative to the U.S. dollar and the euro, the currency has fallen in strength.

Best Buys

Although you may find a bargain at the tourist-oriented shops along the Royal Mile, the more unique gifts are to be found at the shops in the city's various national galleries or in the Museum of Scotland. See chapter 8, "Exploring Edinburgh," for addresses and phone numbers of galleries and museums.

Edinburgh Shopping

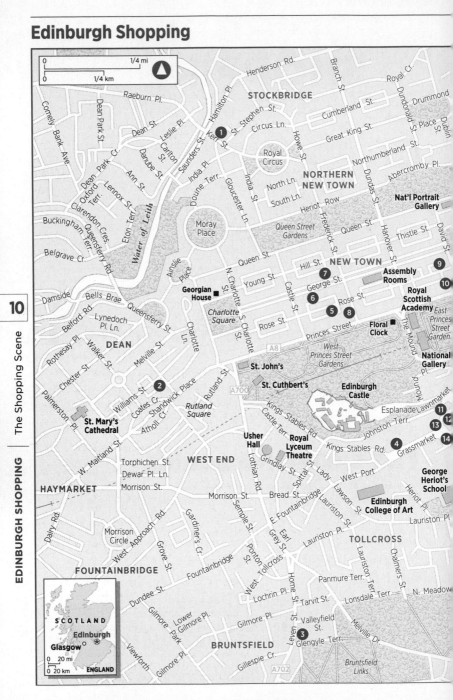

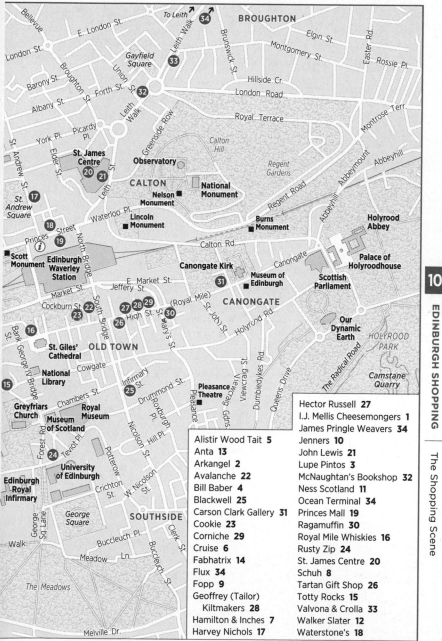

Alistir Wood Tait **5**
Anta **13**
Arkangel **2**
Avalanche **22**
Bill Baber **4**
Blackwell **25**
Carson Clark Gallery **31**
Cookie **23**
Corniche **29**
Cruise **6**
Fabhatrix **14**
Flux **34**
Fopp **9**
Geoffrey (Tailor)
    Kiltmakers **28**
Hamilton & Inches **7**
Harvey Nichols **17**

Hector Russell **27**
I.J. Mellis Cheesemongers **1**
James Pringle Weavers **34**
Jenners **10**
John Lewis **21**
Lupe Pintos **3**
McNaughtan's Bookshop **32**
Ness Scotland **11**
Ocean Terminal **34**
Princes Mall **19**
Ragamuffin **30**
Royal Mile Whiskies **16**
Rusty Zip **24**
St. James Centre **20**
Schuh **8**
Tartan Gift Shop **26**
Totty Rocks **15**
Valvona & Crolla **33**
Walker Slater **12**
Waterstone's **18**

Shopping Complexes

Ocean Terminal Although it was designed by the Conran group, which gave the world Habitat, this is ultimately just another modern indoor mall. Debenhams, French Connection, Gap, and others have set out their stalls at this retail cathedral, which gets a lot of footfall from tourists because the royal yacht *Britannia* is moored nearby. Open till 8pm Monday to Friday. Ocean Drive, Leith. ℂ **0131-555-8888.** www.ocean terminal.com.

Princes Mall There's something for everyone—except a leading department store—at this tri-level mall next to Waverley Station and beneath the city's main tourist information center. There are about 80 shops selling fashions, accessories, gifts, books, jewelry, and beauty products; and a food court with typical fast-food outlets. Princes St. ℂ **0131/557-3759.** www.princesmall-edinburgh.co.uk.

St. James Centre Slightly more upmarket than the Princes Mall, this shopping center is anchored by the John Lewis department store, along with Dorothy Perkins, River Island, and Topshop. There are frequent discussions over whether the rather monstrous-looking mall should be torn down and replaced with something more architecturally attractive. Leith St. (at east end of Princes St.). ℂ **0131/557-0050.** www.stjames shopping.com.

SHOPPING A TO Z

Shopping hours in central Edinburgh are generally from 9 or 10am to 6pm Monday through Wednesday and on Friday and Saturday. On Sunday, shops open at 11am or noon and close around 5pm. On Thursdays, many shops remain open until 7 or 8pm.

Antiques

Carson Clark Gallery ★★ If you're in the market for a bit of history and a unique souvenir, check out this specialist in antique maps and sea charts. One of my favorite works is an early 19th-century pictorial and graphic depiction of the origins, topography, and length of Scotland's major rivers. In addition to fascinating old maps, there are also smart reproductions of historic etchings and prints. 181 Can-ongate. ℂ **0131/556-4710.** www.carsonclarkgallery.co.uk.

Books

Blackwell Once an outlet of the venerable, homegrown James Thin bookshop (which alas went out of business), this store near the Royal Mile still has a knowledgeable staff and wide-ranging stock of fiction and nonfiction, despite being part of a large U.K. chain operation now. 53 South Bridge. ℂ **0131/622-8222.** www.blackwell.co.uk.

McNaughtan's Bookshop ★★ Trading since 1957, this is one of the city's best antiquarian and second-hand book purveyors. A key stop for book lovers. 3a Haddington Place (at the top of Leith Walk near Gayfield Sq.). ℂ **0131/556-5897.** www.mcnaughtansbookshop.com.

Waterstone's ★ The giant Barnes & Noble-like operation with plenty of stock and lots of soft seats is the most prominent book retailer in the city center. It has a good Scottish section on the ground floor and branches in New Town at the western end of Princes Street and on George Street. 128 Princes St. (near Waverley Station). ℂ **0131/226-2666.** www.waterstones.com.

Clothing

FASHION

Corniche One of the more sophisticated boutiques in Edinburgh; if it's the latest in Scottish fashion, expect to find it here. Racks have included "Anglomania kilts" created by Vivienne Westwood, as well as fashions by Gautier, Katherine Hamnett, and Yamamoto. Men's clothes are in the neighboring shop. 2 Jeffrey St. (near the Royal Mile). ✆ **0131/556-3707.** www.corniche.org.uk.

Cruise ★ Commonly associated with Glasgow, this home-grown fashion outlet began in Edinburgh's Old Town—not generally considered fertile ground for the avant-garde. There is still a shop off the Royal Mile, but this New Town outlet is the focus for haute couture. 94 George St. ✆ **0131/226-3524.** www.cruisefashion.co.uk.

MENSWEAR

Walker Slater ★ Well-made and contemporary (if understated) men's clothes, made of tweed or cotton, and dyed in rich, earthy hues, rule the roost here. It also carries Mackintosh overcoats and accessories for the smart gentleman about town. 20 Victoria St. (near George IV Bridge). ✆ **0131/220-2636.** www.walkerslater.com.

STANDOUT BOUTIQUES

Arkangel William Street in the city's affluent West End offers a host of boutique shops. This one specializes in labels apparently exclusive not only to the Scottish capital but to all of Scotland. U.K. clothes designers include Clara Collins. 4 William St., West End. ✆ **0131/226-4466.** www.arkangelfashion.co.uk.

Cookie As would be expected on Cockburn Street, this funky women's clothing shop has t-shirts from the likes of Ruby Walk and Sugarhill. Bargains compared with similar stock elsewhere. 29 Cockburn St. ✆ **0131/622-7260.**

Totty Rocks Established by two former students from the Edinburgh School of Art who went on to work in design in London, Milan, and Hong Kong, this shop features its own label line of contemporary clothing for women. The stock includes other labels (and some serious prices, too) such as Bebaroque hosiery. 40 Victoria St. ✆ **0131/226-3232.** www.tottyrocks.com.

VINTAGE

Rusty Zip Smaller sister outlet to Armstrong's in the Grassmarket (80 Grassmarket ✆ 0131/220-5557), this vintage clothing outlet still packs a lot in, whether retro fashion or party accessories such as feather boas or image-rearranging wigs. 14 Teviot Place ✆ **0131/226-4634.** www.armstrongsvintage.co.uk.

Department Stores

Harvey Nichols ★ Opened in 2002, the advent of Harvey Nics in Edinburgh was highly celebrated but a tad slow to catch on. Perhaps traditional shoppers were not quite prepared for floors of expensive labels and designers such as Jimmy Choo or Alexander McQueen. But they've since learned. 30-34 St. Andrew's Sq. ✆ **0131/524-8388.** www.harveynichols.com.

Jenners ★ Opened in 1838, this shop's neo-Gothic facade is almost as much of a landmark as the Scott Monument just across Princes Street. The food hall offers a wide array of gift-oriented Scottish products, including heather honey, Dundee marmalade, and a vast selection of shortbreads. 48 Princes St. ⓒ **0870/607-2841.** www. houseoffraser.co.uk.

John Lewis The largest department store in Scotland, this branch of John Lewis is many people's first choice when it comes to shopping for clothes, appliances, furniture, toys, and more. St. James Centre (near Picardy Place at the top of Leith Walk). ⓒ **0131/556-9121.** www.johnlewis.com.

Food & Wine

I.J. Mellis Cheesemongers ★★ This shop sells award-winning British and Irish cheeses, and the staff really know their stuff. There are other similar shops in Old Town on Victoria Street (convenient to the Royal Mile), as well as on Morningside Road on the Southside. Bakers Place (Kerr St.). ⓒ **0131/225-6566.** www.mellischeese. co.uk.

Lupe Pintos ★ A compact shop in the Tollcross neighborhood, chock full of Mexican food stuffs from fresh tortillas to bottles of hot sauce and a unique tequila selection. It also stocks a good supply of North American goods, as well as some exotic treats from the Far East. 24 Leven St. (near the King's Theatre). ⓒ **0131/228-6241.** www. lupepintos.com.

Valvona & Crolla ★★ This Italian deli has an excellent reputation across the U.K., thanks to a wonderful range of European cheeses and Italian cured meats, fresh fruit and vegetables (often flown in from the Milan market), plus superb wines and baked goods—from rolls to real sourdough loaves. 19 Elm Row (Leith Walk). ⓒ **0131/556-6066.** www.valvonacrolla.co.uk.

Gifts

Flux ★ This little shop in the heart of Leith offers a nice collection of Scottish crafts, ethically conscious gifts, and an excellent card collection. Flux is the ideal antidote to the typical tartan tat found in so many gift shops. 55 Bernard St. ⓒ **0131/554-4075.** www.get2flux.co.uk.

Ness Scotland On the Royal Mile, Ness is not a twee woolen shop. It has two outlets filled with knitwear, skirts, T-shirts, and whimsical accessories, scoured from areas around the country from the Orkney Islands to the Borders. You'll find hand-loomed cardigans and tasteful scarves, amid much more. In addition to the outlet near the castle, there is another on the High Street. 336 Lawnmarket. ⓒ **0131/225-8155.** www.nessbypost.com.

Tartan Gift Shop Tartan Gift Shop has a chart indicating the place of origin (in Scotland) of family names, accompanied by a bewildering array of hunt and dress tartans for men and women, sold by the yard. There's also a line of lamb's wool and cashmere sweaters and all the accessories. 54 High St. ⓒ **0131/558-3187.**

Hats

Fabhatrix ★ Not just any hat shop, this place has a variety of modern millinery wonders and some classic chapeaus, too. There are hundreds of handmade felt hats and caps, many practical as well as attractive, and some downright frivolous but extremely fun. Keep your head warm, and your whole body will stay warm. Given the occasionally gusty weather in Edinburgh, that's a saying worth keeping in mind. 13 Cowgatehead, Grassmarket. ✆ **0131/225-9222.** www.fabhatrix.com.

Jewelry

Alistir Wood Tait   This jewelry store has a reputation for Scottish gems and precious metal such as agates, Scottish gold, garnets, and sapphires. Victorian collections include "Scottish Pebble" brooches, while contemporary designs include Celtic bangles and Cairngorm handmade pins. 116A Rose St. ✆ **0131/225-4105.** www.alistirtaitgem. co.uk.

Hamilton & Inches ★   Since 1866, the prestigious Hamilton & Inches has sold gold and silver jewelry, porcelain and silver, and gift items. The company workshop is located above the shop, producing limited-production pieces or custom-made jewelry. The watch selection is second only to Bond Street, London. 87 George St. ✆ **0131/225-4898.** www.hamiltonandinches.com.

Kilts & Tartans

Anta ★   Some of the most stylish tartans, especially cool minikilts and silk *earasaids* (oversize scarves) for women, are found at Anta. Woolen blankets and throws are woven from Shetland sheep wool. Crocket's Land, 91-93 West Bow. ✆ **0131/225-4616.** www.anta.co.uk.

Geoffrey (Tailor) Kiltmakers   Past customers have included Sean Connery, Charlton Heston, Dr. Ruth Westheimer, members of Scotland's rugby team, and Mel Gibson (who apparently favors the "Hunting Buchanan" tartan). It stocks 200 of Scotland's best-known clan patterns and is revolutionizing the kilt by creating so called "21st century kilts" in different patterns such as pinstripe. 57-59 High St. ✆ **0131/557-0256.** www.geoffreykilts.co.uk.

Hector Russell   Bespoke clothes made from tartan can be ordered from this well-known Highland-based kiltmaker, with a shop on the Royal Mile and Princes Street. 137-141 High St. ✆ **0131/558-1254.** www.hector-russell.com.

James Pringle Weavers   The Leith mills produce a large variety of wool items, including cashmere sweaters, tartan and tweed ties, travel rugs, tweed hats, and tam-o'-shanters caps. In addition, it boasts a clan ancestry center with a database containing more than 50,000 family names. There's an outlet on the Royal Mile, as well. 70-74 Bangor Rd., Leith. ✆ **0131/553-5161.**

Knits & Woolens

Bill Baber   This workshop turns out adaptations of traditional Scottish patterns for both men and women. Expect to find traditional knits spiced up with strands of Caribbean-inspired turquoise or aqua; rugged-looking sweaters suitable for treks through the moors; and dressy tailored jackets for women. 66 Grassmarket. ✆ **0131/225-3249.** www.billbaber.com.

Ragamuffin   The staff here sells what is termed "wearable art," created by some 150 designers from all over the U.K. The apparel here is unique. Well, nearly: Ragamuffin also has a shop way up north on the Isle of Skye. 276 Canongate, The Royal Mile. ✆ **0131/557-6007.** www.ragamuffinonline.co.uk.

10

Music

Avalanche ★ A bunch of harmless goth kids often hang out in front of the branch of this excellent indie music CD shop where the steep steps of the Fleshmarket Close meet Cockburn Street. It's best for new releases of Scottish and U.K. bands and second-hand CDs. Another shop is on West Nicolson Street. 63 Cockburn St. (near the Royal Mile). (✆) **0131/225-3939.** www.avalancherecords.co.uk.

Fopp Discount DVDs; rock, pop, jazz, and dance CDs; books; and more are found in Fopp's Rose Street branch. Open until 9pm. 7-15 Rose St. (✆) **0131/220-0310.** www.foppreturns.com.

Shoes

Schuh Schuh (pronounced "shoe") has the latest in footwear, including some yellow, red, and blue plaid boots made famous by a local rugby team. Expect fierce, funky finds as well as name brands. 6 Frederick St. (✆) **0131/220-0290.** www.schuh.co.uk.

Tartans

See "Kilts & Tartans," above.

Whisky

Royal Mile Whiskies ★★ The stock at this rather small shop on the Royal Mile is huge: Some 1,000 different Scotch and other nation's whiskies are available. Prices range from around £20 to £900. Staff know their stuff, so tell them what you prefer (smoky, peaty, sweet, or whatever) and they'll find a bottle to please you. 379 High St. (✆) **0131/622-6255.** www.royalmilewhiskies.com.

EDINBURGH AFTER DARK

E very summer, the Scottish capital becomes the cultural capital of Europe—and the envy of every other tourist board in the U.K.—when it hosts the **Edinburgh Festival,** which encompasses the **Fringe, International Festival, Book Festival,** and **Jazz Festival**. All totaled, they bring in thousands upon thousands of visitors to see hundreds upon hundreds of acts—in comedy, dance, drama, music, and more. In August, the Scottish capital becomes a proverbial "city that never sleeps."

While the yearly Festival (www.edinburghfestivals.co.uk) is no doubt the highlight of the year, Edinburgh offers a good selection of after-dark entertainment and activities year-round: from cinema, clubs, and pubs, to theater, opera, and the ballet.

The West End is the cradle of theater and music, with the legendary and innovative **Traverse Theatre,** as well as the **Royal Lyceum Theatre** and, for concerts, the classic and acoustically excellent **Usher Hall.** Nearby, the **Filmhouse** offers the best in independent and art-house cinema. Other venues for drama include the **Playhouse** and **Festival** theaters. The folk scene centers on a couple of pubs—**Sandy Bell's** and the **Royal Oak.** Two of the most active areas for bars and pubs are the **Grassmarket** in Old Town and **Broughton Street** in New Town, although the university precincts on the south side of the city are lively, as are the pubs on the waterfront in the port of **Leith.**

For a complete rundown of what is happening in Edinburgh, pick up a copy of *The List,* a biweekly magazine available at all major newsstands and bookshops. Or visit its website, www.list.co.uk. It previews, reviews, and gives the full details of arts events here—and in Glasgow.

Edinburgh After Dark

The Abbotsford **6**
All Bar One **4**
The Bailie Bar **1**
The Beehive Inn **11**
Black Bo's **33**
Blue Moon Cafe **23**
Bongo Club **32**
Bow Bar **10**
Cabaret Voltaire **34**
Cafe Royal Circle Bar **30**
Cameo **17**
C. C. Bloom's **25**
Cineworld **20**
Corn Exchange **19**
Deacon Brodie's Tavern **8**
Edinburgh Festival
  Theatre **37**
Edinburgh Playhouse **26**
Filmhouse **16**
Guildford Arms **31**
HMV Picturehouse **15**
The Jazz Bar **35**
Jongleurs Comedy Club **29**
Kings Theatre **18**
The Liquid Room **9**
Opal Lounge **3**
The Outhouse **27**
Planet Out **24**
Po Na Na **2**
The Pond Bar **21**
Queen's Hall **39**
Ross Theatre **7**
Royal Lyceum Theatre **12**
The Royal Oak **36**
Sandy Bell's **38**
The Shore **22**
The Stand **5**
Traverse Theatre **13**
Usher Hall **14**
Vue Edinburgh **28**

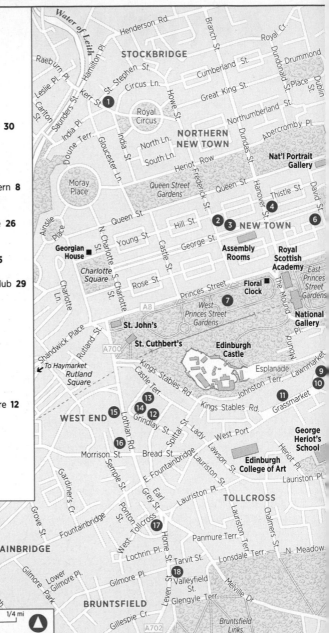

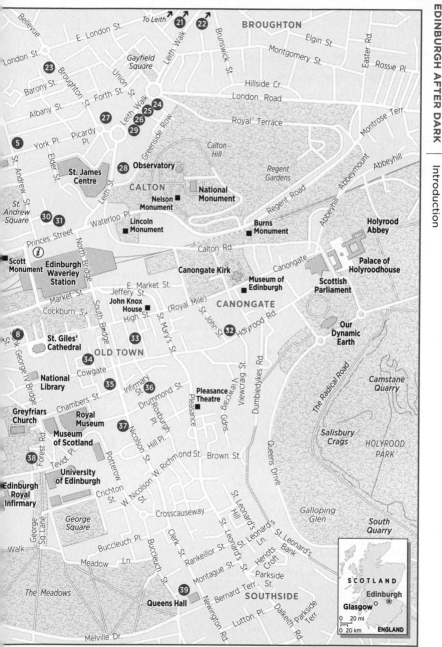

To Leith 21 22

BROUGHTON

E. London St.
Bellevue
Elgin St.
Brunswick St.
Montgomery St.
Easter Rd.
Rossie Pl.
Gayfield Square
London St.
Broughton St.
Barony St.
23
Hillside Cr.
London Road
Forth St.
Albany St.
Royal Terrace
Leith Walk
27 24
25
26
29
York Pl.
Picardy Pl.
5
Elder St.
St. Andrew Square
Calton Hill
Regent Gardens
Montrose Terr.
Abbeyhill
St. James Centre
28 Observatory
CALTON
Nelson Monument
National Monument
Abbeyhill
Holyrood Abbey
30 31
Waterloo Pl.
Lincoln Monument
Regent Road
Burns Monument
Abbeyhill
Princes Street
Calton Rd.
Scott Monument
Edinburgh Waverley Station
North Bridge
Canongate Kirk
Canongate
Palace of Holyroodhouse
Market St.
E. Market St.
Jeffery St.
Museum of Edinburgh
Scottish Parliament
Cockburn St.
South Bridge
John Knox House
High St.
(Royal Mile)
CANONGATE
Holyrood Rd.
8
St. Giles' Cathedral
33
St. Mary's St.
St. John St.
32
Our Dynamic Earth
Bank St.
George IV Bridge
OLD TOWN
34
Cowgate
National Library
35
Infirmary St.
36
Drummond St.
Pleasance Theatre
Viewcraig St.
Viewcraig Gdns.
Dumbiedykes Rd.
The Radical Road
Camstane Quarry
Greyfriars Church
Chambers St.
Royal Museum
37
Roxburgh Pl.
Pleasance
Salisbury Crags
HOLYROOD PARK
Forrest Rd.
Museum of Scotland
38
Teviot Pl.
Potterow
Nicolson St.
Hill Pl.
W. Richmond St.
Brown St.
Queens Drive
University of Edinburgh
Crichton St.
W. Nicolson St.
Edinburgh Royal Infirmary
Crosscauseway
George Sq. Lane
George Square
Galloping Glen
South Quarry
Walk
Buccleuch Pl.
Clerk St.
Buccleuch St.
Rankeillor St.
St. Leonard's Hill
St. Leonard's St.
St. Leonard's Ln.
St. Leonard's Bank
St. Leonard's
Meadow Ln.
The Meadows
Montague St.
Heriots Croft
Parkside St.
SOUTHSIDE
39
Queens Hall
Newington Rd.
Bernard Terr.
Lutton Pl.
Dalkeith Rd.
Parkside Terr.
Melville Dr.

SCOTLAND
Edinburgh
Glasgow
0   20 mi
0   20 km
ENGLAND

THE PERFORMING ARTS

The following venues are organized on the basis of the primary forms of performance—drama, opera, ballet, and such—that they host. But obviously, a stage that offers Shakespeare one week might be the home of Handel on another.

Classical Music, Ballet, & Opera

Edinburgh Festival Theatre   This 1,900-seat theater was formerly the Art Deco Empire, which dated to the 1920s. After extensive renovations in 1994, it reopened in time for the Edinburgh Festival (hence the name). Located on the south side of the city center, about a 10-minute walk from the Royal Mile and near the University of Edinburgh Old Campus, it has performances by Scotland's national opera and ballet, as well as touring companies and orchestras. 13–29 Nicolson St. ✆ **0131/529-6000** for the box office, or 0131/662-1112 for administration. www.eft.co.uk. Tickets £6–£45. Bus: 5, 7, 8, or 29.

Concert Halls

Queen's Hall   About a mile or so south of the Royal Mile, the Queen's Hall dates to the 1820s and began life as the Hope Park Chapel, but was altered in the 1970s (coinciding with Queen Elizabeth's silver jubilee) to accommodate concerts. Primarily a venue for classical works, it is particularly busy during Edinburgh's Jazz and International festivals. Occasionally it also hosts high-brow and brainy rock acts, such as Nils Lofgren and Joan Armatrading. Clerk St. ✆ **0131/668-2019.** www.thequeens hall.net. Bus: 5, 7, 8, or 29.

Ross Theatre   The city council-managed stage toward the western end of Princes Street Gardens, with the castle as dramatic backdrop, is open during the summer for outdoor concerts and sometimes Scottish country-dancing dos, usually in the long, languid evenings. For Hogmanay, this is the premier stage for leading pop and rock acts. West Princes St. Gardens. ✆ **0131/220-4351.** www.edinburgh.gov.uk. Bus: 3, 4, or 25.

Usher Hall ★★   Built in the 1890s, thanks to the bequest of distiller Andrew Usher, this Beaux Arts building is Edinburgh's equivalent of Carnegie Hall. During the International Festival, the horseshoe-shaped auditorium hosts such orchestras as the London Philharmonic. But it is not only a venue for classical music, with top touring jazz, world music, and pop acts also playing here through the year. 71 Lothian Rd. ✆ **0131/228-1155.** www.usherhall.co.uk. Bus: 1, 10, 15, or 34.

Theater

Edinburgh Playhouse   Located at the top of Leith Walk, this venue is best known for hosting popular plays or musicals and other mainstream acts when they come to town, whether *Miss Saigon* or *Lord of the Dance.* Formerly a cinema, it is, apparently, the largest theater of its type in Great Britain with more than 3,000 seats. 18–22 Greenside Place. ✆ **0131/524-3333.** www.edinburgh-playhouse.co.uk. Tickets £8–£35. Bus: 5 or 22.

Kings Theatre   This 1,300-seat Edwardian venue, with a domed ceiling and Glasgow-style stained-glass doors and red-stone frontage, is more than 100 years old. Located on the edge of Tollcross, southwest of the castle, it offers a wide repertoire, including traveling West End plays, productions by the National Theatre of Scotland, ballet, and opera. During December and January, it is the premier theater for popular pantomime productions in Edinburgh. 2 Leven St. ✆ **0131/529-6000.** www.eft. co.uk. Tickets £5–£25. Bus: 11, 15, or 17.

Royal Lyceum Theatre ★   No doubt, the Lyceum (built 1883) has a most enviable reputation, with presentations that range from the most famous works of Shakespeare to new Scottish scribes. The Lyceum is also the leading theater production company in the city, often hiring the best Scottish actors such as Brian Cox, Billy (*Lord of the Rings*) Boyd, and Siobhan Redmond—when they are not preoccupied with Hollywood scripts, that is. Grindlay St. ✆ **0131/248-4848** for the box office, or 0131/238-4800 for general inquiries. www.lyceum.org. Tickets £8–£30. Bus: 1, 10, 15, or 34.

Traverse Theatre ★★   Around the corner from the Royal Lyceum, the Traverse is something of a local legend. Beginning in the 1960s as an experimental theater company that doubled as a bohemian social club, it still produces some of Scotland's best contemporary drama—as well as premiering work by the best of the country's young playwrights. The Traverse bar is the place to find some of the hippest dramatists and actors hanging out (as well as their courtiers in tow). 10 Cambridge St. ✆ **0131/228-1404.** www.traverse.co.uk. Tickets £5–£16. Bus: 1, 10, 15, or 34.

THE CLUB & MUSIC SCENE
Comedy

Jongleurs Comedy Club   A corporate-owned entity from down south, with more than a dozen venues across the U.K., Jongleurs came to Scotland a few years back, pulling in its own cadre of house funny men (and women) as well as some touring comedians from overseas. Omni Centre, Greenside Place (top of Leith Walk). ✆ **0870/787-0707.** www.jongleurs.com. Tickets £5–£20. Bus: 7 or 22.

The Stand ★★   The Stand, just down the hill from St. Andrew Square, is Edinburgh's premier, purpose-built comedy venue. Big acts are reserved for weekends, while local talents try their jokes and tales during the week. Given the importance today of the Edinburgh Festival Fringe's comedy lineup, where good shows can launch a career, the stand-up comedian is, umm, taken very seriously in the Scottish capital. On Sunday you can combine laughs with brunch. 5 York Place. ✆ **0131/558-7272.** www.thestand.co.uk. Tickets £1.50–£10. Bus: 8 or 17.

Folk

Although internationally touring folkies—performers such as Americans Gillian Welsh or Nanci Griffith are big in Scotland—usually get booked into one of the music halls, the day-to-day folk scene in Edinburgh takes place in unassuming public houses. *Ceilidhs*—gatherings for music, stories, and especially Scottish country dancing—are hosted at places such as the **Assembly Rooms** on George Street in New Town (✆ **0131/220-4349**).

The Royal Oak   The Royal Oak, with ground floor and basement bars, is a key venue for live Scottish folk music. On most Sundays from 8:30pm, various guests play at the "Wee Folk Club." Open most nights until 2am (4am during the Festival), this pub, where Old Town meets the Southside, is just a few minutes' walk from the Royal Mile. 1 Infirmary St. ✆ **0131/557-2976.** www.royal-oak-folk.com. Tickets from £3 Sun. Bus: 3, 5, 8, or 29.

Sandy Bell's Live folk or traditional music is played here virtually every night from about 9pm and all day Saturday and Sunday. This small and unassuming pub near the Museum of Scotland is a landmark for Scottish and Gaelic culture. 25 Forrest Rd. © **0131/225-2751.** Bus: 2 or 42.

Rock, Pop & Jazz

Usher Hall (p. 136) hosts some major rock and pop acts. Although not listed below, **Murrayfield Stadium,** the Scottish national rugby stadium, hosts the biggest of international acts—such as Oasis or rock dinosaurs like the Rolling Stones.

Corn Exchange About 3.6km (2 miles) from the city center, this venue was meant to compete with the likes of Glasgow's Barrowland ballroom. No comparison, really, but it is a good medium- to small-size hall (3,000 capacity) to see rock and pop performers, such as Radiohead and Travis, and acts with more cultlike followings, such as Amy MacDonald, the Streets, and Interpol. 11 New Market Rd. © **0131/477-3500.** www.ece.uk.com. Bus: 35. Suburban train: Slateford.

HMV Picturehouse The building here has had a few incarnations as a nightclub over the years, but now it seems well established as a place for gigs by the likes of Dizzee Rascal, Little Boots, or Seth Lakeman. Club nights occupy the space when there's no live music. 31 Lothian Rd. © **0131/221-2280.** www.edinburgh-picturehouse.co.uk. Bus: 1, 22, 30, or 34.

The Jazz Bar ★ This basement bar is owned by a jazz drummer, who occasionally sits in with performers (a few of them internationally renowned). The only purpose-built space dedicated to jazz in the city. 1A Chambers St. © **0131/220-4298.** www.thejazzbar.co.uk. Cover £3–£10. Bus: 3, 5, 8, or 29.

The Liquid Room With space for less than 1,000, this is probably Edinburgh's best centrally located venue for seeing the sweat off the brows of live acts. Both local bands and international acts, such as the Lee "Scratch" Perry, play here. Shut due to a fire in 2009, its reopening was anticipated in 2010. 9c Victoria St. © **0131/225-2564.** www.liquidroom.com. Bus: 35.

Dance Clubs

Clubbing is not quite as huge as it was in the 1980s and 1990s, but it probably draws more people than the folk, jazz, and classical music scene combined. Here is just a sampling of what is typically going on in the clubs around Edinburgh.

Bongo Club Offering a varied music policy throughout the week—funk, dub, and experimental—this venue has more reasonably priced drinks than many. Open daily 10pm to 3am. Moray House, 37 Holyrood Rd. © **0131/558-7604.** www.thebongoclub.co.uk. Cover up to £8. Bus: 35.

Cabaret Voltaire This club's mix includes house, indie, and techno—plus live bands 10 times a month. 36-38 Blair St. © **0131/220-6176.** www.thecabaretvoltaire.com. Cover up to £12. Bus: 35.

Po Na Na This is the Edinburgh branch of a successful chain of clubs in Britain. The theme is a Moroccan casbah with decor to match, thanks to wall mosaics, brass lanterns, and artifacts shipped in from Marrakech. The dance mix is hip-hop and funk or disco and sounds of the '80s. 43B Frederick St. © **0131/226-2224.** www.ponana.co.uk. Daily til 3am. Cover up to £5. Bus: 80.

✎ Late-Night Eats

Okay, it's Friday or Saturday night. You've been out to a play, the pub, or dance club, and now you're utterly starving, but it's somewhere between 11pm and 1am. You're not exactly sure—food will help. The area around Edinburgh University is your best bet. Try

Negociants (45 Lothian St.; ✆ 0131/225-6313). It serves food until midnight during the week and until 2am on Friday and Saturday nights (that is, Sat and Sun mornings). My favorite late night eatery is **Kebab Mahal** (see p. 82).

PUBS & BARS

New Town

The Abbotsford ★ Abbotsford bartenders have been pouring pints since around 1900. The gaslight era is virtually still alive here, thanks to the preservation of dark paneling and ornate plaster ceiling. The ales on tap change about once a week, and there is a good selection of single malt whiskies, too. Drinks are served Monday through Saturday from 11am to 11pm. Platters of food are dispensed from the bar Monday through Saturday from noon to 3pm and in an upstairs dining space from 5:30 to 10pm, too. Located near the eastern end of Rose Street, just a short walk from Waverley Station. 3-5 Rose St. ✆ 0131/225-5276. www.theabbotsford.co.uk. Bus: 3, 28, or 45.

All Bar One In general, I resist the urge to promote characterless chain pubs, but the All Bar One operation is a well-run business, and the smart bar in New Town (a second outlet is off Lothian Rd.) offers a good selection of wines by the glass. Drinks are served Monday to Thursday from 11:30am to midnight; Friday and Saturday from 11:30am to 1am; and Sunday from 12:30 to 11pm. Food is available daily from opening until 9 or 10pm. 29 George St. ✆ 0131/226-9971. www.allbarone.co.uk. Bus: 24, 28, or 45.

The Bailie Bar ★ The Bailie is at the heart of the village of Stockbridge and feels as if it could substitute as a public meeting hall for the neighborhood. Often there is plenty of banter between the regulars and the staff, and the music never drowns out the conversation. A bit of live folk is often played on Sunday evenings, and a dining room is adjacent to the main lounge with its island bar. Drinks are served Monday to Thursday from 11am to midnight, Friday and Saturday from 11am to 1am, and Sunday from 12:30 to 11pm. Food is available Monday to Thursday 11am to 10pm, Friday and Saturday from 11am to 5pm, and Sunday from 12:30 to 5pm. 2 St. Stephen St., Stockbridge. ✆ 0131/225-4673. www.bailiebar.co.uk. Bus: 24, 29, or 42.

Cafe Royal Circle Bar ★★ Another well-preserved, Victorian-era pub, the Cafe Royal was nearly demolished in the late 1960s. Thankfully, it was spared. Spacious booths create a comfortable and historically stylish place to drink. Hours for the bar are Monday through Wednesday from 11am to 11pm, Thursday from 11am to midnight, Friday and Saturday from 11am to 1am, and Sunday from 12:30 to 11pm. Above-average food from the same kitchen as the neighboring oyster bar/restaurant is served daily until about 1pm. 19 W. Register St. ✆ 0131/556-1884. www.caferoyal.org.uk. Bus: 8 or 17.

Guildford Arms ★   This pub dates to the late 19th century, designed by architect Robert Macfarlane Cameron. Through the revolving door, you will find seven arched windows with etched glass and exquisite cornices. It's reasonably large and bustling, with a good deal of character. Separate dining facilities are upstairs on the mezzanine. The pub is open Monday through Thursday from 11am to 11pm, Friday and Saturday from 11am to midnight, and Sunday from 12:30 to 11pm. 1-5 W. Register St. ✆ **0131/556-4312.** www.guildfordarms.com. Bus: 8 or 17.

Opal Lounge   If you want a sense of the so-called "style bar," then this is an excellent example of the genre. After opening in 2001, the Opal became the haunt of Prince William, when the handsome heir to the British throne attended St. Andrew's University. Several other stylish bars have popped up in its wake on trendy George Street, such as **Candy Bar** (113 George St.) and **Tigerlily** (125 George St.). The Opal draws a predominantly young, well-dressed, and affluent crowd, combining a long list of cocktails with a Tardis-like underground space that has several compartments around a central room, which eventually becomes the dance floor. Drinks are served from noon to 3am daily. 51a George St. ✆ **0131/226-2275.** www.opallounge.co.uk. Bus: 24, 29, or 42.

The Outhouse   Broughton Street has a mix of traditional places and modern bars, keeping it one of the more lively streets to drink in Edinburgh. It's a good district for a compact pub crawl. The Outhouse, just down a lane off the street, is one of the more contemporary outfits. During good spells of weather, a beer garden out back offers an excellent open-air retreat, and some outdoor heaters help take the chill off the night. Drinks are served daily from 11am to 1am. 12a Broughton St. Lane. ✆ **0131/557-6688.** www.outhouse-edinburgh.co.uk. Bus: 8 or 17.

Old Town

The Beehive Inn   The Grassmarket is chock-a-block with bars, and this one's hardly exceptional. But there is plenty of space in three different rooms and, unlike so many others along the drag, the Beehive isn't trying to flog any dubious historic connections to a gullible public. The literary pub tours of Edinburgh begin at the Beehive, which has a beer garden in the back as well as street-side seating. Drinks are served Monday to Sunday from 11am to 1am. Food is served until about 9pm. 18-20 Grassmarket. ✆ **0131/225-7171.** Bus: 2.

Black Bo's ★   A stone's throw from the Royal Mile, this small bar is slightly unconventional: It is neither a traditional pub nor a particularly stylish place. Many will find its dark walls and mix-and-match furniture downright plain, but it does have a certain unforced hipness. And, due to its proximity to Blackfriars Street's hostels, Black Bo's often has chatty groups of college-age foreigners enjoying a pint or two. DJs play from Wednesday to Saturday; next door the owners run a vegetarian restaurant—although no food is served in the bar itself. Drinks are served daily from 5pm to 1am. 57 Blackfriars St. ✆ **0131/557-6136.** www.black-bos.com. Bus: 35.

Bow Bar ★   Below Edinburgh Castle near the Grassmarket, the compact Bow Bar is a rather classic Edinburgh pub, which appears little changed by time or tampered with by foolish trends. Surprise: It's only a few more than a dozen years old. Never mind. The pub looks the part and features some eight cask-conditioned ales, which change regularly. The gantry stocks some 140 single malt whiskies, as well. Food is limited to meat pies and toasties, served until they run out. Big groups will have trouble squeezing in and aren't generally encouraged. Open Monday through Saturday from noon to 11:30pm and Sunday from 12:30 to 11pm. 80 W. Bow. ℭ **0131/226-7667.** Bus: 2 or 35.

Deacon Brodie's Tavern   Deacon Brodie's Tavern is primarily populated by tourists wandering the Royal Mile and by members of the legal fraternity who come over from the nearby courts. Its name, of course, perpetuates the memory of William Brodie, good citizen by day and nasty robber by night: A real-life character of the 18th century, he may have inspired Robert Louis Stevenson's fictional Dr. Jekyll and Mr. Hyde. Certainly this traditionally styled pub would like you to think so. Open Sunday through Thursday from 10am to midnight and Friday and Saturday from 10am to 1am. Food is served in the bar from 10am to 10pm; in the restaurant upstairs, from noon to 10pm. 435 Lawnmarket. ℭ **0131/225-6531.** Bus: 23, 27, 28, 35, 41, or 42.

Leith

The Pond Bar ★   A bit off the beaten track in Leith, between Salamander Street and the Edinburgh Dock, the Pond has been described as a transplanted Amsterdam brown bar. The name refers to the "water feature" in the ramshackle patio area at the rear. The decor of the pub inside is eclectic—as if furnished by the purchase of a lot in a blind auction. The highlights of the drinks selection are draft and bottled European lagers. No food is served. Drinks available Monday to Thursday 4pm to 1am, Friday and Saturday 2pm to 1am, and Sunday 12:30pm to 1am. 2-4 Bath Rd. ℭ **0131/467-3825.** Bus: 12.

The Shore ★★   Looking out on the oldest docks in Leith, this pub fits seamlessly into Leith's seaside port ambience, without resorting to a lot of the usual decorations of cork and netting. The place is small, but on nice days they put a few seats out front to soak in the afternoon sun. On 3 nights of the week, you'll find live folk and jazz music. Drinks are served Monday to Saturday from 11am to midnight and Sunday from 12:30pm to midnight. Food is served both in the bar and the adjoining dining room (p. 84). Monday to Friday from noon to 2:30pm and 6:30 to 10pm; Saturday and Sunday from 12:30 to 3pm and 6:30 to 10pm. 3-4 The Shore. ℭ **0131/553-5080.** www.theshore.biz. Bus: 16 or 36.

GAY & LESBIAN EDINBURGH

The heart of the gay community is an area near **Calton Hill,** incorporating the top of **Leith Walk** around the Playhouse Theatre and **Broughton Street,** though it is hardly a distinct gay quarter to rival districts such as Manhattan's Christopher Street or San Francisco's Castro.

Blue Moon Cafe   The Blue Moon is an icon of gay cultural life on Broughton Street: It is allegedly the oldest gay cafe in Britain. It is also linked to the Lesbian, Gay, and Bisexual Centre, which is a useful resource for residents and visitors alike. It is open daily from 10am to 10pm. 36 Broughton St. ℭ **0131/556-2788.** www.bluemooncafe.co.uk. Bus: 8 or 17.

C. C. Bloom's   This club, named after Bette Midler's character in *Beaches,* is one of Edinburgh's long-running and enduringly popular gay night spots. Given that there is no cover charge, the place is usually packed. The dancing is to a wide range of music. Open Monday to Sunday from 10:30pm to 3am. Next door, the glitzy **Habana,** 22 Greenside Place (℃ **0131/556-4349**), is a bar that draws a mixed gay crowd daily from noon to 1am. 23-24 Greenside Place. ℃ **0131/556-9331.** Bus: 7 or 22.

Planet Out This bright bar draws a mixed crowd, attracting a slightly higher percentage of lesbians than most of its nearby competitors. It manages to combine a good, relaxed daytime trade—sort of a neighborhood pub—with a heady, hedonistic, late-night vibe after dark with popular local DJs such as Trendy Wendy offering preclub warm-ups. Open Monday through Friday from 4pm to 1am and Saturday and Sunday from 2pm to 1am. 6 Baxters Place. ℃ **0131/524-0061.** Bus: 7 or 22.

CINEMA

Cameo ★ Periodically threatened with closure for the sake of urban redevelopment, the Cameo is a classic venue showing a mix of Hollywood and indie cinema for local and visiting cineastes. 38 Home St. ℃ **0871/704-2052.** www.picturehouses.co.uk. Tickets £7-£9. Bus: 10, 11, 16, or 24.

Cineworld Part of a chain of multiplex cinemas across the U.K., Cineworld combines big releases and Hollywood blockbusters with art house and some foreign movies, as well. Fountainpark, 130 Dundee St. ℃ **0871/200-2000.** www.cineworld.co.uk. Tickets £6. Bus: 34 or 38.

Filmhouse ★★ The capital's most important cinema, the Filmhouse is the focus of the Edinburgh Film Festival—one of the oldest annual film festivals in the world. The movies here are foreign and art house, classic and experimental, documentary and shorts. Plus, the Filmhouse hosts discussions and lectures with directors. The cafe-bar stays open late and serves drinks and light meals. This is a must stop for any visiting film buff. 88 Lothian Rd. ℃ **0131/228-2688.** www.filmhousecinema.com. Tickets £1.50-£6.50. Bus: 10, 22, or 30.

Vue Edinburgh The big glass-fronted multiplex below Calton Hill at the roundabout near the top of Leith Walk is the most recent addition to the cinema scene, quickly changing its original name of Warner Village to Vue. It offers first-run, big commercial releases. Omni Centre, Greenside Place. ℃ **0871/224-0240.** www.myvue.com. Tickets £6. Bus: 7 or 22.

SIDE TRIPS FROM EDINBURGH

Although Edinburgh has a full complement of attractions and plenty of activities, there are also a number of worthwhile side trips you can take into the surrounding countryside. Whether in the Lothians (which surround Edinburgh), south toward the Borders, or north across the Firth of Forth into the Kingdom of Fife—many attractions are no more than an hour's drive from the city.

The nearest sights are in West and East Lothian, on either side of the city. The highlights here include the impressive ruins of **Linlithgow Palace,** a favorite of the Stuart dynasty; 18th-century **Hopetoun House;** and the seaside town of **North Berwick,** with its views of Bass Rock. Further afield, south in the Borders, the historic **Jedburgh** and **Melrose Abbeys** and **Abbotsford,** Sir Walter Scott's majestic home, beckon day-trippers.

But one of the most popular excursions from the Scottish capital is north to Fife and places such as the golfing mecca of **St. Andrews,** with the oldest university in Scotland.

LINLITHGOW & WEST LOTHIAN

In 1542, Mary, Queen of Scots was born in Linlithgow, some 26km (16 miles) west of Edinburgh. Trains frequently depart from Edinburgh's Waverley Station, and the 20-minute ride to the ancient royal burgh costs about £8.50 for a standard return (round-trip) ticket, though you have to complete your trip on the same day. If you're driving from Edinburgh, follow the M8 toward Glasgow, taking exit 2 onto the M9, following the signs to Linlithgow.

Hopetoun House ★ On the margins of South Queensferry, amid beautifully landscaped grounds, Hopetoun House is one of Scotland's best examples of palatial Georgian architecture, with original design work by Sir William Bruce in 1699. It was enlarged as well as substantially redesigned in 1721 by no less than three members of the architecturally talented Adam family. You can wander through splendid reception rooms filled with period furniture, Renaissance paintings, statuary, and other artworks. The views of the Firth of Forth are panoramic from the rooftop observation deck. After touring the house, visitors should try to take in the grounds, some 60 hectares (150 acres) of parkland with a walled garden, shorefront trail, and deer park. Last entry is 1 hour before closing.

South Queensferry. © **0131/331-2451.** www.hopetounhouse.com. Admission to house and grounds £8 adults, £7 seniors, £4.25 children, £22 family. MC, V. Easter weekend to last weekend in Sept daily 10:30am–5pm (groups by appointment year round). 3km (2 miles) from the Forth Rd. Bridge near South Queensferry, 16km (12 miles) from Edinburgh off A904.

Linlithgow Palace ★   In the 15th and 16th centuries, this was one of the favorite residences of Scotland's royal Stuarts. It was the first building to be called a palace in the country. Today, it is one of Scotland's most poignant ruins, but visitors can still get an idea of how grand the place once was. Most of the structure was built by King James I between 1425 and 1437. In 1513, Queen Margaret (part of the ruling Tudor family in England) waited in vain here for husband James IV to return from the ruinous battle of Flodden, where England's forces routed the Scots, killing the king and much of his court. When their son, James V (also born here) wed Mary of Guise, the palace fountain ran with wine. Their daughter, the now iconic Mary, Queen of Scots, was later the last Scottish monarch born here. More than 200 years later in 1746, a fire gutted the building when government troops, who were in pursuit of Bonnie Prince Charlie's army, were barracked in Linlithgow. Last admission is 45 minutes before closing.

Linlithgow. © **01506/842-896.** www.historic-scotland.gov.uk. Admission £5.20 adults, £4.20 seniors, £3.10 children. AE, MC, V. Apr–Sept daily 9:30am–5:30pm; Oct–Mar 9:30am–4:30pm.

Rosslyn Chapel ★   In no small part thanks to Dan Brown's blockbuster novel, *The Da Vinci Code,* and the Hollywood film, the elaborately carved Rosslyn Chapel is firmly on the trail of those who seek to retrace the historic and mythical path of the Knights Templar. The chapel was founded in 1446 by Sir William St. Clair and has been long noted for its architectural and design idiosyncrasies (though it doesn't have all of those mentioned in Brown's tome). While undergoing long-term restoration, the chapel remains open to the public. Guided tours can be arranged and last admission is 30 minutes before closing.

Off the A701 in the village of Roslin, about 10km (6 miles) south of central Edinburgh. © **0131/440-2159.** www.rosslynchapel.org.uk. Admission £7.50 adults, £6 seniors, £4 students in groups. AE, MC, V. Mon–Sat 9:30am–6pm; Sun noon–4:45pm. Closed Christmas and New Year.

St. Michael's Parish Church   Next to Linlithgow Palace stands the medieval kirk of St. Michael, site of worship for many a Scottish monarch after its consecration in 1242. The biggest pre-Reformation parish church in Scotland, it was mostly constructed in the 15th century. In St. Catherine's Aisle, just before the battle of Flodden, King James IV apparently saw an apparition warning him against fighting the English. Perhaps he should have listened. Despite being ravaged by the more zealous disciples of Protestant reformer John Knox (who chided followers for their "excesses") and transformed into a stable by Cromwell's forces, this remains one of Scotland's best

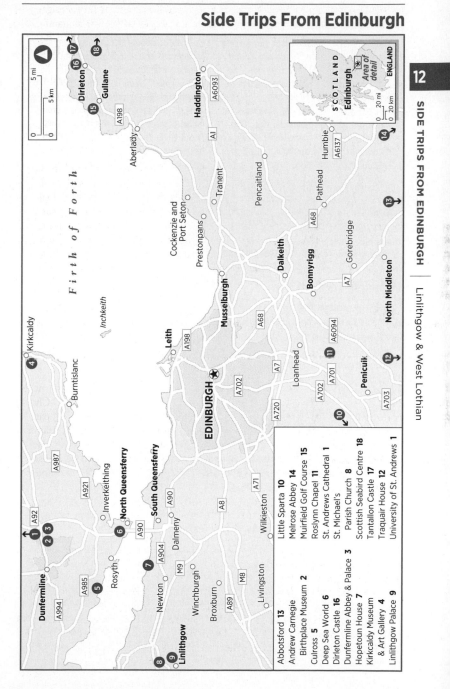

Abbotsford **13**
Andrew Carnegie
  Birthplace Museum **2**
Culross **5**
Deep Sea World **6**
Dirleton Castle **16**
Dunfermline Abbey & Palace **3**
Hopetoun House **7**
Kirkcaldy Museum
  & Art Gallery **4**
Linlithgow Palace **9**

Little Sparta **10**
Melrose Abbey **14**
Muirfield Golf Course **15**
Roslynn Chapel **11**
St. Andrews Cathedral **1**
St. Michael's
  Parish Church **8**
Scottish Seabird Centre **18**
Tantallon Castle **17**
Traquair House **12**
University of St. Andrews **1**

Spa Hotel Breaks

If you are looking for a bit of pampering out of town, head for **Dalhousie Castle** hotel, in Bonnyrigg. Here they have created "Aqueous," a hydro spa: It combines therapeutic treatments, Jacuzzi-like massage pool, Turkish bath, and room for mud cleansing, too. The "total experience" costs about £200. Dalhousie Castle is on the A7 south of Edinburgh. (c) **01875/820-153.**

www.dalhousiecastle.co.uk. Another recommended spa is that of the **Macdonald Marine Hotel & Spa** in North Berwick, East Lothian. There is an exercise pool, health and fitness program, and "thermal suite." The Spa Day rate (which includes facial, scalp massage, and more) costs about £170. The hotel is on Cromwell Rd., North Berwick. (c)**0844/879-9130.** www.macdonaldhotels.co.uk/marine.

examples of a parish church. While providing a dramatic focal point on the landscape, the aluminum spears projecting from the tower were added in the 1960s.

Adjacent to Linlithgow Palace, off the A706, on the south shore of Linlithgow Loch, 1km (½ mile) from Linlithgow railway station. (c) **01506/842-188.** www.stmichaelsparish.org.uk. Free admission. May-Sept daily 10:30am-4pm; Oct-Apr 10:30am-1pm (except during services, funerals, or weddings).

Where to Dine

The Boat House ★★ FISH/SEAFOOD   What a vista. This restaurant is down a few steps from the main street of South Queensferry, which means diners are closer to the sea and have views of the marvelous Forth rail and suspension road bridges. Typical dishes are innovative but not overcomplicated. They might include grilled herring or monkfish, roasted with rosemary, garlic, and olive oil.

22 High St., South Queensferry. (c) **0131/331-5429.** Reservations recommended. Fixed-price lunch £16; main courses £12-£18. MC, V. Mon-Sun noon-2:30pm and 5:30-10pm (8pm Sun).

Champany Inn ★ SCOTTISH   You'll find some of the best beef in Britain in this converted mill. The restaurant, a Michelin star holder since 2008, also serves oysters, salmon, and lobsters, but steaks are the main reason why people dine here. Meat is properly hung before butchering, which adds greatly to its flavor and texture. Next to the main dining room is the Chop House, offering somewhat less expensive cuts. The wine list—around 2,000 bins—has won an award for excellence from the magazine *Wine Spectator.* The inn also has some 16 handsomely furnished guest rooms.

Champany Corner. Take M9 until junction 3, then A904 until you reach the restaurant, 3km (2 miles) northeast of Linlithgow. (c) **01506/834-532.** www.champany.com. Reservations required. Fixed-price lunch £20; main courses £25-£50. AE, DC, MC, V. Mon-Fri 12:30-2pm; Mon-Sat 7-10pm. Main restaurant closed Sun.

Livingston's MODERN SCOTTISH/FRENCH   This restaurant down an alley off the main street of Linlithgow includes a conservatory that overlooks a tidy little garden. On a seasonally changing menu, Highland venison is a favorite dish. Seared scallops with black pudding may appear on the menu, or perhaps wild duck breast and duck leg confit. An elegant dessert selection has, in the past, included Mrs. Livingston's home-grown apples prepared three ways. Diners can wash it all down with a selection from the ample wine and whisky lists.

52 High St., Linlithgow. ℭ **01506/846-565.** www.livingstons-restaurant.co.uk. Reservations recommended. Fixed-price lunch £20, fixed-price dinner £38. MC, V. Tues–Sat noon–2pm and 6–9pm. Closed first 2 weeks in Jan, 1 week in June, and 1 week in Oct.

NORTH BERWICK & EAST LOTHIAN

The royal burgh of North Berwick (*bear*-ick, the "w" is silent) dates to the 14th century. But in more modern Victorian and Edwardian times, it served as an upmarket holiday resort, drawing visitors to its beaches, harbor, and golf courses where the Firth of Forth meets the North Sea. About 36km (21 miles) east of Edinburgh, the town is on a direct rail line from Edinburgh; the trip takes about 30 minutes. Standard one-way fare is about £6. Bus service from Edinburgh takes a little more than an hour. An all-day ticket to North Berwick and the region around it costs around £8. If you're driving, take the coastal road east from Leith, or use the A1 (marked THE SOUTH and DUNBAR) to the A198 (via Gullane) to North Berwick.

At the year-round **tourist office,** Quality St. (ℭ **01620/892-197**), you can get information on boat trips to offshore islands, including **Bass Rock,** a breeding ground inhabited by about 10,000 gannets, the second-largest colony in Scotland, as well as puffins and other birds. It's possible to see the rock from the harbor, but the viewing is even better at **Berwick Law,** a volcanic lookout point that rises up behind the town.

Dirleton Castle ★ Run by Historic Scotland, the castle dates to the 13th century, with surrounding gardens that are apparently just as ancient. It is reputed to have been completely sacked by Cromwell in 1650, but another story holds that the building was only partially destroyed by his army but was further torn down by a local family who desired a romantic ruin on their land. It is a rather grand garden feature. Highlights include the imposing gate house, vaulted arcades, and a 16th-century dovecot that resembles a beehive. The grounds include a herbaceous border that the *Guinness Book of Records* ranks as the longest in the world.

Dirleton, 5km (3 miles) west of North Berwick on the A198. ℭ **01620/850-330.** www.historic-scotland.gov.uk. Admission £4.70 adults, £3.80 seniors, £2.80 children. AE, MC, V. Apr–Sept daily 9:30am–5:30pm; Oct–Mar 9:30am–4:30pm.

Scottish Seabird Centre ☺ From this popular attraction situated on a craggy outcropping in North Berwick, you can watch all the bird action out on Bass Rock, whether gannets and puffins, as well as guillemots on the island of Fidra or colonies

---

Dirleton: Prettiest Village in Scotland?

Dirleton, midway between North Berwick and Gullane, has been cited as the prettiest village in Scotland. It is so picture-postcard perfect, it's hard to believe it's a real village at all—it appears almost to have been created for a movie set. But it is genuine. Because the main road bypasses the village, there is little traffic. Each cottage looks like it's waiting to be photographed, and the standards of home maintenance are undoubtedly very high.

of seals thanks to live video links. The Seabird Centre also has a cafe/bistro and activities geared to the family.

The Harbour, North Berwick. © **01620/890-202.** www.seabird.org. Admission £7.95 adults, £6 seniors, £4.50 children. MC, V. Apr–Sept daily 10am–6pm; Nov–Jan Mon–Fri 10am–4pm, Sat–Sun 10am–5:30pm; Oct, Feb–Mar Mon–Fri 10am–5pm, Sat–Sun 10am–5:30pm.

Tantallon Castle ★   After its construction in the 14th century on a bluff right above the sea, this became the stronghold of the powerful and somewhat trouble-making Douglas family—the Earls of Angus, who tended to side with England in their wars and disputes with Scotland in the 15th and 16th centuries. Both Stuart kings James IV and James V dispatched troops to Tantallon. Like most castles in the region, it endured a fair number of sieges, but the troops of Oliver Cromwell well and truly sacked it in the mid-1600s. Nevertheless, the ruins remain formidable, with a square five-story central tower.

Off the A198 (5km/3 miles east of North Berwick). © **01620/892-727.** www.historic-scotland.gov.uk. Admission £4.70 adults, £3.80 seniors, £2.80 children. Apr–Sept daily 9:30am–5:30pm; Oct–Mar Sat–Wed 9:30am–4:30pm.

Gullane & the Muirfield Golf Course

Lying 8km (5 miles) west of North Berwick, about 28km (16 miles) east of Edinburgh in East Lothian, the pleasant and attractive village of Gullane (pronounced "*gill*-in" by many, "*gull*-an" by others) is another resort with a fine beach and a famous golf course. On the edge of the village, **Gullane Hill** provides a nature reserve and bird sanctuary, where more than 100 species of birds have been spotted. Visitors cross a small wooden footbridge from the car park to enter the reserve. There's no rail service into Gullane, but the station at Drem is only about 4km (2½ miles) away; the train journey there from Edinburgh takes about 25 minutes. Buses for Gullane depart from the Edinburgh bus terminal near St. Andrew's Square (© **0800/232-323** for information). They take about an hour.

Dunbar: Birthplace of John Muir

Go to the wild places, and listen to what they have to say. Take time to look at the pattern of veins on a leaf, the perfect flight of a bird. Hear the music of the wind in the pines. Feel the life around you and in you.

—John Muir

The man who dedicated himself to protecting California's Yosemite Valley, founded the Sierra Club, and lobbied for establishing a U.S. national park system, was born April 21, 1838, in the humble harbor town of Dunbar about 15km (9 miles) southeast of North Berwick.

Pioneering conservationist John Muir left the country as a child and only recently have Scots begun to recognize, celebrate—and also capitalize on—Muir's international stature as an explorer and naturalist. Ironically, Scotland is well behind when it comes to establishing national parks of its own amid the frequently spectacular countryside. There are two: The Cairngorms and Loch Lomond (with the Trossachs). In Dunbar, you can visit Muir's birthplace (126 High St.; © **01368/865-899;** www.jmbt.org. uk), which now houses a museum.

GUIDED minitours FROM EDINBURGH

Sightseeing tours from Edinburgh can give tourists a taste of the often stunning countryside as they whisk visitors on 1-, 2-, and 3-day excursions, whether to Stirling and Loch Lomond (see chapter 20) or farther north to Glen Coe and the shores of Loch Ness. **Timberbush Tours** (555 Castlehill; ✆ **01312/266-066;** www. timberbush-tours.co.uk) use minibuses to take small groups to the Highlands. Prices for a 2-day tour range from around £65 in low season to £80 at the height of summer, and the prices only cover transportation and guide. **Heart of Scotland Tours** (37 Logie Green Rd.; ✆ **01315/588-855;** www.heartofscotlandtours.co.uk) offers 1-day minibus tours of different regions, such as Loch Lomond, the Borders, or Fife. They depart from Waterloo Place near Calton Hill at 8 or 9am, returning to Edinburgh between 6 and 8pm. Prices average about £35. More intrepid adventurers might want to consider a "hop-on, hop-off" hostel bus service offered by **MacBackpackers** (105 High St.; ✆ **01315/ 589-900;** www.macbackpackers.com). This bus does a circuit of Scotland stopping at Pitlochry, Inverness, Kyle of Lochalsh, Fort William, Oban, and Glasgow. The basic price is £75.

Muirfield Golf Course ★   Ranked among the world's greatest golf courses, Muirfield has hosted the Open Championship in Great Britain 15 times. This is the home of the Honourable Company of Edinburgh Golfers—the world's oldest club—which began at the five-hole Leith Links in Edinburgh and whose records date to 1744, when the first rules of golf were written. Developed on a boggy piece of low-lying land in 1891, Muirfield was originally a 16-hole course designed by the legendary Old Tom Morris. Visitors with certified handicaps are welcomed on Tuesdays and Thursdays. Greens fees are steep: Except in winter, expect to pay about £185 for a single round and £240 for two rounds in one day. Tee times go quickly, but there can be availability from mid-October to the end of March if you enquire in the summer.

Duncur Rd., Gullane. ✆ **01620/842-123.** Fax 01620/842-977. www.muirfield.org.uk. Visitor tee times 8:30–9:50am. From Edinburgh, take the A1 (marked The South and Dunbar) to the A198 and Gullane.

Where to Dine & Stay

Creel Restaurant MODERN SCOTTISH/SEAFOOD   A two-story stone building near the harbor in Dunbar is home to the Creel Restaurant. The casual bistro with modern decor emphasizes locally sourced produce whenever possible, including meat from a North Berwick butcher and cheese from nearby cheesemakers. Expect main courses in the evening such as lamb, chargrilled steak, and specials featuring fresh fish.

25 Lamer St., Dunbar. ✆ **01368/863-279.** www.creelrestaurant.co.uk. Reservations recommended. Fixed-price lunch £17.25; main courses £11–£15. MC, V. Thurs–Mon noon–2pm and 6:45–9pm.

La Potinière FRENCH   At this multi-award-winning restaurant, the three-course lunches and four-course dinners offer dishes that are mainly French-inspired, but with international flourishes. The menu is seasonal, and the produce is usually purchased locally, with everything freshly made on the premises.

Main St., Gullane. ☏ **01620/843-214.** www.la-potiniere.co.uk. Reservations recommended. Fixed-price lunch £22.50; fixed-price dinner £40. MC, V. Wed–Sun 12:30–1:30pm and 7–8:30pm.

The Open Arms   Just across the road from Dirleton Castle, this traditional stone-built hotel has some rooms that overlook the castle's romantic ruins, while others offer vistas of the town. It specializes in golfing packages, so links masters often stay here.

Main St. ☏ **01620/850-241.** www.openarmshotel.com. 12 units. £146–£164 double with breakfast. AE, MC, V. **Amenities:** Restaurant; bar; lounge.

THE BORDERS

The romantic ruins of Gothic abbeys in the **Borders** region stand as mute reminders of the battles that once raged between England and Scotland, as well as between Protestants and Catholics. For a long time, the "Border Country" was a no-man's land of plunder and destruction, lying south of the Moorfoot, Pentland, and Lammermuir hill ranges.

The Borders is also the land of Sir Walter Scott, master of romantic adventure, who topped the bestseller lists in the 19th century. Because of its abundant sheep-grazing land, the Borders is home of the cashmere sweater and the tweed suit. And plans to re-establish a railway line between Edinburgh and the Borders are moving forward, however slowly.

Melrose

Rich in history, the town of Melrose ★, about 60km (37 miles) southeast of Edinburgh, is one of the highlights of the region. It has one of the most beautiful ruined abbeys in the country, as well as nearby Abbotsford, home of Sir Walter Scott, which is about 3km (2 miles) west. Melrose is on the Southern Upland Way, a trail that snakes across lower Scotland from Portpatrick in the southwest to the North Sea. You can take a hike along the section that runs near Melrose—a delightful and scenic trek. Among sports fans in the U.K., the town is most famous for its annual "Rugby Sevens" tournament, which began in 1883.

Visitors may prefer to take the bus to Melrose from Edinburgh. Travel time is at least 90 minutes, departing twice an hour or so. Call ☏ **0870/608-2608** for information. If you're driving from Edinburgh, you can reach the town by going southeast along the A68 or the more winding A7, which runs past the town.

The tourist office is at Abbey House, Abbey Street (☏ **01896/822-555**). It's open Monday through Saturday from April to October.

Abbotsford ★   Sir Walter Scott's home from 1817 until death, this is the mansion that he built and like his novels it quotes from history, too. Designed in the Scots baronial style, it has an entrance that mimics the porch at Linlithgow palace and a door from Edinburgh's tolbooth. Scott was a very keen souvenir hunter, scouring the land for artifacts associated with the historical characters he rendered into fiction. Hence, Abbotsford contains many relics and mementos—whether Rob Roy's sporran or a sword given to the Duke of Montrose by Charles I. Especially popular is Scott's small study, with writing desk and chair, where he penned some of his most famous works. There are also extensive gardens and grounds to visit, plus the private chapel, added after Scott's death.

B6360, near Galashiels; 3km (2 miles) west of Melrose; just off the A6091. 🄯 **01896/752-043.** www. scottsabbotsford.co.uk. Admission £7 adults, £3.50 children, £18 families. MC, V. Mid-Mar–end of Oct, Mon–Sat 9:30am–5pm, Mid-Mar–May, Oct Sun 11:00am–4pm, June–Sept Sun 9:30am–5pm. Nov to mid-Mar group bookings only.

Little Sparta ★★ 🏠 Not highlighted by many guidebooks, this garden was devised by one of Scotland's most intriguing artists in the 20th and 21st centuries, the late Ian Hamilton Finlay, who died on March 27, 2006. It is a surprisingly lush plot of land, given the harsh terrain of the Pentland Hills all around it. Dotted throughout the garden are stone sculptures (many with Finlay's pithy sayings and poems) created in collaboration with master stonemasons and other artists. Little Sparta has been called the "only original garden" created in Great Britain since World War II. During the Edinburgh Festival, minibus transport from Edinburgh is usually provided.

Stonypath, near Dunsyre, off the A702; 32km (20 miles) southwest of Edinburgh. 🄯 **01899/810-252.** www.littlesparta.co.uk. Admission £10. Mid-June–end of Sept Wed, Fri, and Sun 2:30–5pm.

Melrose Abbey ★★ These lichen-covered ruins, among the most evocative in Europe, are all that's left of an ecclesiastical community established by Cistercian monks in the 12th century. The tall walls still standing today follow the lines of the original abbey, but they were largely constructed in the 15th century. The Gothic design moved Sir Walter Scott to write in the *Lay of the Last Minstrel,* "If thou would'st view fair Melrose aright, go visit in the pale moonlight." The author was also instrumental in ensuring that the decayed remains were preserved in the 19th century. You

SIR WALTER SCOTT: INVENTOR OF historical novels

It may be hard to imagine the fame that Walter Scott, novelist and poet, enjoyed as the best-selling author of his day. His works are no longer so widely read, but Scott (1771–1832) was thought to be a master storyteller and he is now regarded as one of the inventors of the historical novel. Before his Waverley series was published in 1814, no modern English author had spun such tales from actual events, examining the lives of individuals who played roles—large and small. He created lively characters and realistic pictures of Scottish life in works such as *The Heart of Midlothian.*

Born on August 14, 1771 into a Borders family that later settled in Edinburgh, Scott was permanently lame due to polio, which he contracted as a child. All his life he was troubled by ill health and later by ailing finances as well. He spent his latter years writing to clear enormous debts incurred when his publishing house and printers collapsed in bankruptcy.

Scott made Scotland and its scenery fashionable with the English, and he played a key role in bringing Hanoverian King George IV to Edinburgh in 1822. It had been decades since a British monarch had set foot in Scotland.

In 1831, heavily in debt and suffering from the effects of several strokes, Scott set out on a Mediterranean cruise to recuperate. He returned the following year to Abbotsford, where he died on September 21, 1832. Scott is buried at Dryburgh Abbey, sited in a loop of the Tweed River.

can still view its sandstone shell, filled with elongated windows and carved capitals, and the finely decorated masonry. It is believed that, per his wishes, the heart of Robert the Bruce is interred in the abbey.

Abbey St., Melrose. ✆ **01896/822-562.** www.historic-scotland.org.uk. £5.20 adults, £4.20 seniors, £3.10 children. AE, MC, V. Apr–Sept daily 9:30am–5:30pm; Oct–Mar daily 9:30am–4:30pm.

Traquair House ★   Little changed since the beginning of the 18th century and dating in part to the 12th century, Traquair House is among Scotland's most romantic mansions. The Stuarts of Traquair still live in the great mansion, making it, they say, the oldest continuously inhabited home in Scotland. One of the most poignant exhibits is in the King's Room: An ornately carved oak cradle, in which Mary, Queen of Scots rocked her infant son, who was to become James VI of Scotland and James I of England. Other treasures include embroideries, silver, manuscripts, and paintings. Of particular interest is the brewery, still producing very fine ales. On the grounds are craft workshops—such as wrought ironwork and woodturning—as well as a hedge maze and woodland walks. There are three rather sumptuous overnight rooms, too, at £180, including full breakfast.

Innerleithen; 47km (29 miles) south of Edinburgh. ✆ **01896/830-323.** www.traquair.co.uk. Admission to house and grounds £7.50 adults, £6.80 seniors, £4 children, £18 families. MC, V. April, May, and Sept daily noon–5pm; June–Aug daily 10:30am–5pm; Oct daily 11am–4pm; Nov Sat–Sun 11am–3pm. Closed Dec–Feb.

Where to Dine & Stay

Burt's Hotel SCOTTISH   Within walking distance of Melrose Abbey, this family-run inn was built in 1722. All guest rooms are well furnished and equipped with shower-only bathrooms. Alternative accommodations are offered across the street at the Townhouse Hotel. The restaurant menu offers main courses such as baked halibut with crab and pea risotto or pan-seared pheasant with butter bean purée. In addition to the more formal dining room, Burt's serves meals in the bistro/bar.

Market Sq., Melrose. ✆ **01896/822-285.** Fax 01896/822-870. www.burtshotel.co.uk. Reservations recommended. Fixed-price dinner £36; bistro main courses £9–£14. 20 units. £130 double with breakfast. AE, DC, MC, V. Free parking. **Amenities:** Restaurant; bar; babysitting; room service. *In room:* TV, hair dryer.

Chapters Bistro SCOTTISH/INTERNATIONAL   You only need to cross a footbridge over the River Tweed to reach this unassuming bistro near Melrose, run by Kevin and Nicki Winsland. The menu ranges from the house stroganoff and red snapper to scallops St. Jacques and venison with juniper berries.

Main St. (off the A6091), Gattonside by Melrose. ✆ **01896/823-217.** Main courses £10–£16. MC, V. Tues–Sat noon–2pm, 6:30–10pm.

FIFE

North of Edinburgh, the region of Fife still likes to call itself a "kingdom," a distinction dating to Pictish prehistoric times when Abernethy was Fife's capital. Some 14 of Scotland's 66 royal burghs lay in this rather self-contained shire on a broad peninsula between the Forth and Tay rivers. The highlight for golfers is St. Andrews, which many consider the most sacred spot of the sport. But the town, named after the country's patron saint, is also of ecclesiastic and scholarly importance. St.

Andrews is the site of Scotland's first university, founded in 1413. Closer to Edinburgh, Dunfermline was once the capital of Scotland, and its abbey witnessed the births of royalty and has the burial grounds for several, as well.

St. Andrews: Golf's Hallowed Ground

The medieval royal burgh of **St. Andrews** in northeast Fife, about 80km (50 miles) from Edinburgh, was once filled with monasteries and ancient buildings, but only a few ruins of its early history survive. Once a revered place of Christian pilgrimage, the historic town by the sea is now best known for golf, which has been played here at least as early as the 1600s, though some believe much earlier. Today, the rules of the sport are reviewed, revised, and clarified in St. Andrews by the Royal and

HITTING THE links

There are five 18-hole courses at St. Andrews (www.standrews.org.uk) and one course with only 9 holes for beginners and children, all owned by a trust and open to the public. They are:

1. **Old Course,** which is where the Open is frequently played and dates to the 15th century.
2. **New Course,** designed by Old Tom Morris in 1895.
3. **Jubilee Course,** opened in 1897 in honor of Queen Victoria.
4. **Eden Course,** opened in 1914.
5. **Strathyrum Course,** the least testing 18 holes, designed for those with high handicaps.
6. **Balgove,** the 9-hole course designed for beginners and hackers. No reservations, just turn up and play (or turn up and wait during busy times at weekends and holidays).

For the New Course, you should try to reserve your tee time at least 1 month in advance. To play Jubilee, Eden, or Strathyrum, tee times can be reserved 24 hours ahead (if you're lucky). The reservation office is at (*C*) **0133/446-6666.** Online bookings for the New Course, Jubilee, Eden, and Strathyrum can be made by logging on to www.linksnet.co.uk.

The Old Course, which hosted the Open in 2010, is a different kettle of fish:

First you need a handicap of 24 for men and 36 for women. You apply in writing 1 year in advance and, even then, there are no guarantees. There is a daily ballot or lottery, which gives out about 50% of the tee times for the following day's play. Apply in person or by telephone before 2pm on the day before play. By post, send applications to Reservations Office, Pilmour House, St. Andrews KY16 9SF, Scotland. Single golfers wishing to play the Old Course should contact the reservations department at reservations@standrews.org.uk.

Greens fees vary from course to course and depending on the time of year. Generally speaking, for the 18-hole courses expect to pay between £16 to £125. From November to March, it costs around £70 to play the Old Course, using mats that protect the fairways.

Facilities for golfers in St. Andrews are legion. Virtually every hotel in town provides assistance to golfers. The **Royal and Ancient Golf Club,** founded in 1754, remains more or less rigidly closed as a private-membership men's club, however. It does traditionally open the doors to the public on St. Andrews Day to view the trophy room. This usually falls on November 30.

Ancient Golf Club, while its Old Course is perhaps the most famous 18 holes in the world. Golfers consider this town to be hallowed ground.

There is no train station in St. Andrews, but there is a stop some 13km (8 miles) away at the town of Leuchars. The trip from Edinburgh takes about an hour; the fare is about £20 for a standard return (round-trip) ticket. Once at Leuchars, you can take a bus for the 10-minute ride to St. Andrews. The bus service from Edinburgh takes approximately 2 hours, and the same-day return fare is around £10. For information, call ✆ **0870/608-2608.** If you're driving from Edinburgh, head north across the Forth Road Bridge. Take the A921 to the junction with the A915 and continue northeast until you reach St. Andrews. Less scenic is the A92 north to the A914 via Cupar. The tourist information center is at 70 Market St. (✆ **01334/472-021**). It's open Monday to Saturday all year and on Sunday, too, during the high season.

St. Andrews Cathedral ★ Near the Celtic Church of Blessed Mary on the Rock, by the sea at the east end of town, St. Andrews Cathedral was once the largest church in Scotland. Founded in 1161, the Cathedral certified the town as the ecclesiastical capital of the country. But the ruins can only suggest its former beauty and importance. There's a collection of early Christian and medieval monuments, as well as artifacts discovered on the Cathedral site. Admission allows entry to nearby **St. Andrews Castle,** where the medieval clergy lived.

A91, off The Pends ✆ **01334/472-563.** www.historic-scotland.gov.uk. Admission cathedral and castle £7.20 adults, £5.80 seniors, £4.30 children. MC, V. Apr–Sept daily 9:30am–5:30pm; Oct–Mar daily 9:30am–4:30pm.

University of St. Andrews This is the oldest university in Scotland and the third oldest in Britain after Oxford and Cambridge. Of its famous students, the most recent graduate was Prince William, heir to the throne after his father, Charles, Prince of Wales. At term time, you can see packs of students in their characteristic red gowns. The university spreads throughout the town today, but the original site was centered in the districts just west of the Cathedral. The gate tower of St. Salvador College on North Street dates to the 15th century.

St. Andrews, Fife. ✆ **01334 476161.** www.st-andrews.ac.uk.

Dunfermline & Its Abbey

The ancient town of Dunfermline, 23km (14 miles) northwest of Edinburgh, was a place of royal residence as early as the 11th century. The last monarch to be born in Scotland, Charles I, came into the world at Dunfermline. However, when Scottish and English crowns were joined 3 years later in 1603, the royal court departed for London and the burgh's fortunes declined—a process aided by a fire in 1624. Linen

---

Historic Scotland Explorer Pass

You may have noticed that many of the attractions in this chapter are run by the Scottish Government's Historic Scotland organization. If you are planning to visit several of them in a few days, it's worth getting an "Explorer Pass." For 3 days entry, it costs £22 for an adult, £17 for a senior, and £12 for a child. A 3-day family pass is £44. For more information, go to www.historic-scotland.gov.uk.

Culross: Step Back in Time

Thanks largely to the National Trust for Scotland, this town near Dunfermline shows what a Scottish village in the 17th and 18th centuries was like. With its cobbled streets lined by stout cottages featuring crow-stepped gables, Culross ★★ may also have been the birthplace of St. Mungo, who went on to establish the Cathedral in Glasgow.

James IV made this port on the Firth of Forth a royal burgh in 1588. The National Trust runs a visitor center (✆ 01383/880-359; www.nts.org.uk) that is open daily noon to 5pm from Good Friday to the end of September, which provides access to the town's palace and other sites. Adult admission is £8.50.

manufacturing in the 18th and 19th centuries provided a boost. In America, its most famous product, however, is Andrew Carnegie, born in a weaver's cottage in 1835.

Dunfermline is on the "Fife Circle" train route from Edinburgh to the north, which means twice hourly connections to the Scottish capital on a 30-minute ride. By bus, the trip from Edinburgh takes about 40 minutes. If you're driving from Edinburgh, take the A90 west, cross the Forth Road Bridge, and follow the signs north to the center of Dunfermline.

Andrew Carnegie Birthplace Museum   In 1835, American industrialist and philanthropist Andrew Carnegie was born just down the hill from Dunfermline Abbey. This museum comprises the 18th-century cottage where he lived as a child and a memorial hall funded by his widow, Louise. Displays tell the story of the weaver's son, who emigrated to the United States and became one of the richest men in the world.

Moodie St., Dunfermline. ✆ 01383/723-638. www.carnegiebirthplace.com. Free admission. Mar–early Dec Mon–Sat 10am–5pm, Sun 2–5pm.

Dunfermline Abbey & Palace   This abbey was constructed on the site of a Celtic church and a priory church built under the auspices of Scotland's first Queen Margaret around 1070. Some 50 years later work began on a new priory, which is today part of the Romanesque "Medieval Nave." Abbey status was bestowed in 1150, and thereafter a string of Scottish royalty, beginning with David I, was buried at the abbey, including Robert the Bruce (except for his heart). The newest sections of the abbey church were built in 1818; the pulpit was placed over the tomb of – and a memorial to – the Bruce. The remains of the royal palace are adjacent to the abbey. Only the southwest wall remains of this once-regal edifice.

St. Margaret's St., off the M90. ✆ 01383/739-026. www.historic-scotland.gov.uk. Admission £3.70 adults, £3 seniors, £2.20 children. MC, V. Apr–Sept daily 9:30am–5:30pm; Oct–Mar daily 9:30am–4:30pm.

Kirkcaldy

Kirkcaldy Museum & Art Gallery ★   The art collection in the second-floor galleries here is among the single best gathering of works by Scottish artists. An entire room is devoted to the brightly hued still-life paintings and landscapes by "colourist" S. J. Peploe. There is more art by Hornel, Hunter, and Fergusson. Another highlight of the collection is a range of paintings by William McTaggart. In addition, you can compare the abstract beauty of, say, Joan Eardley's "Breaking Wave" to a portrait by Scotland's currently best-selling, if critically panned, contemporary painter, Jack Vettriano. This unassuming and humble attraction is arguably the best provincial art museum in Great Britain. What's more, all they request are donations from visitors.

War Memorial Gardens, next to the train station. ℂ **01592/412-860.** Free admission. Mon–Sat 10:30am–5pm; Sun 2–5pm.

North Queensferry

Deep Sea World ☺   In the early 1990s, a group of entrepreneurs sealed the edges of an abandoned rock quarry under the Forth Rail Bridge, filled it with sea water, and positioned a 112m (370-ft.) acrylic tunnel on the bottom. Stocked with a menagerie of creatures, this bit of artificial sea is Scotland's most comprehensive aquarium. Now, compared to what you'll find in cities such as Orlando, this may seem amateurish. But from the submerged tunnel, you view kelp forests; sandy flats favored by bottom-dwelling schools of stingray, turbot, and sole; and murky caves that shelter conger eels and small sharks. Curiously, the curvature of the tunnel's thick clear plastic makes everything seem about 30% smaller than it really is. For £155, you can also arrange a "shark dive," however, and see them full size.

Battery Quarry, North Queensferry. ℂ **01383/411-880.** www.deepseaworld.com. Admission £12 adults, £10.25 seniors, £8.25 children, £38.50 families. AE, MC, V. Mon–Fri 10am–5pm; Sat–Sun 10am–6pm.

Where to Dine & Stay

Keavil House Hotel   This tranquil country hotel in the Best Western chain is set on a dozen acres of forested land and gardens. The superior doubles are generous in size and well appointed. Master bedrooms contain four-poster beds. The hotel offers dining in its **Cardoon** restaurant.

Main St., Crossford. Take the A994, 3km (2 miles) west of Dunfermline; the hotel is off the main street at the west end of the village. ℂ **01383/736-258.** Fax 01383/621-600. www.keavilhouse.co.uk. 47 units. £120 double with full breakfast. AE, DC, MC, V. Free parking. **Amenities:** Restaurant; bar; babysitting; health club; room service. *In room:* TV, hair dryer.

Old Course Hotel   This aptly named hotel overlooks the 17th fairway—the infamous "Road Hole"—of St. Andrews Old Course (to which the inn has no formal connections). The rooms and facilities are world-class and have price tags to match. The eating options encompass the contemporary **Sands** seafood bar and restaurant and fine dining at the **Road Hole Grill,** where gentlemen are encouraged to wear jackets to dinner.

Old Station Rd., St. Andrews. ℂ **01334/474-371.** Fax 01334/477-668. www.oldcoursehotel.co.uk. 144 units. £220 double with full breakfast. Children 11 and under stay free in parent's room. AE, DC, MC, V. **Amenities:** Restaurant; bar; pool; pro shop; spa; Jacuzzi; steam rooms; salon; room service; massage; babysitting; laundry service. *In room:* TV, minibar, coffeemaker, hair dryer.

Ostlers Close ★ MODERN SCOTTISH   Fife has a host of good restaurants, and this charming one in a 17th-century building is among the best. Located in the town of Cupar, west of St. Andrews, Ostlers Close emphasizes fresh and local produce. The daily-changing menus can feature dishes such as seared Isle of Mull scallops, roast saddle of venison, or roast filet of Pittenweem cod.

25 Bonnygate, Cupar. © **01334/655-574.** www.ostlersclose.co.uk. Reservations recommended. Main courses £10–£20. AE, MC, V. Tues–Fri 7–9:30pm; Sat 12:15–1:30pm and 7–9:30pm. Closed 2 weeks mid-May.

Peat Inn ★★ MODERN SCOTTISH/FRENCH   The Peat Inn (which dates to 1760) came under new ownership in 2006. Luckily, it was taken over by Chef Geoffrey Smeddle, who earned a Michelin star in 2010. Meals highlight local, seasonal ingredients in dishes such as seared scallops with fennel purée, roast filet of beef with chanterelle mushrooms, or tayberry and elderflower tart. The Peat Inn, about 10km (6 miles) from St. Andrews, has eight overnight suites.

Near Lathones. © **01334/840-206.** Fax 01334/840-530. www.thepeatinn.co.uk. Reservations recommended. Fixed-price lunch £16, fixed-price dinner £32. Tues–Sat 12:30–1:30pm and 7–9pm. 8 units. £175 suite with continental breakfast. AE, MC, V. **Amenities:** Restaurant; bar; bike rental; limited room service. *In room:* TV.

The Seafood Restaurant FISH/SEAFOOD   This St. Andrew's restaurant is a second branch for owner Tim Butler and his business partner, chef Craig Millar, who began farther down the coast in St. Monans. Here, the location on the seafront is spectacular, and given the restaurant is essentially housed in a glass box, there is no missing the views. Dishes range from crab risotto to pan-seared scallops, with plenty of fancy accompaniments on the side.

The Scores, St. Andrews. © **01334/479-475.** www.theseafoodrestaurant.com. Fixed-price lunch £16, dinner £30. AE, MC, V. Daily noon–2:30pm and 6–10pm.

The Wee Restaurant MODERN SCOTTISH   As the name implies this is a small place (room for 34 diners in total) but it has an ever-growing reputation. Chef and owner Craig Wood has made his restaurant a spot worth heading for: whether for fresh seafood dishes or robust meals using local ingredients from the land.

17 Main Street, North Queensferry. © **01383/616-263.** www.theweerestaurant.co.uk. Main courses £16–£22. MC, V. Tues–Sat noon–2pm and 6:30–9pm; Sun noon–3pm.

GETTING TO KNOW GLASGOW

Glasgow is only about 74km (46 miles) west of Edinburgh, but the contrast between the two cities is significant. Glasgow (pronounced "*glaaz*-go" by natives) doesn't have the fairy-tale setting that Edinburgh does, but it compensates with a lively culture, metropolitan feel, and gregarious locals.

Glasgow's origins are ancient, making Edinburgh seem comparatively young. Archaeologists have uncovered evidence of Roman settlements. In the 6th century, St. Kentigern (or St. Mungo) is believed to have begun a monastery at the site of **Glasgow Cathedral,** a hillside along a *burn* (creek) that feeds into the River Clyde. The site was logical for a settlement, as it was at an opportune point to ford the mighty Clyde before it widens on its way to the sea some 30km (20 miles) away. According to some translations, Glasgow, or *glascau,* means "dear green place."

Aside from the Cathedral itself, practically none of this once-important medieval ecclesiastical center (including a university) remains. That's a shame, as Glasgow was considered one of the prettiest towns in all of 17th-century Europe. And much of its historical records (kept at the Cathedral) were swept away and lost during the Reformation.

The city became an economic powerhouse in the 18th century and quickly grew to be Scotland's largest city (as well as the fourth-most populous in the U.K.). The boom began in earnest with the tobacco trade to the New World, where Glasgow outpaced rivals such as London or Bristol. The city then became famous worldwide for shipbuilding and docks that produced the *Queen Mary* and other fabled ocean liners. It was the Second City of the Empire. But postindustrial decline gave Glasgow a poor reputation—particularly in contrast to the enduring charms of Edinburgh.

In the 1980s, the city reversed its fortunes, becoming Scotland's contemporary cultural capital and drawing talent from across the U.K., whether in art or rock 'n' roll. Decades of grime were sandblasted away from its monumental Victorian buildings, and one of Europe's best collections of art—the

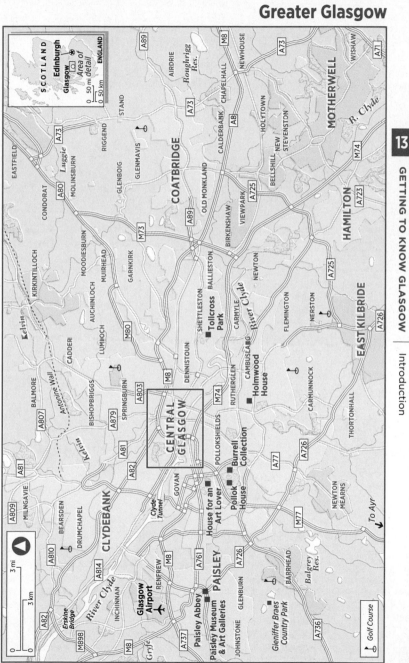

Impressions

The town of Glasgow [sic], though not so big, nor so rich, yet to all seems a much sweeter and more delightful place than Edinburgh.

—Daniel Defoe, 1650

Burrell—found a permanent home. In 1990, the city was named European Capital of Culture.

That said, Glasgow is not a metropolis without flaws. Pockets of poverty remain in the city's peripheral housing projects (estates or schemes). A major motorway cuts a scar through the center of town—and, not learning the lessons of its harmful effects, the city has another new freeway slashing its way through Glasgow's Southside. Although the city still appears to prefer knocking buildings down and erecting new structures at the slightest opportunity, the splendor of what architectural critics hailed as "the greatest surviving example of a Victorian city" is still evident. The next big event to come to the city is the 2014 Commonwealth Games.

On Glasgow's doorstep is the scenic estuary of the **Firth of Clyde,** with attractive coastal peninsulas and atmospheric islands only short drives and ferry rides away. In addition, Glasgow is a good gateway for exploring **Burns Country** in Ayrshire to the southwest. From Glasgow, visitors can easily tour Loch Lomond and see some of the southern fringes of the Highlands or travel less than an hour away to Stirling and the Trossach mountains.

ORIENTATION

Arriving

For information about arriving in Glasgow by plane, train, bus, or car, see "Getting to Edinburgh & Glasgow," p. 25 in chapter 3.

Visitor Information

The **Greater Glasgow and Clyde Valley Tourist Board,** 11 George Sq. (© **0141/204-4400;** www.seeglasgow.com; Underground: Buchanan St.), has a full range of services, from hotel reservations to currency exchange. In addition to piles of brochures, there is a small bookshop. During peak season it is open Monday to Saturday from 9am to 7pm and Sunday from 10am to 6pm. Hours are more limited during winter months. Getting full information about traveling around Glasgow can be a bit frustrating. Traveline (© **0871/200-2233;** www.traveline.org.uk) offers bus and rail timetable information but cannot tell you costs.

MAIN ARTERIES & LANDMARKS

Virtually all evidence of Glasgow's medieval existence was demolished by some well-meaning—if heritage-destroying—urban renewal schemes of late Georgian and Victorian Glasgow. So, no narrow alleys and cobbled streets remain in the original city center around the High Street. Still standing on the hill at the top of High Street is Glasgow Cathedral, an excellent example of pre-Reformation Gothic architecture next to the hill-filling Central Necropolis. Down the High Street, no longer the city's main street, you'll find the Tolbooth Steeple (1626) at Glasgow (or Mercat) Cross. The Mercat Cross was the hub of the city until the 18th century. This area is now generally called Merchant City and it flows rather seamlessly into Glasgow's commercial center. Both are laid out in a grid system, so navigation is reasonably easy along primary arteries such as Buchanan Street, Argyle Street, Bath Street, Sauchiehall Street, and St. Vincent Street. Stretches of a few of these are traffic-free and full of pedestrians.

The city's salubrious and leafy West End is just a short journey from central Glasgow, on the other side of the M8. The late Georgian terraces of Woodlands Hill, rising to Park Circus, afford excellent views. Nearby, the tower of the University of Glasgow dominates the skyline. For the West End and Glasgow in general, Byres Road is a primary social and entertainment destination, full of restaurants, cafes, bars, and shops.

The city's Southside sprawls from the River Clyde and is largely residential. The commercial heart of the Southside is Shawlands, which offers an increasing number of good restaurants, and nearby Queens Park is a hilly classic of Victorian planning. Glasgow's East End is slowly redeveloping after the boom of its industrial heyday went bust. Visitors to one primary East End artery, the Gallowgate, should visit the flea-market stalls of the Barras at the weekend. A few neighborhoods, such as Dennistoun, which is east down Duke Street from the Cathedral area, are gradually drawing young, creative types who can no longer afford apartments in the West End or on the Southside: A renaissance is simmering.

Glasgow Neighborhoods in Brief

CITY CENTER

Cathedral (Townhead) This is where St. Mungo apparently settled in A.D. 543 and built his little church in what's now the northeastern corner of the city center. **Glasgow Cathedral** was once surrounded by a variety of prebendal manses (residences), and the so-called Bishop's Castle stood between the Cathedral's west facade and the Provand's Lordship, which still exists largely in its original form. East of the Cathedral is one of Britain's largest Victorian cemeteries, Glasgow's Central Necropolis.

Merchant City The city's first New Town development—today southeast of the city's core—Merchant City extends from the boulevard called the Trongate and Argyle Street in the south to George Street in the north. As the medieval lanes and alleys off High Street were regarded as festering sores, the affluent moved to develop areas to the west. Merchant's warehouses largely replaced the houses, and everyone was shifted out. Ironically, now the district has become one of the few inner-city areas of Glasgow where people reside in any density.

Finding an Address

Glasgow was built in various sections over the years, and some historic districts, such as the infamous Gorbals, south of the city center, have been torn down in the name of slum clearance: Streets have been completely reconfigured to accommodate modern traffic flows. Other neighborhoods have fallen prey to freeway development. Luckily for visitors, the city center is primarily laid out on a grid, which makes it easier to navigate.

Get a detailed map of Glasgow before setting out. Always find the nearest cross street, and then look for your location from there. If it's a hotel or restaurant, the sign of an establishment is often more prominent than the number.

Glasgow Neighborhoods

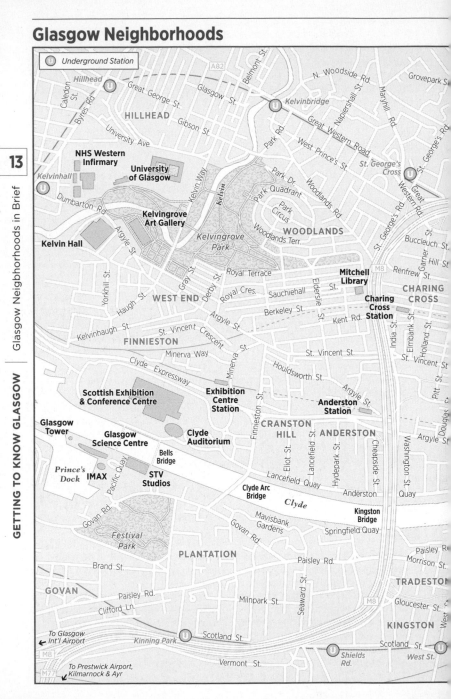

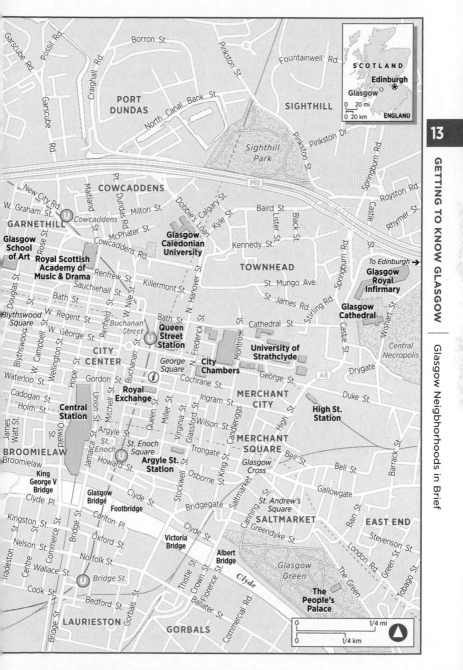

Gallowgate The Gallowgate, the principal street running east from the Trongate and Glasgow Cross, and its surrounding district is best known for the Barras weekend flea markets; Barrowland, a one-time ballroom that now is a popular live-music venue for rock groups; and Glasgow Green public park. The street was once one where prosperous city businessmen strolled. The Saracen's Head Inn stood here and received such distinguished guests as Dr. Samuel Johnson and James Boswell in 1774 after the duo's famous tour of the Hebrides.

Saltmarket While the first settlements in Glasgow were on the hill by the Cathedral, almost as early were dwellings in this area at the opposite end of High Street along the banks of the Clyde. It served as the trading post where the river could be forded. The Bridgegate (the road to the bridge) leads to Victoria Bridge—constructed in the 1850s and the oldest Clyde crossing in Glasgow.

Commercial Center The biggest of the central districts of Glasgow, it includes areas of 19th-century development such as **Blythswood** and **Charing Cross** (although the latter was severed by the M8 freeway). This area offers Victorian architecture at its finest, although the city once had a mind to tear it down before realizing that the buildings had international importance.

Broomielaw It has been said: "The Clyde made Glasgow." From the docks that once existed here, Glasgow imported tobacco, cotton, and rum, and shipped its manufactured goods around the world. Today the Broomielaw, after becoming a rather lost and neglected part of the city center, is targeted for renewal.

Garnethill Up the steep slopes north of Sauchiehall Street, this neighborhood is best known for the Charles Rennie Mackintosh–designed Glasgow School of Art. Developed in the late 1800s, Garnethill offers good views of the city and is also home to the first proper synagogue built in Scotland. A prosperous late 19th-century suburb, Garnethill is now one of the few concentrations of residential properties in Glasgow city center.

WEST END

Woodlands Centering on Park Circus at the crown of Woodlands Hill, this neighborhood is a mix of residential tenements and retail stretches, particularly on Woodlands and Great Western roads. South of the river lies the district of **Finnieston.** Its most visible landmark is the old shipbuilding crane, standing like some giant dinosaur. Along the Clyde is the Scottish Exhibition Centre. West of Woodlands is **Kelvingrove,** with the Art Gallery and Museum and the impressive park. Glasgow allegedly has more green spaces per resident than any other European city.

Hillhead With the Gilmorehill campus of the University of Glasgow, Hillhead is rather dominated by academia. Its main boulevard is Byres Road, which is the Main Street of the West End.

Partick The railway station at Partick is one of the few in the city to translate the stop's name into Gaelic: Partaig. Indeed there is a bit of Highland pride to the neighborhood, although no particular evidence that Highland people have settled here in great masses. Partick is one of the less pretentious districts of the central West End. To the north are leafy and affluent **Hyndland** and **Dowanhill.**

SOUTHSIDE

Gorbals This neighborhood, just across the Clyde from the city center, developed a reputation for mean streets and unsanitary tenements; so, the city demolished it in the early 1960s, erecting sets of modern high-rise apartment towers, which, in turn, developed a reputation for unsavory and unpleasant conditions. Today they are gradually coming down and a New Gorbals has been developed on a more human scale, although the fabric of the place still seems torn and frayed. It is home to the Citizens Theatre (p. 237), one of the most innovative and democratic in the U.K.

Govan Until 1912, Govan (*guv*-an) was an independent burgh and one of the key shipbuilding districts on the south banks of the Clyde. It was settled as early as the

10th century—another ecclesiastical focal point along with St. Kentigern's north of the river. The first shipyard, Mackie & Thomson, opened in 1840. But with the demise of shipbuilding, the fortunes of Govan fell too. Today, it is hoped that the Science Centre and other developments, such as a new Transport Museum and BBC Scotland's headquarters, will revive Govan's fortunes.

Pollokshaws Along with **Strathbungo, Queens Park, Pollokshields,** and **Crosshill,** these neighborhoods form the heart of the city's more modern Southside suburbs. Pollok Park and the Burrell Collection are the primary tourist attractions, and Queens Park is perhaps better and more verdant than Kelvingrove Park, even if it lacks the monuments and statues of the West End's oasis.

GETTING AROUND

One of the best ways to explore Glasgow is by foot. (See chapter 17 for walking tours.) The center of town is laid out on a grid, which makes map reading relatively easy. However, some of the city's significant attractions, such as the Burrell Collection, are in surrounding districts, and for those, you'll need to rely on public transportation or a car.

Glasgow by Bus

Glasgow has an extensive (if somewhat confusing) bus service run by the privately owned **First Group.** The buses can be embarrassingly litter-strewn by the end of the day, and routes tend to run between east and west or north and south, with almost all buses coming through the city center on busy thoroughfares such as St. Vincent, Hope, Argyll, and Sauchiehall streets. Service is frequent during the day. After 11pm it is curtailed on most routes, but some (for example, 40 or 62) run all night long (at least on weekends), although there is a premium put on tickets. Typically, one-way (single) fares are about £1.80, and for £3.75 you can use the buses (after 9:30am) all day long with few restrictions. A weeklong ticket costs £16. The city bus station is the **Buchanan Street Bus Station.** The "Traveline" number (© **0871/200-2233**) gives timetable information (but not fares); you can also log on to www.firstgroup.com.

"FirstDay" Bargain on the Buses

For £3.75, at time of writing, you can buy a FirstDay ticket that allows you to hop on and off buses run by the main bus company all day long. The ticket is valid daily from 9:30am to midnight. It's sold by drivers. For more information, check www.firstgroup.com.

Glasgow by Underground & Suburban Train

Glasgow's Underground, which in a nod to the city's American cousins is officially called the **Subway,** offers a 15-stop circular system linking the city center, West End, and a bit of the Southside. There are no stops east of the city center. During the day there is generally no more than a 5- to 8-minute wait for trains. Trains run on longer intervals on Sunday and at night. The one-way adult fare is £1.10. Alternatively, you can purchase an all-day Discovery Ticket for £3.50 or a 20-trip ticket

Glasgow Underground

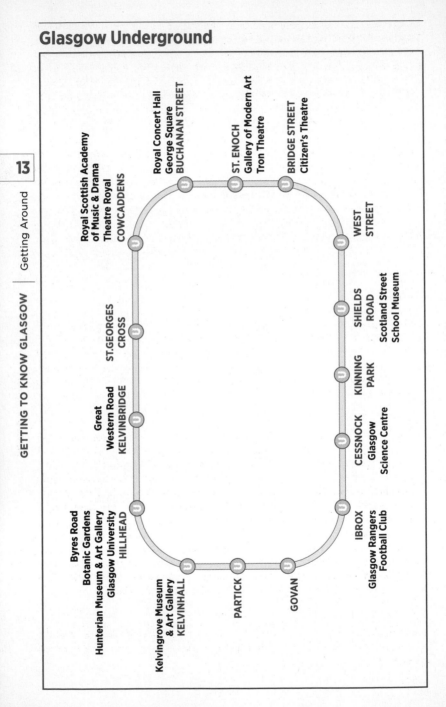

booklet for £19. The underground runs Monday to Saturday 6:30am to about 11:30pm and Sunday 11am to about 6pm.

The **Transcentre** (local ticket sales only) at the St. Enoch underground station, two blocks from the Central Station, is generally open Monday to Saturday from 8:30am to 5:30pm, but it closes early on Wednesday. On Sunday, the hours are 10am to 5pm.

Glasgow and the region have the largest train network in Great Britain after London, operated by the private franchise holder First ScotRail and the quasi-public body now called the **Strathclyde Partnership for Transport (SPT).** Local train services to both Central (upper and lower levels) and Queen Street (lower level only) stations run as frequently as every 10 minutes or so during the day to destinations in the West End and on the Southside. Service is less frequent after the evening rush hour, and the system shuts down around midnight. While extensive, the trains are not cheap by European standards. A typical round-trip fare is £3 to £5.50.

For families on an excursion, the **Daytripper** ticket is excellent. For £17.50, two adults and up to four children (5–15 years old) can travel anywhere in the system (including broad swaths of Ayrshire) by suburban train, the underground, most buses, and even a few ferries. For one adult and two children, the fare is £9.80.

The main SPT switchboard is ✆ **0141/332-6811.** Hours are Monday to Saturday 9am to 5pm, or visit www.spt.co.uk.

Glasgow by Taxi

Metered taxis are the same excellent ones found in Edinburgh or London: the Fast Black, which you can hail or pick up at taxi ranks in the city center. Alternatively you can also reserve one by calling **Glasgow Taxis Ltd. (**✆ **0141/429-7070).** Most taxi trips within the city cost between £6 and £16. A surcharge is imposed for late-night/early-morning runs. There are also **Glasgow Private Hire** cars, but they cannot be hailed. Call ✆ **0141/774-3000.**

Glasgow by Car

Glasgow, in reality, goes a long way toward encouraging car use with several multi-story parking lots offering parking prices cheaper than public transport tickets. But traffic at times is absolute murder. Metered street parking is available, but expensive. Some zones in residential areas are marked PERMIT HOLDERS ONLY—your vehicle may be towed if you lack a permit. A double yellow line along the curb indicates no parking at any time. A single yellow line along the curb indicates restrictions, too, so be sure to read the signs for details of limitations.

If you want to rent a car, it's best to arrange it in advance. But if you want to rent a car locally, most companies will accept your foreign driver's license. All the major rental agencies are represented at the airport. In addition, **Avis Rent-a-Car** is at 70 Lancefield St. (✆ **0870/608-6339); Budget Rent-a-Car** is at 101 Waterloo St. (✆ **0800/212-636);** and **Arnold Clark** is at multiple locations (✆ **0845/607-4500).**

Glasgow by Bicycle

Though bikes are not as widely used in Glasgow as in Edinburgh, most parts of the city are fine for biking. For more information on cycle hire and rentals, see p. 206 in chapter 16.

WHERE TO STAY IN GLASGOW

14

The tourist trade in Glasgow is less distinctly seasonal than in Edinburgh, a city that sees a vast number of visitors every summer thanks to its internationally renowned Festival. However, for Glasgow, the increase in budget-airline flights from the European continent has increased the overall number of tourists, while the city continues to be a popular spot for business conferences. If, therefore, an international association of dermatologists is in town, finding accommodation can be more difficult.

Whenever you're coming, it's a good idea to reserve rooms in advance. Some business-trade oriented hotels offer bargains at weekends, and the overall number of moderate and budget options has increased. Of course, the Internet can be a real treasure trove of reduced room rates, albeit with cancelation penalties. Multiple-night stays can also bring price cuts. The Glasgow and Clyde Valley tourism office (www.seeglasgow.com) in conjunction with VisitScotland (www.visitscotland.com) offers an **Information & Booking Hot Line** (© **0845/225-5121** from within the U.K., or 44-1506/832-121 from outside the U.K.; fax 0150/683-2222). Lines are open (local time) Monday to Friday from 9:30am to 6:30pm, Saturday from 9am to 5pm. The fee for this booking service is £4.

The Scottish tourist board is also a source of hotel ratings, which are based largely on amenities, like TVs in the rooms and wireless Internet in the lobby. The stars can be limited for smaller operations that may not offer all the modern conveniences, but these establishments are still perfectly good places to stay. The prices or tariffs listed in this chapter are generally the standard rates, which can potentially be reduced with advance or Internet bookings. All hotels, B&Bs, and guesthouses are completely nonsmoking, although some will offer smoking areas outside.

BEST HOTEL BETS

- **Best Boutique Hotel: Hotel du Vin at One Devonshire Gardens,** 1 Devonshire Gardens, Glasgow G12 0UX (℗ **0141/339-2001**), is one of the finest operations in Scotland, with some extremely sumptuous suites. See p. 175.
- **Best Spa Facilities: Blythswood Square,** 11 Blythswood Sq., Glasgow G2 4AD (℗ **0141/208-2458**), is not only the best in this category: It's the best new operation in a long time. See p. 173.
- **Best Merchant City Hotel: Brunswick Hotel,** 106–108 Brunswick St., Glasgow G1 1TF (℗ **0141/552-0001**), is one of the hippest hotels in the city. See p. 169.
- **Best Hotel with Pub: Babbity Bowster,** 16–18 Blackfriars St. (off High St.), Glasgow G1 1PE (℗ **0141/552-5055**), is in a class all of its own. See p. 172.
- **Best Traditional Luxury Hotel: Hilton Glasgow Hotel,** 1 William St., Glasgow G3 8HT (℗ **800/445-8667** in the U.S. and Canada, or **0141/204-5555**), ticks all the boxes for a top-class international hotel. See p. 172.
- **Best B&B/Guesthouse: Alamo Guest House,** 46 Gray St., Glasgow G3 7SE (℗ **0141/339-2395**), has only one known downside, which is shared bathrooms. See p. 176.
- **Best Designed Hotel: Radisson Blu,** 301 Argyle St., Glasgow G2 8DL (℗ **0141/204-3333**), is an arresting sight in Glasgow city center. See p. 174.
- **Best Budget West End Hotel: Ambassador Hotel,** 7 Kelvin Dr., Glasgow G20 8QJ (℗ **0141/946-1018**), offers good value for money in a leafy district of the city. See p. 175.
- **Best Boutique Chain Hotel: Malmaison,** 278 W. George St., Glasgow G2 4LL (℗ **0141/572-1000**), has lost little of its glamour and allure. See p. 173.

WHERE TO STAY IN GLASGOW

Merchant City

MERCHANT CITY

Moderate

Brunswick Hotel ★   In the heart of Merchant City, this is one of the hippest places to stay. The modern, minimalist design has aged well since the Brunswick opened in the 1990s. It remains one of relatively few independently and locally run hotels in town. The unit sizes vary and some of the "compact rooms" are on the small side but all are soothing and inviting with neutral tones, comfortable mattresses, and adequate bathrooms. There is also a three-bedroom apartment. Brutti Ma Buoni is the in-house cafe and bar, which has a fairly artistic and lively clientele.

106–108 Brunswick St., Glasgow G1 1TF. ℗ **0141/552-0001.** Fax 0141/552-1551. www.brunswickhotel. co.uk. 18 units. £50–£100 double with continental breakfast. AE, DC, MC, V. Parking on street. Underground: Buchanan St. **Amenities:** Restaurant; bar; 24-hr. reception. *In room:* TV, Internet.

Merchant Lodge Hotel   Located in a historic building, tucked down a narrow street in the heart of Merchant City, this hotel is attractively priced. Overall the location is great, but one recurring complaint from guests (and, indeed, the hotel itself) is the occasional sound of late-night revelry when a local nightclub dispenses its guests.

52 Virginia St., Glasgow G1 1TY. ℗ **0141/552-2424.** Fax 0141/552-4747. www.merchantlodgehotel.com. 40 units. £80 double with breakfast. AE, MC, V. Underground: Buchanan St. *In room:* TV, hair dryer.

Where to Stay in Glasgow

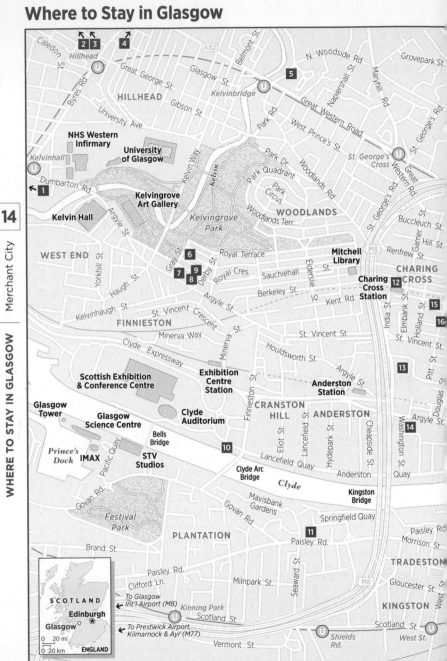

Caledon St.

2 **3**

4

Hillhead

Byres Rd

Great George St.

A82

Glasgow St.

Kelvinbridge

Belmont St.

N. Woodside Rd.

5

Grovepark St.

Maryhill Rd.

Great Western Road

West Prince's St.

St. George's Rd.

HILLHEAD

Gibson St.

Park Rd.

Woodlands Rd.

Naplershall Rd.

University Ave.

NHS Western
Infirmary

University
of Glasgow

Kelvin Way

Kelvin

Park Dr.

Park Quadrant

Park
Circus

St. George's
Cross

Great Western Rd.

St. George's Rd.

Kelvinhall

Dumbarton Rd.

1

Kelvingrove
Art Gallery

Kelvingrove
Park

Woodlands Terr.

WOODLANDS

Buccleuch St.

Garner St.

Hill St.

Kelvin Hall

Argyle St.

Gray St.

Derby St.

Royal Terrace

Royal Cres.

Sauchiehall St.

Mitchell
Library

M8

Renfrew St.

CHARING
CROSS

WEST END

Yorkhill St.

6

7 **9**

8

Eldersie St.

Charing
Cross
Station

12

15

Haugh St.

Kelvinhaugh St.

St. Vincent Crescent

Berkeley St.

Kent Rd.

India St.

Elmbank St.

Holland St.

16

FINNIESTON

Minerva Way

Argyle St.

Minerva St.

St. Vincent St.

St. Vincent St.

13

Pitt St.

Clyde Expressway

Houldsworth St.

Argyle St.

Washington St.

Argyle St.

Scottish Exhibition
& Conference Centre

Exhibition
Centre Station

Finnieston St.

CRANSTON
HILL

Anderston
Station

ANDERSTON

Douglas St.

Glasgow
Tower

Glasgow
Science Centre

Clyde
Auditorium

Eliot St.

Lancefield St.

Hydepark St.

Cheapside St.

14

Pacific Quay

Bells
Bridge

10

Lancefield Quay

Anderston

Washington St. Quay

Prince's
Dock

IMAX

STV
Studios

Clyde Arc
Bridge

Clyde

Kingston
Bridge

Govan Rd.

Mavisbank
Gardens

Springfield Quay

Festival
Park

Govan Rd.

PLANTATION

11

Paisley Rd.

Seaward St.

Paisley Rd.

Morrison St.

TRADESTON

Brand St.

Paisley Rd.

M8

Gloucester St.

West St.

Clifford Ln.

Milnpark St.

KINGSTON

SCOTLAND

Edinburgh

Glasgow

0 20 mi

0 20 km

ENGLAND

To Glasgow
Int'l Airport (M8)

To Prestwick Airport,
Kilmarnock & Ayr (M77)

Kinning Park
Scotland St.

Vermont St.

Scotland St.

Shields
Rd.

Scotland St.

West St.

ABode **19**
Alamo Guest House **6**
Albion Hotel **5**
Ambassador Hotel **4**
Argyll Hotel **7**
Babbity Bowster **27**
Blythswood Square **17**
Brunswick Hotel **25**
City Inn **10**
Devoncove Hotel **8**
Etap Hotel **11**

Glasgow Loft
  Apartments **18**
Hilton Glasgow Hotel **13**
Hotel du Vin at One
  Devonshire Gardens **3**
Hotel Ibis **15**
Kelvingrove Hotel **9**
Kirklee Hotel **2**
Malmaison **16**
Manor Park Hotel **1**
Marks Hotel **20**

Menzies Hotel **14**
Merchant Lodge Hotel **23**
Millennium Hotel
  Glasgow **22**
Park Inn **21**
Premier Inn **26**
Premier Inn Charing Cross **12**
Premier Inn City
  Centre South **29**
Rab Ha's **24**
Radisson Blu **28**

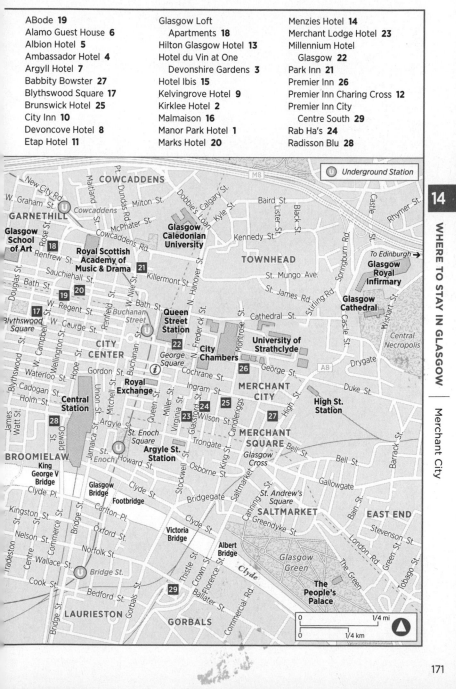

Rab Ha's 🎁 Similar in size to the Babbity (see below), this small boutique hotel above a popular and urbane pub has a quartet of overnight rooms. They feature dark slate flooring in the bathrooms, specially commissioned glass, photographic prints, and flat-screen televisions. The location in Merchant City, southeast of George Square, is excellent for the city center.

81 Hutcheson St., Glasgow G1 1SH. ✆ **0141/572-0400.** Fax 0141/572-0402. www.rabhas.com. 4 units £80–£90 double with continental breakfast. AE, DC, MC, V. Parking on street. Underground: Buchanan St. **Amenities:** Restaurant; bar. *In room:* TV, MP3 dock, Wi-Fi.

Inexpensive

Babbity Bowster ★ Housed in a reconstructed late-18th-century "five-bay house," the Babbity Bowster is a small inn, pub, and restaurant with plenty of character. The guest rooms are modest if reasonably well appointed, and there is no lobby for residents. But the Babbity Bowster is designed to appeal to travelers who do not spend too much time in their rooms or lolling about hotel lounges. The ground-level pub of the same name (p. 241) is convivial and notably civilized, with a sheltered beer garden.

16–18 Blackfriars St. (off High St.), Glasgow G1 1PE. ✆ **0141/552-5055.** Fax 0141/552-7774. 5 units. £60 double. AE, MC, V. Free parking. Train: High St. Bus: 40. **Amenities:** Restaurant; bar.

Premier Inn Backing onto a peaceful old churchyard, this former tax office (Montrose House) is a branch of the inexpensively priced Premier Inn chain. As such, it is functional if not full of character and individuality. Rooms that overlook the kirkyard are preferable to those facing busy George Street and the Strathclyde University parking lot across the road.

187 George St., Glasgow G1 1YU. ✆ **0870/238-3320.** Fax 0141/553-2719. www.premierinn.com. 254 units. £65 double without breakfast. AE, DC, MC, V. Parking on street. Underground: Buchanan St. **Amenities:** Restaurant; bar. *In room:* TV, hair dryer.

COMMERCIAL CENTER
Very Expensive

Hilton Glasgow Hotel ★ Glasgow's first-class Hilton is centrally located but oddly situated, towering over the M8 freeway. Still, it is a dignified and modern hotel, one that has a good deal of class and shine. Many of the numerous overnight rooms—plush and conservative—offer fine city views. The spa facilities include a 15-m (49-ft.) pool. Dining options include a casual New York deli-style buffet, Minsky's, as well as the posh Camerons with first-rate and expensive modern Scottish cuisine.

1 William St., Glasgow G3 8HT. ✆ **800/445-8667** in the U.S. and Canada, or **0141/204-5555.** Fax 0141/204-5004. www.hilton.co.uk/glasgow. 331 units. £140–£200 double with breakfast. AE, DC, MC, V. Parking £5. **Amenities:** 2 restaurants; bar; babysitting; concierge; exercise room; indoor pool; room service; sauna; massage. *In room:* A/C, TV/DVD, hair dryer, Internet, minibar.

Expensive

ABode This boutique hotel in the city center, formerly known as the Arthouse, was originally built in the Edwardian era to house Glasgow's school board. Part of a chain of U.K. luxury hotels, ABode particularly prides itself on its fine-dining restaurant, **Michael Caines @ ABode** (p. 184). It is under the direction of a Michelin-starred chef who is based in England, while a more casual cafe bistro is located in the basement.

129 Bath St., Glasgow G2 2SZ. ☏ **0141/221-6789.** Fax 0141/221-6777. www.abodehotels.co.uk/glasgow. 65 units. £100–£170 double with breakfast. AE, DC, MC, V. Parking on street. Underground: Buchanan St. **Amenities:** 2 restaurants; bar; room service. *In room:* TV/DVD, hair dryer, Internet.

Blythswood Square ★★ This most recent addition to the upper end of the market comes from Edinburgh's vaunted Townhouse Group. Extensive renovations have turned the one-time Royal Scottish Automobile Club into a luxury spa hotel. Opening in progression, The much-promoted spa (free allocated time slots, excluding treatments, for all guests) was still under construction as we went to press but will be open by Autumn 2010, although the hotel overnight rooms and well-received restaurant and bar were accepting visitors.

11 Blythswood Sq., Glasgow G2 4AD. ☏ **0141/208-2458.** www.townhousecompany.com/blythswood square. £120–£245 double with breakfast. AE, MC, V. Underground: Buchanan St. **Amenities**: Restaurant; bar; concierge; gym; room service; spa; swimming pool. *In room:* TV/DVD, hair dryer, Wi-Fi.

Glasgow Loft Apartments 🛏 These serviced guest suites near the heart of Glasgow offer the comforts of home: Range and oven, fridge, dishwasher, washing machine. All the modern one- and two-bedroom flats have floor-to-ceiling windows that face back to the city center, appointed in black leather upholstered sofas, power shower/Jacuzzi bathrooms, and dining tables that seat six.

134 Renfrew St., Glasgow G3 6ST. ☏ **0141/332-1976.** www.glasgowloftapartment.co.uk. 10 units. £145–£155 apartment for two. MC, V. Parking £18. Underground: Cowcaddens.

Malmaison ★ Today there are hip and sophisticated Malmaisons across the U.K., but the chain began in Scotland. This converted church has sleek and modern decor. Rooms vary in dimensions—and if size matters to you, rooms in the original church conversion are bigger with high ceilings (though there is no lift to the older part of the hotel). In the vaulted space below reception is the popular brasserie of the same name and a champagne bar.

278 W. George St., Glasgow G2 4LL. ☏ **0141/572-1000.** Fax 0141/572-1002. www.malmaison-glasgow. com. 72 units. From £100–£140 double with breakfast. AE, DC, MC, V. Train: Charing Cross. **Amenities:** Restaurant; 2 bars; babysitting; exercise room; room service. *In room:* A/C, TV/DVD, hair dryer, Internet, minibar.

Millennium Hotel Glasgow Adjacent to Queen Street Station, this classic hotel has a conservatory space for dining and drinks that faces onto the city's central plaza, George Square. The most desirable rooms are at the front of the building, too; those in the rear offer no memorable views. The ground-floor restaurant, Brasserie on George Square, offers an elegant—but not stuffy—dining ambience.

George Sq., Glasgow G2 1DS. ☏ **0141/332-6711.** Fax 0141/332-4264. www.millenniumhotels.com. 117 units. From £145–£198 double with breakfast. AE, DC, MC, V. Parking £5. Underground: Buchanan St. **Amenities:** Restaurant; 2 bars; babysitting; concierge; room service. *In room:* A/C, TV, hair dryer, Internet.

Park Inn This modern hotel is opposite the Glasgow Royal Concert Hall and next to the central bus station. A medley of bedrooms is available, in various shapes, sizes, and configurations—and each attempts to offer a certain amount of flair. It is in a busy spot, and late-night noise might be a nuisance for some. Good central city location, though.

2 Port Dundas Place, Glasgow G2 3LD. (*) **0141/333-1500.** Fax 0141/333-5700. www.rezidorparkinn. com. 100 units. From £110 double with breakfast. AE, DC, MC, V. Parking nearby. Underground: Buchanan St. **Amenities:** Restaurant; bar; exercise room; massage; sauna; spa; room service. *In room:* TV, hair dryer, minibar.

Moderate

Marks Hotel Formerly Bewleys, this modern boutique-style inn is centrally located around the corner from the Mackintosh-designed Willow Tea Rooms. The hotel rises impressively from the street, with oddly angled windows that appear to look down on the ground below. It is reasonably priced with a posh feeling once in your room. Great location.

110 Bath St., Glasgow G2 2EN. (*) **0141/353-0800.** Fax 0141/353-0900. www.markshotels.com. 103 units. £100 double with breakfast. AE, DC, MC, V. Underground: Buchanan St. **Amenities:** Restaurant; bar; limited room service. *In room:* TV, hair dryer, Wi-Fi.

Menzies Hotel The advertised "Feng Shui bedrooms" may or may not appeal to the average visitor to Glasgow, but the Menzies Hotel in the Broomielaw district can be justifiably proud of its excellent mid-price range in-house restaurant: The Brasserie. Families should note that children under 16 are not allowed to use the gym facilities. In addition to 129 en-suite rooms, there are 12 split-level apartments.

27 Washington St., Glasgow, G3 8AZ. (*) **0141/222-2929.** www.menzies-hotels.co.uk. 141 units. From £110 double with breakfast. AE, MC, V. Parking £3 per day. Underground: St. Enoch. **Amenities:** Restaurant; bar; fitness facility; pool. *In room:* TV, hair dryer, Internet.

Radisson Blu ★ Since its November 2002 opening, Glasgow's Radisson has set down architectural markers for other hotels. Its shiny facade is just a stone's throw from Central Station, and contemporary units with blonde wood details and Scandinavian cool have all the modern conveniences. The 1,394-sq.-m (15,000-sq.-ft.) club and fitness facility includes a 15m (49-ft.) pool and state-of-the art gym.

No Frills in the City Center

For basic, inexpensive accommodation from the better-known chains, Glasgow has a few options. Near Sauchiehall Street in the Charing Cross district is the **Hotel Ibis** (220 West Regent St., G2 4DQ; (*) **0141/225-6000**), www. ibishotel.com, with rooms from £50 plus a restaurant and bar. Just across the Clyde in the gentrified New Gorbals, the **Premier Inn** group has colonized the Tulip Inn (80 Ballater St., G5 0TW; (*) **0870/423-6452**), www. premierinn.com, offering double rooms from around £60 and lots of free car parking. Above the Charing Cross railway stop there is another 278-unit outlet (10 Elmbank Gardens, G2 4PP; (*) **0870/990-6312**) with rooms at similar prices. Opened in 2007, the **Etap Hotel** (Springfield Quay, G5 8NP; (*) **0141/429-8013**, www.etaphotel. com) has rooms for around £36.

301 Argyle St., Glasgow G2 8DL. ☎ **0141/204-3333.** Fax 0141/204-3344. www.radissonsas.com. 250 units. From £150 double with breakfast. AE, DC, MC, V. Reduced-rate parking nearby. Underground: St. Enoch. **Amenities:** 2 restaurants; 2 bars; fitness facility; pool. *In room:* TV, minibar, Internet.

THE WEST END

Expensive

Hotel du Vin Bistro at One Devonshire Gardens ★★★   This hotel (which most still call simply One Devonshire) has been the most glamorous the city has to offer for more than a decade. It's the place where the great and good traditionally stay. Of the guest rooms, the "Balfour" (aka the luxury town house) is the most impressive, with a sitting room, sauna, dining space, exercise room, and more. "Hush Heath," fashioned after a Kentish Manor House, is not far behind. The "Vettriano Suite" has a luxury freestanding bathtub in the bedroom. The hotel has an excellent fine-dining modern restaurant, **Bistro at One Devonshire Gardens** (p. 187), and for all the obvious luxury it is also family-friendly.

1 Devonshire Gardens, Glasgow G12 0UX. ☎ **0141/339-2001.** Fax 0141/337-1663. www.hotelduvin.com. 38 units. From £145 double with breakfast. AE, DC, MC, V. Free parking. Underground: Hillhead. **Amenities:** Restaurant; bar; concierge; outdoor smoking pavilion; room service. *In room:* TV/DVD, CD, fridge, hair dryer, minibar.

Moderate

Albion Hotel   This unpretentious small hotel was originally two nearly identical beige-sandstone row houses in a leafy district of the West End. High-ceilinged guest rooms have modern furniture and a shower-only bathroom. If your hotel requirements are straightforward, you'll likely be happy here, where they particularly pride themselves on friendliness.

405–407 N. Woodside Rd., Glasgow G20 6NN. ☎ **0141/339-8620.** Fax 0141/334-8159. www.glasgow hotelsandapartments.co.uk. 20 units. £90 double with breakfast. AE, DC, MC, V. Free parking. Underground: Kelvin Bridge. **Amenities:** Bar. *In room:* TV (DVD on request), hair dryer, Internet.

Ambassador Hotel ★ 🍴   Across from the Botanic Gardens and overlooking the River Kelvin, this small hotel in a circa-1900 Edwardian town house is owned by the same people as the Albion (above). Suites are spacious enough to accommodate five to seven guests. The hotel is well situated for exploring the West End, with many good restaurants or brasseries nearby on Byres Road.

7 Kelvin Dr., Glasgow G20 8QJ. ☎ **0141/946-1018.** Fax 0141/945-5377. www.glasgowhotelsand apartments.co.uk. 16 units. £90 double with breakfast. AE, DC, MC, V. Free parking. Underground: Hillhead. **Amenities:** Bar. *In room:* TV (DVD on request), fridge, hair dryer.

Argyll Hotel ☺   Only a short walk to the University or the Kelvingrove Art Gallery and Museum, the Argyll lives up to its Scottish name—full of tartan and the like. There is a clutch of spacious family rooms, and one double has a firm four-poster bed and corner-filling bathtub.

969–973 Sauchiehall St., Glasgow G3 7TQ. ☎ **0141/337-3313.** Fax 0141/337-3283. www.argyllhotel glasgow.co.uk. 38 units. £80 double with breakfast. AE, MC, V. Limited free parking. Underground: Kelvin Hall. Bus: 18, 62, or city sightseeing bus. **Amenities:** Restaurant; bar; room service (till 10pm); Wi-Fi. *In room:* TV, hair dryer.

City Inn   Right on the River Clyde and near the conference and exhibition center, this smart hotel with its waterside terrace is not exactly in the heart of the action. But neither is it very far away. Part of a small chain, City Inns are modern and contemporary with good facilities. Rooms have power showers.

Finnieston Quay, Glasgow G3 8HN. ✆ **0141/240-1002.** www.cityinn.com. 164 units. £139 double with breakfast. AE, DC, MC, V. Limited free parking. Train: Exhibition Centre. **Amenities:** Restaurant; bar; health club; room service. *In room:* A/C, TV, hair dryer, Internet.

Devoncove Hotel   At the Devoncove, rooms are comfortable if not huge, although by some local standards the singles here are downright roomy; no need to stand on the bed in order to open the closet door. The more spacious rooms face the street, which is typically quite busy, although double-pane windows muffle most of the noise.

931 Sauchiehall St., Glasgow G3 3TQ. ✆ **0141/334-4000.** Fax 0141/339-9000. www.devoncovehotel. com. 73 units. £105 double with breakfast. AE, MC, V. Free parking. Bus: 18, 62, or city sightseeing bus. **Amenities:** Restaurant; bar; Wi-Fi. *In room:* TV, fridge, hair dryer.

Kelvingrove Hotel ★ 🛍   Three generations of women in the Somerville family have made a difference to this guest house since buying it in October 2002. They are welcoming hoteliers with nearly 40 years of experience orienting new arrivals, answering questions, booking cabs, or just generally conversing with visitors. The rooms are comfortable with mainly modern furnishings.

944 Sauchiehall St., Glasgow G3 7TH. ✆ **0141/339-5011.** Fax 0141/339-6566. www.kelvingrove-hotel. co.uk. 22 units. £60 double with breakfast. MC, V. Parking on street. Bus: 18, 62, or city sightseeing bus. *In room:* TV.

Kirklee Hotel ☺   A red-sandstone Edwardian terraced house, with elegant bay windows, near the West End's diverse night life on Byres Road and the Botanic Gardens, the Kirklee is often recommended locally. Overlooking a private garden, the Edwardian guest lounge has period furniture. The high-ceilinged bedrooms are average in size, but some are large enough to accommodate families.

11 Kensington Gate, Glasgow G12 9LG. ✆ **0141/334-5555.** Fax 0141/339-3828. www.kirkleehotel.co.uk. 9 units. £75 double with breakfast. MC, V. Parking nearby. Underground: Hillhead. **Amenities:** Bar. *In room:* TV, hair dryer.

Manor Park Hotel   This impressive West End town house, built in 1895 (in the slightly out of the way Broomhill district) was converted into a hotel in 1947. Decor offers a blend of modern and traditional furnishings, including beechwood pieces set against a background of floral wallpaper. Each guest room comes with a neat little bathroom with either tub or shower; top floor units are the largest.

28 Balshagray Dr., Glasgow G11 7DD. ✆ **0141/339-2143.** Fax 0141/339-5842. www.manorparkhotel. com. 9 units. From £60 double with breakfast. AE, DC, MC, V. Free parking. *In room:* TV, coffeemaker, hair dryer, trouser press.

Inexpensive

Alamo Guest House 🖋   This highly regarded small hotel faces toward Kelvingrove Park, the Art Gallery, and Glasgow University. The period furniture and Victorian interior design details (especially in the entrance hallway) are particularly impressive for the price. Most rooms share bathroom facilities, however.

46 Gray St., Glasgow, G3 7SE. ✆ **0141/339-2395.** www.alamoguesthouse.com. 12 units. £66 double with breakfast. MC, V. Underground: Kelvinhall. *In room:* TV, coffeemaker.

WHERE TO DINE IN GLASGOW

L ike Edinburgh, the dining scene in Glasgow is diverse and there are some outstanding places to dine out. The recession of 2008/9 hit the industry rather hard, but the choice of restaurants remains good, from the Merchant City district right across to the West End. Although the city cannot boast about any Michelin stars (in contrast to Edinburgh), this also means that Glasgow's best is less costly, while the city has an eclectic mix of seriously stylish dining rooms, budget-minded bistros, and ethnic eateries.

Today some of the best fresh Scottish produce is served in Glasgow, whether it is shellfish and seafood from the nearby West Coast sea lochs, Ayrshire meat such as pork and lamb, or Aberdeen Angus steaks. There is an ever-increasing number of ethnic restaurants. The immigrant groups who have traditionally most influenced cuisine in the city are Italians and South Asians (especially Punjabis). There is a good choice of Far East, Chinese, and Spanish-influenced restaurants, too.

The hours listed here are when food is served. Bars on the premises may stay open longer.

For more ideas on dining options, buy *The List* magazine's annual *Eating & Drinking Guide,* a fantastically comprehensive review of hundreds of eateries in Glasgow (and Edinburgh). You can also visit the magazine's website: www.list.co.uk.

PRICES Dining out in Scotland is rarely cheap. Still, there is a range of choices for most budgets. If you're looking for bargains, inquire about fixed-price lunches or pre-theater special menus, which can be half the cost of the regular dinner menu. Visit **www.5pm.co.uk** for a selection of restaurants offering early dining deals.

SMOKING Smoking is prohibited by law from all enclosed public spaces in Scotland, which includes restaurants and bars. Some, however, may provide outdoor seating where smoking is allowed.

BEST DINING BETS

- **Best Overall Dining Experience: Bistro at One Devonshire Gardens,** Hotel du Vin at One Devonshire Gardens, 1 Devonshire Gardens (✆ **0141/339-2001**), matches first-class cuisine with a classy ambience. See p. 187.
- **Best Fish Restaurant: Gamba,** 225a W. George St. (✆ **0141/572-0899**), is one of Frommer's favorites in any category cuisine. See p. 184.
- **Best Cafe Bistro: Café Gandolfi,** 64 Albion St. (✆ **0141/552-6813**), has been a Merchant City favorite for some 30 years. See p. 182.
- **Best Indian Restaurant: Mother India,** 28 Westminster Terrace, Sauchiehall St., at Kelvingrove St. (✆ **0141/221-1663**), has many, many fans, not only from Glasgow but further afield. See p. 189.
- **Best Italian Restaurant: La Parmigiana,** 447 Great Western Rd. (✆ **0141/334-0686**), sets the standard for the city's main Italian restaurants to match. See p. 187.
- **Best Budget Restaurant: Wee Curry Shop,** 7 Buccleuch St., near Cambridge St. (✆ **0141/353-0777**), is tiny indeed from the premises to the final check. See p. 186.
- **Best Newcomer to the Scene: Dining Room,** 104 Bath St. (✆ **0141/332-6678**), is under the direction of one of the city's most talented chefs. See p. 183.

RESTAURANTS BY CUISINE

ASIAN
Wagamama (Commercial Center, $$, p. 186)

CAFE
Where the Monkey Sleeps (Commercial Center, $, p. 186)

CHINESE
Dragon-i ★ (Commercial Center, $$, p. 185)
Ho Wong (Commercial Center, $$$, p. 184)

CONTINENTAL
Café Gandolfi ★ (Merchant City, $$, p. 182)

FISH/SEAFOOD
City Merchant (Merchant City, $$$, p. 179)
Crabshakk (West End, $$, p. 188)
Gamba ★★ (Commercial Center, $$$, p. 184)

Harry Ramsden's (Southside, $$, p. 191)
Mussel Inn (Commercial Center, $$, p. 185)
Rogano (Commercial Center, $$$, p. 184)
Two Fat Ladies ★ (West End, $$, p. 189)

FRENCH
Brian Maule at Chardon d'Or (Commercial Center, $$$, p. 183)
La Vallee Blanche (West End, $$$, p. 188)
Michael Caines @ ABode (Commercial Center, $$$, p. 184)
Schottische (Merchant City, $$, p. 182)

GREEK
Konaki (West End, $$, p. 189)

KEY TO ABBREVIATIONS:
$$$$** = Very Expensive   **$$$** = Expensive   **$$** = Moderate   **$ = Inexpensive

INDIAN

Balbir's ★ (West End, $$, p. 188)
The Dhabba ★ (Merchant City, $$,
  p. 182)
Mother India ★ (West End, $$, p. 189)
Wee Curry Shop ★★ (Commercial
  Center, $, p. 186)

INTERNATIONAL

Cookie (Southside, $$, p. 190)
Stravaigin Café Bar ★ (West End, $$,
  p. 190)

ITALIAN

Bella Napoli (Southside, $$, p. 190)
Fratelli Sarti (Commercial Center, $$,
  p. 185)
La Parmigiana ★ (West End, $$$,
  p. 187)

JAPANESE

Nanakusa ★ (Commercial Center, $$,
  p. 186)
Wagamama (Commercial Center, $$,
  p. 186)

RUSSIAN

Café Cossachok ★ (Merchant City, $$,
  p. 179)

SCOTTISH

Art Lover's Café (Southside, $,
  p. 190)
Bistro at One Devonshire Gardens ★★
  (West End, $$$, p. 187)
Brian Maule at Chardon d'Or (Commer-
  cial Center, $$$, p. 183)
Café Gandolfi ★ (Merchant City, $,
  p. 182)
City Merchant (Merchant City, $$$,
  p. 179)
Dining Room (Commercial Center, $$$,
  p. 183)
Schottische (Merchant City, $$,
  p. 182)
Stravaigin Café Bar ★ (West End, $$,
  p. 190)
Two Fat Ladies ★ (West End, $$,
  p. 189)
Ubiquitous Chip ★ (West End, $$$,
  p. 188)
Windows Restaurant (Commercial
  Center, $$, p. 186)

VEGAN/VEGETARIAN

Mono (Merchant City, $, p. 183)

MERCHANT CITY

Expensive

City Merchant FISH/SCOTTISH   This restaurant in the heart of Merchant City combines friendly service and menus that highlight fresh fish, seafood, and Scottish meat. Not exactly old-fashioned but certainly favored by businessmen and by those celebrating a family event, it is also convenient if you're attending a performance at the City Halls, which are just across the street. The seared scallops and the classic smoked haddock soup, known as Cullen skink, are both tempting. But if you're not in the mood for fruits of the sea, roast breast of duck, rack of lamb, or an escalope of venison can substitute.

97–99 Candleriggs. ✆ **0141/553-1577.** www.citymerchant.co.uk. Reservations recommended. Fixed price lunch £12; main courses £16–£22. AE, DC, MC, V. Mon–Sat noon–10:30pm; Sun 1–9pm. Underground: Buchanan St.

Moderate

Café Cossachok ★ 🍴 RUSSIAN   Back to its original address on King Street, but completely redesigned now and integrated into the arts/educational center known as Trongate 103, Café Cossachok is better than ever. It's a combination of restaurant and Russian cultural center, where live music is frequently played at supper time

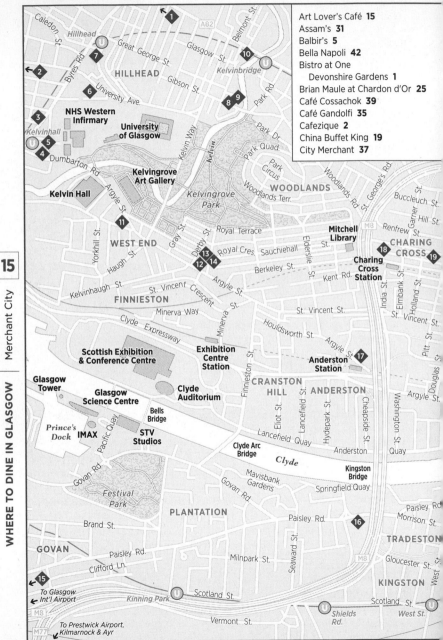

Art Lover's Café **15**
Assam's **31**
Balbir's **5**
Bella Napoli **42**
Bistro at One
   Devonshire Gardens **1**
Brian Maule at Chardon d'Or **25**
Café Cossachok **39**
Café Gandolfi **35**
Cafezique **2**
China Buffet King **19**
City Merchant **37**

Cookie **43**
Crabshakk **12**
The Dhabba **36**
Dining Room **27**
Dragon-i **21**
Fratelli Sarti **28**
Gamba **29**
Harry Ramsden's **16**
Ho Wong **41**
Konaki **13**
La Parmigiana **10**
La Vallée Blanche **6**

Michael Caines
@ ABode **26**
Mono **38**
Mother India **14**
Mother India's Café **11**
Mussel Inn **30**
Nanakusa **18**
Rogano **40**
Schottische **34**
Stravaigin Café Bar **8**
Tchai-Ovna
House of Tea **9**

Two Fat Ladies **4**
Two Fat Ladies
at the Buttery **17**
Two Fat Ladies
in the City **23**
Ubiquitous Chip **7**
University Café **3**
Wagamama **32**
Wee Curry Shop **20**
Where the Monkey Sleeps **24**
Willow Tea Rooms **22**
Windows Restaurant **33**

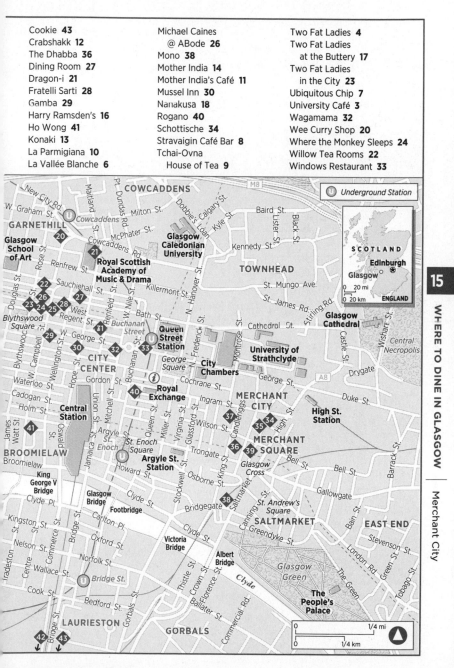

while diners enjoy heaping plates of hearty Slavic fare: Primarily Russian, Georgian, and Ukrainian specialties. Come here to feast on famous dishes such as borscht beetroot soup with sour cream or some savory blini (the Russian equivalent of pancakes). In addition, for the full Russian experience, a variety of vodka bottles inhabit the freezer for a refreshing shot to throw down with your meal.

10 King St. ℂ **0141/553-0733.** www.cossachok.com. Reservations recommended. Fixed-price lunch £7; main courses £7–£12. MC, V. Tues-Sat 11am–11pm; Sun 4–10pm. Train: High St.

Café Gandolfi ★ CONTINENTAL/SCOTTISH   For many local foodies in Merchant City, this is their all-time favorite: It offers solid cooking at the right price and a friendly atmosphere. Owner Seumas MacInnes hails from a Highland/Hebredian family and so the black pudding comes from Stornoway on the Isle of Lewis while the haggis hails from the western Highland town of Dingwall. Particularly recommended is the black pudding, Gandolfi's creamy Cullen skink (smoked haddock chowder), or one of the light pasta dishes. Although if you're really hungry, go for the steak sandwich. The ground-floor room has original, organic, and comfortable wooden furniture created by the Tim Stead workshop in Scotland. Above the premises is **Bar Gandolfi,** which is a bit livelier, and up the street is **Gandolfi Fish,** the owner's dedicated fish restaurant (84 Albion St., ℂ **0141/552-9475**).

64 Albion St. ℂ **0141/552-6813.** www.cafegandolfi.com. Reservations recommended. Main courses £8–£12. MC, V. Daily 9am–11:30pm. Train: High St.

The Dhabba ★ INDIAN   Glaswegians love Indian food, as visitors can tell from the number of Indian restaurants alone. This one, which opened in late 2002, however, is not your typical Glasgow curry house. It is a bit more refined, slightly more expensive, and considerably more stylish than the norm. It specializes in North Indian dishes and largely foregoes the bright food coloring that so many other restaurants use. In addition to spicy dishes featuring lamb, chicken, and shrimps, there is also an excellent selection of vegetarian dishes, which are noticeably less costly than the meat options. Marinated fish cooked in tandoori spices is recommended, as are the many baked breads, whether *naan, rotis,* or *parathas.* Up Candleriggs and on the other side of the street is Dhabba's sister restaurant, **Dakhin** (ℂ **0141/553-2585**), which specializes in South Indian food, with excellent rice flour *dosas.*

44 Candleriggs. ℂ **0141/553-1249.** www.thedhabba.com. Reservations recommended. Fixed price lunch £10; main courses £8–£20. AE, MC, V. Mon-Fri noon–2pm and 5–11pm; Sat and Sun 1–11pm. Underground: St. Enoch.

Schottische SCOTTISH/FRENCH   Housed above the popular Babbity Bowster (p. 241) pub in the small hotel of the same name, Schottische has a rustic feel with a coal fire at one end of the cozy room and handwritten menus. The ingredients are typically Scottish in origin, whether lamb, venison, or sea bass. But given that the chef was born in France, the cuisine usually displays hearty Gallic influences—in addition to excellent wines. For simpler but tasty meals from the same kitchen, stick to the pub on the ground floor.

16–18 Blackfriars St. (off High St.) ℂ **0141/552-5055.** Reservations recommended. Main courses £10–£14. AE, MC, V. Tues-Sat 6:30–9pm. Train: High St.

Inexpensive

Mono VEGAN/VEGETARIAN In the Saltmarket district near the River Clyde, Mono offers dairy-free and meat-free meals in laid-back surroundings. Not only a cafe/restaurant with a bar, Mono also houses a fantastic CD and LP shop with the latest in indie rock and non-mainstream music (p. 232). The cafe/bar is a welcoming and casual place with a mixed and varied clientele. Homemade soups or veggie burgers with fries are typical. The owners also stock a selection of organic wines. Live music, mostly but not exclusively of an acoustic nature, is featured regularly, and the kitchen may close early on gig nights.

12 Kings Court. ✆ **0141/553-2400.** Main courses £5–£7. AE, MC, V. Daily noon–9pm (bar open until midnight). Underground: St. Enoch.

COMMERCIAL CENTER

Expensive

Brian Maule at Chardon d'Or ★ FRENCH/SCOTTISH Chef Brian Maule was born in Ayrshire near Glasgow, but he trained as a young man with some of the best chefs in France and became head chef at the vaunted Michelin-star-winning Gavroche restaurant, owned by the highly respected Roux brothers in London. He decided to return to Scotland and opened his own restaurant in Glasgow in 2001. It is considered to be among the finest in the city, with excellent ingredients and an ambience that is classy but not at all stuffy. Fresh fish and lamb dishes come highly recommended, and in the evenings, Maule inevitably comes out to meet his diners.

176 W. Regent St. ✆ **0141/248-3801.** www.brianmaule.com. Reservations required. Fixed-price lunch £16.50; main courses £20–£26. AE, MC, V. Mon–Fri noon–2:30pm and 6–10pm; Sat 6–10:30pm. Underground: Buchanan St.

Dining Room ★ MODERN SCOTTISH One of the best new arrivals on Glasgow city center's restaurant scene, the Dining Room marks the return of chef Jim Kerr after a spell in the hinterlands—in partnership with Alan Tomkins (co-owner of Gamba). Some predict there could be Michelin recognition, but even without that, it is pretty exceptional. Kerr's sashimi starter of delicate slices of fish

 FAMILY-FRIENDLY fare

China Buffet King Just like in Edinburgh, the buffet-only Chinese restaurant has taken Glasgow by storm. This one is centrally located, at 349 Sauchiehall St. (✆ **0141/333-1788**), with a good variety of Chinese food and some European dishes at all-you-can-eat discount prices that are even lower for children. Open daily noon to 11pm.

University Café I scream, you scream, we all scream for ice cream. "Knickerbocker Glory" is the king of the ice-cream sundae in Scotland, and few places do it better than this Art Deco landmark at 87 Byres Rd., in the west of Glasgow (✆ **0141/339-5217**), with all original features from booths to counters. Open every day except Tuesday from 9am to 10pm (or so).

is made more memorable with strands of ginger, tomato, chives, soya, and tart citrus yuzu fruit juice. Main courses might include rump of Shetland lamb or roast guinea fowl. Staff are relaxed but totally professional.

104 Bath St. ✆ **0141/332-6678.** www.diningroomglasgow.com. Reservations recommended. Fixed-price lunch £13.50; main courses £15–£24. AE, MC, V. Mon–Sat noon–2:30pm and 5–10pm; Sun 5–10pm. Underground: Buchanan St.

Gamba ★★ FISH/SEAFOOD   For many, Gamba is Glasgow's best restaurant on the strength of its fresh fish and seafood dishes prepared by chef and co-owner Derek Marshall. The basement venture is modern and stylish without feeling excessively fancy. Starters include Marshall's signature fish soup or a pseudo-Japanese style sashimi, with succulent slices of salmon and scallops. Main courses may include whole lemon sole in browned butter or delicate pan-seared sea bream. And desserts are not an afterthought either, whether a smooth panna cotta or ice cream infused with Scotch whisky. If you're on a tight budget, however, try the lunch or pre-theater fixed-price menu. The great food is complemented by professional and cordial staff.

225a W. George St. ✆ **0141/572-0899.** www.gamba.co.uk. Reservations required. Fixed-price lunch £17; main courses £20–£26. AE, MC, V. Mon–Sat noon–2:30pm and 5–10:30pm. Underground: Buchanan St.

Ho Wong CHINESE   One of the city's fanciest Chinese restaurants, this classy establishment is on a rather inauspicious block between the river and Argyle Street, just southwest of Glasgow's Central Station. The ambience is refined and even a bit romantic. There are traditionally at least eight duck dishes on the menu, along with a few types of fresh lobster, plenty of fish options, and some sizzling platters as well. If you have trouble deciding, the banquet option makes life easier.

82 York St. ✆ **0141/221-3550.** www.ho-wong.com. Reservations recommended. Fixed-price lunch £10.50; main courses £14–£22. AE, MC, V. Mon–Sat noon–2pm; daily 6–11:30pm; Sun 5–10:30pm. Underground: St. Enoch.

Michael Caines @ ABode FRENCH   When it opened in 2005, this restaurant had ambitions to be the best in the city. Chef/owner Michael Caines appears on British TV and had already earned Michelin stars in England. It didn't happen here but still it is hard to find fault with the cooking and presentation of dishes, such as salmon with spinach ravioli or saddle of venison with "boulangère" (slow-cooked) potatoes, squash puree, and red cabbage. The dining room is modern and stylish, as you would expect in a boutique hotel such as ABode (p. 173). In addition to this fine-dining restaurant, there is a cafe/bar in the basement.

129 Bath St. ✆ **0141/221-6789.** www.michaelcaines.com. Reservations required. Fixed-price lunch £12.95; fixed-price dinner £19. AE, MC, V. Tues–Sat noon–2:30pm and 6–10pm. Underground: Buchanan St.

Rogano FISH/SEAFOOD   A landmark dining establishment, Rogano boasts a reasonably well-preserved and still impressive Art Deco interior that was patterned after the *Queen Mary* ocean liner. Much of what you see dates back to the opening of an oyster bar here in 1935. Since then, the space has expanded, and Rogano has hosted virtually every visiting celebrity to Glasgow. Service is attentive and informed. The menu emphasizes seafood, such as halibut or lobster, often in traditional if possibly old-fashioned recipes. Alas, the food doesn't always live up to expectations raised by these prices. A less expensive menu is offered downstairs in Cafe Rogano, where the price for a main course hovers around the £12 mark.

11 Exchange Place. ☎ **0141/248-4055.** www.roganoglasgow.com. Reservations recommended. Fixed-price lunch £16.50; main courses £17–£34. AE, DC, MC, V. Daily noon–2:30pm and 6–10:30pm. Underground: Buchanan St.

Moderate

Assam's INDIAN   Opened in 2009 by a long-standing manager at one of Glasgow's most loved and critically acclaimed Indian restaurants, Assam's shows that Assam Rashid was paying attention and ready to strike out on his own. The basement space is not ideal but it's comfortable, and the one-page menu provides welcome contrast to the typically long-winded selections at most Indian restaurants. Good quality and value-for-money prices should ensure that Assam's goes on to join the higher ranks of Glasgow's already impressive collection of Indian restaurants.

51 W. Regent St. ☎ **0141/331-1980.** www.assams.co.uk. Reservations recommended. Fixed-price lunch £7.50; main courses £7–£12. MC, V. Daily noon–11pm (midnight Fri and Sat). Underground: Buchanan St.

Dragon-i ASIAN/CHINESE   Convenient for the Theatre Royal, which is virtually across the street, this contemporary Chinese/Far Eastern restaurant is always packed before a show. Expect the unexpected at the elegant Dragon-i, whose cuisine never falls into the bland or typical chow mein or sweet-and-sour standards. Instead, the menu has dishes such as tiger shrimps with asparagus in a garlic chardonnay sauce or chicken with sautéed apples and pineapples. The wine list is also excellent, and the pre-theater menu is good value (just make sure you have a booking if there is a performance across the street).

313 Hope St. ☎ **0141/332-7728.** www.dragon-i.co.uk. Reservations recommended. Main courses £11–£16. AE, MC, V. Mon–Fri noon–2pm and 5–11pm; Sat and Sun 5–10pm. Underground: Cowcaddens.

Fratelli Sarti ☺ ITALIAN   Owned by the Sarti brothers, this dual restaurant and cafe feels like a family-run cafe/bistro crossed with a delicatessen. Indeed, you can still buy dry goods and wines here, although they discontinued the deli meats and cheeses a couple of years ago. The pizza is excellent, with a thin, crispy crust and modest amounts of sauce, cheese, and toppings, which prevent it from becoming a sloppy mess. Pasta dishes, such as "al forno" with penne, sausage, and spinach, are filling. If you desire a slightly more formal setting in the evening, try the Fratelli Sarti at 42 Renfield Street (☎ **0141/572-7000**).

133 Wellington St. ☎ **0141/204-0440.** www.sarti.co.uk. Reservations recommended. Main courses £8–£12. AE, MC, V. Mon–Fri 8am–10pm; Sat 10am–10pm; Sun noon–10pm. Underground: Buchanan St.

Mussel Inn FISH/SEAFOOD   Sister restaurant to the original on Rose Street in Edinburgh, this restaurant has the distinction of being owned by shellfish farmers in the west of Scotland. The kilo pot of mussels you eat here on any given day could have been harvested within the last 24 hours. The feel at the Glasgow unit is casual, with an open kitchen, light wood tables, and high ceilings—re-creating a seaside look in the city. In addition to the house specialty of steamed mussels served with a choice of broths (from spicy to white wine with garlic), the queen scallop salad is fine and refreshing, creamy chowders hearty and filling, and the menu always features a fresh "catch of the day."

157 Hope St. ☎ **0141/572-1405.** www.mussel-inn.com. Main courses £8–£14. AE, MC, V. Mon–Thurs noon–2:30pm and 5:30–10pm; Fri–Sat noon–10pm; Sun 5–10pm. Underground: Buchanan St.

15

WHERE TO DINE IN GLASGOW

Commercial Center

Nanakusa ★ JAPANESE   New in 2007, this locally owned restaurant tries to present the full range of Japanese cuisine, from sushi and sashimi to teppanyaki and tempura; not to mention bento boxes, rice dishes, side plates such as *gyoza*, and big steamy, slurpy noodle bowls. It's casual and stylish, often buzzing with customers, with helpful staff to help everyone negotiate the large and varied menu. Portions are usually generous and because it draws a mix of customers, it is quite a lively place, too.

441 Sauchiehall St. ℭ **0141/332-6303.** Fixed-price lunch £6; main courses £7–£10. MC, V. Mon–Thurs noon–2:30pm and 5–11pm; Fri–Sat noon–midnight; Sun 5–11pm. Train: Charing Cross.

Wagamama ASIAN/JAPANESE   A chain operation based in London, where there are several outlets, the Wagamama Japanese noodle bar formula has proved successful at its first venture into Scotland. Casual seating is at long tables and benches, where waiting staff key your order into handheld devices that transmit it to the cooks. Dishes come as they are prepared, rather than as starters and main courses. It is one of the best places in the city center to get a quick bite before a show or the cinema—unless the line is going out the front door.

97–103 W. George St. ℭ **0141/229-1468.** www.wagamama.com. No reservations. Dishes £5–£10. Daily noon–11pm (till 10pm Sun). Underground: Buchanan St.

Windows Restaurant SCOTTISH   Unlike Edinburgh, Glasgow doesn't have many restaurants with views overlooking the city. In fact, it has one—this one. Here, on the top floor of the Carlton George Hotel, Windows is aptly named, as it gives diners panoramic views of Glasgow's city center near George Square and the City Chambers. The menu includes such dishes as roast chicken supreme or grilled filet of Scottish beef with mushrooms.

In the Carlton George Hotel, 44 W. George St. ℭ **0141/354-5070.** Reservations recommended. Main courses £13–£16. AE, MC, V. Daily noon–2:30pm and 5–9:30pm. Underground: Buchanan St.

Inexpensive

Wee Curry Shop ★★ 🔪 INDIAN   This tiny place is hardly big enough to swing a cat in, but the aptly named Wee Curry Shop offers the best, low-cost Indian dishes in the city. Just about five tables are crammed between the front door and the open kitchen, where the chefs prepare everything to order. The menu is concise with a clutch of opening courses, such as fried *pakora,* and a half dozen or so main courses, such as spicy chili garlic chicken. Portions are large even if prices are cheap. While it may feel off the beaten track, the Wee Curry Shop is actually only a short walk from the shopping precincts of Sauchiehall Street. There are other branches in the West End on Ashton Lane and Byres Road.

7 Buccleuch St. (near Cambridge St.). ℭ **0141/353-0777.** Reservations recommended. Fixed-price lunch £5.25; main courses £6.50–£8. No credit cards. Mon–Sat noon–2pm and 5:30–10pm; Sun 5:30–10pm. Underground: Cowcaddens.

Where the Monkey Sleeps CAFE   Downstairs near Blythswood Square, this singular cafe is one of the best daytime places for cappuccinos, soups, and sandwiches in the commercial center of Glasgow. You know you've found it when you see the bikes of messengers who seem to live here when they are not on the streets delivering special letters and business packages. As the name might indicate, this is no ordinary cafe. Sandwich names appear to resemble those of the hard rock acts so beloved by the owner, and the hit of the mix is probably the "Stoofa," which is a

For tea and a snack, why not join the rest of the tourists in Glasgow and try to secure a table at the landmark **Willow Tea Rooms,** 217 Sauchiehall St. ((℗ **0141/332-0521;** Underground: Buchanan St.). When the famed Mrs. Cranston opened the Willow Tea Rooms in 1904, it was something of a sensation due to its unique Charles Rennie Mackintosh design. The building's white facade still stands out from the crowd more than 100 years later. The dining room, one floor above street level, is open Monday to Saturday 9am to 5pm and Sunday noon to 5pm. A second branch on Buchanan Street is similarly appointed if less authentic.

For a more contemporary experience, in the West End overlooking the River Kelvin, **Tchai-Ovna House of Tea,** 42 Otago St. ((℗ **0141/357-4524;** Underground: Kelvinbridge), has a selection of some 80 teas, served in fairly eccentric and bohemian surroundings. Food is vegetarian. In the evenings, there may be live music, poetry, or comedy. Tchai-Ovna is open daily from 11am to 11pm.

panini with free-range chicken, sage, thyme, red onion, mayo, and balsamic vinegar. Be patient, the place is busy at peak time but it's worth the wait.

182 W. Regent St. (℗ **0141/226-3406.** www.wtms.co.uk. Soups £2.50; sandwiches £3–£6. MC, V. Mon-Fri 8am–5pm; Sat 10am–5pm. Underground: Buchanan St.

THE WEST END

Expensive

Bistro at One Devonshire Gardens ★★ MODERN SCOTTISH   In the luxurious Hotel du Vin (p. 175), this restaurant sets the bar nearly as high as the world-class lodgings. Chef du Cuisine Paul Tamburrini takes care of the food, with dishes such as braised oxtail terrine, shellfish and smoked haddock soufflé, or butter roasted loin of roe deer. The wine list is large, and the house selections are both diverse and relatively affordable, the surroundings feel elegant but not stuffy, and staff are relaxed but informed. While the restaurant at this landmark address hasn't quite achieved the heights to which it once soared under the guidance of Michelin-starred chef Andrew Fairlie, it is certainly flying in the right direction.

Hotel du Vin at One Devonshire Gardens, 1 Devonshire Gardens. (℗ **0141/339-2001.** www.hotelduvin. com. Reservations required. Fixed-price lunch £14.50; main courses £20–£25. AE, MC, V. Mon-Fri 7–10:30am, noon–2.15pm, and 6–10pm; Sat 7–11am and 6–10pm; Sun 7–11am, 12.30–2.45pm, and 6–10pm. Rail: Hyndland.

La Parmigiana ★ ITALIAN   This remains the favorite fine-dining Italian restaurant in Glasgow, providing a cosmopolitan and Continental atmosphere. A well-established, quarter-of-a-century-old business belonging to the Giovanazzi family, Parmigiana is often recommended for its fish and meat dishes, whether grilled salmon with honey-roasted vegetables, pan-fried pork cutlet with caramelized apple, or roast breast of guinea fowl stuffed with porcini mushrooms. A highlight of the pasta options is lobster ravioli with basil cream sauce.

447 Great Western Rd. © **0141/334-0686.** www.laparmigiana.co.uk. Reservations required. Fixed-price lunch £14.50; main courses £16–£22. AE, DC, MC, V. Mon–Sat noon–2:30pm and 5:30–10:30pm; Sun noon–7:30pm. Underground: Kelvinbridge.

La Vallée Blanche FRENCH   Opening just before the worst recession on record is awkward timing, but this restaurant at the top of Byres Road appears to have weathered the storm and has more critics happy than before. Named after a glacial gorge, La Vallée Blanche gently mimics Alpine aesthetics with wood paneling and lanterns, but the food is not especially rustic. Dishes such as braised pig cheeks, scallops with black pudding and artichoke sauce, and roast guinea fowl are well executed and refined. The set-price lunches emphasize French classics.

360 Byres Rd. © **0141/334-3333.** www.lavalleeblanche.com. Reservations recommended. Fixed-price lunch £13; main courses £16–£20. MC, V. Tues–Fri noon–2pm and 5:30–10:30pm; Sat and Sun noon–10pm. Underground: Hillhead.

Ubiquitous Chip ★ MODERN SCOTTISH   No other restaurant has been more responsible for the culinary renaissance in Scotland than the Ubiquitous Chip. Opening the "Chip" in 1971, the late Ronnie Clydesdale (1936–2010) was way ahead of the curve. Although not a professional chef, he had the idea of bringing the best Scottish ingredients into his kitchen—and then to the attention of diners. To this day, the menus state the provenance of the produce, a practice now common-place in most of the better restaurants. The menu may feature Rothesay black pudding, Hebridean Soay lamb, Ardnamurchan venison, Aberdeen Angus filet steak, or Scrabster-landed lythe; the wine list is epic. Upstairs, there's a friendly pub and a brasserie that serves similar quality fare at a fraction of the price.

12 Ashton Lane, off Byres Rd. © **0141/334-5007.** www.ubiquitouschip.co.uk. Reservations required for restaurant, recommended for brasserie. Fixed-price lunch £25; fixed-price dinner £40. AE, DC, MC, V. Daily noon–2:30pm and 5:30–11pm. Underground: Hillhead.

Moderate

Balbir's ★ INDIAN   After taking a break from running restaurants in Glasgow, Balbir Singh Sumal returned in 2005 to open this sprawling place, serving first-class curries and other Indian specialties. Dishes are lighter than the norm, as his chefs eschew ghee in favor of low-cholesterol rapeseed oil. The tandoori oven is used to good effect with dishes, especially a starter of barbecued salmon, served with freshly made chutney. 2010 saw a renovation of the interiors. If on Glasgow's Southside, check out his **Saffron Lounge** at 61 Kilmarnock Road (© **0141/632-8564**). Open evenings only.

7 Church St. © **0141/339-7711.** www.balbirsrestaurants.co.uk. Main courses £8–£14. AE, MC, V. Daily 5–10:30pm. Underground: Kelvinhall.

Crabshakk 🍴 FISH/SEAFOOD   Established in 2009 by a family with links to Scotland's Western Isles, the only confusing thing about this newcomer is the decision to misspell the name. The menu ranges from moderately priced fish dishes, such as smoked mackerel and horseradish or a fish club sandwich with chips, to more pricey whole crab or lobster. And they're only available if found fresh in the market that week. Crab cakes are a signature dish and they're wonderfully lacking any potato filler. Langoustines are sold cold or grilled, in small or larger portions. The

Finnieston district of Glasgow is a growing foodie destination, but for visitors this may feel a bit off the beaten track.

1114 Argyle St. ✆ **0141/334-6127.** www.crabshakk.com. Reservations recommended. Main courses £7–£17. MC, V. Tues–Sat noon–10pm; Sun noon–6pm. Underground: Kelvinhall. Bus: 62.

Mother India ★ INDIAN   After more than a decade in business, this restaurant has established itself as the most respected Indian restaurant in Glasgow. The menu is not overloaded with hundreds of different dishes—just a dozen or so and there's not a poor option among them. Oven-baked fish, which comes wrapped in foil, is seasoned with aromatic spices, while chicken and zucchini squash is served with a sauce that favors pan-roasted cumin and cardamom. Whether seated on the ground floor or in the dining room above, you will find the staff to be courteous and attentive. Down the road, toward the heart of the West End, a second branch—**Mother India's Café** ★ (1355 Argyle St.; ✆ **0141/339-9145**)—offers less expensive, tapas-style dishes.

28 Westminster Terrace (Sauchiehall St. at Kelvingrove St.). ✆ **0141/221-1663.** www.motherindia glasgow.co.uk. Reservations required. Fixed-price lunch £9.50; main courses £7.50–£12. MC, V. Mon–Tues 5:30–10pm; Wed–Fri noon–2:30pm, and 5–10:30pm; Sat 1–10:30pm; Sun 4:30–10pm. Underground: Kelvinhall.

Two Fat Ladies ★ FISH/SCOTTISH   This ranks high on the list of many locals' favorite restaurants. The "Two Fat Ladies" is a reference to its street number—a nickname for the number 88 when called out in bingo games. Dishes might include red-onion-and-goat-cheese tart, pan-seared bream, or filet of sea bass served on mashed potatoes with spring onions. In addition to the neighborhoody West End flagship, there's a more cosmopolitan outlet, **Two Fat Ladies in the City** ★, at 118a Blythswood St. (✆ **0141/847-0088**); for a more formal setting go to **Two Fat Ladies at the Buttery** ★ 🎁 (652 Argyle St.; ✆ **0141/221-8188**).

88 Dumbarton Rd. ✆ **0141/339-1944.** www.twofatladiesrestaurant.com. Reservations recommended. Fixed-price lunch £13.50; main courses £14–£18. MC, V. Mon–Sat noon–3pm and 5pm; Sun 1–9pm. Underground: Kelvinhall.

Inexpensive

Cafezique ★ 🎁 CAFE/BISTRO   You're not likely to stumble across Cafezique, but West End locals will know how to find this modern, split-level cafe in the Partick neighborhood of the West End. Up the hill from Dumbarton Road and Mansfield Park (which hosts the farmers' markets every fortnight), this eatery serves up everything from spicy Bloody Marys, cappuccinos, and scones with jam to knock-out eggs Benedict, alongside a decent range of main courses. There's not an inch of unused space, but the staff manages to make all feel welcomed. A great wee place.

66 Hyndland St. ✆ **0141/339-7180.** Reservations recommended. Main courses £6–£12. MC, V. Daily 9am–10pm. Underground: Kelvinhall.

Konaki GREEK   This simple and unassuming Greek taverna midway between the city center and the heart of the West End—convenient for the several moderately priced hotels and guesthouses nearby—has developed a reputation for good, hearty food at relatively inexpensive prices. The menu includes phyllo pastry stuffed with goat's cheese, slow-cooked meats, and chargrilled kebabs. For a sample of Greek delicacies such as stuffed grape leaves and hummus dip, opt for the meze platter.

920 Sauchiehall St. ☎ **0141/342-4010.** www.konakitaverna.co.uk. Fixed-price lunch £7; main courses £10. MC, V. Mon–Sat noon–11pm; Sun 5–10pm. Underground: Kelvinhall.

Stravaigin Café Bar ★ 🍴 SCOTTISH/INTERNATIONAL   "Think global, eat local" is the motto of Stravaigin, which roughly means "wanderin'" in Scots. While the basement restaurant here is an award-winning enterprise, the ground-level pub/ cafe offers less expensive but still memorable food. Scottish produce gets international twists: For example, cheese and herb fritters with sweet chili sauce or roast lamb served with coriander couscous. But there are also staples such as hearty beer-battered fish and fluffy Maris Piper fries. The atmosphere is always cordial, and prices are lower still during the busy pre-theater seating. If you like Stravaigin, you might consider its sister bistro near Byres Road, called appropriately enough, **Stravaigin 2** (8 Ruthven Lane; ☎ **0141/334-7156**).

28 Gibson St. ☎ **0141/334-2665.** www.stravaigin.com. Fixed-price lunch £13; main courses £8–£12. AE, MC, V. Daily 11am–10:30pm. Underground: Kelvinbridge.

THE SOUTHSIDE
Moderate

Bella Napoli ITALIAN   Set in the heart of the Shawlands district, the main commercial area of Glasgow's Southside, Bella Napoli looks from the street to be a bright, shiny Italian cafe. But to the rear and down a few steps, a more refined but still casual dining room is hidden. The family-run business is friendly, and the staff is efficient as well. Starters include melon with shrimps or minestrone soup, with the rest of the menu offering a range of pasta dishes as well as risotto and meaty main courses. Up front, the diner is best for lunch food such as *calzones* filled with vegetables, cheese, and tomato sauce.

85 Kilmarnock Rd. ☎ **0141/362-4222.** www.crolla.com. Reservations suggested for restaurant. Main courses £6–£17. MC, V. Daily 9am–11pm (with lunch and dinner hours kept in restaurant). Train: Cross-myloof. Bus: 38.

Cookie 🍴 INTERNATIONAL   Opened late in 2009, this cool bistro with graffiti art and a tiny shop for kitchen gadgets offers a menu chalked on the board. Owner Domenico del Priore likes using fresh, seasonal produce and hopes you will, too—so far so good as people have been flocking here. Cookie's goal is to connect diners with cooks, food producers, farmers, and local allotment growers. Del Priore's own family in Umbria grows the olives that end up in the oil here. Expect dishes such as wild mushroom risotto, pork loin with savoy cabbage, or house-made vanilla ice cream. The wine selection is virtually unique and almost all are sold by the glass as well.

72 Nithsdale Rd. ☎ **0141/423-1411.** www.cookiescotland.com. Main courses £8.50–£15. MC, V. Tues–Sat 9am–10pm; Sun and Mon 10am–6pm. Train: Queens Park. Bus: 38 or 44.

Inexpensive

Art Lover's Café SCOTTISH   The House for an Art Lover (p. 200) is a creation by contemporary builders and architects working with some very basic drawings left by Charles Rennie Mackintosh. In addition to being a stop for hardcore Mackintosh fans, it's also home to a popular cafe. Next to the gift shop, a stylish, ivory-colored dining room has arching windows that look out on to a garden. The cafe's modern

Scottish cuisine—dishes such as salad of seared scallops, black pudding, and crisp pancetta—is occasionally inspired, and the place at lunchtime on the weekend is rarely less than full.

House for an Art Lover, Bellahouston Park, 10 Dumbreck Rd. © **0141/353-4779.** Reservations recommended. www.houseforanartlover.co.uk. Main courses £6–£8. AE, MC, V. Daily noon–4pm. Train: Dumbreck. Bus: 9, 36, 38, 54, or 56.

Harry Ramsden's ☺ FISH   Harry Ramsden's is something of a British institution. The restaurant chain began humbly in the north of England, with branches spreading in all directions today. While fish and chips in Scotland (more commonly called a "fish supper" if ordered to go and a "fish tea" when eating in) usually involves battered and deep-fried haddock, in England the common white fish used is cod. Here at Harry's you can get either—as well as plaice and other options. For children, there is a special menu and an outdoor play area.

251 Paisley Rd. © **0141/429-3700.** www.harryramsdens.co.uk. Main courses £7–£10. AE, MC, V. Daily noon–10pm. Bus: 9 or 54.

PICNIC FARE

This leafy city has no shortage of spots for a picnic, whether along the Clyde near the city center in sprawling Glasgow Green; Kelvingrove Park or the Botanic Gardens in the West End; or Pollok Country Park and Queens Park, both of which are on the Southside.

If you're in the city center, gravitate toward **Pekhams** in Merchant City near George Square, 61 Glassford St. (© **0141/553-0666**), which has a full delicatessen, fresh bread, and a wine shop. Another possibility in this district is **Berits & Brown,** a cafe and small deli at 6 Wilson St. (© **0141/552-6980**).

In the West End, the options include the exceptional **Heart Buchanan Fine Food and Wine** ★★, near the Botanic Gardens at 380 Byres Rd. (© **0141/334-7626**), which also has a small cafe. **Delizique** ★, 70 Hyndland St. (© **0141/339-2000**), is another superior food shop, while there's another branch of **Pekhams** at 124 Byres Rd. (© **0141/357-1454**). Nearby is the cafe and deli, **Kember & Jones Fine Food Emporium** ★, 134 Byres Rd. (© **0141/337-3851**).

For some of the best cheese in the U.K., visit the **I. J. Mellis Cheesemonger** ★★ branch in Glasgow on Great Western Rd. (© **0141/339-8998**), and just further toward the city center is the Glasgow branch of **Lupe Pintos** ★, 313 Great Western Rd. (© **0141/334-5444**), for Mexican and American foodstuffs. On the Southside in the Shawlands district near Queens Park, the **1901 Deli,** 11 Skirving St. (© **0141/632-1630**), has a good supply of goodies for any outdoor feast.

EXPLORING GLASGOW

Glasgow is a reasonably compact and contiguous city—roughly the size of Amsterdam or San Francisco. As its 19th-century expansion was inspired in part by American cities such as Chicago, Glasgow's city center is laid out U.S.-style on a grid. Not very European, but at least the heart of the city is user-friendly. Most visits begin here, amid the rich Victorian architecture, whether it be 19th-century banks (many of which have been converted to other uses such as restaurants and bars), office buildings, warehouses, and churches.

Culturally, the options in the heart of Glasgow include architect Charles Rennie Mackintosh's **School of Art,** the city-owned **Gallery of Modern Art (GOMA),** and the **Tron Theatre.** There is also the Gothic medieval **Glasgow Cathedral** and the splendid Victorian **Theatre Royal.** These attractions are all within a fairly short walking distance of each other. Three main boulevards—Argyle, Buchanan, and Sauchiehall streets—form a Z shape and have been made into predominantly car-free pedestrian zones, which offer a wealth of shopping opportunities.

Adjacent to the commercial center is Merchant City, where loft conversions over the past 25 years have created a hip, happening quarter with many lively bars and restaurants. The affluent and urbane West End has the city's top university, its most desirable homes, and plenty of restaurants, bars, and shops. This area is trendy and lively, with some of the city's best nightlife. Leafy and attractive, with the **Kelvingrove Art Gallery & Museum** fabulously refurbished and now one of the most visited attractions in Britain, the West End is many visitors' favorite place to explore.

A river runs through Glasgow, and the modern city has yet to capitalize fully on the real potential of the **Clyde.** The shipbuilding industry that made the river famous is long gone. There isn't even an active, attractive marina for leisure boats today. At least, not yet. But bits of the waterfront have been improved and there is a certain urban charm to the riverbank, which has a national cycle path.

On the opposite side of the Clyde from the city center and West End, the Southside spreads out with well-established suburban neighborhoods.

Some say this is the "real" Glasgow. While mostly residential, it is home to at least one major, arguably world-class, attraction—the **Burrell Collection**—that merits an excursion south of the River Clyde.

Suggested Itineraries

IF YOU HAVE 1 DAY

From George Square, the city's main plaza in front of Glasgow City Chambers, catch one of the open-topped **tour buses.** The trip, from historic **Glasgow Cathedral** in the east to **Glasgow University** and trendy **Byres Road** in the west, can be as entertaining as it is informative. It's also the best way to get oriented. Tickets are valid for 24 hours, and you can get off and on as much as you desire. Visit at least one of the city-run museums (they're free) and a bona-fide Glasgow pub, such as the **Horse Shoe** (p. 241).

IF YOU HAVE 2 DAYS

Follow one of the strolls outlined in chapter 17. Try to take in a bit of real **Charles Rennie Mackintosh** architecture, whether as an organized tour of the **Art School** on Garnethill in the city center or by visiting the interiors of his family house reconstructed at the **Hunterian Art Gallery** on the University of Glasgow campus in the West End. While you're in the area, check out the **Kelvingrove Art Gallery & Museum.** Head south and visit the vaunted **Burrell Collection.** Its art and artifacts from ancient to modern are the pride of the city, housed in an attractive, contemporary building amid verdant Pollok Country Park.

IF YOU HAVE 3 DAYS

Architecture buffs should discover more about **Alexander "Greek" Thomson,** who preceded Mackintosh by two generations and was equally innovative and important. Try **Holmwood House** on the city's South-side. After London, Glasgow is the second city for shopping in the U.K. But don't be content with the familiar department stores: Seek out the designer labels in Merchant City or some funky shop off Byres Road in the West End. Don't miss the Cathedral, and if the weather's fine, hike around the nearby **Central Necropolis.** The city's main graveyard occupies a hill, so the views are grand.

IF YOU HAVE 4 DAYS OR MORE

Those more interested in social history might visit the **People's Palace** museum; visitors with kids should gravitate to the **Science Centre;** while those attuned to contemporary arts have not only the **CCA** but also the **Arches** to consider. In addition, **Trongate 103,** which opened in 2009, is a well-conceived cultural center on the edge of Merchant City. On the weekend, lovers of car boot sales (or trunk sales) and flea markets owe the **Barras** stalls a visit. An excursion away from the city is in order, either down the Clyde toward the sea and across to the western peninsulas and islands, or up the road to **Loch Lomond** and the beginnings of the Highlands. In most directions, it takes under 30 minutes to find wide-open countryside.

TOP ATTRACTIONS
City Center & Merchant City

The proverbial heart of Glasgow is **George Square,** at the doorstep of the seat of local government, the **City Chambers,** which Queen Victoria opened in 1888. The building's interiors have been used for movie sets (sometimes to represent the Kremlin), and the lavishly decorated **Banqueting Hall** is occasionally open to the public. Of the several statues in George Square, the most imposing is the 25-m (80-ft.)

Glasgow Attractions

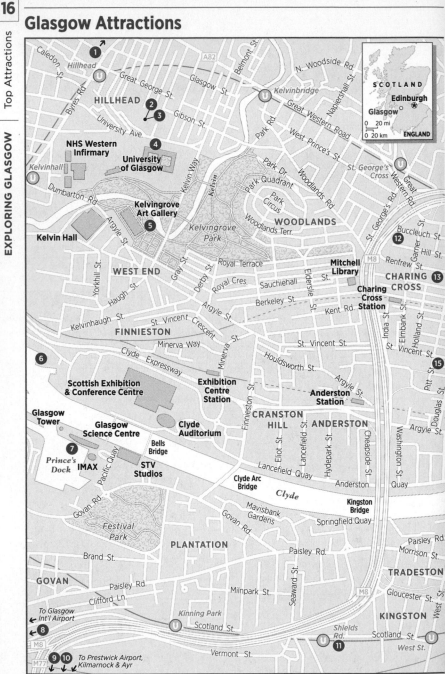

Caledon St.

1

Hillhead

Byres Rd.

Great George St.

Glasgow St.

A82

Belmont St.

N. Woodside Rd.

Kelvinbridge

Great Western Road

Napiershall St.

HILLHEAD

2

3

Gibson St.

University Ave.

Park Rd.

West Prince's St.

St. George's Western Rd.

SCOTLAND

Edinburgh

Glasgow ✸

ENGLAND

0   20 mi

0   20 km

NHS Western Infirmary

4

University of Glasgow

Kelvin Way

Kelvin

Park Dr.

Park Quadrant

Woodlands Rd.

St. George's Cross

Kelvinhall

Dumbarton Rd.

Kelvingrove Art Gallery

5

Kelvingrove Park

Park Circus

Woodlands Terr.

WOODLANDS

Buccleuch St.

12

Kelvin Hall

Argyle St.

Yorkhill St.

WEST END

Gray St.

Derby St.

Royal Terrace

Royal Cres.

Sauchiehall St.

Elderslie St.

Mitchell Library

M8

Garner

Hill St.

Renfrew St.

CHARING CROSS

13

Haugh St.

Kelvinhaugh St.

St. Vincent Crescent

Berkeley St.

Argyle St.

Kent Rd.

Charing Cross Station

India St.

St. Vincent St.

Elmbank St.

Holland St.

FINNIESTON

Minerva Way

Minerva St.

St. Vincent St.

Houldsworth St.

Argyle St.

Pitt St.

Douglas St.

Argyle St.

15

6

Clyde Expressway

Finnieston St.

CRANSTON HILL

ANDERSTON

Anderston Station

Cheapside St.

Washington St.

Scottish Exhibition & Conference Centre

Exhibition Centre Station

Eliot St.

Lancefield St.

Hydepark St.

Glasgow Tower

Glasgow Science Centre

Clyde Auditorium

Bells Bridge

Lancefield Quay

Anderston Quay

7

Prince's Dock

IMAX

Pacific Quay

STV Studios

Clyde Arc Bridge

Clyde

Kingston Bridge

Govan Rd.

Mavisbank Gardens

Govan Rd.

Springfield Quay

Festival Park

PLANTATION

Paisley Rd.

Paisley Rd.

Morrison St.

TRADESTON

Brand St.

GOVAN

Paisley Rd.

Clifford Ln.

Milnpark St.

Seaward St.

M8

Gloucester St.

West St.

KINGSTON

To Glasgow Int'l Airport

8

Kinning Park

Scotland St.

Shields Rd.

11

Scotland St.

West St.

M8

M77

9 10

To Prestwick Airport, Kilmarnock & Ayr

Vermont St.

Botanic Gardens **1**
The Burrell Collection **9**
Central Necropolis **21**
Centre for
  Contemporary Art (CCA) **13**
Gallery of Modern Art **17**
Glasgow Cathedral **20**
Glasgow Green **24**
Glasgow School of Art **14**
Holmwood House **23**

House for an Art Lover **8**
Hunterian Art Gallery **2**
Hunterian Museum **4**
Kelvingrove Art Gallery
  & Museum **5**
The Lighthouse **16**
Mackintosh House **3**
People's Palace **25**
Pollok Country Park **10**
Provand's Lordship **18**

St. Mungo Museum of
  Religious Life & Art **19**
St. Vincent Street Church **15**
Science Centre **7**
Scotland Street
  School Museum **11**
The Tall Ship at
  Glasgow Harbour **6**
Tenement House **12**
Trongate 103 **22**

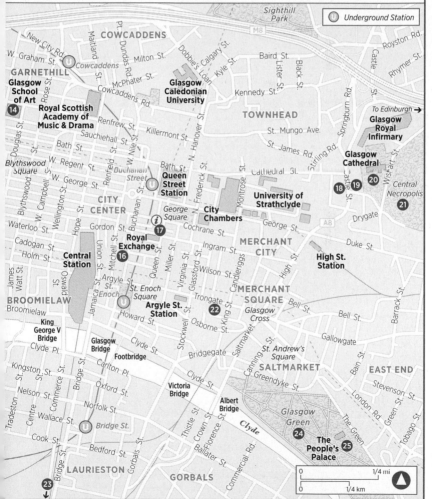

Doric column with Sir Walter Scott at the top. It was the first such monument built in the author's honor, about 5 years after his death.

Gallery of Modern Art ★ GOMA, as it is better known, is housed in the former Royal Exchange in Royal Exchange Square, where Ingram Street meets Queen Street. The building—originally surrounded by farmland—was built as a mansion for an 18th-century tobacco magnate. Later it was expanded by one of the city's busy 19th-century architects, David Hamilton, who added a dramatic portico to the front. Now the pile and its square are at the heart of the city, near George Square and Buchanan Street. The galleries on different floors are slightly pretentiously named after earth, fire, air, and water. The permanent collection has works by Euan Uglow, Stanley Spencer, and John Bellany, as well as art from the "new Glasgow boys" who emerged in the 1980s, such as Peter Howson, Ken Currie, and the late Steven Campbell. Before controversially becoming a museum in the mid-1990s, the pile was used as a public library and recently the basement was converted to that function again.

Royal Exchange Sq., Queen St. *(C)* **0141/287-3050.** www.glasgowmuseums.com. Free admission. Mon–Wed and Sat 10am–5pm; Thurs 10am–8pm; Fri and Sun 11am–5pm. Underground: Buchanan St. Bus: 12, 18, 40, 62, or 66.

Glasgow Cathedral ★★ Also known as the Cathedral of St. Kentigern or St. Mungo's, Glasgow Cathedral dates to the 13th century. The edifice is mainland Scotland's only complete medieval cathedral—the most important ecclesiastical building of that era in the entire country. Unlike other cathedrals across Scotland, this one survived the Reformation practically intact, although 16th-century protestant zeal did purge it of all Roman Catholic relics (as well as destroying plenty of historical documents). Later, misguided architectural "restoration" led to the demolition of its western towers, forever altering the Cathedral's appearance.

The lower church is where Gothic design reigns, with an array of pointed arches and piers. The Laigh Kirk (lower church), whose vaulted crypt is said to be one of the finest in Europe, also holds St. Mungo's tomb. Mungo's death in 612 was recorded, but the annals of his life date only to the 12th century. Other highlights of the interior include the Blackadder aisle and the 15th-century nave with a stone screen (unique in Scotland) showing the seven deadly sins.

For one of the best views of the Cathedral (and the city, too, for that matter), cross the ravine (through which the Molendinar Burn once ran before being diverted underground) into the **Central Necropolis ★**. Built on a proud hill and dominated by a statue of John Knox, this graveyard (patterned in part on the famous Père Lachaise cemetery in Paris) was opened in the 1830s. It is emblematic of the mixing of ethnic groups in Glasgow, as the first person to be buried here was Jewish, as Jews were the first to receive permission to use part of the hill for burial grounds.

Glasgow Cathedral, Cathedral Sq., Castle St. *(C)* **0141/552-6891.** www.historic-scotland.gov.uk. Free admission. Apr–Sept Mon–Sat 9:30am–6pm, Sun 1–5pm; Oct–Mar Mon–Sat 9:30am–4pm, Sun 1–4pm. Sun morning service at 11am. Train: High St. Bus: 11, 36, 37, 38, 42, or 89.

Glasgow School of Art ★★★ Architect Charles Rennie Mackintosh's global reputation rests in large part on this magnificent building on Garnethill above Sauchiehall Street, a highlight of the Mackintosh trail that legions of his fans from across the world follow through the city. Completed in two stages (1899 and 1909), the building offers a mix of ideas promoted by the Arts and Crafts and Art Nouveau

FROMMER'S FAVORITE GLASGOW experiences

Taking the Mackintosh "Trail" and Discovering "Greek" Thomson Architecture in Glasgow has not always been appreciated, and city planners after World War II had a mind to accomplish what German bombers had not: That is, knock down the city's glorious Victorian structures. Luckily they were stopped. In the 19th century, the city spawned two singular stars of architecture: The now-famous Charles Rennie Mackintosh as well as the lesser-known, but equally talented, Alexander "Greek" Thomson.

Visiting the Kelvingrove Art Gallery and the Burrell Collection The artistic *pièces de résistance* of Glasgow (and some say in all of Scotland), the Kelvingrove—restored in 2006—and Burrell are two of the city's major attractions. The former showcases the excellent municipal art collection. The latter shows what a virtually unlimited budget, acquired during the lifetime of shipping baron Sir William Burrell, can purchase.

Hanging Out in the West End From dining in trendy bistros to shopping at vintage clothing or antiquary bookshops—or just strolling the streets near the University and around the Botanic Gardens, Glasgow's West End is bound to have something to interest the erudite explorer.

Downing a Dram in a Glasgow Bar Whether sipping a 12-year-old single malt whisky from the island of Islay or nursing a pint of lager, you should find that Glasgow's many bars are the best places to connect with the local population. In contrast to the essay by the 20th-century poet Hugh MacDiarmid, the city's drinkers are generally not "dour" but rather friendly if occasionally direct.

movements. Given its quality, what's more amazing is that Mackintosh was not yet 30 when he designed the place. It is still a working—and much respected—school, whose graduates continue to make their mark in the international art world. Guided tours are the only way to see the entire building, a highlight of which has to be the library. The airy landing one flight up serves as the school's exhibition space: The Mackintosh Gallery, while the basement has a new, well-stocked shop.

167 Renfrew St. ✆ **0141/353-4526.** www.gsa.ac.uk. Tours £8.75 adult, £7 seniors and students, £4 children, £23.50 family. AE, MC, V. Advance reservations recommended. Apr–Sept daily 10am, 11am, noon, 2, 4, and 5pm; Oct–Mar daily 11am and 3pm. The Mackintosh Shop Apr–Sept daily 9:30am–6:30pm, Oct–Mar daily 10am–5pm. Underground: Cowcaddens. Train: Charing Cross. Bus: 16, 18, 44, or 57.

St. Vincent Street Church ★

This should be a three-star, must-see attraction, but access to the public is limited by the evangelic reformed Free Kirk of Scotland congregation that worships here. Nevertheless, the church remains the most visible landmark attributed to the city's other great architect, Alexander "Greek" Thomson. Built in 1859, the stone edifice offers two classic Greek porticos facing north and south, aside which a clock tower rises, decorated in all manner of exotic yet curiously sympathetic Egyptian, Assyrian, and even Indian-looking motifs and designs. The interior is surprisingly colorful.

265 St. Vincent St. Sun services at 11am and 6:30pm. www.greekthomsonchurch.com/our-building. Bus: 62.

Tenement House ★ 🏛 Run by the National Trust for Scotland, this "museum" is a typical Glasgow flat, preserved with all the fixtures and fittings from the early part of the 20th century: Coal fires, box bed in the kitchen, and gas lamps. Indeed, the resident, Miss Agnes Toward, apparently never threw out anything from 1911 to 1965, so there are displays of all sorts of memorabilia, from ticket stubs and letters to ration coupons and photographs from trips down the Clyde.

145 Buccleuch St. ℂ **0141/333-0183.** www.nts.org.uk/visits. Admission £5.50 adults, £4.50 children and seniors, £15 family. MC, V. Mar–Oct daily 1–5pm. Closed Nov–Feb. Underground: Cowcaddens. Bus: 11, 20, 66, 118, or 159.

Trongate 103 ★★ Opened in 2009, this is an exciting, well-considered artistic development from the City Council. It combines no less than four existing galleries, including the always excellent Glasgow Print Studio, as well as the kinetic sculptures of the Sharmanka Theatre and a Russian Cultural Centre in Café Cossachok. As a locus of creativity, there are also workshops and studios for Glasgow artists. On the first Thursday of the month, the complex opens all doors and stays open later.

103 Trongate. ℂ **0141/276-8380.** www.trongate103.com. Free admission. Mon–Sat 10am–5pm; Sun noon–5pm (some galleries are closed Mon). Underground: St. Enoch. Bus: 62

West End

Hunterian Art Gallery ★ The University of Glasgow inherited the artistic estate of American-born James McNeill Whistler, with some 60 of his paintings bestowed by his sister-in-law and many hanging in this gallery on the university campus. The main gallery space also exhibits 17th- and 18th-century paintings (Rembrandt to Rubens) and 19th- and 20th-century Scottish works, including those by the so-called "Glasgow Boys" and the Scottish Colourists, such as Cadell, Hunter, and Fergusson. Temporary exhibits, selected from Scotland's largest collection of prints, are hung in the print gallery upstairs. The Hunterian also boasts a collection of Charles Rennie Mackintosh furnishings, and one wing of the building has a re-creation of the architect's Glasgow home from 1906 to 1914—startling then and a little less so today. The **Mackintosh House** ★★ covers three levels, decorated in the original style of the famed architect and his artist wife, Margaret Macdonald. All salvageable fittings and fixtures were recovered from the original home before it was demolished in the mid-1960s. The aspect of this re-creation mimics the original house; the sequence of the rooms is identical.

University of Glasgow, 22 Hillhead St. ℂ **0141/330-5431.** www.hunterian.gla.ac.uk. Free gallery admission. Mackintosh House admission £3; free Wed after 2pm. Mon–Sat 9:30am–5pm. Closed Sun and public holidays. Underground: Hillhead. Bus: 44 or 59.

Hunterian Museum First opened in 1807, this is Glasgow's oldest museum. It's named after William Hunter, its early benefactor, who donated his private collections in 1783. The original home was a handsome Greek revival building near High Street across town on the Old College campus, none of which survives today. Now housed in the main Glasgow University buildings, the collection is wide-ranging: From dinosaur fossils to coins to relics of the Roman occupation and plunder by the Vikings. The story of Captain Cook's voyages is pieced together in ethnographic material from the South Seas.

University of Glasgow, Main/Gilbert-Scott Building. ℂ **0141/330-4221.** www.hunterian.gla.ac.uk. Free admission. Mon–Sat 9:30am–5pm. Closed Sun and public holidays. Underground: Hillhead. Bus: 44 or 59.

Kelvingrove Art Gallery & Museum ★★　 Along with The Burrell Collection (see below), the Kelvingrove Art Gallery and Museum presents the stirring soul of the city's art collection, one of the best amassed by a municipality in Europe. Reopened in 2006 after a 3-year and several-million-pound refurbishment, the Kelvingrove can boast that it is the most visited gallery and museum in Scotland—the most popular in the U.K. outside of London. The space features French impressionists and 17th-century Dutch and Flemish paintings. One painting of particular note is *Christ of St. John the Cross* by Spanish surrealist Salvador Dalí. Other highlights include paintings by the Scottish Colourists and the Glasgow Boys, a wing devoted to Mackintosh, as well as more recent art by Anne Redpath and Joan Eardley. But there is more than art, with exhibits on Scottish and Glasgow history, armory and war, as well as natural history and nature—often mixing to good educational effect, for example showing how human armor copied the natural protection of some animals, such as the armadillo. There are plenty of interactive displays and touches of humor, too. The building itself, built for the 1901 Glasgow International Exhibition, is magnificent, as well. There is a new cafe/restaurant in the semi-basement.

Argyle St. © **0141/276-9599.** www.glasgowmuseums.com. Free admission, except for some temporary exhibits. Mon–Thurs and Sat 10am–5pm; Fri and Sun 11am–5pm. Underground: Kelvinhall. Bus: 9, 16, 18A, 42, or 62.

Southside

The Burrell Collection ★★　 This custom-built museum houses many of the 9,000 treasures left to Glasgow by Sir William Burrell, a wealthy ship owner and industrialist who had a lifelong passion for art and artifacts. He started collecting at age 14 and only stopped when he died at the age of 96 in 1958. His tastes were eclectic: Chinese ceramics, French paintings from the 1800s, tapestries, stained-glass windows from churches, even stone doorways from the Middle Ages. Here you can see a vast aggregation of furniture, textiles, ceramics, stained glass, silver, art objects, and pictures. Ancient artifacts, Asian art, and European decorative arts and paintings are featured. It is said that the collector "liked just about everything," and landed one of the very few original bronze casts of Rodin's *The Thinker*. From Sir William's home, Hutton Castle at Berwick-upon-Tweed, the dining room, hall, and drawing room have also been reconstructed and furnished here. There is a cafe on site, and you can roam through surrounding Pollok Country Park, some 5km (3 miles) south of the River Clyde.

　Nearby **Pollok House** (© **0141/616-6521**) dates to the 18th century. Now managed by the National Trust for Scotland on behalf of Glasgow, it features interiors as they were in the Victorian/Edwardian era. Open daily with an admission of £8 for adults.

Pollok Country Park, 2060 Pollokshaws Rd. © **0141/287-2550.** www.glasgowmuseums.com. Free admission. Mon–Thurs and Sat 10am–5pm; Fri and Sun 11am–5pm. Train: Pollokshaws West. Bus: 45 or 57.

Holmwood House ★★ 🎁　 This villa, designed by Alexander "Greek" Thomson and built in 1858, is probably the best example of his innovative style as applied to stately Victorian homes. Magnificently original, its interior restoration (which is ongoing) has revealed that the architect was apparently concerned with almost every element of the house's design, right down to the wallpaper and painted friezes. Now operated by the National Trust for Scotland, visitors have access to most parts of the building and surrounding gardens. Most impressive is the overall exterior design, as well as the home's parlor, with its circular bay window, the cupola over the staircase, and the detailed cornicing around the ceiling in the dining room. There are also 2 hectares (5 acres) of grounds and a small kitchen garden.

61–63 Netherlee Rd., Cathcart (about 6km/4 miles south of the city center). © **0141/637-2129.** www. nts.org.uk. Admission £5.50 adults, £4.50 seniors, students, and children, £15 family. MC, V. Mid-Mar–Oct Thurs–Mon noon–5pm. Closed Tues–Wed and Nov–Mar. Train: Cathcart. Bus: 44 or 66.

ADDITIONAL ATTRACTIONS

Centre for Contemporary Art (CCA)   Housed in a building designed by Alexander "Greek" Thomson, the CCA is one of three premier venues in Glasgow for the exhibition of contemporary art—usually of a conceptual nature by both local artists and those of international reputation. The central atrium-like space is given over to the CCA's popular cafe, but there are other exhibition rooms, plus a small theater, where art-house and foreign films coordinated by the Glasgow Film Theatre are screened.

350 Sauchiehall St. © **0141/352-4900.** www.cca.org. Free admission. Tues–Fri 11am–6pm; Sat 10am–6pm. Closed Sun–Mon and 2 weeks during Christmas and New Year holidays. Underground: Cowcaddens. Train: Charing Cross. Bus: 16, 18, 44, or 57.

House for an Art Lover ♨   This house, which opened in 1996, was based on—or rather inspired by—an unrealized and incomplete 1901 competition entry by Charles Rennie Mackintosh. The building, with its elegant interiors, is therefore really a modern architect's interpretation of what Mackintosh had in mind. The tour includes the main hall, the dining room, with its gesso panels, and the music room. Mackintosh devotees flock here, but it is not the same as the real thing. On the plus side, however, is the popular **Art Lover's Cafe** (p. 190), as well as gift shop, all surrounded by a parkland setting adjacent to Victorian walled gardens.

Bellahouston Park, 10 Dumbreck Rd. © **0141/353-4770.** www.houseforanartlover.co.uk. Admission £4.50 adults; £3 seniors, students, and children, £12 family. AE, MC, V. Apr–Sept Mon–Wed 10am–4pm, Thurs–Sun 10am–1pm; Oct–Mar Sat–Sun 10am–1pm, call for weekday times. Cafe and shop daily 10am–5pm. Underground: Ibrox. Bus: 9 or 54.

Museum of Transport   This museum and its collection of many forms of transportation and related technology is closed until summer 2011, when it is expected to reopen in completely new premises as part of the Riverside Museum. For updates on its progress, visit www.riversideappeal.org.

People's Palace ☺   This museum covers the social history of Glasgow, with exhibits on how "ordinary people" have lived in the city, especially since the industrial age. It also attempts to explain the Glasgow vernacular, speech patterns, and expressions that even Scottish folk from outside the city have trouble deciphering. Also noteworthy are the murals painted by new "Glasgow Boy" Ken Currie. In front of the museum is the recently restored Doulton Fountain, which was moved here from another spot on Glasgow Green. The spacious **Winter Gardens,** to the rear of the building in a restored Victorian glass house with cafe facility, offer a good retreat.

Glasgow Green. © **0141/554-0223.** www.glasgowmuseums.com. Free admission. Mon–Thurs and Sat 10am–5pm; Fri and Sun 11am–5pm. Bus: 16, 18, 40, 61, 62, 64, or 263.

AHEAD OF his time: CHARLES RENNIE MACKINTOSH

Although he is legendary today, Charles Rennie Mackintosh (1868–1928) was largely forgotten in Scotland at the time of his death. His approach to design, poised between Arts and Crafts and the Art Nouveau eras, had its fans, however, and certainly history has compensated for any slights he received during his lifetime. Mackintosh's work is recognized today as one of the city's great architectural treasures.

Born in 1868, Mackintosh began his career as a draftsman for the architectural firm of Honeyman & Keppie. Glasgow had become the "second city" of the British Empire, and the era marks a golden age in the city's architectural heritage. In 1896, Mackintosh's design for the **Glasgow School of Art** won a prestigious competition. Forms of nature, especially plants, inspired his interior design motifs, which offered a pared down simplicity and harmony that was far from the Victorian fashions of the day. Acclaim came from Central Europe and the Vienna Secessionists, in particular, as well as the Arts and Crafts movement in England and America. The reaction in Glasgow was mixed, and he left the city in 1914.

Other landmark Mackintosh buildings in the city include the exterior of the old Glasgow Herald building, now **The Lighthouse;** the **Willow Tea Rooms** on Sauchiehall Street; the **Scotland Street School;** and the **Mackintosh Church at Queens Cross,** HQ for the Charles Rennie Mackintosh Society (www.crm society.com). His own West End home (1906–14), with wife and collaborator Margaret Macdonald, was itself a work of art, eschewing the fussy clutter of the age for clean, elegant lines. Its interiors have been re-created by the University of Glasgow's Hunterian Gallery. In Helensburgh, 40km (25 miles) west of Glasgow, is perhaps his greatest singular residential achievement: **Hill House** (p. 246), which was designed for publisher Walter Blackie in 1902.

Leaving Glasgow, he moved to Walberswick on the southern coast of England (where friendships with German-speaking artists caused undue concern during World War I) and later to Port-Vendres in France. In both places, lacking architecture or design commissions, his artistic talents were put in a different direction. He painted watercolors of flowers and landscapes that are nearly as distinctive and individual as his architectural and interior design work. His hand as a master draftsman was confirmed. For more information on the buildings to visit, go to the website of the Charles Rennie Mackintosh Society, or call ℂ **0141/946-6600.**

Provand's Lordship Glasgow's oldest house, built in the 1470s, and the only survivor from what would have been clusters of medieval homes and buildings in this area of the city near Glasgow Cathedral. It is named after a church canon who once resided here. Thanks to the 17th-century furniture from the original collection of Sir William Burrell, it shows what the interiors would have been like around the date 1700.

3 Castle St. ℂ **0141/552-8819.** www.glasgowmuseums.com. Free admission. Mon–Thurs and Sat 10am–5pm; Fri and Sun 11am–5pm. Train: High St. Bus: 11, 36, 37, 38, 42, or 89.

UNAPPRECIATED genius: ALEXANDER "GREEK" THOMSON

Although architect and designer Charles Rennie Mackintosh (1868–1928) is well known and his worldwide popularity has spurred a cottage industry of "mock-intosh" imitations from jewelry to stationery, a precursor to him was perhaps even more important and innovative. Alexander "Greek" Thomson (1817–75) brought a vision to Victorian Glasgow that was unrivaled by his contemporaries. While the influence of classical structures—the Greek Revival—was nothing new, Thomson did not so much replicate Grecian design as hone it to essentials, and then mix in Egyptian, Assyrian, and other Eastern-influenced motifs. Like Mackintosh later, Thomson increasingly found himself out of step with fashion, which architecturally was moving toward Gothic Revival (such as the University of Glasgow on Gilmorehill, which Thomson apparently despised).

While a number of structures created by the reasonably prolific and successful Thomson have been tragically lost to the wrecker's ball, some key works remain: Terraced houses, such as **Moray Place** (where he lived) on the city's Southside and **Eton Terrace** in the West End; churches, such as the embarrassingly derelict **Caledonian Road Church** and still-used **St. Vincent Street Church;** detached homes, such as the **Double Villa** or **Holmwood House;** and commercial structures, such as the **Grecian Buildings** (which today houses the CCA) or **Egyptian Halls** near Central Station. Just as a Mackintosh trail has been created so that fans can revisit his works, Thomson deserves no less and, in time, may receive his full due.

Ironically, for all of his interest in the exotic, Thomson himself never traveled abroad. He was planning to visit Italy when he died in his home on Moray Place on March 22, 1875, at the age of 57. Less than a decade later, the "Alexander Thomson Travelling Studentship" was created in his honor to send young architects abroad. The second recipient was none other than 22-year-old Charles Rennie Mackintosh.

St. Mungo Museum of Religious Life & Art   Opened in 1993, this eclectic museum of spirituality is next to Glasgow Cathedral on the site where the Bishop's Castle once stood. It embraces a collection that spans the centuries and highlights various religious groups. It has been hailed as rather unique in that Buddha, Ganesha, and Shiva, among other spiritual leaders, saints, and historic figures are treated equally. A more recent acquisition is Kenny Hunter's statue of Jesus. The grounds include a Zen garden of stone and gravel.

2 Castle St. ⓒ **0141/553-2557.** Free admission. Mon–Thurs and Sat 10am–5pm; Fri and Sun 11am–5pm. Train: High St. Bus: 11, 36, 38, 42, or 89.

Science Centre ☺   On the banks of the River Clyde and opposite the Scottish Exhibition and Conference Centre, the futuristic-looking buildings of the Science Centre are a focal point in Glasgow's redevelopment of the once rundown former docklands. The overall theme of the exhibitions is to document 21st-century challenges, as well as Glasgow's contribution to science and technology in the past, present, and future. Families should enjoy the hands-on and interactive activities, whether taking a three-dimensional head scan or starring in their own digital video.

The Science Centre is also home to a planetarium and the silver-skinned **IMAX Theatre.** The planetarium and theater charge separate admissions.

50 Pacific Quay. ✆ **0141/420-5010.** www.glasgowsciencecentre.org. Admission £9.95 adults, £7.95 students and seniors; additional £2.50 for IMAX or tower. MC, V. Daily 10am–5pm. Underground: Cessnock. Train: Exhibition Centre and walk across the footbridge over the Clyde. Bus: 89 or 90.

Scotland Street School Museum   Another of Charles Rennie Mackintosh's designs, this building, commissioned by the local school board, celebrated its centenary in 2005. Given that it is surrounded by light-industrial parks and faces the M8 motorway, it seems an odd location for a school. But that's only because all of the surrounding apartment buildings were torn down, which is why the school had only about 90 pupils when it closed in 1979. The museum that occupies this admittedly lesser but still fascinating work from the great architect is devoted to the history of education in Scotland, with reconstructed examples of classrooms from the Victorian, World War II, and 1960s' eras. It also has displays of Mackintosh's designs for the building.

225 Scotland St. ✆ **0141/287-0500.** www.glasgowmuseums.com. Free admission. Mon–Thurs and Sat 10am–5pm; Fri and Sun 11am–5pm. Underground: Shields Rd. Bus: 89 or 90.

Maritime Glasgow

The Tall Ship at Glasgow Harbour   Restored in 1999, the SV *Glenlee* is one of only five Clyde-built sailing ships that remain afloat. Built in 1896, it circumnavigated Cape Horn 15 times and a video offers black-and-white film showing just how rough the journey could be. Check out the logbook in the poop cabin. It offers a more grim picture of life onboard as the captain's diary documents how one particular sailor was taken ill, recovered, and then died. You can explore the ship and, while onboard, take in an exhibition detailing cargo-trading history.

100 Stobcross Rd. ✆ **0141/222-2513.** www.glenlee.co.uk. Admission £5.95 adults, £4.65 seniors, students, and children. MC, V. Mar–Oct daily 10am–5pm; Nov–Feb daily 10am–4pm. Train: Exhibition Centre. Bus: Tour buses.

GARDENS & PARKS

Botanic Gardens 📷   Glasgow's Botanic Gardens are not as exemplary as the Royal Botanic Gardens in Edinburgh (p. 101), but they nevertheless cover some 11 hectares (28 acres). There is an extensive collection of tropical plants in Kibble Palace, the Victorian cast-iron glasshouse, which has been restored. The plant collection includes some rather acclaimed orchids and begonias. This is a good place to unwind and wander, whether through the working vegetable plot or along the banks of the River Kelvin. The Botanic Gardens are open daily from dawn to dusk. The greenhouses are open 10am to 4:45pm (until 4:15pm in the winter).

Great Western Rd. ✆ **0141/334-2422.** Free admission. Daily 7am–dusk. Underground: Hillhead. Bus: 20, 66, or 90.

Glasgow Green ☺   This is the city's oldest park by some distance and dates in part probably to medieval times. Running along the River Clyde, southeast of the commercial center, this huge stretch of green had paths laid and shrubs planted in the middle of the 18th century but formally became a public park some 100 years later. Its landmarks include the People's Palace (p. 200) social history museum and adjoining Winter Garden, Doulton Fountain, and Nelson's Monument. At the eastern end, the influence of the Doge's Palace in Venice can be seen in the colorful facade of the old Templeton Carpet Factory. Near here is a large children's play area. The southern side of Glasgow Green offers dulcet walks along the river.

Greendyke St. (east of Saltmarket). © **0141/287-5098.** www.glasgow.gov.uk. Free admission. Daily dawn–dusk. Underground: St. Enoch. Bus: 16, 18, 40, 61, 62, or 64.

Pollok Country Park ☺ On the Southside of the city, this hilly and large expanse of open space is the home to both The Burrell Collection and Pollok House (p. 199) but merits a visit for its own attributes. Rhododendrons, Japanese maples, and azaleas are part of the formal planting—created at the end of the 19th century by Sir John Stirling Maxwell, whose family long-resided in Pollok House—but the park is best known for its glens and pastures, which have Highland cattle grazing.

2060 Pollokshaws Rd. © **0141/632-9299.** www.glasgow.gov.uk. Free admission. Daily dawn–dusk. Train: Pollokshaws West. Bus: 45 or 57.

ORGANIZED TOURS

City Sightseeing Glasgow These brightly colored and open-topped buses depart from George Square, and in addition to live commentary, which can be quite entertaining and informative, visitors can hop on and off at some 22 designated stops such as Glasgow Green, the University, or the Royal Concert Hall. Passes are good for two consecutive days.

153 Queen St. at George Sq. © **0141/204-0444.** www.scotguide.com. Tickets £11 adults, £5 children, £25 family. Apr–Oct 9:30am–5pm (every 20 min.); Nov–Mar 9:30am–4:30pm (every 30 min.). Underground: Buchanan St.

Mercat Glasgow Fancy acquainting yourself with the more ghoulish aspects of Glasgow? Mercat are happy to oblige with a Horror Walking Tour. Guides re-create macabre Glasgow with a parade of goons such as hangmen, ghosts, murderers, and body snatchers. The tours take about 60 minutes, departing normally from the Tourist Information Centre at George Square. The company also does a 90-minute Historic Glasgow tour for those not interested in a fright.

25 Forth Rd., Bearsden. © **0141/586-5378.** Tickets £10. Advance reservations essential. Underground: Buchanan St.

SPECIAL EVENTS

Celtic Connections ★ The best-attended annual festival in Glasgow, and the largest of its kind in the world, Celtic Connections music festival covers Gaelic, folk, roots, alt-country, Americana, and more. It kicks off the year every January. The main venue for performances is the Royal Concert Hall, which produces the event.

✆ **0141/353-8000.** www.celticconnections.com.

Doors Open Days ★ 🍴 For a couple of weekends every September, this event arranges for the doors at buildings normally closed to the public to be opened. Thus it affords visitors rare opportunities to see the interiors of architecturally significant and historic edifices across the city.

✆ **0141/248-1188.** www.doorsopendays.org.uk.

Glasgow International Jazz Festival This annual event, usually running from the last week of June through the first days of July, brings a few top jazz acts to Glasgow. In recent years, the festival featured saxophonist David Murray and singer/songwriter Van Morrison, as well as showcasing more locally based talent, such as singers Carol Kidd and Tommy Smith. Free events are always included in the "Fringe" schedule.

✆ **0141/552-3552.** www.jazzfest.co.uk.

Piping Live! A lone piper playing a Scottish lament in a Highland glen can bring a tear to the eye, for sure. But a band full of bagpipes blown in unison is one of the most stirring sounds on the planet. The best pipers from around the world converge on Glasgow in August of every year for the **World Pipe Band Championships** on Glasgow Green, the culmination of a weeklong festival with concerts across the city.

30–34 McPhater St. ✆ **0141/353-8000.** www.pipingfestival.co.uk.

West End Festival The city's West End celebrates every summer with a host of music and cultural events for 2 weeks in June. The centerpiece is a Mardi Gras Carnival and parade that draws thousands if it turns out to be a hot day.

✆ **0141/341-0844.** www.westendfestival.co.uk.

SPORTS & OUTDOOR ACTIVITIES

Football (Soccer)

Glasgow's Southside is the site of Scotland's national football stadium, **Hampden Park** (✆ **0141/620-4000;** Bus: 75 or 89). It seats more than 52,000 fans and is used for Scotland internationals as well as annual cup matches. There is also a football museum here.

The city's two big clubs are **Celtic** and **Rangers.** As any international soccer fan knows, these are the two largest professional soccer teams in Scotland—indeed, among the biggest in Europe. Collectively called the "Old Firm," they have passionate, even fanatical, followers, a portion of whom can be violent in their desire to show their loyalty. Celtic play in the East End at their stadium in Parkhead (℡ **0141/556-2611;** www.celticfc.net). Rangers are based south of the Clyde at Ibrox Stadium (℡ **0870/600-1972;** www.rangers.co.uk). Two relatively smaller soccer clubs also play their home games in Glasgow: Partick Thistle at Firhill in the West End and Queen's Park at Hampden.

Other Activities

CYCLING

In principle you can cycle from Glasgow east to Edinburgh, west to the Clyde coast, and north to Loch Lomond and beyond to Inverness using the national cycle routes. They combine off-road paths and on-road lanes, the latter of which are sometimes poorly marked. The tourist office, however, provides maps with overviews and details.

Rentals are available off Byres Road at **West End Cycles,** 16–18 Chancellor St. (℡ **0141/357-1344;** Underground: Hillhead or Kelvinhall; Bus: 9 or 18). It is close to the National Cycle Trail that leads to Loch Lomond and rents bikes well-suited to the hilly terrain of Glasgow and surrounding areas. The cost is as low as £4 per hour. In the city center, **Alpine Bikes,** in the TISO Outdoor Centre, 50 Couper St., near Buchanan Bus Station (℡ **0141/552-8575**), offers limited cycle rental. Prices start at £8.

GOLF

The city of Glasgow operates five municipal golf courses of a reasonable standard. The best-kept 18-hole courses are probably the 5,005-yard **Linn Park,** on the Southside (℡ **0141/633-0337**), and 6,364-yard **Littlehill,** north of the city center (℡ **0141/772-1916**). Two 9-hole courses are **Alexandra Park,** Alexandra Parade (℡ **0141/556-1294**), and **Knightswood,** Lincoln Avenue (℡ **0141/959-6358**). None have dress codes, and greens fees are modest: £10 adults and £5 kids between 5 and 17 during the week for 18-hole courses and about half those rates for the 9-hole courses. For additional information, log onto **www.glasgow.gov.uk.**

Of course, Glasgow has private clubs and around the city are a host of other courses. Southwest of Glasgow, Ayrshire offers the best concentration of links-style golf in the country (see chapter 20).

SPORTS COMPLEXES, GYMS & POOLS

Kelvin Hall International Sports Arena is on Argyle Street (℡ **0141/357-2525;** Underground: Kelvinhall), near the River Kelvin. This is the country's major venue for national and international indoor sports competitions; check with the tourist office for any events scheduled for the time of your visit. The facility is open daily with a weight room and fully equipped gym.

Scotstoun Leisure Centre, further west on Danes Drive (℡ **0141/959-4000;** Bus: 9), offers a gym, indoor and outdoor tennis, and a five-lane pool. In the East End, **Tollcross Park Leisure Centre** (℡ **0141/763-2345;** Bus: 61) has the city's 50-m (164-ft.) Olympic-size swimming pool. For hours, admission, and further information, log onto **www.glasgow.gov.uk.**

CITY STROLLS IN GLASGOW

G lasgow is set on some fairly gentle hills, which rise from the basin created by the River Clyde. Thus, it's a city amenable to walking. Most of the following perambulations don't involve the scaling of many steep streets—although in order to obtain good vistas, a climb is sometimes obligatory. Like in any bustling metropolis with roads often clogged with traffic, pedestrians should exercise caution. Glasgow drivers (including those behind the wheels of city buses) can be a tad aggressive at times. Still, some streets in the city center have been made into vehicle-free pedestrian zones.

It is quite easy to get off the beaten track and away from crowds, should you desire. Plus, the city has plenty of parks and open spaces. And given the multitude of bus routes, the circular subway, and various suburban trains, getting back to where you began is typically easy if you tire of walking. Should you have a half-day free, walks 1 to 3 listed below can be combined to create one pleasant stroll right across Glasgow from Merchant City to West End.

WALKING TOUR 1: MERCHANT CITY & EAST END

START:	**Central Necropolis.**
FINISH:	**Royal Exchange Square.**
TIME:	**About 1 to 2 hours.**
BEST TIME:	**Daytime.**
WORST TIME:	**Late at night.**

This walk takes in Glasgow's historic heart, whose medieval districts were first lost to the designs of the city's initial "New Town" developments in the 1700s—the beginnings of the area now known as Merchant

City. But there are hints to the past, and Merchant City is almost to Glasgow as SoHo is to Manhattan, with loft apartments and trendy bars.

Start the walk at:

1 The Necropolis

As big graveyards go—with monuments, crypts, and views—Glasgow's Central Necropolis is difficult to beat. Fashioned on Paris's famous Père Lachaise, it was the third of its kind in Britain, opening in 1833 (after St. James's in Liverpool and London's Kensal Green), although a Jewish burial ground had been established at the base of the hill 3 years earlier. The most sought-after plots of the day were near the monument to John Knox, which had been standing on the hill since 1825.

Cross the bridge to Cathedral Square and:

2 Glasgow Cathedral

The Cathedral (p. 196) is considered one of the best examples of medieval religious architecture in Scotland, although there's unfortunately no evidence of the settlement that once surrounded it. Across High Street, the building known as Provand's Lordship (p. 201) was built in 1471 by Bishop Andrew Muirhead. It miraculously managed to avoid demolition during Glasgow's robust urban renewals of the 19th and 20th centuries. The tall and modern buildings beyond it to the west are part of Strathclyde University.

Walk south on High Street to:

3 Glasgow Cross & Tolbooth

Down gently curving High Street, the red sandstone tenements you pass are exemplary of those constructed in the late-Victorian era by the Civic Improvement Trust. After crossing Duke Street comes the College Bar (nearly opposite the High Street railway station), whose name is a reminder that the original Glasgow University campus was nearby. The towering landmark at the base of the street and historic Glasgow Cross is the eight-story **Tolbooth Steeple,** completed in 1627, around which traffic up and down High Street snakes today.

At the steeple go east (left) and walk along the:

4 Gallowgate

"Gate" in Scottish essentially means "road to": Today, the Gallowgate is one of the main avenues leading to the working-class bastions of Glasgow's East End. If it's a weekend, visit the Barras (or Barrows) market, full of antiques, collectables, junk, and Glasgow character. The old dancing ballroom called Barrowland has become one of the most famous and popular places to see rock bands in Scotland. Also worth noting is the Saracen Head (or as the locals say, Sarry Heid) pub. It has historic connections to an inn of the same name that hosted Johnson and Boswell and also Wordsworth. Alas, it is only open sporadically these days.

Walking Tour: Merchant City & East End

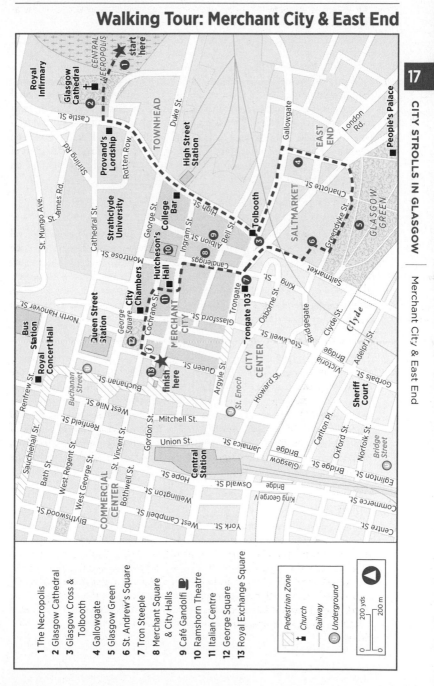

1 The Necropolis
2 Glasgow Cathedral
3 Glasgow Cross & Tolbooth
4 Gallowgate
5 Glasgow Green
6 St. Andrew's Square
7 Tron Steeple
8 Merchant Square & City Halls
9 Café Gandolfi
10 Ramshorn Theatre
11 Italian Centre
12 George Square
13 Royal Exchange Square

Pedestrian Zone
Church
Railway
Underground

200 yds
200 m

Walk south from Gallowgate, crossing London Road to:

5 Glasgow Green

Running along the River Clyde, this huge stretch of green became a public park in the middle of the 19th century, although paths had been laid and shrubs planted out 100 years earlier. Its landmarks include the red sandstone **People's Palace** social history museum (p. 200) and adjoining Winter Garden, Doulton Fountain, and Nelson's Monument. To the east, the influence of the Doge's Palace in Venice is obvious in William Leiper's colorful facade of the old Templeton Carpet Factory, which has a great brewery/bar, WEST (p. 241), on the ground floor. The southern side of Glasgow Green offers walks along the river as it begins its upstream meandering and the northwestern flank now features modern apartments opened in the late 1990s as the so-called "City for the Future."

Walk west on Greendyke Street, turning right (north) on Turnbull Street to:

6 St. Andrew's Square

Styled after St-Martin-in-the-Field, London, and indeed once surrounded by open space, the impressive sandstone St. Andrew's parish church was completed in 1756, making it the oldest post-Reformation kirk in Glasgow. Today, it houses a center for traditional Scottish music and dance. Around the corner, the only remaining bit of 18th-century residential property is no. 52 Charlotte Street, now available as overnight accommodation from the National Trust for Scotland.

Make your way back to Glasgow Cross and proceed west on the Trongate to:

7 Tron Steeple

The steeple with arches through which pedestrians can walk on the south side of the Trongate dates to 1592, although the original Tron or Laigh Kirk was founded 8 years before Columbus sailed to the New World. The tron was a beam used for weighing goods. The Tron Theatre, which occupies the site today, favors inventive new plays, as well as hosting musical events (p. 237). The theater's modern bar (facing Chisholm St.) and Victorian-style pub and restaurant are well-known hangouts for creative people. This neighborhood also now boasts the new cultural center called Trongate 103 (p. 198).

Cross the Trongate and go north (right) on Candleriggs to Bell Street and the:

8 Merchant Square & City Halls

The old covered markets of Glasgow have been converted into trendy gathering spots. The old Cheese Market is now a bar and nightclub, while more of the original character of the former Fruit Market has been retained by the Merchant Square development. A diverse array of bars and restaurants share the communal and cavernous interior space on the cobbles. Just north of it are the renovated City Halls, with acoustically celebrated performance spaces (p. 236). Since the 1980s, warehouses in this area have been turned into loft apartments, while newer flats have been constructed more recently.

From the east exit of Merchant Square, cross Albion Street and stop by:

9 Café Gandolfi 🍴

In a bit of the old Cheese Market, Café Gandolfi (64 Albion St.; ℂ 0141/552-6813) is one of the more popular places in Merchant City. It is relaxed, friendly, and at times very busy. But with a bar on the top floor, you can almost always find space. Food is Scottish and European. See p. 182 for a full review.

Return to Candleriggs and continue north to Ingram Street and the:

10 Ramshorn Theatre

This is another former church (St. David) that has been turned into an arts venue, hosting mainly student productions. Round the side and to the rear of this handsome Gothic revival by Thomas Rickman (built in the 1820s) is an atmospheric graveyard that dates to 1719.

Go west on Ingram Street to John Street and the:

11 Italian Centre

Shopping, anyone? The facade of this mid-19th-century warehouse has been retained while an interior courtyard, apartments, and retail space for flashy clothing shops were created in the late 1980s. The Italian Centre is now home to Emporio Armani, while car-free and cobbled John Street is where outdoor dining and drinking are possible. At the corner of Ingram and John streets is Hutcheson's Hall, designed by David Hamilton in 1802 to combine French neoclassical with English baroque.

Walk north on John Street, turn left (west) on Cochrane Street, and continue to:

12 George Square

This is the city's main civic plaza, dating to 1782. More recently, it was repaved in a red, spongy material—and the color is oddly appropriate as this is the historic focal point of militant left-wing demonstrations. Rising majestically at the eastern side of George Square is Glasgow City Chambers, designed by William Young in 1882 as the seat of municipal authority. Facing the western end of the plaza are attractive Victorian and Edwardian-era buildings, which were originally uniform in height. Inside Queen Street railway station, the arching iron roof over the high-level platforms is impressive, but the exterior that faces the square is an eyesore. The square's statues include Robert Burns (whose plinth includes reliefs depicting a few of his tales), the bulky Cenotaph (honoring war casualties), the seated figure of Scottish engineering pioneer James Watt, and the towering monument to Sir Walter Scott.

Leave George Square from the southwest corner and go south on Queen Street to:

13 Royal Exchange Square

Invariably, the statue of the Duke of Wellington in front of the city's Gallery of Modern Art (GOMA) in Royal Exchange Square will be wearing an orange traffic cone on his head. No one knows who started this tradition, but invariably some student makes certain it's there: Symbolic perhaps of Glasgow's irreverent side as well as a bit of Dada-esque art itself. The pile that Wellington guards was originally built in 1778 as a mansion on what was then farmland. In 1832, architect David Hamilton converted the building into the Royal

Exchange. He added an imposing classical portico to the front and a matching "newsroom" to the back. The building sits squarely in the middle of the square, surrounded by cafes with outdoor seating and shops.

WALKING TOUR 2: **THE COMMERCIAL CENTER**

START:	**Royal Exchange Square.**
FINISH:	**Charing Cross.**
TIME:	**About 1½ to 2 hours.**
BEST TIME:	**Daytime.**
WORST TIME:	**Late at night.**

There is no definitive route to see Glasgow city center. For some visitors, it may be better to simply wander. Given the grid system, anyone with a map would be hard-pressed to get completely lost. The pride of the city is its Victorian architecture. Many—indeed most—of the city's stone facades have been cleaned of decades of grime. This stroll includes buildings by the city's two greatest architects: Charles Rennie Mackintosh and Alexander "Greek" Thomson.

This walk begins at the west side of:

1 Royal Exchange Square

At the west end of the square, behind the Gallery of Modern Art, are two archways, both leading to Buchanan Street. Just past the southern one is a restaurant landmark: The Rogano. Its Art Deco interiors were fashioned after the *Queen Mary* ocean liner in 1935. The building between the arches is the former Royal Bank of Scotland (from Charles Wilson's 1850 designs), which faces Gordon Street, leading to Central Station.

Go through one of the arches, and north (right), walking up Buchanan Street to:

2 St. Vincent Street

Buchanan Street was turned into a car-free pedestrian zone in the mid-1970s, although it has long been a primary shopping street. At the intersection with St. Vincent Street is a bronze, table-high scale model of central Glasgow's streets and buildings. To the east (toward George Square) runs St. Vincent Place and its handsome late-19th- and early-20th-century buildings. Mid-block, the former Anchor Line office includes some maritime-themed interiors by the same designer who worked on rooms for the ill-fated SS *Lusitania*. Running west is St. Vincent Street. Its commercial architecture, which replaced terraced houses in the mid-1800s, has been rightfully called "monumental."

Continue north up Buchanan Street to:

3 Nelson Mandela Place

Just before St. George's Tron Church, on the left (west) side of Buchanan Street, is the attractive sandstone and Gothic facade of the former Stock Exchange by John Burnet in 1875. Roundels commemorate the contributions of Science, Art, and Engineering. The slender square (formerly St. George's Place and renamed in honor of the South African leader while he was still

Walking Tour: The Commercial Center

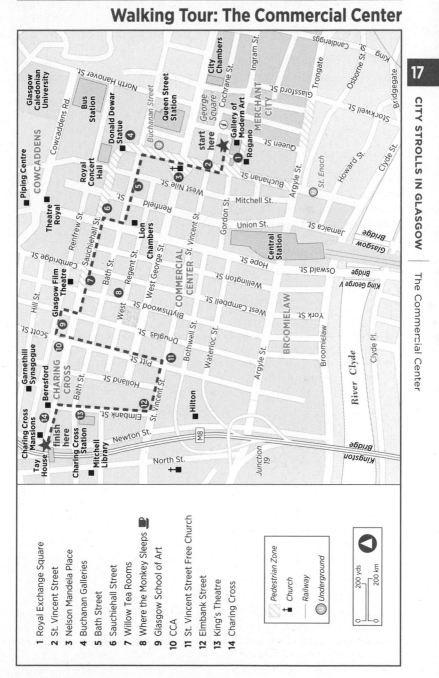

1 Royal Exchange Square
2 St. Vincent Street
3 Nelson Mandela Place
4 Buchanan Galleries
5 Bath Street
6 Sauchiehall Street
7 Willow Tea Rooms
8 Where the Monkey Sleeps
9 Glasgow School of Art
10 CCA
11 St. Vincent Street Free Church
12 Elmbank Street
13 King's Theatre
14 Charing Cross

Pedestrian Zone
Church
Railway
Underground

0 200 yds
0 200 km

imprisoned) that engulfs the church dates to 1810. Mandela was awarded the Freedom of the City in August 1981.

Continue up Buchanan Street to:

4 Buchanan Galleries

Before the next intersection, after entrances to the underground, comes the southern wing of the rather unremarkable Buchanan Galleries shopping center. Indoors, it is equally predictable, a mall that could be almost anywhere in the capitalist world. Ahead is the modern and brutalist Royal Concert Hall, which now terminates Buchanan Street—effectively cutting off a direct path to the bus station and Glasgow Caledonian University beyond. The concert hall's outdoor steps, however, provide a suntrap and offer good views down Buchanan Street toward St. Enoch Square and the River Clyde. Just in front of those broad stairs is a statue of Scotland's first First Minister, Donald Dewar, who opened the new Scottish Parliament in 1999 but died before his initial term in office was over.

Turn left (west) and proceed on:

5 Bath Street

Bath Street got its name from the public baths that opened here in the early 19th century. Today, it is home to several popular bars and restaurants. At the next intersection, West Nile Street, looking south (left), one can see the first of three buildings by Alexander "Greek" Thomson (p. 202) on this walk. Today housing a barbershop, this modest warehouse displays some design signatures of Thomson, Glasgow's underappreciated yet visionary Victorian-era architect. At the intersection after the next, again just south of Bath Street, is another minor architectural landmark at 172 Hope Street: The Lion Chambers. Now trussed in chicken wire after many years behind scaffolding, the eight-story gabled building resembles a Scottish castle keep. It is built on a plot measuring only 10 × 14m (33 × 46 ft.) with artist studios at the top.

At Hope Street, turn right (north) 1 block to:

6 Sauchiehall Street

Sauchiehall Street is probably Glasgow's most famous street. Today, for several blocks west of Buchanan Street, it is pedestrianized and popular for shopping. Beyond, it is a locus of drinking and dining with door-to-door restaurants and bars. Just over the rise of Hope Street to the north, one gets a glimpse of the Italian styling of the Piping Centre (formerly St. Stephen's church). Nearby is the Theatre Royal (p. 236).

Go left (west) on Sauchiehall Street and continue to:

7 Willow Tea Rooms

On the south side of Sauchiehall Street, between West Campbell and Blyth-swood streets, is one of the signature works by architect Charles Rennie Mack-intosh (p. 201). The spare white exterior, clean lines, and asymmetrically arranged windows certainly stand out from anything else on the street. The ground floor is now a jeweler's shop, but above are tea rooms in Mackintosh's ground-breaking 1904 design. Much of it has been reconstructed, but a few original details have been preserved, as well. Around the corner and north up Rose Street is the Glasgow Film Theatre, the city's dedicated art film and repertory cinema (p. 243) with an Art Deco design. In the other direction, two blocks away, is Blythswood Square, a tidy bit of open space that was part of a New Town development that dates to the 1820s.

Near Blythswood Square down some steps to:

8 Where the Monkey Sleeps ☕

Where the Monkey Sleeps (182 West Regent St.; ✆ 0141/226-3406) is no ordinary cafe. It is an atmospherically arty hangout and gallery space, serving excellent cappuccino and freshly prepared sandwiches. See p. 186 for a full review.

Our walk continues west on Sauchiehall Street to Dalhousie Street, turning right (north), and climbing steep Garnethill to the:

9 Glasgow School of Art

Our second Mackintosh masterpiece, the Glasgow School of Art, is on the left as you ascend Garnethill via Dalhousie Street. Even from this approach, along the most austere side of the building, the ingenuity of its design is apparent. Completed in two stages (1899 and 1909), the building offers a mix of ideas promoted by both the Arts and Crafts and the Art Nouveau movements. Facing Renfrew Street, the wide facade offers huge studio windows. This is still a key campus building, so immediate public access is limited to the reception hall, shop, and a second-floor gallery space in a large landing beneath exposed timber beams. To see more, take a guided tour (p. 196), which includes the impressive library: A place that anyone would happily spend hours in. Another room has original art and drawings by Mackintosh. Nearby on Hill Street is Garnethill Synagogue, the first Jewish temple built in Scotland. Before descending Garnethill, take in the views, particularly south toward the Clyde.

At the west side of the Art School, turn left (south) and come down Scott Street to the:

10 CCA

To the right as you come down Scott Street, admire the stonework, such as acanthus leaf motifs, so typical of Alexander Thomson's buildings. Redeveloped in 2001, the home for Glasgow's Centre for Contemporary Art (CCA) is the architect's 1865 Grecian Building (although most of the detailing has more to do with Egypt). The structure incorporated one of the older villas built on the hillside and inside you can see the facade of that earlier building. Stand at the corner of Sauchiehall and Scott streets and look back up the hill: This is a unique spot in Glasgow, where works by both the city's most innovative architects stand almost side by side.

Cross Sauchiehall Street and proceed south on Pitt Street to:

11 St. Vincent Street Free Church

Only four streets away is Thomson's most impressive temple—what some have called his "magnum opus." Built for the United Presbyterians in 1859, the stone church offers two classic Greek porticos facing north and south, aside which a clock tower rises decorated in all manner of exotic yet sympathetic

Egyptian, Assyrian, and even Indian-looking motifs and designs. A similar Thomson church stands in inexcusable disrepair on Caledonian Road on the city's Southside, although there are promises to restore it.

Turn right (west) on St. Vincent Street to:

12 Elmbank Street

Looking west from the windswept corner of Elmbank and St. Vincent streets, visitors might begin to appreciate the impact of the M8 motorway, which passes noisily nearby. In the near but seemingly unreachable distance across the motorway, the prow of St. Patrick Roman Catholic Church pokes up above the concrete infrastructure. Going up Elmbank Street, admire the figures of Cicero, Homer, Galileo, and Watt on the facade of the old Glasgow High School. At the corner of Elmbank Crescent, offices of the Scottish Opera occupy the handsome former Institute of Engineers and Shipbuilders. If you go left here and cross the street, you'll be at an entrance to the Charing Cross station and can catch a train back one stop to Queen Street station and George Square.

Otherwise proceed up Elmbank Street to the:

13 King's Theatre

Over a century old, the red sandstone King's Theatre regularly stages comedy and light drama that appeals to a range of generations. On the opposite northeast corner is the Griffin pub (originally the King's Arms), whose exterior displays some recently repaired Glasgow-style Art Nouveau design.

Continue up Elmbank Street to Sauchiehall Street and:

14 Charing Cross

The boldly Art Deco Beresford, built in the 1930s as a hotel, faces back down Elmbank Street. This stretch of Sauchiehall Street is the one loaded with bars, nightclubs, and eateries. On the northern side of the street at the intersection with St. Georges Road (technically a motorway off-ramp) is the curving red sandstone Charing Cross Mansions by J. J. Burnet in 1889. Across Sauchiehall Street, Tay House is a rather brutal modern office building that bridges the freeway. The edifice was built on stilts originally designed for another flyover with high-speed traffic.

WALKING TOUR 3: THE WEST END

START:	**Charing Cross.**
FINISH:	**Botanic Gardens.**
TIME:	**About 2 to 3 hours.**
BEST TIME:	**Daytime.**
WORST TIME:	**Late at night.**

This walk will give visitors a sense of Glasgow's salubrious and trendy West End, while hitting some of its landmarks as well. The stroll begins in Charing Cross on Sauchiehall Street, but on the western side of the M8 motorway, which is set in a

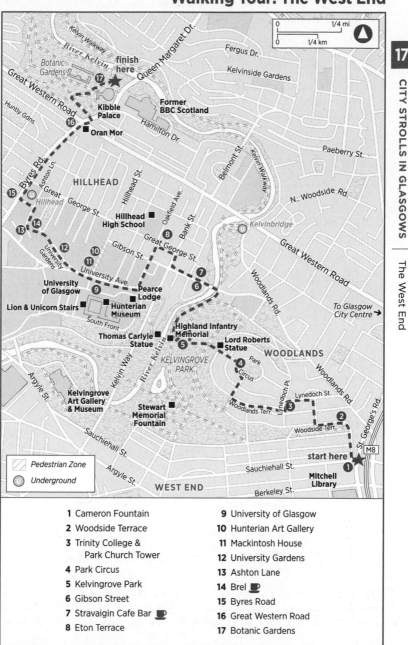

1 Cameron Fountain
2 Woodside Terrace
3 Trinity College &
Park Church Tower
4 Park Circus
5 Kelvingrove Park
6 Gibson Street
7 Stravaigin Cafe Bar
8 Eton Terrace

9 University of Glasgow
10 Hunterian Art Gallery
11 Mackintosh House
12 University Gardens
13 Ashton Lane
14 Brel
15 Byres Road
16 Great Western Road
17 Botanic Gardens

canyon as it bores through the city center. The West End's development began in the 19th century, as the booming city needed more space to house its ever-growing population, which made Glasgow the Second City of the British Empire.

Start at:

1 Cameron Fountain

From the red stone fountain, built in 1896 and listing considerably eastward, detour briefly a few streets south on North Street to see the Mitchell Library, among the largest public reference libraries in Europe, with its prominent dome.

From the fountain walk up Woodside Crescent to:

2 Woodside Terrace

This late Georgian row of homes (designed by George Smith in the 1830s) began an exemplary New Town development. Here you'll find Greek Doric porticos unlike any in the city. But most of the credit for the overall elegance and charm of Woodlands Hill goes to Charles Wilson, whose designs in the middle of the 19th century are mostly responsible for the terraces up the hillside to Park Circus.

Continue on Woodside Terrace, turning right (north) on Lynedoch Terrace to Lynedoch Street and proceed left (west) to:

3 Trinity College & Park Church Tower

The former Trinity College (now Trinity House) is a landmark whose three towers are visible from many approaches to the city. Designed by Wilson, it was constructed in 1857 as a Free Church College. Most of the original interiors were lost when the complex was converted to flats in the 1980s. Across the broad triangular intersection is the cream-colored Park Church Tower. Part of J. T. Rochead's 1856 design, it is the other feature of the neighborhood recognizable from some distance. Alas, the church that went with the tower was razed in the late 1960s. Similar to the Tolbooth and the Tron Church at Glasgow Cross, only a steeple remains.

From here, go left (south) and follow the gentle curve (west) of Woodlands Terrace, turning right (north) at Park Street South to:

4 Park Circus

This oval of handsome and uniform three-story buildings around a small central garden is the heart of Wilson's plans, designed in 1855. No. 22 (the so-called "Marriage Suites" where the city conducts civil marriages and other ceremonies) offers remarkable interiors with Corinthian columns and an Art Nouveau billiards room. Attendants are not impressed when uninvited visitors just wander in, however. Luckily, the external door is impressive enough. At the western end of Park Circus is Park Gate, leading to an entrance to Kelvingrove Park. This promontory offers excellent views toward the University and south to the River Clyde.

Enter:

5 Kelvingrove Park

Originally West End Park, the development of this hilly and lush open space on the meandering banks of the River Kelvin was commissioned to Sir Joseph Paxton in 1854, although construction apparently began a year before he produced his plans. At this elevated entrance is the statue of Lord Roberts on his steed. Down the hill to the left, the Gothic Stewart Memorial Fountain includes signs of the zodiac and scenes that depict the source of the city's main supply of water: Loch Katrine. Crossing the river below Park Gate at the Highland Light Infantry Memorial is the faded red sandstone Prince of Wales Bridge. Across the bridge looking back at you is the head of historian/writer Thomas Carlyle emerging from the roughly hewn stone.

If facing the bridge at the infantry memorial, go right (north) and follow one of the two paths that run along the river and exit the park at:

6 Gibson Street

Leaving the park, turn left (west) and cross the short road bridge that brings you into the Hillhead district, which includes the main campus of the University of Glasgow on Gilmorehill, and the NHS Western Infirmary.

7 Stravaigin Cafe Bar 🍵

On Gibson Street, Stravaigin Cafe Bar (28 Gibson St.; ℂ 0141/334-2665) is an ideal place to stop for a coffee, a bite to eat, or a drink. "Stravaig" means "to wander" in Scots. The basement restaurant is one of the most innovative and well-regarded in the city, and the same chefs prepare food on the less adventurous but still excellent cafe/bar menu. Alternatively, if you just want a coffee or cup of tea, try Offshore Café across the street. See p. 190 for a full review of Stravaigin.

Continue west on Gibson Street to Bank Street, go right (north) 1 block to Great George Street, then left (west) 1 block to Oakfield Avenue and:

8 Eton Terrace

Here, on the corner across from Hillhead High School, is the unmistakable hand of Alexander "Greek" Thomson on an impressive (if rather poorly maintained) terrace of eight houses completed in 1864 (following his similarly designed Moray Place; see "Walking Tour 4: The Southside," p. 221). Two temple-like facades serve as bookends—both pushing slightly forward and rising one floor higher than the rest—which have double porches fashioned after the Choragic Monument of Thrasyllus in Athens. For all his admiration of Eastern design, Thomson ironically never traveled outside the U.K.

Return to the corner of Great George Street and follow Oakfield Avenue, crossing Gibson Street to University Avenue, then turn right up the hill to the:

9 University of Glasgow

While aficionados rightfully bemoan the loss of the original campus east of the High Street—which may have offered the best examples of 17th-century architecture in Scotland—the university moved here in the 1860s. The city could have done worse—a lot worse. The setting high above Kelvingrove Park is befitting of a center of learning. Englishman Sir George Gilbert Scott (who designed the hotel at London's St. Pancras Station) won the commission. His Gothic revival is punctuated by a 30-m (100-ft.) tower, which rises from the double quadrangle, and provides a virtual beacon on the horizon of the West End. There are fragments of the original university brought from across town, too. For example, the facade of Pearce Lodge, as well as the salvaged Lion and Unicorn Stair at the chapel. The cloistered vaults and open columns under the halls between the two quads evoke a sense of meditation and reflection. From here you can enter the Hunterian Museum, whose exhibits include ancient coins, as well as geological and archaeological discoveries (p. 198).

Cross University Avenue north to Hillhead Street and view the:

10 Hunterian Art Gallery

Built in the 1980s next to the university library, the Hunterian Art Gallery (p. 198) houses the school's permanent collection, which includes 18th- and 19th-century Scottish art as well as many works by American James McNeill Whistler. Scottish-Italian pop art pioneer, the late Eduardo Paolozzi, designed the chunky, cast-aluminum internal doors to the main exhibition space.

Incorporated into the building past the gift shop is:

11 Mackintosh House

Charles Rennie Mackintosh's and his wife, Margaret Macdonald's, West End home (originally nearby and demolished by the university in the 1960s) has been replicated here, with furniture and interiors designed by the pair. Visitors to the Mackintosh House (p. 198) enter from the side (the front door is actually several feet above the level of the plaza outside) to see the entry hall, dining room, sitting room with study, and the couple's bedroom. On the top floor is the replica of a bedroom he designed for a house in England: His final commission.

Return to University Avenue, exit turning right to:

12 University Gardens

This fine row of houses was designed primarily by J. J. Burnet in the 1880s, but it is worth stopping for—especially to admire no. 12, which was done by J. Gaff Gillespie in 1900 and exemplifies Glasgow Style and the influences of Mackintosh and Art Nouveau.

Continue down University Gardens past Queen Margaret Union and other university buildings, going left down the stairs just past the Gregory Building. At the bottom, follow the sidewalk and turn right onto:

13 Ashton Lane

This cobbled mews is the heart of West End nightlife, although it bustles right through the day, too, with a mix of students, university instructors and staff as well as local residents. The host of bars, cafes, and restaurants includes the venerable Ubiquitous Chip, which can be credited for starting (in 1971) the ongoing renaissance of excellent cooking of fresh Scottish produce (p. 188).

Continue onwards to:

14 Brel ☕

Especially welcome on nice days, Brel (39–43 Ashton Lane; ✆ 0141/342-4966), a bar and bistro, provides both outdoor and conservatory seating in the back. It has a Belgian theme, serving mussels and European beers. See p. 241 for full review.

Go left past the Ubiquitous Chip down the narrow lane to Byres Road. Here is an underground station, and you can catch the train back to the city center. Otherwise, turn right onto:

15 Byres Road

Full of bars, cafes, restaurants, and a panoply of shops, this is the proverbial Main Street of Glasgow's West End. Rarely less than buzzing, the road, for many, exemplifies the lively district. If you're not in a hurry, the tree-lined streets running west from Byres Road, such as Huntly Gardens, merit a detour to see the proud town houses.

Proceed north up Byres Road to:

16 Great Western Road

It took an 1836 Act of Parliament in London to create this street, then a new turnpike road into the city. Today, its four lanes remain a main thoroughfare in and out of Glasgow. A stroll west for five or six blocks from this intersection at the Botanic Gardens will reveal the opulent terraces (including one by "Greek" Thomson) along the boulevard's southern flank. Going in the opposite direction takes you to more retail shops. At this corner, the former Kelvinside Parish Church has been converted into a bar, restaurant, and center for the performing arts called Oran Mor.

Cross Great Western Road to the:

17 Botanic Gardens

Neither as extensive nor as grand as the Royal Botanic Gardens in Edinburgh, this hilly park is pleasant nonetheless. One main attraction is the extensively refurbished Kibble Palace, a giant, domed, cast-iron-and-glass Victorian conservatory with exotic plants. Other greenhouses contain orchid collections, while the outdoor planting includes a working vegetable plot, roses, and rhododendrons, and beds with lots of flowering perennials.

WALKING TOUR 4: THE SOUTHSIDE

START:	**Tramway.**
FINISH:	**Kilmarnock Road.**
TIME:	**About 1 hour.**
BEST TIME:	**Afternoon.**
WORST TIME:	**Late at night.**

The Southside of Glasgow is mostly residential and thus presumably of less interest to visitors—although some consider it to represent the real Glasgow, and Southsiders can be very attached to their patch of the city. It encompasses a large area. This relatively short walk provides only a small sample of the various neighborhoods south of the River Clyde.

Take the train one stop from Central Station upper level to the Pollokshields East station. Exit at the rear of the platform, come up the steps, and go right on Albert Drive to the:

1 Tramway

The one-time Coplawhill Tramway Works and Depot was built in the late 1800s. After the city's fleet of electric streetcars was mothballed, the sprawling industrial building became a Museum for Transport before becoming another of the city's centers for cutting-edge art and performance. More recently, it became the rehearsal space for the Scottish Ballet. Behind the building is a recently constructed park—called the Hidden Gardens—with contributions from contemporary artists. With a mixture of structured landscaping, wildflower meadow, and specimen planting, it is an urban oasis.

Exit Tramway, turning right to Pollokshaws Road, where you turn right (southwest) and stop by:

2 Heraghty's 🍺

(708 Pollokshaws Rd.; ✆ 0141/423-0380) is an Irish pub, but not the invented type with a phony atmosphere: This one's for real. Many of Glasgow's Irish immigrants settled on the city's Southside. Even if families have since moved to the outer suburbs, they often come back to this friendly, traditional pub for a pint of Guinness.

Continue southwest on Pollokshaws Road and go right (northeast) onto:

3 Nithsdale Road (Titwood Place)

Originally Titwood Place in the old village of Strathbungo, this street has a fairly long row of tenements probably designed by Alexander "Greek" Thomson, if executed after his death by a less than ambitious business partner. Although the buildings are rather plain, experts see the repetitive use of design and the manner in which the row terminates with a single-story shop as confirming Thomson's hand. Around the corner from the single-story shop is more evidence of Thomson's influences with acanthus leaves and square columns. Although tenements have a reputation as moldy, poor places to live, many built in the 1800s were the models of middle-class living. Thomson's best tenement, Queens Park Terrace on Eglinton Street north of here, was a victim of neglect and shamelessly demolished by the city in 1981.

To the left (west) of the roundabout at the end of Nithsdale Road is:

4 Moray Place

Nos. 1 to 10 Moray Place, facing the railway tracks, is the first terrace of houses designed by Alexander "Greek" Thomson, and the first house became the great architect's home in the 1860s. Like Eton Terrace (see "Walking Tour 3: The West End," p. 216), the structure has two "temples" at either end of a row of two-story town houses. A colonnade of some 52 square columns dominates the upper floor's facade. The original chimney pots were fashioned after lotus flowers, which are repeated in urns at the front of nos. 5 and 6. The terraces along

Walking Tour: The Southside

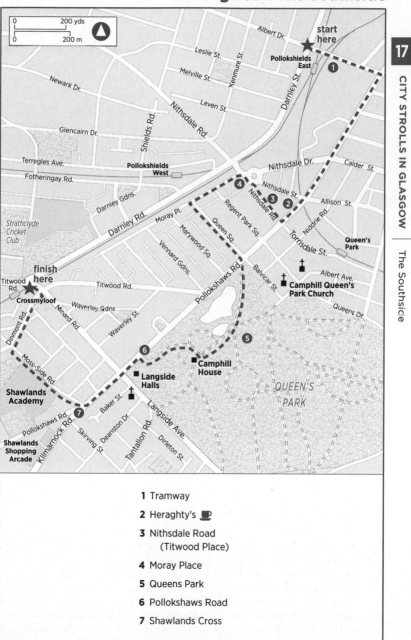

1 Tramway

2 Heraghty's ☕

3 Nithsdale Road
  (Titwood Place)

4 Moray Place

5 Queens Park

6 Pollokshaws Road

7 Shawlands Cross

the rest of Moray Place to the west only attempt to live up to Thomson's achievement.

Continue along Moray Place, go left on Queen Square to Pollokshaws Road, and cross to:

5 Queens Park

Although opened in 1862, this large hilly park was not named after Queen Victoria but rather Mary, Queen of Scots. Near here, her disastrous Battle of Langside was fought. The Gothic steeple, constructed of light colored stone, is part of William Leiper's Camphill Queen's Park Church, finished in 1883. By walking parallel to Pollokshaws Road, past the upper pond with resident swans on its island, and up a slight rise, you will come to Camphill House. Built toward the beginning of the 19th century with fluted Ionic columns at the front portico, it was once a costume museum.

To the right of Camphill House, follow the tree-lined drive past the compact soccer pitches back to:

6 Pollokshaws Road

One of the main thoroughfares leading to and from the city, Pollokshaws Road points directly at Glasgow Cathedral as it nears the city center. At this end of the boulevard, you'll find more of the city's distinctive red sandstone tenements. Nos. 988 to 1004 Camphill Gate, offer some distinctive Glasgow Style design work, from the lettering to cupolas and the iron railing along the roof. At the corner of the park is Langside Halls, which originally stood in the city center on Queen Street. It was moved lock, stock, and barrel to this location and rebuilt. The exterior decoration is by the same man who worked on London's Houses of Parliament.

Cross Langside Avenue and continue southwest on Pollokshaws Road to the fork with Kilmarnock Road and:

7 Shawlands Cross

This is the proverbial heart of the Southside, with lots of shops, pubs, and restaurants. This is especially the case going south on Kilmarnock Road, though the west side of the street is largely occupied with the unattractive 1960s-style Shawlands Shopping Arcade. On nearby Moss-side Road, the onetime Waverley Cinema, with its Egyptian-style columns, has been converted into a sprawling bar, restaurant, and nightclub called Tusk.

Go northwest on Moss-side Road, taking a right at Dinmont Road to Crossmyloof station and catch the suburban train back to the city center.

GLASGOW SHOPPING

After London, the capital of the U.K. and a city at least 10 times its size, Glasgow brags about having the second-most retail space in all of the U.K. (Birmingham begs to differ). Whatever the fact, Glasgow is a true shopping mecca in Scotland and, apparently, a reason for people to visit from northern England, too, as Glasgow's Buchanan Street is closer to them than London's Oxford Street.

The mainstream area for retail therapy in Glasgow is defined by the predominantly pedestrian zones of Argyle, Buchanan, and Sauchiehall streets, which join together and form a Z shape right in the heart of the city. But for more unique shops and fashions, it pays to venture into Merchant City and the West End. And perhaps the city's most unique shopping experience is at the flea-market-like stalls at the weekend Barras market in the East End.

THE SHOPPING SCENE

Glaswegians are notorious shoppers and their taste for labels is reflected in the range of shops across the city center. For quirkier finds, go into Merchant City and the West End, which has a growing number of hip and boutique outlets.

Best Buys

Among the retail goods that are high-quality *and* priced competitively are fine **wool knits,** particularly cashmere. Goods produced within the country (with the exception of whisky, which is taxed as heavily as all alcoholic products) should be less expensive than outside the U.K.: From **smoked salmon** and **shortbread** to **tweed** and **Caithness glass**. Finally, given the number of artists in the country, getting an original piece of **art** to take home might represent the most value for your money.

Shopping Complexes

Princes Square (Buchanan St.; ✆ **0141/204-1685;** www.princes square.co.uk) is the city's most stylish and upmarket shopping center.

Glasgow Shopping

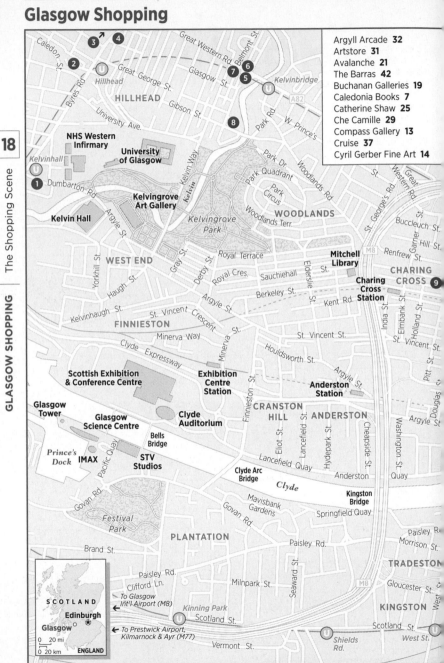

Argyll Arcade **32**
Artstore **31**
Avalanche **21**
The Barras **42**
Buchanan Galleries **19**
Caledonia Books **7**
Catherine Shaw **25**
Che Camille **29**
Compass Gallery **13**
Cruise **37**
Cyril Gerber Fine Art **14**

Debenhams **34**
Eunice Whyte **1**
Felix & Oscar **5**
Fopp **4**
Geoffrey (Tailor) Kiltmakers
   & Weavers **9**
Glasgow Print Studio **39**
Heart Buchanan Fine
   Food & Wine **3**
Hector Russell **26**
House of Fraser **28**

I.J. Mellis Cheesemonger **6**
James Pringle Weavers **22**
Jigsaw **36**
John Lewis **18**
Mackintosh Shop **10**
Marks & Spencer **12**
Mr. Bens **41**
Monorail **40**
Moss **24**
Niche Optical Tailor **38**
Peckham's **35**

Princes Square **30**
Roger Billcliffe Fine Art **11**
St. Enoch Shopping Centre **33**
Schuh **17**
SoleTrader **20**
Starry Starry Night **2**
Thomas Pink **27**
Urban Outfitters **23**
Victorian Village **16**
Voltaire & Rousseau **8**
Waterstone's **15**

Within a modernized and renovated Victorian building, the mall has many specialty stores, men's and women's fashion outlets, as well as restaurants, cafes, and bars.

If you're after a fancy watch or gold ring, go to the **Argyll Arcade,** the main entrance to which is at 30 Buchanan St. Even if the year of its construction (1827) wasn't posted above the entrance, you'd still know that this collection of shops beneath a curved glass ceiling is historic. The L-shaped, Parisian-style arcade contains one of the largest concentrations of retail **jewelers,** both antique and modern, in all of Europe. It's considered lucky by some to purchase a wedding band here.

Nearby, between Argyle Street and the River Clyde is the **St. Enoch Shopping Centre** (© 0141/204-3900; www.stenoch.com), which was being revamped and expanded in 2010. It is a fairly conventional indoor shopping mall with a couple of major department stores and a food court at one end.

The **Buchanan Galleries** (© 0141/333-9898; www.buchanangalleries.co.uk) are at the top of Buchanan Street. Completed in 1999, this mammoth development is hardly ground-breaking but it does include a **John Lewis** department store.

On the outskirts of town, the **Braehead Shopping Centre** (© 0141/885-1441; www.braehead.co.uk) is between the city and the airport. Its major draw is a sprawling Ikea store. In south Glasgow, the **Silverburn** shopping center (© 0141/880-3200; www.silverburn.com) is a recent addition. These malls appear to be taking shoppers away from the city center, in part because they are consistently open later in the evening.

SHOPPING A TO Z

In general, retail outlets in the city center are open from 9am until 6pm, though on Thursday evenings, shops in the heart of the city can stay open until 8pm. Most established stores are now open in the afternoon on Sunday.

Unless otherwise indicated, the shops below are in the commercial center of Glasgow and are within walking distance of either the Buchanan Street or St. Enoch underground stations.

Antiques

Victorian Village   This warren of shops offers a pleasantly claustrophobic array of goods. Some of the merchandise isn't particularly noteworthy, but there are some worthwhile pieces if you know what you're after and are willing to go hunting. 93 W. Regent St. © **0141/332-0808.**

Art

Compass Gallery   Opened by Cyril Gerber (see below), this gallery is run as a cooperative, featuring many affordable pieces of contemporary art by local artists. You could find something special for as little as £20. The pre-Christmas sale is particularly good. 178 W. Regent St. (near Blythswood Sq.). © **0141/221-6370.** www.compassgallery.co.uk.

Cyril Gerber Fine Art ★   One of Glasgow's best small galleries, it veers away from the avant-garde, specializing in British painting of the 19th and 20th centuries. It has good Scottish landscapes and cityscapes as well as works by Colourists and the Glasgow Boys. Gerber is the city's most respected art authority for several decades, with lots of contacts in art circles throughout Britain and Europe. 148 W. Regent St. © **0141/221-3095.** www.gerberfineart.co.uk.

Glasgow Print Studio ★★   In new premises as part of the Trongate 103 cultural center (p. 198), GPS sells limited-edition etchings, wood blocks, aquatints, and screen prints by members of the prestigious collective, as well as other notable artists. The prices are good and there is a framing facility on the premises. 97-101 Trongate. © **0141/552-0704.** www.gpsart.co.uk.

Roger Billcliffe Fine Art   Another fine fine-art shop with several floors of works, whether original contemporary paintings by Scottish and English artists or delicate ceramics. 134 Blythswood St. (just off Sauchiehall St.). © **0141/332-4027.** www.billcliffegallery.com.

Art Supplies

Artstore   If Glasgow's wealth of art and architecture, combined with the steely northern light, inspires you to make a bit of your own art, then this shop in the heart of the city will provide all the supplies you'll need. 94 Queen St. (across from the Gallery of Modern Art). © **0141/221-1101.** www.artstore.co.uk.

Books

Caledonia Books ★★   One of few remaining second-hand and antiquarian shops in the city of Glasgow, Caledonia Books is charming and well run. The stock tends to favor quality over quantity. 483 Great Western Rd., West End. © **0141/334-9663.** www.caledoniabooks.co.uk. Underground: Kelvinbridge.

Voltaire & Rousseau   This shop in an out-of-the-way location near the River Kelvin says it is the longest-running second-hand bookstore in the city. And if you found this place, you might as well visit nearby **Thistle Books** (61 Otago St.; © **0141/334-8777**). 18 Otago Lane (near Gibson St.), West End. © **0141/339-1811.** Underground: Kelvinbridge.

Waterstone's   A giant operation with plenty of stock, a cafe, and lots of soft seats. A good Scottish section. 174 Sauchiehall St. © **0141/248-4814.** www.waterstones.co.uk.

Clothing
FASHION

Cruise   Bring your credit cards for a selection of designer togs. Labels include Prada, Armani, D&G, Vivienne Westwood, and more. At the second branch nearby

(223 Ingram St.), the Oki-Ni shop within the shop offers limited-edition Adidas and Levis. 180 Ingram St. (at the Italian Centre), Merchant City. ℂ **0141/572-3232.**

Urban Outfitters Those familiar with Manhattan will recognize the stock in this popular store for youth, with a balance of metro-retro, kitsch, and chic clothing. 157 Buchanan St. (at Nelson Mandela Sq.). ℂ **0141/248-9203.** www.urbn.com.

MENSWEAR

Thomas Pink This is perhaps Glasgow's closest thing to that U.S. temple of preppy sensibilities: Brooks Brothers. This is the place for the finest button-down Oxford shirts that a man could possibly hope for—and a silk tie to match. 1 Royal Bank Place (next to Borders, just off Buchanan St.). ℂ **0141/248-9661.** www.thomaspink.com.

VINTAGE

Mr. Bens Clothing from this shop recently began to appear in newspaper fashion pages, but really it is one of the oldest purveyors of vintage clothing in the city. Expanded from its originally cramped premises, it nevertheless remains packed with wares, with an emphasis on 1960s' and 1970s' styles. 101 King St. ℂ **0141/553-1936.**

Starry Starry Night Those Victorians and Edwardians were surely tiny, but they wore some pretty stunning gowns, and this shop (with a branch in the Barras at the weekend) normally has a few worth dusting off. Also available are second-hand kilts and matching attire. 19 Dowanside Lane (off Ruthven Lane and Byres Rd.), West End. ℂ **0141/337-1837.** Underground: Hillhead.

WOMENSWEAR

Che Camille This is the place for bespoke, one-off fashion-led clothing. Run by a young designer, Che Camille is a clothes shop, design studio, and gallery in one—the kind of place that can make old-fashioned tweed look cutting-edge. 6th floor, Argyll Chambers, 34 Buchanan St. ℂ **0141/221-9620.** www.checamille.com.

Jigsaw Under the glorious dome of the baroque former Savings Bank of Glasgow are the displays of this outpost of the fashionable U.K. chain of womenswear, junior styles, and accessories. Using its own design team in Kew, West London, Jigsaw opened its first shop in Hampstead some 30 years ago. 177 Ingram St. (at Glassford St.). ℂ **0141/552-7639.** www.jigsaw-online.com.

Department Stores

Debenhams Sturdy department store with mid-range prices. St. Enoch Shopping Centre, 97 Argyle St. ℂ **0844/561-6161.** www.debenhams.com.

House of Fraser Victorian-era glass arcade rises up four stories, and on the various levels you'll find everything from clothing to Oriental rugs, from crystal to handmade local artifacts of all kinds. 45 Buchanan St. (at Argyle St.). ℂ **0870/160-7243.** www.houseoffraser.co.uk.

John Lewis Quality brand names, assured service, and an excellent returns policy on damaged or faulty goods. Buchanan Galleries, 220 Buchanan St. ℂ **0141/353-6677.** www.johnlewis.com.

Marks & Spencer Still the leading department store across Great Britain, "Marks & Sparks" carries on with clothing and a very good food hall. Two branches in Glasgow on Argyle and Sauchiehall streets. 172 Sauchiehall St. ℂ **0141/332-6097.** www.marksandspencer.com.

Bring That Passport!

Take along your passport when you go shopping in case you make a purchase that entitles you to a **VAT (value-added tax) refund.**

Food & Wine

Heart Buchanan Fine Food & Wine ★ Perfect for picnic nosh to take to the nearby Botanic Gardens, this is Glasgow's premier fine food shop. It also has a small cafe. 380 Byres Rd., West End. ✆ **0141/334-7626.** http://heart buchanan.co.uk. Underground: Hillhead.

I.J. Mellis Cheesemonger ★★ The Glasgow branch of this excellent Edinburgh-based cheese specialist offers an outstanding selection of British and Irish cheeses. 492 Great Western Rd., West End. ✆ **0141/339-8998.** Underground: Kelvinbridge.

Peckham's A full delicatessen with fresh bread and a good wine shop in the basement. 61 Glassford St. ✆ **0141/553-0666.** www.peckhams.co.uk.

Gifts & Design

Catherine Shaw Named after a long-deceased matriarch of the family owners, Catherine Shaw is a somewhat cramped gift shop that has cups, mugs, postcards, jewelry, and souvenirs. It's a good place for easy-to-pack gifts. Look for another branch at 31 Argyll Arcade (✆ **0141/221-9038**). 24 Gordon St. ✆ **0141/204-4762.**

Felix & Oscar ★ This shop stocks off-beat cards and toys, kitsch accessories, fuzzy bags, perfumes and toiletries, as well as a selection of T-shirts that you're not likely to find anywhere else in Glasgow. In addition to the flagship shop, there is another on Cresswell Lane. 459 Great Western Rd., West End. ✆ **0131/339-8585.** www.felix andoscar.co.uk.

Mackintosh Shop This shop, recently moved to the basement of Glasgow School of Art, prides itself on a stock of limited-edition art, books, cards, stationery, mugs, glassware, and sterling-and-enamel jewelry created from or inspired by the original designs of Charles Rennie Mackintosh. Only authorized Mackintosh goods are sold here, so quality is assured. Glasgow School of Art, 167 Renfrew St. ✆ **0141/353-4500.**

Kilts & Tweeds

Geoffrey (Tailor) Kiltmakers & Weavers Both a retailer and manufacturer of tartans, which means they have all the clans and have also created their own range of 21st-century-style kilts—for better or worse. 309 Sauchiehall St. (across from the CCA). ✆ **0141/331-2388.** www.geoffreykilts.co.uk.

Hector Russell Founded in 1881, Hector Russell is Scotland's long-established Inverness-based kiltmaker. Crystal and gift items are sold on street level, but the real heart and soul of the place is below, where impeccably crafted and reasonably priced tweed jackets, tartan-patterned accessories, waistcoats, and sweaters made from top-quality wool for men and women are displayed. 110 Buchanan St. ✆ **0141/221-0217.** www.hector-russell.com.

James Pringle Weavers In business since 1780, this shop is known for its traditional clothing that includes well-crafted, bulky wool sweaters, and a tasteful selection of ties, kilts, and tartans. Some of the merchandise is unique to this shop. Ever slept in a tartan nightshirt? 130 Buchanan St. ✆ **0141/221-3434.**

Kilt Hire

Moss You might just wish to don a kilt during your stay, and renting one is a heck of a lot less expensive than buying one. This clothing store has a good stock and will sometimes reduce the price of a rental for those making last-minute hires. 25 Renfield St. (near Central Station). ✆ **0141/248-7571.**

Music

Avalanche ★ The indie rock store to beat all others? Small and cramped perhaps but Avalanche is possibly the best for the latest releases by everybody from White Stripes to Yo La Tengo or local stars Franz Ferdinand and up-and-comers such as Sons and Daughters. 34 Dundas St. (near Queen St. Station). ✆ **0141/332-2099.** www.avalanche records.co.uk.

Fopp Glasgow's largest independent CD outlet, saved from closure a couple of years back by the HMV Group, stocks a good number of re-releases priced at only £5. In addition to the West End flagship, there is a larger, multistory branch in the city center on Union Street (✆ **0141/222-2128**) near Central Station. 358 Byres Rd., West End ✆ **0141/357-0774.** www.fopp.co.uk.

Monorail ★★ Located within the vegan restaurant and bar called Mono (p. 183), this is the most individual of independent CD and record outlets in the city. Glasgow is alight with young musicians, and this shop specializes in new music from up-and-coming local acts, as well as the best of cutting-edge bands from elsewhere. 10 King St. ✆ **0141/553-2400.**

Shoes

Schuh Pronounced "shoe," this shop has the biggest range of shoes in the city, from stilettos to sneakers, Converse high-tops to "Doc" Martens. 9 Sauchiehall St. (near Buchanan Galleries). ✆ **0141/353-1990.**

SoleTrader A more fashion-conscious selection of European designers and makers, such as Birkenstock. 164a Buchanan St. (at Dundas Lane). ✆ **0141/353-3022.**

Spectacles

Niche Optical Tailor ★ Arguably the leading optician in Scotland when it comes to stylish specs, the range of glasses includes all the coolest designers and many frames not found elsewhere. 119 Candleriggs, Merchant City. ✆ **0141/553-2077.**

Tartans

See "Kilts & Tweeds," above.

Woolen Knits

Eunice Whyte 👜 This small, locally owned shop is not sewn into the primary shopping districts. But come here for an excellent selection of wool sweaters and cardigans, scarves, and hats; some real bargains on occasion, too. 109 Dumbarton Rd., West End. ✆ **0141/339-2534.**

GLASGOW AFTER DARK

Some say that it is Glasgow—not Edinburgh—that is the center of contemporary culture in Scotland. It is an arguable, not to say locally controversial, point of view. But there is no doubt that Glasgow has seen the most progress since the middle of the 20th century, when the shipping boom went bust, giving way to an image of profound decline that began to reverse in the 1980s. Its local arts scene was always alive, however.

Although the Scottish capital to the east hosts a world-famous festival and is home to the country's national art galleries and museums, Glasgow is where the respected and accomplished **Scottish Opera** and **Scottish Ballet** companies—as well as the **Scottish National Orchestra**—are based. It is also the city where young talent is nurtured at the **Royal Scottish Academy of Music & Drama.** There are several theaters, including two that rank highly in the U.K. for staging ground-breaking drama: The **Citizens** and the **Tron.** Even more experimental performances can be seen at the **Arches.**

But for all this "high art," Glasgow has the reputation for being an unsurpassed spawning ground in Scotland for diverse pop and rock groups, such as Primal Scream, Paolo Nutini, Franz Ferdinand, Snow Patrol, and Belle and Sebastian. **Barrowland,** a former ballroom, has to be one of the best venues (that is, sweaty and vibrating) in all of Britain for seeing live contemporary music. Additionally, there is the **Academy** on the city's Southside and in the city center, **ABC,** a former cinema that was redeveloped into an excellent mid-size music venue in 2005. There are also at least four bars—**King Tut's Wah Wah Hut** (where the band Oasis was apparently "discovered"), **Nice 'n' Sleazy, the 13th Note,** and **Stereo**—that provide Glasgow with smaller dedicated performance spaces. They attract rising bands and acts preferring cozy confines.

Then, of course, there are the city's many other pubs and bars, the best of which are listed toward the end of this chapter. They are friendly places, and don't be surprised if the locals strike up a conversation. Remember, all indoor public places, including bars, are completely non-smoking. For a complete rundown of what is happening in Glasgow, pick

Glasgow After Dark

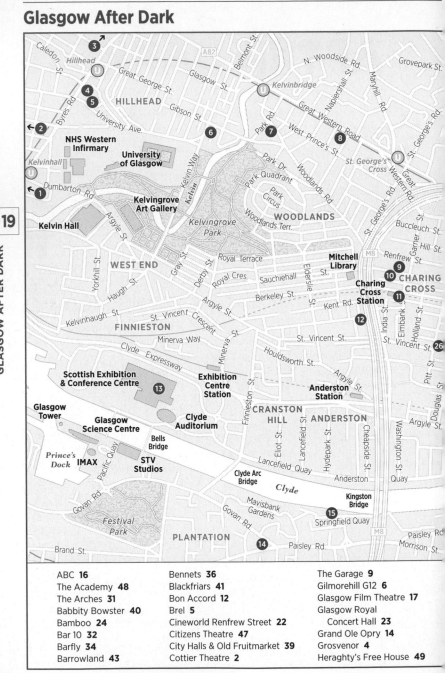

ABC **16**	Bennets **36**	The Garage **9**
The Academy **48**	Blackfriars **41**	Gilmorehill G12 **6**
The Arches **31**	Bon Accord **12**	Glasgow Film Theatre **17**
Babbity Bowster **40**	Brel **5**	Glasgow Royal
Bamboo **24**	Cineworld Renfrew Street **22**	Concert Hall **23**
Bar 10 **32**	Citizens Theatre **47**	Grand Ole Opry **14**
Barfly **34**	City Halls & Old Fruitmarket **39**	Grosvenor **4**
Barrowland **43**	Cottier Theatre **2**	Heraghty's Free House **49**

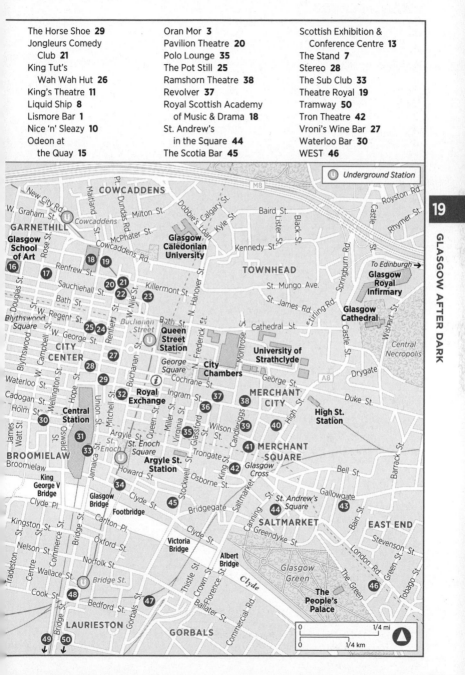

The Horse Shoe **29**
Jongleurs Comedy
  Club **21**
King Tut's
  Wah Wah Hut **26**
King's Theatre **11**
Liquid Ship **8**
Lismore Bar **1**
Nice 'n' Sleazy **10**
Odeon at
  the Quay **15**

Oran Mor **3**
Pavilion Theatre **20**
Polo Lounge **35**
The Pot Still **25**
Ramshorn Theatre **38**
Revolver **37**
Royal Scottish Academy
  of Music & Drama **18**
St. Andrew's
  in the Square **44**
The Scotia Bar **45**

Scottish Exhibition &
  Conference Centre **13**
The Stand **7**
Stereo **28**
The Sub Club **33**
Theatre Royal **19**
Tramway **50**
Tron Theatre **42**
Vroni's Wine Bar **27**
Waterloo Bar **30**
WEST **46**

up a copy of *The List,* a biweekly magazine available at all major newsstands and bookshops, or go online to www.list.co.uk.

THE PERFORMING ARTS
Ballet & Opera

Theatre Royal ★★★ This is the home theater for the ambitious, well-respected **Scottish Opera,** as well as the recently ascendant **Scottish Ballet.** The Royal also hosts visiting companies from around the world. Called only slightly exaggeratedly by the *Daily Telegraph,* "the most beautiful opera theatre in the kingdom," the auditorium does offer splendid Victorian plasterwork and some glittering chandeliers. However, it's not the decor but the repertoire—Wagner's *Ring* cycle, *La Bohème,* or *Don Giovanni*—that traditionally has attracted operagoers. 282 Hope St. ℂ **0870/060-6647.** www.theatreroyalglasgow.com. Ballet tickets £3.50 (standby) to £55; opera tickets £28–£180; touring company tickets £10–£25. Underground: Cowcaddens.

Concert Halls

City Halls & Old Fruitmarket ★★ This set of smaller halls, which date to the 1840s, is perhaps the most acoustically perfect in Glasgow. Home to the **BBC's Scottish Symphony Orchestra** and the **Scottish Chamber Orchestra,** the Merchant City venue is now a key venue in the annual Celtic Connections Festival and the International Jazz Festival, as well. Candleriggs and Albion streets, Merchant City. ℂ **0141/353-8000.** www.glasgowcityhalls.com. Underground: Buchanan St.

Glasgow Royal Concert Hall Situated at the top of Buchanan Street, there is very little that's subtle about this modern music hall, which houses the largest bespoke performance space in the city and is home to the **Royal Scottish National Orchestra,** which plays its yearly Winter–Spring series and Pops seasons in the main auditorium. The hall also produces the city's annual Celtic Connections Festival every January. 2 Sauchiehall St. ℂ **0141/353-8000.** www.grch.com. Underground: Buchanan St.

Royal Scottish Academy of Music & Drama This mouthful is usually shortened to its acronym: The RSAMD. A fine auditorium in this clunky brick structure compensates for any sins of the external architecture. 100 Renfrew St. ℂ **0141/332-4101.** www.rsamd.ac.uk. Underground: Cowcaddens.

Theater

Although hardly competition for a drama giant such as London, Glasgow's theater scene is equal to, if not a step ahead of, Edinburgh's. Young Scottish playwrights often make their debuts here, and from the established dramatic repertoire you're likely to see anything from Steinbeck's *The Grapes of Wrath* to Beckett's *Crapp's Last Tape.*

The Arches ★ Located within the vaulted brick arches beneath the railway lines in and out of Central Station, the Arches offers a range of inexpensive drama and performances. However, it also offers a fairly full schedule of live music of all descriptions, regular dance clubs, and visual art exhibits. Although it receives grants from government arts bodies, it is an independent, not-for-profit entity. The cafe/bar at the Arches is, like at the Traverse in Edinburgh, a scene unto itself. 253 Argyle St. ℂ **0870/240-7528.** www.thearches.co.uk. Tickets £4–£10. Underground: St. Enoch.

Citizens Theatre ★★   Perhaps the prime symbol of Glasgow's verve and democratic approach to theater is the well-known "Citz." Located in the Gorbals, just across the River Clyde from the commercial center of Glasgow, it's home to a repertory company, and the facility has three performance spaces: A main auditorium and two smaller theaters. Prices are always reasonable. 119 Gorbals St. (at Ballater St.). ℂ **0141/429-0022.** www.citz.co.uk. Tickets £5–£15. Underground: Bridge St. Bus: 5, 12, 20, or 66.

Cottier Theatre   This 350-seat, nonprofit theater is housed in the former Dowanhill Parish Church in the Hyndland district of the city's West End. Small-scale productions and community theater are usually staged here. The complex includes a pub with verdant beer garden. 935 Hyndland St. ℂ **0141/357-3868.** www.thecottier.com. Tickets £4–£20. Underground: Kelvinhall.

Gilmorehill G12   Run by the University of Glasgow, and often just called G12 (the local postal code), productions by the university's drama students and other college and independent companies are staged here. 9 University Ave. ℂ **0141/330 5522.** www.gilmorehillg12.co.uk. Tickets £3–£12. Underground: Kelvinbridge.

King's Theatre   The over-a-century-old King's Theatre generally offers popular and light entertainment, whether comedies, musicals, or family-oriented plays. This red-sandstone hall is also the place where touring Broadway and West End spectacles, such as *Miss Saigon,* are likely to appear. During December and January, the King's is best noted for its over-the-top pantomime presentations, often starring well-known Scottish actors. 297 Bath St. ℂ **0870/060 6648.** www.kings.glasgow.co.uk. Tickets £6–£26. Train: Charing Cross. Bus: 16 or 18.

Pavilion Theatre   After the King's Theatre, this equally historic theater (if less architecturally distinguished) specializes in family entertainment, variety shows, light drama, tribute acts and bands, as well as comedy. It's another prime location for pantomime around Christmas time. 121 Renfield St. ℂ **0141/332-1846.** www.pavilion theatre.co.uk. Tickets £10–£25. Underground: Buchanan St. Bus: 21, 23, or 38.

Ramshorn Theatre   Another church conversion, this performance space is used primarily for student productions of nearby Strathclyde University and for touring companies. Ticket prices are typically low. 98 Ingram St. ℂ **0141/552-3489.** Tickets £2.50–£8. Underground: Buchanan St.

Tramway   This postindustrial, huge hangar of an arts venue is one of the only places in Glasgow able to stage sprawling performance art and modern theater, such as Peter Brook's *The Mahabharata,* which came here in the late 1980s. 25 Albert Dr., Pollokshields. ℂ **0141/422-2023.** www.tramway.org. Tickets £4–£12. Train: Pollokshields East. Bus: 38 or 45.

Tron Theatre ★★   Housed in part of the former Tron Church, which dates back to the 15th century, the Tron Theatre is one of Scotland's leading venues for new and sometimes experimental dramatic performances. The stage is often the place where contemporary local companies, such as Cryptic or Vanishing Point, debut works that go on to tour in the U.K. and even internationally. In addition to theater, the hall is used for music and dance. The Tron also has a modern bar/cafe as well as a beautifully restored Victorian bar/restaurant serving lunch and dinner, including

📎 **Finding Out What's On**

For a complete rundown of what is happening in the city, pick up a copy of *The List,* a biweekly magazine available at all major newsstands and bookshops. It reviews, previews, and gives the details of the arts and events in Glasgow and Edinburgh. For the online version, go to www.list.co.uk.

vegetarian dishes, as well as a fine selection of beer and wine. 63 Trongate. ✆ **0141/552-4267.** www.tron.co.uk. Tickets £3–£20. Underground: St. Enoch.

THE CLUB & MUSIC SCENE

Comedy

Jongleurs Comedy Club   A corporate-owned entity from England, with more than a dozen venues across the U.K., Jongleurs came to Scotland a few years back bringing along its own cadre of house funny men (and women), as well as some touring comedians from overseas. The acts tend to be mainstream. Renfield St. and Renfrew St. ✆ **0870/787-0707.** Cover £12. Underground: Buchanan St.

The Stand ★   After starting and thriving in Edinburgh, The Stand opened a second venue in Glasgow—the city's only purpose-built comedy club. Its presence has helped to establish an annual International Comedy Festival every spring in the city. Usually Tuesday night, entitled "Red Raw," is reserved for amateurs. 333 Woodlands Rd. ✆ **0870/600-6055.** www.thestand.co.uk. Cover £2–£10. Underground: Kelvinbridge.

Dance Clubs

Glasgow has one of the most active dance club scenes in Great Britain. Listed below are just a few selected venues. In local parlance, "venues" are distinct from the actual "clubs"—such as Optimo (techno/post-punk) or Pressure (house and techno)—which are associated with a specific style, DJ, or team of DJs. They can move around to different venues. It all makes perfect sense to those in the know.

Bamboo   This stylish basement club has three distinct rooms, one of which is a rather posh cocktail lounge. The "Disco Badger" club, playing a mix of house and R&B, gets good reviews. It's open from 10pm to 3am. 51 West Regent St. ✆ **0141/332-1067.** www.bamb0051.com. Cover £5–£8; free before 10:30pm. Underground: Buchanan St.

The Garage   A big student crowd tests the limits of the 1,478-person capacity here at weekends. In the downstairs area, surrounded by rough stone walls, you get the impression you're in a castle with a Brit pop and indie soundtrack. Most regulars, however, gravitate to the huge main dance floor. Open daily 11pm to 3am. 490 Sauchiehall St. ✆ **0141/332-1120.** Cover £2–£7. Underground: Buchanan St.

The Sub Club ★   The city's best-known "underground" club is possibly better than ever, with DJs such as the long-standing kings of house, Harri and Dom of Subculture, Sunday night's famous Optimo, and occasional live acts such as L.A.'s No Age. Open daily 10pm to 3am. 22 Jamaica St. ✆ **0141/248-4600.** www.subclub.co.uk. Cover £3–£10. Underground: St. Enoch.

Folk

Oran Mor   Oran Mor is an ambitious center for the performing arts that includes a bar and restaurant as well as different spaces for live music—often but not always in a Scottish folk vein. An afternoon drama in the popular "Play, Pie, and a Pint" series includes lunch. Contact Oran Mor for cover and ticket prices, and a schedule of events. Byres Rd. and Great Western Rd. ℂ **0141/357-6200.** www.oran-mor.co.uk.

St. Andrew's in the Square   This sympathetically converted early- to mid-18th-century church is the city's venue dedicated to folk, Celtic, and traditional Scottish music. The program includes concerts and *ceilidhs* (Scottish country dance) in the main hall upstairs. In the basement, **Café Source** serves wholesome Scottish nosh and hosts regular sessions of Scottish music, which can be rather reverentially listened to by the patrons; and jazz, too. 1 St. Andrew's Sq. (off Saltmarket near Glasgow Cross). ℂ **0141/559-5902.** www.standrewsinthesquare.com. Tickets £4–£8. Underground: St. Enoch. Bus: 16, 18, 64, or 263.

The Scotia Bar   Along with the nearby **Clutha Vaults** bar, this low-ceilinged pub frequently offers live music, which includes a good dose of folk. 112 Stockwell St. ℂ **0141/552-8681.** http://scotiabar.net. No cover. Underground: St. Enoch.

Rock, Pop & Jazz

ABC ★   Opened in 2005, this is an excellent venue for bands visiting Glasgow. The main hall has room for about 1,250, allowing audiences to get a bit closer to the musicians. The building itself dates to 1896 and reputedly screened the first film ever shown in Scotland, although it also housed a permanent circus before reverting to a film house in the 20th century. 300 Sauchiehall St. ℂ **0870/400-0818.** www.abcglasgow.com. Underground: Cowcaddens.

The Academy   A 2,500 capacity ex-cinema, this venue was expressly designed to compete with Barrowland. But it cannot, honestly. Part of the 02 chain currently, it has booking strength with touring bands. 121 Eglinton Rd. ℂ **0141/418-3000.** Underground: Bridge St.

Late-Night Eats

Famished at 4 minutes past midnight? Several Indian restaurants are open until 1am, but a couple trump the lot by staying open until 4am. **Charcoals** is in the city center (26 Renfield St.; ℂ **0141/221-9251**), while **Spice Gardens** is on the southern bank of the River Clyde (Clyde Place near Bridge St.; ℂ **0141/429-4422**).

Barfly   Part of a chain of small clubs devoted mostly to indie bands, Barfly draws some of the best in local and national talent. Cover charge varies. Tickets for shows should be purchased in advance. 260 Clyde St. ℂ **0141/204-5700.** www.barflyclub.com. Underground: St. Enoch.

Barrowland ★★   No seats and often stinking of beer, this former ballroom remains the most exciting place in the city to see visiting bands, although there is some talk of the owners selling it. The hall rocks, and groups who play here rank it among the best venues in the U.K. in which to perform. With room for about 2,000, it is not exactly intimate, but if you can withstand the mosh pit, you'll feel the sweat of the performers. 244 Gallowgate. ℂ **0141/552-4601.** Train: High St. Bus: 40, 62, or 262.

Grand Ole Opry 🎁 Country-western music has a strong cult following in Glasgow, and this club, 2.5km (1½ miles) southwest of the city center, is the largest of its type in Europe devoted to that genre. There is a bar, bingo, and "shoot-out," as well as a mildly offensive night-ending paean to the American Confederacy—but mainly plenty of dancing (Texas line) plus a "chuck-wagon" eatery. 2-4 Govan Rd., Paisley Toll Rd. ⓒ **0141/429-5396.** Underground: Shields Rd. Bus: 9.

King Tut's Wah Wah Hut ★ This sweaty, crowded rock venue has been in business for more than a decade. It's a good place to check out the Glasgow music and arts crowd, as well as local bands and cult international acts, such as Holly Golightly. Successful Scottish acts, such as Teenage Fan Club, got their starts here. Open Monday to Saturday noon to midnight and Sunday 6pm to midnight. Tickets for shows can be purchased in advance at the bar. 272 St. Vincent St. ⓒ **0141/221-5279.** www.kingtuts.co.uk. Train: Charing Cross. Bus: 40, 61, or 62.

Nice 'n' Sleazy This bar books live acts to perform in the dark basement space. The cover is quite reasonable, but it can get expensive if you catch a more established act. Holding some 200 patrons, it provides a rare opportunity to catch such musicians in an intimate setting. The ground-floor bar has the city's best jukebox, and DJs spin an eclectic mix of music. Open daily 11:30am to 11:45pm. 421 Sauchiehall St. ⓒ **0141/333-9637.** Train: Charing Cross. Bus: 16, 44, or 66.

Scottish Exhibition & Conference Centre ✋ Incorporating the slightly more intimate Clyde Auditorium (or Armadillo because of its exterior design), the Clydeside SECC may indeed be lacking charm, but it provides Scotland with the only indoor space large enough to host major touring acts, from Ozzy Osbourne to Justin Timberlake. Finnieston Quay. ⓒ **0141/275-6211.** www.secc.co.uk. Train: Exhibition Centre.

Stereo Below a vegan cafe/bar is this spare performance space for indie acts/alternative bands, such as Cate Le Bon or the Slits, and club nights, as well. 22-28 Renfield Lane. ⓒ **0141/222 2254.** www.stereocafebar.com. Train: St. Enoch.

BARS & PUBS
Commercial Center

Bar 10 Perhaps the granddaddy of the Glasgow style bar, it has mellowed after two-plus decades into a comfortable place for drinking. The coolish design is still apparent, but more important is the good mix of folk and the convenient city center location. Food is comforting and served from noon to about 5pm. Drinks are served Monday to Saturday from noon to midnight and Sunday from 12:30pm to midnight. DJs play at the weekend. 10 Mitchell Lane. ⓒ **0141/572-1448.** Underground: Buchanan St.

Bon Accord This amiable pub, just west of the city center on the other side of the M8 freeway, is among the best in the city for cask-conditioned real ale. There's an array of hand-pumps—a dozen devoted to English and Scottish ales—while the rest of the draft and bottled beers and stouts hail from the Czech Republic, Belgium, Germany, Ireland, and Holland. The pub is likely to satisfy your taste in malt whisky, as well, and offers affordable pub food. Open Monday to Saturday noon to midnight, Sunday noon to 11pm. 153 North St. ⓒ **0141/248-4427.** Train: Charing Cross.

The Horse Shoe ★   If you could only visit one pub in central Glasgow, I might suggest this one. It is the last unscathed "Palace Pub," which opened around the turn of the 20th century. The circular, island bar is one of the longest in Europe, and the place draws an interesting cross-section of Glaswegians. Drinks are served Monday to Saturday noon to midnight and Sunday from 12:30pm to midnight. The buffet is open until 7:30pm daily except Sunday, when it closes at 5pm. 17 Drury St. (btw. Renfield and W. Nile streets). ℂ **0141/229-5711.** Underground: Buchanan St.

The Pot Still   Previously called the Cask & Still, this pub is the best place for sampling superior malt whiskies. You can taste from a selection of hundreds and hundreds of them, with a variety of styles (peaty or sweet), strengths, and maturities. Open Monday to Thursday noon to 11pm, Friday and Saturday noon to midnight, Sunday 12:30 to 11pm. 154 Hope St. ℂ **0141/333-0980.** www.thepotstill.co.uk. Underground: Buchanan St.

Vroni's Wine Bar   If you favor the grape over the grain, Bordeaux over brown ale, Sancerre rather than cider, then Vroni's selection of red, white, and sparkling wines, sold by the glass or the bottle, should satisfy you. The feeling of this small bar is Continental with banquette seating and candle-lit tables. Open Monday to Saturday from 10am to midnight and Sunday from 12:30pm to midnight; food is served at lunchtimes. 47 W. Nile St. ℂ **0141/221-4677.** Underground: Buchanan St.

Merchant City

Babbity Bowster ★   A civilized place for a pint, with no pounding soundtrack of mindless pop to distract you from conversation. The wine selection is good, and the food is worth sampling, as well. Outdoor seating is available, although it is rarely in full sun. Folk musicians often drop in for a bit of spontaneous jamming. Drinks are served daily from noon to midnight; food until about 9pm. 16 Blackfriars St. ℂ **0141/552-5055.** Train: High St.

Blackfriars   Real ales are less plentiful in Glasgow when compared to Edinburgh, but this basic Merchant City pub has a decent selection of rotating beers, including some from the Continent. Jazz is featured in the basement space, as is comedy. Drinks are served Monday to Saturday from noon to midnight and Sunday from 12:30pm to midnight. 36 Bell St. ℂ **0141/552-5924.** Underground: St. Enoch.

East End

WEST ★   This brewery and bar is modeled after Munich beer halls. In the basement they produce the best, freshest lager in Scotland following strict German laws for purity and using chemical-free processes. Don't let the name fool you, however, as WEST is at the east end of Glasgow Green in the former wool-winding room of the Templeton Carpet Factory (near the People's Palace museum). Food leans toward hearty Bavarian dishes; drinks are served from noon to midnight; food until about 9pm. Glasgow Green. ℂ **0141/550-0135.** www.westbeer.com. Bus: 16, 43, or 64.

West End

Brel ★   Ashton Lane is full of pubs and bars, but this one is possibly the best. It has a Belgian theme—with beers and cuisine favoring that French-speaking country—but it is not overplayed. The music policy is eclectic, with DJs and live acts adding atmosphere to the former stables. The bar is open daily from 10am to midnight. Food is served Monday to Friday from noon to 3pm and from 5 to 10:30pm, and on Saturday and Sunday from noon to 10:30pm. 39-43 Ashton Lane. © **0141/342-4966.** www.brelbarrestaurant.com. Underground: Hillhead.

Liquid Ship 🍴   Given its location, you're most likely to meet locals at Liquid Ship. Owned by the same people who run Stravaigin (p. 190), it is unpretentious and smart with the main bar up a few steps and a lounge in the basement. Drinks are served Monday to Thursday from noon to 11pm, Friday and Saturday from noon to midnight, and Sunday from 12:30 to 11pm. Light fare is served daily from noon until about 8pm. 171 Great Western Rd. © **0141/331-1901.** Underground: St. George's Cross.

Lismore Bar   Decorated in a modern manner that still recognizes traditional Highland culture, the Lismore is a relaxed and laid-back bar. The whisky selection is excellent, and the malt of the month is always a bargain. There is often Scottish and Gaelic music on Tuesday and Thursday nights. The bar is open Sunday to Thursday from 11am to 11pm and Friday and Saturday from 11am to midnight. No food is served. 206 Dumbarton Rd. © **0141/576-0103.** Underground: Kelvinhall.

Southside

Heraghty's Free House 🍴   The trend for Irish theme pubs has left its mark on Glasgow, but if you want the real McCoy, come to this traditional bar on the city's Southside. It serves up perfect pints of Guinness and Irish *craic* (banter) in almost equal portions. No food, though. Open Monday to Thursday from 11am to 11pm, Friday and Saturday from 11am to midnight, and Sunday from 12:30 to 11pm. 708 Pollokshaws Rd. © **0141/423-0380.** Train: Queens Park. Bus: 38, 45, or 56.

GAY & LESBIAN

Glasgow and its environs are said to have the largest concentration of gays and lesbians in the U.K. outside of London. The Merchant City is the only identifiable district in the city where the gay and lesbian community is particularly concentrated, dubbed the "gay triangle."

Bennets   Self-described as the city's "premier gay and lesbian night club," Bennets is the most consistently popular club in the gay scene. The club extends over two levels, with chart and full-on dance music. Open Tuesday to Sunday 11:30pm to 3am. 80 Glassford St. © **0141/552-5761.** Cover £3–£10. Underground: Buchanan St.

Polo Lounge   Gay but hetero-friendly, the Polo is often described as a cross between an urbane gentleman's club and a Highland country lodge. It is both a bar and club, with dancing downstairs. Open daily from 5pm to 1am (until 3am Fri–Sat). 84 Wilson St. © **0141/553-1221.** Cover after 10pm £5. Underground: Buchanan St.

Revolver   Gay-owned and -operated, the Revolver bar has always tried to be a bit more grown-up and to dismiss some of the more cheesy and stereotypical elements of the gay scene. But that doesn't mean that it is not fun or popular. Conversation generally rules, and the jukebox is free. Drinks are served daily from noon to midnight. 6A John St. © **0141/553-2456.** Underground: Buchanan St.

Waterloo Bar   Attracting a slightly older crowd, this place is the longest-standing gay bar in town. Away from the heart of the scene in Merchant City, it's located west of Central Station. Open from noon to midnight Monday to Saturday and from 12:30 to 11pm on Sunday. 306 Argyle St. ℂ **0141/221-7359.** Underground: St. Enoch.

CINEMA

Cineworld Renfrew Street ★ The towering building in the city center, the screens at this multiplex formerly known as the UGC are dominated by blockbusters and big releases, but a couple of the theaters are reserved for foreign films and independent art house features. 7 Renfrew St. ℂ **0871/200-2000.** www.ugccinemas.co.uk. Tickets £4.50–£6.50.

Glasgow Film Theatre ★★ Two screens are used for a well-programmed daily output of independent, foreign, repertory, and art house films. The cinema was originally called the Cosmo, an Art Deco theater built in the late 1930s. Near the box office is Café Cosmo, a good place for pre- or post-movie beverages. 12 Rose St. ℂ **0141/332-8128.** www.gft.org.uk. Tickets £4–£6. Underground: Cowcaddens.

Grosvenor Refurbished and restored on Ashton Lane in the West End, the Grosvenor is possibly the only neighborhood cinema still operating in Glasgow, with a bar and two downstairs screening rooms with comfy big leather chairs and sofas that you can rent. The cinema screens a mix of mostly mainstream and a clutch of independent movies. Ashton Lane. ℂ **0141/339-8444.** www.grosvenorcinema.co.uk. Tickets £2.50–£6.50. Underground: Hillhead.

Odeon at the Quay A modern multiplex movie house on the south bank of the River Clyde, showing Hollywood films and other mainstream movies. Springfield Quay, Paisley Rd. ℂ **0141-418-0111.** Tickets £4.50–£6.50.

SIDE TRIPS FROM GLASGOW

One of Glasgow's attractions is its proximity to a diverse array of rural scenery, whether the hills and mountains to the north or the sea coasts to the west. A short journey in almost any direction will present visitors with open spaces and fresh air.

As Sir Walter Scott dominates Lothian and the Borders, the prominence of 18th-century poet **Robert Burns** is felt southwest of Glasgow in Ayrshire. The heart of "Burns Country" is there, although it extends to Dumfries, as well. Down the Clyde coast is another popular tourist attraction: **Culzean Castle.** Pronounced approximately "cul-lane," it is more of a mansion than a castle, with extensive and picturesque gardens and woods all around.

Some of the world's great links golf courses are in this region, including world-famous **Royal Troon** and **Turnberry,** with windswept coastal views and gorse-filled dunes. Although the heyday of resort towns such as Rothesay on the Isle of **Bute** or Brodick on the Isle of **Arran** may be gone, these islands in the broad Firth of Clyde are great relaxing places to visit. Or, go a bit further afield to the peninsulas further west—such as **Kintyre**—where you might be lured by the scenery into spending more than a night or two. Short of that, day-trippers can easily reach Helensburgh and visit one of architect Charles Rennie Mackintosh's singular achievements: The residence known as **Hill House.**

Glasgow is also an excellent gateway to explore the southern reaches of the **Highlands.** Within an hour, you can be on the bonnie banks of **Loch Lomond,** with the mountains looming in the distance. Finally, the city of **Stirling** and the **Trossachs** range of mountains can be visited in a single day. See p. 49 for a map with an overview of excursions from Glasgow ("Glasgow & Side Trips" in 1 week, chapter 4).

WEST COAST HIGHLIGHTS ★★

Some fairly spectacular scenery can be found by exploring the coastal regions west of Glasgow. The **Firth of Clyde** begins the display, but as you keep going, the terrain gets less populated and wilder. Depending

Side Trips from Glasgow

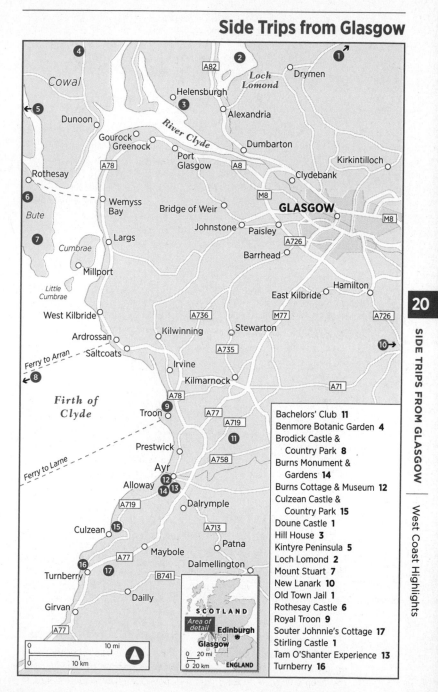

20

Cowal

4

A82

2

Loch
Lomond

Drymen

1

Helensburgh

3

Alexandria

5

Dunoon

River Clyde

Gourock

Greenock

Port
Glasgow

Dumbarton

Kirkintilloch

A78

Clydebank

Rothesay

6

Bute

Wemyss
Bay

Bridge of Weir

M8

GLASGOW

M8

7

Cumbrae

Largs

Johnstone

Paisley

A726

Barrhead

Millport

Little
Cumbrae

Hamilton

East Kilbride

West Kilbride

A736

M77

A726

Kilwinning

Stewarton

Ardrossan

A735

Saltcoats

Ferry to Arran

8

Irvine

Kilmarnock

A71

*Firth of
Clyde*

A78

Troon

9

A77

A719

10

11

Prestwick

A758

Ayr

12

Alloway

14

13

A719

Dalrymple

Culzean

15

A713

Patna

Maybole

Dalmellington

Turnberry

16

17

B741

Dailly

Girvan

A77

Legend

Bachelors' Club **11**
Benmore Botanic Garden **4**
Brodick Castle &
  Country Park **8**
Burns Monument &
  Gardens **14**
Burns Cottage & Museum **12**
Culzean Castle &
  Country Park **15**
Doune Castle **1**
Hill House **3**
Kintyre Peninsula **5**
Loch Lomond **2**
Mount Stuart **7**
New Lanark **10**
Old Town Jail **1**
Rothesay Castle **6**
Royal Troon **9**
Souter Johnnie's Cottage **17**
Stirling Castle **1**
Tam O'Shanter Experience **13**
Turnberry **16**

0   10 mi
0   10 km

SCOTLAND

Area of
detail

Edinburgh
✹

Glasgow
◉

0   20 mi
0   20 km

ENGLAND

upon your stamina and interest, it is worth doing a bit of "island hopping" from the mainland to **Arran** or **Bute** and then into **Argyll** and onto the **Cowal** and **Kintyre** peninsulas, finally getting as far as the small island of **Gigha,** the most southerly of Scotland's Hebridean islands. The distances are not great, and the ferry trips cut down the driving times, as well. Sunsets over the western seas rarely fail to disappoint on a good evening.

Helensburgh

Hill House ★★★   Designed by Charles Rennie Mackintosh for publisher Walter Blackie, this timeless house on the hill above the town of Helensburgh has been lovingly restored and opened to the public by the National Trust for Scotland. Inspired by Scottish Baronial style, Hill House is still pure Mackintosh: The asymmetrical juxtaposition of windows and clean lines that blend sharp geometry and gentle curves. Inside, the sumptuous but uncluttered interior has bespoke details by both the architect and his artist wife Margaret Macdonald, such as glass inlays, fireplace tiles, and decorative panels. Built at the beginning of the 20th century but still looking modern today, practically the entire house is open to the public. The garden, overgrown when the National Trust took over the property in the early 1980s, has been restored to its original state thanks to photography from a German design magazine published in 1905.

Upper Colquhoun St., Helensburgh; 48km (30 miles) west of Glasgow; off the A814. Half-hourly train service from Glasgow Queen Street Station. 🕐 **01436/673-900.** www.nts.org.uk/visits. Admission £8.50 adult; £5.50 students and seniors; £21 family. Apr–Oct daily 1:30–5:30pm. Closed Nov–Mar.

Arran

The Isle of Arran, in the Firth of Forth off the coast of Ayrshire, is often called "Scotland in Miniature," primarily because its geology mimics the country at large. But increasingly locals involved in tourism (www.visitarran.com) prefer to call it "Arran, the Island." Either way, it is a fine place to visit. There's a castle (see below) and some great hiking up to the top of craggy Goat Fell (874m/2,867 ft.), or in the majestic valley of Glen Rosa, near the main port of Brodick. Along the rugged southern coastline near Kildonan, you're almost guaranteed to see seals and perhaps even a dolphin or two and on the west side of the island you can see standing stones at Machrie Moor. There are also some excellent food producers on Arran, including the Island Cheese Company and Creelers smoked Scottish seafood. The primary ferry services depart (5–6 per day) from Ardrossan in Ayrshire to Brodick (50 min. crossing). A single passenger pays about £6 and about £40 for a car. There's a seasonal ferry from Claonaig near Skipness (on the Kintyre peninsula) to Arran's northern port of Lochranza. For ferry information, contact **CalMac** (🕐 **0870/565-0000;** www.calmac.co.uk). Call 🕐 **0870/608-2608** for linking public transportation information.

Brodick Castle & Country Park ★   The oldest bit of this proud mansion goes back to the 13th century, but it has had several additions since then, most of them from the Victorian era. The home and stronghold of the dukes of Hamilton for centuries, and more recently a retreat for the Duke and Duchess of Montrose, the place is full of furnishings and artifacts from both families. The 90-odd stag heads in the main hall are impressive, and the immediate grounds offer lots of trails. From here

In addition to the many hiking possibilities in the area, you could try archery, kayaking, sailing, rock climbing, and more. **Arran Adventure** (✆ **01770/302-244;** www.arranadventure.com), based at the Auchrannie Spa Resort in Brodick, can arrange the works for you. If you fancy a unique golfing challenge, then head west across the island from Brodick to Blackwaterfoot and try your luck at the Shiskine course. It has only 12 holes, but between the driving winds and diverting scenery, it has become a legendary challenge. A round costs about £18. Contact the **Shiskine Golf and Tennis Club** (✆ **01770/860-226;** www.shiskinegolf.com).

you can also hike (or mountain-bike) around an extensive 300-acre country park, as well as joining the paths to Goat Fell and Glen Rosa.

North of Brodick town center, off the A841 near Cladach. ✆ **08444/932-152.** www.nts.org.uk. Admission £10.50 adults, £7.50 seniors and children, £26 family. Parking £2. MC, V. Castle: Apr–Oct daily 11am–4pm. Country park: Daily 9:30am–sunset.

Isle of Bute

Bute is one of the easiest Scottish islands to reach. Ferries depart from the restored Victorian railway terminal in the village of **Wemyss Bay** on the Clyde coast, about 54km (33 miles) southwest of Glasgow. Trains from Glasgow's Central Station depart hourly and the trip takes less than 1 hour. The standard, same-day round-trip fare is about £10. The ferry departs approximately every 45 minutes in the summer and the crossing to **Rothesay**, Bute's main port, takes 35 minutes. Single passengers pay £4 one-way, and cars cost an additional £16. For ferry information, call ✆ **0870/565-0000,** or go to www.calmac.co.uk. Call ✆ **0870/608-2608** for public transportation information.

Mount Stuart ★★   This neo-Gothic mansion (built in the 1870s) belongs to the Marquess of Bute's family (descendents of the Stuart royal line). The interiors reveal the particular interests of John Crichton-Stuart, the Third Marquess (1847–1900), such as a ceiling covered in constellations, reflecting his interest in astrology. The garden is excellent, dating back to the early decades of the 18th century. The extensive grounds have a woodlands park, a huge walled area—ironically called the "wee garden"—and a working vegetable plot, too.

A844 near Scoulag, Isle of Bute, about 8km (5 miles) south of Rothesay. ✆ **01700/503-877.** www.mountstuart.com. Admission for both house and grounds £8 adults, £6.50 seniors, £4 children, £20 family. AE, MC, V. House: May–Sept Sun–Fri 11am–5pm; Sat 10am–2:30pm. Gardens: Daily 10am–6pm.

Rothesay Castle ★   Located in the heart of Rothesay, only a few minutes' walk from the ferry terminal and harbor, this castle is unusual in Scotland for its circular plan. It dates to the beginning of the 13th century, with a large moat encircling the ramparts. Interestingly, the castle plays up the connections that this part of Scotland had with Norse rulers; King Haakon IV in particular. Scandinavia's battles with the native Scots ended with Scotland's eventual victory in the 13th century. Although mostly a restored ruin, the castle has an impressive pigeon tower and chapel within the grassy courtyard. If you dare (and you're thin enough), you can descend from the Gatehouse into a small dungeon once reserved for prisoners.

Rothesay, Isle of Bute. ☎ **01700/502-691.** www.historic-scotland.gov.uk. Admission £4.20 adults, £3.40 seniors, £2.50 children. AmEx, MC, V. Apr–Sept daily 9:30am–5:30pm; Oct–Mar Mon-Wed, Sat-Sun 9:30am–4:30pm.

Cowal & Kintyre Peninsulas

West of Glasgow, the Cowal and Kintyre peninsulas extend their fingers into the sea, creating long salt-water fiords that extend well north up to the Highlands. The main town and ferry port for Cowal is **Dunoon,** which offers a place to stock up on goods. The landscape features magnificent sea lochs, gentle hills, and forested glens. Highlights include the **Benmore Botanic Garden ★** (daily Mar–Oct) 11km (7 miles) north of Dunoon on Cowal. It has giant redwoods and thickets of rhododendrons. The village of **Tighnabruaich** is a mecca for boaters, set in a picturesque natural bay across from the isle of Bute. Indeed, you can get a lesson on splicing the main brace (or at least sailing a dinghy) at the local sailing school.

On Kintyre, the lovely harbor of **Tarbert ★** is where many local fishing boats land. At the ferry slip you can purchase fresh scallops, as well as live crabs and lobsters. Avian populations abound in this region of Scotland, and breeds include black-headed gulls, gannets, oystercatchers, razorbills, and shags (and those are just a few of the seabirds). An observatory is on the island of **Sanda,** just off the tip (or mull) of Kintyre. On the peninsula itself, however, another bird-watching blind is situated near the west coast village of **Machrihanish.**

Where to Stay & Dine

An Lochan ★★ SEAFOOD   This hotel overlooking the sea in Tighnabruaich offers some luxurious rooms, but without a hint of pretension or attitude from the McKie family owners or staff. The "superior sea view" rooms fit the bill, offering huge super king-size beds and ample bathrooms (with tubs and showers), comfy leather-upholstered furnishings, and little goodies such as fresh fruit on arrival (and swallows nesting in the eaves). Meals in the two conservatory dining rooms highlight the excellent locally landed seafood and fish as well as Argyllshire venison and beef.

Tighnabruaich, Argyll. ☎ **01700/811-236.** Fax 01700/811-300. Dinner main courses £18–£20. Reservations required. Mon–Sun noon–3pm and 6–9pm. www.anlochan.co.uk. 11 units. £100–£200 double with breakfast. AE, MC, V. Free parking. **Amenities:** Restaurant; bar. In room: TV, hair dryer.

GIGHA: "THE good isle" ★

Pronounced "*gee*-a" with a hard *g* (as in gear), this small island gets its name from the ancient Norse ruler King Haakon who once dominated this region of Scotland. It means "the good isle." And good, indeed, it is. Tiny and placid, Gigha is best known for its **Achamore Gardens ★** with their exceptional springtime display of rhododendrons and azaleas. But as a quiet place to escape and relax, it is excellent, as well.

There are plenty of rural and coastal walks. Gigha is also particularly noteworthy because on March 15, 2002, the residents established a community trust and assumed ownership of the isle. The 30-minute ferry for Gigha leaves from Tayinloan on the Kintyre peninsula. For overnight dinner, bed, and breakfast accommodations, contact the **Gigha Hotel** (✆ **01583/505-254;** www.gigha. org.uk).

Hunters Quay Hotel ★   Right on the water, north of the Dunoon town center, this up-to-date whitewashed mansion is a very welcoming and comfortable hotel. Guest rooms are individually sized and decorated. Your best option in the immediate vicinity.

Hunters Quay, Marine Parade. ✆ **01369/707-070.** www.huntersquayhotel.co.uk. 10 units. Double £90–£100. AE, MC, V. **Amenities:** Restaurant; bar. *In room:* TV, hair dryer.

Russian Tavern at the Port Royal Hotel 🗽 RUSSIAN/SEAFOOD   You're not likely to find another place like this on your travels in Scotland. In the village of Port Bannatyne just 3km (2 miles) north of Rothesay on the Isle of Bute, the Royal is a family-run inn where the house specialties include Russian cuisine (for example blini, spicy sausage, and pavlova), fresh fish and seafood, and some rarely found Scottish ales served from kegs atop the bar in the small cafe/pub. All meals are cooked to order. Overnight rooms, two with en suite baths, are basic rather than luxurious.

Main St., Port Bannatyne, Bute. ✆ **01700/505-073.** www.butehotel.com. Main courses £16–£24. Mar-Nov Wed–Mon 12:30–10:30pm. Closed winter. 5 units. £50 double. Rates include continental breakfast. MC, V. Parking on street. **Amenities:** Restaurant/bar. *In room:* TV, hair dryer.

The Seafood Cabin ★★ 🗽 SEAFOOD   This place (aka the Crab Shack) south of Tarbert in Skipness is special and worth a detour if you fancy seafood. The meals, prepared in a converted 1950s-style mini-trailer (or caravan) in the shadow of a castle ruin, feature langoustines, queen scallops, mussels, smoked salmon, and more. It's completely unassuming, with chickens and ducks freely wandering on the grass around the picnic tables. There's no better place on a sunny day to have an organic bottle of ale and chow down fresh seafood.

B8001, Skipness, Tarbert, Argyll: 20km (12 miles) south of Tarbert off the A83. ✆ **01880/760-207.** Lunch £8–£16. June–Sept Sun–Fri 11am–6pm.

LOCH LOMOND, STIRLING & THE TROSSACHS ★

One of the benefits of Glasgow is its proximity to wild, open spaces. While a diverse region, Loch Lomond, Stirling, and the Trossachs offer the largest inland body of

Loch Lomond, Stirling & Trossachs

HIKING THE west highland way

One of Scotland's best-known long-distance footpaths is the **West Highland Way** ★★, established in the 1980s. For most people, it begins rather uneventfully northwest of Glasgow in the affluent suburb of Milngavie (pronounced "mill-*guy*"). But as the trail winds its way for some 153km (95 miles), it just gets better and better. North along the eastern shore of Loch Lomond, through the desolate and prehistoric looking Rannoch Moor, and along the breathtaking and historic Glen Coe, ending finally in Fort William, the trail is particularly dramatic. Hikers can backpack and camp along the way or stay at inns conveniently dotted along the trail. There are tour companies, as well, that will haul your luggage from stop to stop along the way. At the northern terminus, you're at the foot of Ben Nevis, Scotland's highest mountain.

Trains run frequently throughout the day from the Queen Street railway station in central Glasgow to Milngavie, the starting point of the walk. The 25-minute trip costs about £3 one-way. In Fort William, you can catch the ScotRail train back to Glasgow. For details, visit www.west-highland-way.co.uk, or contact the National Park Gateway Centre at Loch Lomond Shores (01389 751035; www.lochlomondshores.com).

water not only in Scotland but all of Great Britain (Loch Lomond), as well as the historic burgh of Stirling and its great castle, plus the towering hills and forests of the Trossachs (which are linked to the Highland mountains further northwest).

Loch Lomond

Loch Lomond is only about a half-hour drive or train ride from the city limits of Glasgow. At the southern edge, on the outskirts of the otherwise unremarkable if pleasant town of Balloch, the **Lomond Shores** development (www.lochlomond shores.com) was opened in 2002. The complex includes a shopping mall and an information center (daily 10am–5pm; ✆ **01389/722-199**). The National Park Gateway Centre has guidance on using the adjacent national park—Scotland's first—that extends up the eastern shores of the loch.

If you're hiking, the trails up the eastern shoreline are preferable. This is the route that the West Highland Way (see below) follows. If you are a canoeing or kayaking enthusiast, the Lomond Shores' visitor center has rentals (✆ **01389/602-576;** www.canyouexperience.com) for £15 per hour. Up the western shores, before the notoriously winding road at Tarbet, where the train from Glasgow to Oban stops, visitors can take loch cruises. Golfers will likely be attracted to the Loch Lomond country club, which hosts the annual Scottish Open professional golf championship, near the pleasant resort village of **Luss.**

Stirling & the Trossachs

North-northeast of Glasgow some 42km (26 miles) is historic Stirling, with its **castle** set dramatically on the hill above the town. During the reign of the Stuarts in the 16th century, royalty preferred Stirling to Edinburgh. Stirling Bridge is believed to be the crucial site of a 13th-century battle between English invaders and the rag-tag band of Scots led by William Wallace (forever immortalized—if fictional-ized—in the movie *Braveheart*). High on a nearby hill north of the city center stands the prominent **Wallace Monument** (✆ **01786/472-140;** www.nationalwallace monument.com), which is open daily; admission is £7.50 for adults, £6 for seniors and students, £4.50 for children, and £20 for families. On summer weekends, the story of Wallace is reenacted in costumed dress.

Just outside of the city to the south is another famous battleground: **Bannock-burn.** In these fields, a well-armed English-led force was nevertheless routed by Scottish troops led by King Robert the Bruce in 1314. A heritage center operated by the National Trust for Scotland is open daily March through October; admission is £5.50 for adults, £4.50 for seniors, students, and children, and £15 family.

Northwest of Stirling are the **Trossachs,** a mountain range distinct from the Highlands—appealing for its wooded forests. Two villages that provide gateways to the more mountainous regions north are Callander and Aberfoyle. They can be over-run by bus tours in the high season but offer places to rest, eat, and shop during the day.

First ScotRail trains run frequently to Stirling from Glasgow's Queen Street Sta-tion. The same-day standard round-trip fare is about £10 and takes 30 to 45 minutes depending on the train and the number of stops it has to make in between.

Doune Castle ★ 🏛 Fans of the comedy film *Monty Python and the Holy Grail* (1975) may recognize the exterior of Doune Castle, as it served as a location for several scenes. Visitors (especially those with a good imagination) can get an idea of what living here in the 14th century may have been like. Though unfurnished, the building has low doors, narrow spiral stairs, and a feeling of damp that presumably was part of medieval life. Visitors can clamber through most of the edifice.

Doune, 6.5km (10 miles) northwest of Stirling off the A84. ✆ **01786/841-742.** www.historic-scotland. gov.uk. £4.20 adults, £3.40 seniors, £2.50 children. AE, MC, V. Apr–Sept daily 9:30am–5:30pm; Oct–Mar daily 9:30am–4:30pm.

Old Town Jail ☺ On tours of this Victorian prison, the guides don historic garb, taking you through the paces of penal life here as actors role-play as wardens and inmates. In 1847, this "gaol" replaced a less humane one (condemned as the worst in Britain) across the street in the Tolbooth. Still, a rack-like device hints that penal life was hard. Last admission is 1 hour before closing.

St. John St. ✆ **01786/450-050.** Guided tours £6.50 adults, seniors £5, £4 children, £17 family. MC, V. Apr–Oct daily 9:30am–5pm (4pm in Oct); Nov–Mar daily 10am–3pm.

Stirling Castle ★★ Even if you don't venture inside the walls of this impressive castle, the ramparts and grounds surrounding the well-fortified landmark are impres-sive, particularly the cemetery and the "Back Walk" along a defensive wall. In the castle proper, arguably the grandest in the land, there is a lot of work ongoing to return the buildings to their historic condition (all explained in a museum). High-lights include the Chapel Royal, which was remodeled by James VI (James I of England). Tapestries are being hand-woven in the former stable block to hang in the chapel, and on most days you can watch the intricate process. Quite recently restored, the castle's Great Hall stands out for miles thanks to the creamy, almost yellow exterior that replicates its original color. From Easter 2011, visitors will be allowed to enter the royal Renaissance-era palace of James V. It has six apartments, which have had £12 million worth of work to restore them to their mid-16th-century glory. On the road to the castle is Argyll's Lodging, a well-preserved historic house. Last entry is 45 minutes before closing.

Castle Wynd. Ⓒ **01786/450-000.** www.stirlingcastle.gov.uk. Admission to castle and Argyll's Lodging £9 adults, £7.20 seniors and students, £5.40 children. AE, MC, V. Apr–Sept daily 10am–6pm; Oct–Mar daily 10am–5pm.

Where to Stay & Dine

Cameron House on Loch Lomond ★★
Posh, plush, and perched on the shores of Loch Lomond, the five-star Cameron House hotel offers premier lodgings with Egyptian cotton linens. The mid-range deluxe rooms face the water, while the luxury suites are part of the original house and allow guests to have their meals in the sitting rooms. Dining options include a restaurant under the direction of Edinburgh's Michelin-starred chef Martin Wishart, with a six-course tasting menu at £65.

A82 north of Balloch, Dunbartonshire G83 8QZ. Ⓒ **01389/755-565.** Fax 01389/759-522. www.cameronhouse.co.uk. 95 units. From £180 double with garden view; from £210 double with loch view. Free parking. **Amenities:** 4 restaurants; bars; babysitting; health club; Jacuzzi; room service; sauna; spa; tennis courts; massage. *In room:* TV, DVD, hair dryer, Internet, MP3 dock.

Creagan House ★ FRENCH/SCOTTISH
Cherry and Gordon Gunn have for nearly 25 years run this charming inn housed in a 17th-century farmhouse north of Callander, 25km (15 miles) from Stirling. In the evenings, Gordon cooks guests sumptuous French-influenced meals, using mostly local ingredients. This place is well situated for country walks. A clutch of rooms, including one that has a four-poster bed, start around £120, including full breakfast. If you're coming for dinner, you must have a reservation.

A84, north of Strathyre. Ⓒ **01877/384-638.** www.creaganhouse.co.uk. Reservations required. Fixed-price dinner £30. AE, MC, V. Fri–Tues 7:30–8:30pm. Closed mid-Jan to mid-Mar.

The Cross Keys ★ MODERN SCOTTISH
One of the oldest inns in the region west of Stirling, the Cross Keys' fortunes have been revived over the past few years thanks to new owners. Debby McGregor and her husband/chef Brian provide modern Scottish pub grub—from breast of Guinea fowl to Moroccan lamb stew or a simple but always hand-battered fish with real chips. There are three contemporary rooms for overnight stays, each with their own bathroom.

Main St., Kippen. Ⓒ **01786/870-293.** www.kippencrosskeys.com. Main courses £12. Tues–Fri noon–3pm, 5–9pm; Sat noon–9pm; Sun noon–8pm. No food on Mon. AE, M, V. 3 units. £60–£80 per double with breakfast.

Drover's Inn
The stuffed, snarling, and slightly worn animals near the entrance give a pretty good hint as to the nature of this rustic tavern with restaurant and overnight rooms, located in a building that was established in 1705. The atmospheric pub usually has an open fire going, barmen in kilts, and plenty of travelers nursing their drinks. The pub food is okay, but it's the ambience of the place that makes Drover's a worthwhile stop. There are 10 overnight units in the original house built in 1705, and another 16 rooms have been added in a new building (£58–£78 for a standard double depending on the season).

A82 at Inverarnan by Ardlui. Ⓒ **01301/704-234.** www.thedroversinn.co.uk. Main courses £9–£21. MC, V. Daily 10am–midnight.

The Inn at Kippen MODERN SCOTTISH   About a 15-minute drive west of Stirling on the A811, Kippen is a typical country village in the rolling hills north of Glasgow. The Inn at Kippen is a modernized version of the country tavern and small hotel. The ground-floor pub and restaurant specializes in Scottish fare with contemporary twists. The three overnight rooms are £85 with breakfast.

Fore Rd., Kippen. © **01786/870-500.** www.theinnatkippen.co.uk. Main courses £8–£16. AE, MC, V. Daily noon–2:30pm and 6–9pm.

Mhor ★★ SCOTTISH   Just up the highway from Creagan House is this outstanding hotel/restaurant (formerly the Monachyle Mhor) serving lunch and dinner in an 18th-century farmhouse. The conservatory dining room is modern and so is the cooking. Dinner is expensive (albeit worth it), though lunches are less costly. The adjoining lodge has 11 units with their own bathrooms, starting at around £100, which includes breakfast.

Off the A84, Balquhidder; turn right at Kingshouse Hotel, and drive 9.5km (6 miles). © **01877/384-622.** http://mhor.net. Fixed-price dinner £46. AE, MC, V. Mid-Feb to Dec daily noon–1:45pm and 7–8:45pm. Closed Jan to mid-Feb.

AYRSHIRE & "BURNS COUNTRY"

Ayrshire and southwest Scotland are probably best known as "Burns Country," the region where Scotland's favorite bard, Robert Burns, spent most of his short life from 1759 to 1796. But in addition to the historic sites connected with the famous poet, the region is one of the best places to golf in all of Scotland, especially on its signature sandy links-style courses. Given its southwest exposure to the Gulf Stream influences, this is among the most temperate regions in Scotland. In addition to year-round golf, there is ample hiking and fishing, while the back roads are ideal for road cycling.

The royal burgh of Ayr was once the most popular resort on Scotland's west coast. On the reasonably picturesque Firth of Clyde, it's only some 56km (35 miles) southwest of Glasgow or about an hour by train or by car. For many years it was a busy market town—with a more important and indeed larger port than Glasgow's until the 18th century. Today, it offers visitors some 4km (2½ miles) of beach, cruises, fishing, and golf—as well as the top horse racing in Scotland.

Essentials
GETTING THERE
Trains from Glasgow's Central Station will whisk you to a variety of Ayrshire towns. The trip to Ayr takes less than 1 hour, and a standard round-trip journey, which must be made in the same day, costs about £13. Stagecoach Express runs buses about twice an hour during the week from Glasgow's Buchanan Street bus terminal. Call **Traveline Scotland** (© **0871/200-2233**) for specific journey times. By car, simply take the M77 south out of Glasgow, and it will take you straight to Ayr.

VISITOR INFORMATION
The Ayr **Tourist Information Centre** is at 22 Sandgate, Ayr (© **01292/678-100;** www.ayrshire-arran.com). It's open Monday to Saturday 10am to 5pm.

Burns Heritage Trail

The **Burns Heritage Trail** ★ can be followed by car or on a bus tour. The main destinations are the national poet's places of birth and death, with a few lesser landmarks in and around Ayr thrown in for good measure. Son of a gardener and tenant farmer, Burns was born January 25, 1759, in the village of **Alloway,** which is now part of the suburbs south of the coastal town Ayr. The **Burns Cottage & Museum** exhibits family items. Nearby are the church where his father William is buried (and where the haunted creatures of Burn's *Tam O'Shanter* came to life); the Greek revival **Burns Memorial;** and the arched bridge over the River Doon, the Brig o' Doon, which has been immortalized, for better or worse, by the Lerner and Loewe musical *Brigadoon.*

Further afield in the town of Dumfries is the **Burns' House,** where the bard died July 21, 1796. Here are more relics and items, the most impressive of which may be his signature, scrawled using a diamond in a window of the cottage. Twenty years after his death, Burns was moved to a purpose-built mausoleum in Dumfries, where some of his friends were also interred.

AYR

Ayr is the logical place to begin any journey through Burns Country, and the town has a few associations with the bard itself.

Ayr's 15th-century **Auld Brig** (old bridge), according to the poet, "stood flood an' tide" and he wrote it would still be standing when the New Brig (built in his lifetime) was reduced to a "shapeless cairn [stone heap]." And Burns was correct: The so-called New Brig came down and was replaced in the 19th century. But the Auld Brig remains and is one of the oldest stone bridges in Scotland.

Not far away on the banks of the River Ayr is the **Auld Kirk** (old church), which dates to 1655, when it replaced the 12th-century Church of St. John, which was seized and dismantled by the invading forces of Oliver Cromwell. Robert Burns was baptized in the Auld Kirk. Its greatest curiosity, however, is a macabre series of "mort safes," metal grates which covered freshly filled graves to discourage grave-robbers or, more likely, body snatchers seeking cadavers for sale to medical colleges.

On the High Street, the **Tam O'Shanter Inn** is presumably the site of the tavern ("and ay the ale was growing better") where Tam leaves his drinking buddy Souter Johnnie and sets off riding his trusty gray mare Meg on that infamously stormy evening in Burn's epic and comic poem.

The **Wallace Tower,** also on High Street, rises some 34m (112 ft.). Constructed in 1828, it has a statue of medieval Scottish rebel William Wallace (celebrated by Mel Gibson's film *Braveheart*) by local sculptor James Thom. Legend holds that Wallace was imprisoned here and made a daring escape.

Ayr After Dark

Rabbie's Bar   The walls are highlighted with the pithy verses of Robert Burns, and his portrait is painted directly onto the wall. However, don't come here expecting poetry readings in a quiet corner. The crowd, while not particularly literary, is talkative.

23 Burns Statue Sq. (ℂ) **01292/262-112.** Mon–Sat 11am–12:30am; Sun noon–midnight.

Alloway: Burns' Birthplace

Some 3km (2 miles) south of Ayr, Alloway is where Scotland's national poet was born in a simple cottage—the "auld clay biggin'"—that his father, gardener, and farmer William Burnes (Robert dropped the "e") built by hand in 1757.

Start your visit of the **Burns National Heritage Park** at the **Burns Cottage & Museum.** Just a 10- to 15-minute walk down the road are the simple ruins of the **Alloway Auld Kirk,** celebrated in the poem *Tam O'Shanter:* "Coffins stood round, like open presses/That shaw'd the dead in their last dresses." It stands roofless and allegedly still haunted to this day, with the poet's father buried prominently at the front of the kirkyard. The nearby stone **Brig o' Doon** still arcs elegantly over the River Doon. Admission to the cottage, museum, and video in the **Tam O'Shanter Experience** is £2 for adults and £1.25 for children and seniors.

Burns Cottage & Museum ★ Although historically underfunded and rather basic, this attraction is now undergoing major renovation, due to be completed in 2011. Visitors can take a self-guided tour of the cottage that is kept in the fashion of the poet's early childhood, when livestock shared part of the building with humans. The family lived here for about a decade. After that, the cottage was expanded and used as a pub and inn, before the local Burns Society had it restored to the original, more compact size with features such as the "box bed" in the kitchen where the poet would have been born. Outside of the cottage is the vegetable plot that the self-sufficient Burnes family would have depended on.

The museum has a treasure trove of Burnsiana, keeping the best collection of Burns's manuscripts, first editions of his books—signed in some cases—as well as many letters that Burns wrote and received.

Alloway. 3km (2 miles) south of Ayr on B7024. *(C)* **01292/443-700.** www.nts.org.uk. Admission £4 adults, £2.50 children and seniors, £10 families. MC, V. Apr–Sept daily 10am–5:30pm; Oct–Mar Mon–Sat 10am–5pm.

Burns Monument & Gardens About 1km (½ mile) from the Burns Cottage, just past the old kirk, this Grecian-classical monument was erected in 1823 in a ceremony attended by the poet's widow, Jean Armour. Later, it was replicated in Edinburgh on Calton Hill. The gardens overlook the River Doon and the famous arching bridge.

Alloway. *(C)* **01292/443-700.** Free admission. Apr–Sept daily 10am–5pm; Oct–Mar 10am–4pm.

Where to Stay & Dine

Abbotsford Hotel About a half-mile from the center of Ayr, this small hotel with a popular, civilized pub is curiously named after Sir Walter Scott's mansion rather than associating itself with Burns. The quiet residential neighborhood is less than a 10-minute walk to the shoreline and convenient to the local golf courses, too. Most of the units are smart and comfortable, with flat-screen TVs and modern bathrooms. Family-run and friendly, the Abbotsford offers sound, moderately priced accommodations.

14 Corsehill Rd., Ayr KA7 2ST. *(C)* **01292/261-506.** Fax 01292/261-606. www.abbotsfordhotel.co.uk. £85 double with breakfast. MC, V. Free parking. **Amenities:** Bar; restaurant; beer garden. *In room:* TV.

Enterkine House MODERN SCOTTISH The overnight rooms at this Art Deco country house hotel are five-star quality, while the Woodland Lodge offers a quirkier

BURNS: poet, HUMANITARIAN & SKIRT CHASER

The honest man, tho' e'er sae poor
Is king o' men for a' that
        —Robert Burns, *A Man's a Man*
                for a' That (1795)

Robert Burns (1759–96) continues to hold a sentimental spot in the national consciousness of Scotland. When the new Scottish Parliament opened in 1999, his *A Man's a Man for a' That* was sung. In recent years, Ayrshire has begun to host an annual music and cultural festival, **Burns an' a' That** (www.burns festival.com), to celebrate his life using contemporary Scottish culture. The only slightly surprising matter is why Scotland is reluctant to make *Auld Lang Syne*—surely one of the most recognized songs in the world—its national anthem.

Born on a night so gusty that part of the family cottage came down, he was the son of a simple and pious gardener/tenant farmer who nevertheless encouraged the boy to read and seek an education. So Burns did learn to alliterate, rhyme, and later compose lyrical poetry. But he was, by trade, a hard-working if largely unsuccessful farmer and ended his life employed as a tax collector. Now the world knows him as the author of poetry, often set to song, and acclaimed narrative masterpieces, such as *Tam O'Shanter.* Of it one contemporary critic wrote that Burns displayed "a power of imagination that Shakespeare himself could not have exceeded." In his short life, he wrote hundreds of poems and songs.

But Burns was also a prodigious pursuer of women who fathered numerous children, legitimate and otherwise. He died at 37 of presumed heart disease in the southern town of Dumfries, distinguished even then but resolutely destitute. Almost immediately, however, contributions to his widow and family were made from across Scotland. Burns was buried with some ceremony on the very day that his wife Jean delivered their ninth child.

cottage on the woodland estate. Dining at its highly rated Browne's @ Enterkine restaurant can be a special treat. Menus emphasize local ingredients, whether seasonal game or fish landed at nearby Troon.

Coylton Rd., Annbank KA6 5AL, about 8.5km (5½ miles) east of Ayr, off the B742. ☎ **01292/520-580.** www.enterkine.com. Reservations required. Fixed-price lunch £19, dinner £30. Sun–Fri noon–2:30pm; daily 7–9pm. 8 units. £210 double with breakfast. AE, MC, V. Free parking. **Amenities:** Restaurant; bar/lounge; library. *In room:* TV, hair dryer.

Fairfield House   On the seafront at the edge of Ayr's Low Green, this Victorian mansion/country home has been restored and converted into a four-star hotel. The staff is attentive and, like at the Abbotsford, above, they will help you arrange tee times at nearby golf courses. Rooms in the main building are decorated in a country-house style, while a newer wing offers more modern decor.

12 Fairfield Rd., Ayr KA7 2AR. ☎ **01292/267-461.** Fax 01292/261-456. www.fairfieldhotel.co.uk. 44 units. £130 double with continental breakfast. AE, DC, MC, V. Free parking. **Amenities:** Restaurant; bar; health club; indoor pool; room service; sauna; spa. *In room:* A/C, TV, hair dryer, Internet.

Fouter's Restaurant MODERN SCOTTISH   In the heart of Ayr, this restaurant occupies the cellar of an old bank, retaining the original stone floor and a vaulted ceiling. The restaurant's name derives from the Scottish word used in the expression, "foutering about," which is equivalent to "fiddling around." But they are not goofing around here; the food is excellent.

2A Academy St., Ayr KA7 1HS. ℂ **01292/261-391.** www.fouters.co.uk. Reservations recommended. Main courses £13–£20. AE, MC, V. Tues–Sat noon–2:30pm and 6–9pm.

A Wee Bit More o' Burns

Bachelors' Club   Obtained in 1938 by the National Trust for Scotland, this is the infamous cottage with thatched roofing where Burns and a group of unmarried friends established a society—the Tarbolton Bachelors—to discuss issues of the day. The membership rules were clear: "No haughty, self-conceited person, who looks upon himself as superior to the rest of the club, and especially no mean-spirited, worldly mortal, whose only will is to heap up money, shall upon any pretence be admitted." On Castle Street, in the nearby village of Mauchline, is the **Burns House Museum** (ℂ **01290/550-045;** Tues–Sat 10am–5pm). Burns married his wife Jean Armour here in 1788, and this cottage was their home for a spell. Nearby, two locations, Mossgiel and Lochlea, are where Burns's family farms were run with little success earlier in the poet's life.

Sandgate St., Tarbolton, off A77 south of Kilmarnock. ℂ **01292/541-940.** www.nts.org.uk/visits. Admission £5.50 adults, £4.50 children, £15 family. Apr–Sept Fri–Tues 1–5pm and Burns Day (Jan 25) 1–5pm.

Souter Johnnie's Cottage   A "souter" is a shoemaker and in Kirkoswald, some 19km (12 miles) south of Ayr, is the home of Burns's pal, cobbler John Davidson or Souter Johnnie. Davidson is name-checked in Burns's tale of Tam O'Shanter, who in real life was another friend named Douglas Graham. The cottage, which dates to 1785, contains period furniture and contemporary cobbler's tools. In the nearby kirkyard are the graves of Graham as well as Souter Johnnie and his wife, Ann.

Main Rd., A77, Kirkoswald. ℂ **01655/760-603.** www.nts.org.uk. Admission £5.50 adults, £4.50 children, £15 family. Apr–Sept Fri–Tues 11:30am–5pm and Burns Day (Jan 25) 11:30am–5pm.

CULZEAN

Culzean Castle & Country Park (remember, the "z" in Culzean is silent and the second syllable sounds like lane) is situated on the cliffs above the sea about 20km (12 miles) southwest of Ayr. The attraction provides one of the more scenic and soothing stops in Ayrshire. The "castle" is of relatively recent vintage: Robert Adam designed much of the pile between 1777 and 1792. Adam had a hand in quite a few stately houses of the period, displaying no end of Georgian symmetry and elegance. The country park (Scotland's first) stretches for more than 200 hectares (500 acres). Thanks to the influences of the mild Gulf Stream, the grounds have some exotic plants that one might not expect to find in Scotland.

Culzean Castle ★   This is a fine example of Adam's "castellated" style (i.e., built with turrets and ramparts) for the once powerful Kennedy clan. After World War II, the castle was given to the National Trust for Scotland. Notwithstanding its architectural attributes—whether the celebrated round drawing room or the outstanding Oval Staircase—the pile is of special interest to many Americans because General Dwight D. Eisenhower was given an apartment for life here. He reputedly called Culzean "a place [where] I can relax." Undoubtedly the mansion's location near so many outstanding golf courses, such as Turnberry (see below), also pleased the golf-mad U.S. president. Today, tourists can use his six-room top-floor flat as holiday accommodations. Fans of the Scottish cult horror film, *The Wicker Man,* should recognize that scenes were filmed here. Last entry is 1 hour before closing.

A719, west of Maybole. © **01655/884-455.** www.culzeanexperience.org. www.nts.org.uk. Admission (including entrance to the Country Park) £13 adults, £9 seniors and children, £32 family. MC, V. Apr–Oct daily 10:30am–5pm (visitor center also Nov–Mar Thurs–Sun 11am–4pm).

Culzean Country Park ★★ ☺   The expansive grounds surrounding the castle contain a formal walled garden, an aviary, swan pond, camellia house, an orangery, adventure playground, and restored 19th-century pagoda. Not to mention a deer park, kilometers and kilometers of woodland paths, and a beach, too. Unless you're dead keen on historical houses, the country park is arguably the real highlight of a trip to Culzean on a fine Ayrshire day. The views over the sea to the southwest include the rounded rock of an island called Ailsa Craig. Some 16km (10 miles) offshore, it's a nesting ground and sanctuary for seabirds.

On the land surrounding Culzean Castle. © **01655/884-400.** Included in admission to Culzean Castle. Daily 9am–dusk.

GOLFING HEAVENS: TROON & TURNBERRY

Troon

The town of **Troon,** 11km (7 miles) north of Ayr and about 50km (31 miles) south-west of Glasgow, looks out across the Firth of Clyde toward the Isle of Arran. Troon takes its name from the curiously hook-shaped promontory jutting out into the sea: The trone or "nose." From this port, a ferry sails March to October to Larne in Northern Ireland.

Troon and its environs offer several sandy links courses, most prominently the **Royal Troon Golf Club ★**, Craigend Rd., Troon, Ayrshire KA10 6EP (© **01292/ 311-555;** www.royaltroon.co.uk). Royal Troon is a 7,150-yard seaside course that hosts the prestigious Open Championship, which was last played here in 2004. Hole 8, the famous "Postage Stamp," may be only 123 yards in distance, but depending upon the wind, you may need a wood or wedge to reach the green. A second course, the 6,289-yard Portland, is arguably even more challenging. Visitors, with certificate of handicap (20 for men and 30 for women), can play the course from May through October on Monday, Tuesday, and Thursday. The 1-day fee to play one round on the Old Course and one on Portland is around £240, which includes morning coffee and a buffet lunch. Two rounds on Portland are about half the cost.

A less expensive and still gratifying option is to play one of Troon's municipal courses run by the South Ayrshire Council, such as Darnley or Lochgreen, which runs parallel to Royal Troon at spots. Fees during the weekend range from £18 to £32. Another option is a six-round, 7-day golf pass from the council for £88. Log onto www. golfsouthayrshire.com, or call the South Ayrshire Golf hotline on © **01292/616-255.**

Trains from Glasgow's Central Station stop at Troon several times daily. The trip takes about 40 minutes, and the standard same-day round-trip fare is about £12. Trains and buses also connect Ayr with Troon, which is about a 10-minute ride. Call © **0870/608-2608** for public transportation information.

Where to Stay & Dine

Lochgreen House Hotel   This lovely country-house hotel is set on 12 lush hectares (30 acres) of forest and landscaped gardens. The property opens onto views of the Firth of Clyde and Ailsa Craig. The interior evokes a more elegant era, with detailed cornices, antique furnishings, and elegant oak and cherry paneling.

Monktonhill Rd., Southwood, Troon, Ayrshire KA10 7EN. © **01292/313-343.** Fax 01292/318-661. www. costley-hotels.co.uk. 40 units. £150 double with breakfast. AE, MC, V. Free parking. **Amenities:** 2 restaurants; 2 bars; room service; tennis court. *In room:* TV, hair dryer.

MacCallums of Troon Oyster Bar FISH/SEAFOOD   Near the ferry terminal at the harbor, this seaside bistro has its own fresh fish market, as well. Oysters, whole sardines, grilled langoustines, sole, and combination platters frequently grace the menu.

The Harbour, Troon. © **01292/319-339.** Reservations recommended. Main courses £12–£22. AE, MC, V. Tues–Sat noon–2:30pm and 7–9:30pm; Sun noon–3:30pm.

Piersland House Hotel   Opposite Royal Troon and designed by William Leiper in 1899, this hotel was originally the mansion of Sir Alexander Walker of the Johnnie Walker whisky family. It remained a private residence until 1956. The moderately sized guest rooms have traditional country-house styling; for additional privacy and more space (rooms have small lounges), opt for one of the cottages across the car park.

15 Craigend Rd., Troon, Ayrshire KA10 6HD. © **01292/314-747.** Fax 01292/315-613. www. piersland.co.uk. 30 units. £145 double with breakfast; £190 double with dinner and breakfast. AE, MC, V. Free parking. Drive 3 min. south of the town center on B749. **Amenities:** Restaurant; bar; room service. *In room:* TV, minibar, hair dryer.

> ## Spa Breaks
>
> If you want to take it slow, get pampered, and perhaps, when ready, indulge in a bit of exercise, you'll find a number of good options in the regions around Glasgow. On the Isle of Arran, the Auchranie Spa Resort is open year round. It offers a range of treatments and therapies, plus a 20-m (65-ft.) indoor pool and a games hall for rainy days. It is located on the outskirts of Brodick, © **01770-302-234,** www. auchrannie.co.uk. Another good bet is Turnberry (see below), which has a first-class gym and luxury indoor pool with views of the sea.

Turnberry

The coastal settlement of Turnberry, some 81km (50 miles) southwest of Glasgow on the A77, was once part of the Culzean estate. It began to flourish early in the 20th century with the development of a rail service (now absent), and when a recognized golfing center with a first-class resort hotel was established.

From the original pair of 13-hole golf courses, the complex has developed two championship level courses, Ailsa and Kintyre, known worldwide as the **Turnberry Hotel Golf Courses.** Ailsa's 18 holes have been the scene of British Open tournaments, and after 15 years the Open returned in 2009. Guests of the Westin Turnberry hotel get priority of play, especially on the Ailsa course. The fees vary. Hotel residents should expect to pay between £50 and £150, depending on the course and the season. If you're not staying at Turnberry, rates range from around £100 to £200. Log onto www.turnberry.co.uk, or call © **01655/334-032** for up-to-date details.

Where to Stay & Dine

Glenapp Castle ★   This beautiful mansion south of Turnberry designed in the 1870s by David Bryce, a celebrated architect of his day, offers Victorian baronial splendor with antiques, oil paintings, and elegant touches at every turn. Lounges and dining rooms are elegant, while the spacious bedrooms and suites are individually furnished. The hotel, open seasonally unless by special arrangement, stands on 12 hectares (30 acres) of lovely, secluded grounds with many rare plants.

Ballantrae, Ayrshire KA26 0NZ. Some 30km (20 miles) south of Ayr. ℭ **01465/831-212.** Fax 01465/831-000. www.glenappcastle.com. Apr–Oct. 17 units. £375–£475 double with dinner and breakfast. AE, MC, V. Free parking. **Amenities:** Restaurant; bar; room service (8am–midnight); tennis court. *In room:* TV.

Malin Court Hotel   On one of the most scenic strips of the Ayrshire coast, this well-run hotel fronts the Firth of Clyde and the Turnberry golf courses. It is not a great country house but rather a serviceable, welcoming retreat offering a blend of informality and comfort. Bedrooms are mostly medium in size. The staff can arrange hunting, fishing, riding, sailing, and golf.

Turnberry, Ayrshire KA26 9PB. ℭ **01655/331-457.** Fax 01655/331-072. www.malincourt.co.uk. 18 units. £128 double with breakfast. AE, DC, MC, V. Free parking. **Amenities:** Restaurant; bar; room service. *In room:* TV, hair dryer, Internet.

Turnberry ★   This 1908 pile is a remarkable and well-known landmark. From afar, you can see the hotel's white facade, red-tile roof, and dozens of gables. And right beside is the more famous golf course, which has hosted the Open Championship several times, most recently in 2009. But you don't have to come for the golf. The spa is exceptional. The hotel's public rooms contain Waterford crystal chandeliers, Ionic columns, molded ceilings, and oak paneling. Each guest room is furnished in unique early-1900s' style and has a marble-sheathed bathroom.

Maidens Rd., Turnberry, Ayrshire KA26 9LT. ℭ **01655/331-000.** Fax 01655/331-706. www.turnberry. co.uk. 221 units. £360 double with breakfast. AE, DC, MC, V. Free parking. **Amenities:** 3 restaurants; 2 bars; babysitting; health club; indoor pool; Jacuzzi; room service; tennis courts; sauna; spa; massage. *In room:* TV, minibar, hair dryer, trouser press.

THE CLYDE VALLEY

The River Clyde meanders north to Glasgow from its inland headwaters in the southern uplands of Scotland. The Clyde Valley is best known locally for its garden nurseries and their sometimes quaint tea shops. The main town is **Lanark,** 44km (27 miles) from Glasgow. Trains leave Glasgow Central Station twice an hour, and the trip takes about an hour. Standard same-day round-trip fare is around £10. By car, take the M74 freeway southeast from Glasgow and exit at signs for Lanark at Kirkmuirhill or via the more scenic route through the Clyde Valley on the A72.

New Lanark ★ ☺   A UNESCO World Heritage Site, New Lanark was a progressive industrial mill and village in the early 19th century, offering its workers and families free education, a day-care nursery, social club, and cooperative store. Today, the attraction includes a chair-lift ride that tells the story of what life here was like, as well as self-guided tours of the principal buildings. A pleasant walk upstream will bring visitors to the three-tiered Falls of Clyde.

Braxfield Rd., outside Lanark. ℭ **01555/661-345.** www.newlanark.org. Admission £6.95 adults, £5.95 children and seniors, £28 families. Daily Apr–Sept 10am–5pm, Oct–Mar 11am–5pm.

EDINBURGH & GLASGOW

American Express The American Express office in Edinburgh exchanges money and traveler's checks as well as performing other services for cardholders. It is at 69 George St. ((℃ **0131/718-2501;** Bus: 13, 19, or 41). It's open Monday through Friday from 9am to 5:30pm and Saturday from 9am to 5pm; on Wednesday, the office opens at 9:30am. In Glasgow, the office is at 66 Gordon St. ((℃ **0141/225-2905**), Monday to Friday from 8:30am to 5:30pm and Saturday 9am to noon.

Area Codes The city code for Edinburgh is 0131, and for Glasgow it's 0141. These codes cover some of the surrounding towns. Regional area codes in Scotland are 5 digits long (including the zero). The country code for Scotland is **44.** When phoning from outside the U.K., you drop the zero from the local code.

To make international calls from Scotland, dial 00 and then the country code, local code, and telephone number. The U.S. and Canadian country code is **1,** Australia is **61,** and New Zealand is **63.** If you can't find a number, a directory is available by dialing a variety of numbers (thanks to privatization of the service), including (℃ 118-118 or (℃ 118-800 for domestic numbers and (℃ 118-505 for international numbers. To make collect calls outside the U.K., dial 155 for an international operator.

Business Hours Most businesses are open Monday through Saturday from 9 or 9:30am to 5 or 5:30pm, with some exceptions. Many businesses and shops are closed Sunday, although several shops in the cities open on Sunday afternoons. Most cities also have extended shopping hours on Thursday until 8pm. Outside of Edinburgh and Glasgow, businesses may close for lunch, generally from 12:30 to 1:30pm.

Banks are normally open from 9 or 10am until about 5pm on weekdays. Banks are good places to exchange currency and get credit card cash advances.

Car Rentals For a list of agency websites, see p. 265.

Cash Points/ATM Networks See "Money & Costs," p. 27.

Dentists If you have a dental emergency, go to the **Edinburgh Dental Institute,** 39 Lauriston Place ((℃ **0131/536-4900;** Bus: 35), open Monday through Friday from 9am to 3pm. In Glasgow, go to the Accident and Emergency Department of **Glasgow Dental Hospital,** 378 Sauchiehall St. ((℃ **0141/211-9600**). Its hours are Monday to Friday 9:15am to 3:15pm and Sunday and public holidays 10:30am to noon. For additional assistance, call the **National Health Service** line ((℃ **0800/224-488**).

Doctors You can seek help from the **Edinburgh Royal Infirmary,** 1 Lauriston Place ((℃ **0131/536-1000;** Bus: 35). The emergency department is open 24 hours. In Glasgow, the main hospital for emergency treatment (24 hours) in the city is the Royal Infirmary, 82–86 Castle St. (✆ **0141/211-4000**). For additional assistance, call the **National Health Service** line (✆ **0800/224-488**).

Drinking Laws   You can drink legally on your own at 18. Children with parents can have a low-alcohol drink such as beer or wine with a meal. Beer, wine, and spirits are sold at off-licences (the equivalent of U.S. liquor stores), small groceries licensed to sell alcohol, and supermarkets. By law, off-licence shops can only sell alcohol from 10am to 10pm.

Driving Rules   See "Getting Around," p. 57 and p. 165 in chapters 5 and 13.

Electricity   The electric current in Scotland is 240 volts AC, which is different than the U.S. current, so most small appliances brought from the U.S., such as hair dryers and shavers, don't work (and the current could damage the appliance). If you're considering bringing your laptop or iron from home, check the voltage first to see if it has a range between 110 volts and 240 volts. If the voltage doesn't have a range, the only option is to purchase an expensive converter. If the voltage does have a higher range, then you still need to buy an outlet adapter because your prongs won't fit in the Scottish sockets. You can buy an adapter for about $10 at an appliance store or even at the airport. Wherever you go, bring a **connection kit** of the right power and phone adapters, a spare phone cord, and a spare Ethernet network cable—or find out whether your hotel supplies them to guests.

Embassies & Consulates   Embassies are located in London. Edinburgh has consulates and high commissions for Australia (69 George St.; ✆ **0131/624-3700**), Canada (30 Lothian Rd.; ✆ **0131/245-6013**), and the United States (3 Regents Terrace; ✆ **0131/556-8315**).

Emergencies   For any emergency, contact the police or an ambulance by calling ✆ **999** from any phone. You can also call the National Health Service Helpline (NHS Direct), ✆ **0845-4647,** which offers health-related advice and assistance from 8am to 10pm daily. For emergencies, treatment is free, although you will be billed for long stays.

Gasoline (Petrol)   Like pretty much everywhere in the world, the price of gas and diesel in Scotland has risen considerably in the 2000s. As of mid-2010, the prices were nearly £1.30 for a liter. Taxes are already included in the printed price. One U.S. gallon equals 3.8 liters or .85 imperial gallons. That should put U.S. drivers' complaints about expensive gas into context. It's much more costly in the U.K. If you're not venturing outside Edinburgh or Glasgow, don't bother getting a car and save some cash.

Holidays   Public holidays vary slightly between Scotland and England. In general, they share Christmas, New Year's Day, and Easter. For more information on holidays see the "Calendar of Events," p. 20 in chapter 3.

Hospitals   See "Doctors" above.

Hotlines   **Edinburgh & Lothian Women's Aid** is at ✆ **0131/229-1419. Lothian Gay & Lesbian Switchboard** (✆ **0131/556-4049**) offers advice from 7:30 to 10pm daily; the **Lesbian Line** is ✆ **0131/557-0751.** The **Rape Crisis Centre** is at ✆ **0141/331-1990.** In Glasgow, the **Centre for Women's Health** is at Sandyford Place, Sauchiehall St. (✆ **0141/211-6700**). Gays and lesbians can call the **Strathclyde Gay & Lesbian Switchboard** at ✆ **0141/847-0447.** The **Rape Crisis Centre** is at ✆ **0141/331-1990.**

Insurance   For travel overseas, most U.S. health plans (including Medicare and Medicaid) do not provide coverage, and the ones that do often require you to pay for services upfront and reimburse you only after you return home.

As a safety net, you may want to buy travel medical insurance, particularly if you're traveling to a remote or high-risk area where emergency evacuation might be necessary.

If you require additional medical insurance, try **MEDEX Assistance** (℃ **410/453-6300;** www.medexassist.com) or **Travel Assistance International** (℃ **800/821-2828;** www. travelassistance.com); for general information on services, call the company's **Worldwide Assistance Services, Inc.,** at ℃ **800/777-8710**.

Canadians should check with their provincial health plan offices or call **Health Canada** (℃ **866/225-0709;** www.hc-sc.gc.ca) to find out the extent of their coverage and what documentation and receipts they must take home in case they are treated overseas.

The cost of **travel insurance** varies widely, depending on the destination, the cost and length of your trip, your age and health, and the type of trip you're taking, but expect to pay between 5% and 8% of the vacation itself. You can get estimates from various providers through **InsureMyTrip.com.** Enter your trip cost and dates, your age, and other information, for prices from more than a dozen companies. U.K. citizens and their families who make more than one trip abroad per year may find an annual travel insurance policy works out cheaper. Check **www.moneysupermarket.com,** which compares prices across a wide range of providers for single- and multi-trip policies.

Internet Access   The advent of Wi-Fi means that many cafes, hotel lobbies, and other public buildings will have Internet access. There is an **EasyInternet Cafe** at 58 Rose St., between Frederick and Hanover streets (www.easyeverything.com; Bus: 42), is open daily from 7:30am to 10:30pm. It has some 448 terminals. In Glasgow, try EasyInternet Cafe, 57–61 St. Vincent St. (www.easyeverything.com; Underground: Buchanan St.). This outlet offers more than 350 computers and good rates. Open Monday to Friday from 7am to 10pm; Saturday and Sunday 8am to 9pm.

Laundromats   For your dry-cleaning needs in Edinburgh, the most central service is probably at **Johnson's Cleaners,** 23 Frederick St. (℃ **0131/225-8095;** Bus: 13, 19, or 42), which is open Monday through Friday from 8am to 5:30pm and Saturday from 8:30am to 4pm. In Glasgow, the most central service is **Garnethill Cleaners,** 39 Dalhousie St. (℃ **0141/332-2387;** Underground: Cowcaddens), open Monday to Saturday from about 7:30am to 6:30pm and Sunday from 8am to 5pm.

Lost & Found   Be sure to tell all of your credit card companies the minute you discover your wallet has been lost or stolen, and file a report at the nearest police precinct. Your credit card company or insurer may require a police report number or record of the loss. Most credit card companies have an emergency toll-free number to call if your card is lost or stolen; they may be able to wire you a cash advance immediately or deliver an emergency credit card in a day or two. Both Edinburgh Waverley and Glasgow Queen Street police stations have lost property departments.

Mail   The Edinburgh Branch Post Office, St. James Centre, is open Monday through Saturday from 9am to 5:30pm. In Glasgow, the main branch is at 47 St. Vincent's St. (℃ **0141/204-3689**; Underground: Buchanan St.). It's open Monday to Friday 8:30am to 5:45pm and Saturday 9am to 5:30pm. Smaller branches are open Monday through Friday from 9am to 5pm and Saturday from 9am to noon. Often, however, they will close early on one day of the week. For general postal information, call ℃ **0845/722-3344.**

Newspapers & Magazines   Published since 1817, *The Scotsman* is a quality daily newspaper with a national and international perspective, while its sister publication, the *Evening News,* concentrates more on local affairs. In Glasgow, published since 1783, *The Herald* is the major newspaper with national, international, and financial news, sports, and cultural listings; the *Evening Times* offers local news. The *Daily Record* is for tabloid enthusiasts only. For comprehensive arts and entertainment listings and reviews of local shows, buy *The List* magazine, which is published every other Wednesday—and weekly during the Festival. *Metro,* a free daily (Mon–Fri) available on buses and in train stations, also gives listings of daily events.

Passports   See p. 23 in chapter 3.

Police   See "Emergencies" above.

Public Toilets   Usually costing 20p at rail stations and free in department stores. A few public toilets, often marked wc, are still found in Edinburgh and Glasgow. They're safe and clean but likely to be closed late in the evening.

Smoking   In April 2006, a ban on smoking in all enclosed public spaces—including business offices, restaurants, and pubs—went into effect. Smoking was already prohibited on all trains and buses.

Taxes   A consumption tax of 17.5% is charged on pretty much all goods and services. It's called VAT (value-added tax) and given the U.K.'s budget woes, it may go up after 2010. Tourists from outside the European Union are entitled to a refund, however, VAT is nonrefundable for services such as hotels, meals, and car rentals.

Telephones   Both cities still have pay phones that accept coins and credit cards.

Time   Scotland follows Greenwich Mean Time, which is five time zones ahead of Eastern Standard Time in the United States (8 hours ahead of the Pacific Coast). So, when it's noon in New York, it's 5pm in Glasgow. The clocks are set forward by 1 hour for British summer time in late March, which expires at the end of October. The high latitude blesses the country with long days in the summer, with sunset as late as 10 or even 11pm. But the opposite is true in winter, when the sun sets as early as 3:30 or 4pm.

Weather   For weather forecasts and severe road-condition warnings, call the Met Office *(* **0870/900-0100.** An advisor will offer forecasts for the entire region and beyond.

AIRLINE, HOTEL & CAR-RENTAL WEBSITES

MAJOR U.S. AIRLINES
(*flies internationally as well)

American Airlines*
www.aa.com

ATA Airlines
www.ata.com

Continental Airlines*
www.continental.com

Delta Air Lines*
www.delta.com

Northwest Airlines
www.flynaa.com

United Airlines*
www.united.com

US Airways*
www.usairways.com

MAJOR INTERNATIONAL AIRLINES

Air France
www.airfrance.com

Air India
www.airindia.com

Alitalia
www.alitalia.com

American Airlines
www.aa.com

British Airways
www.british-airways.com

Continental Airlines
www.continental.com

Delta Air Lines
www.delta.com

Emirates Airlines
www.emirates.com

Icelandair
www.icelandair.com
www.icelandair.co.uk (in U.K.)

Lufthansa
www.lufthansa.com

Qantas Airways
www.qantas.com

Swiss Air
www.swiss.com

United Airlines
www.united.com

US Airways
www.usairways.com

Virgin Atlantic Airways
www.virgin-atlantic.com

BUDGET AIRLINES

Aer Lingus
www.aerlingus.com

BMI Baby
www.bmibaby.com

easyJet
www.easyjet.com

JetBlue Airways
www.jetblue.com

Ryanair
www.ryanair.com

Southwest Airlines
www.southwest.com

CAR RENTAL AGENCIES

Advantage
www.advantagerentacar.com

Alamo
www.alamo.com

Auto Europe
www.autoeurope.com

Avis
www.avis.com

Budget
www.budget.com

Dollar
www.dollar.com

Enterprise
www.enterprise.com

Hertz
www.hertz.com

Thrifty
www.thrifty.com

MAJOR HOTEL & MOTEL CHAINS

Best Western International
www.bestwestern.com

Clarion Hotels
www.choicehotels.com

Comfort Inns
www.comfortinnchoicehotels.com

Courtyard by Marriott
www.marriott.com/courtyard

Crowne Plaza Hotels
www.ichotelsgroup.com/
crowneplaza

Days Inn
www.daysinn.com

Embassy Suites
www.embassysuites.hilton.com

Fairfield Inn by Marriott
www.marriott.com/fairfieldinn

Four Seasons
www.fourseasons.com

Hilton Hotels
www.hilton.com

Holiday Inn
www.holidayinn.com

Hyatt
www.hyatt.com

InterContinental Hotels & Resorts
www.ichotelsgroup.com

Loews Hotels
www.loewshotels.com

Marriott
www.marriott.com

Omni Hotels
www.omnihotels.com

Quality
www.qualityinn.choicehotels.com

Radisson Hotels & Resorts
www.radisson.com

Ramada Worldwide
www.ramada.com

Sheraton Hotels & Resorts
www.starwoodhotels.com/sheraton

Westin Hotels & Resorts
www.starwoodhotels.com/westin

Index

See also Accommodations and Restaurant indexes, below.

General Index

Accommodations— Edinburgh and environs

Accommodations— Glasgow and environs

Restaurants— Edinburgh and environs